Contracts

BLACK LETTER OUTLINES

Contracts

SIXTH EDITION

John D. Calamari
Late Wilkinson Professor of Law,
Fordham University

Joseph M. Perillo
Late Distinguished Professor, Emeritus,
Fordham University

Michael P. Malloy
Distinguished Professor
University of the Pacific McGeorge School of Law

BLACK LETTER SERIES®

WEST ACADEMIC

860 Blue Gentian Road, Suite 350
Eagan, MN 55121
1-877-888-1330

Published in the United States of America

ISBN: 978-1-68561-139-2

Summary of Contents

Table of Contents

Capsule Summary

I. INTRODUCTION—SOURCES OF LAW

In contract law, there are multiple sources that often apply in the analysis of issues, and one must be aware of the possibility that they may interact. While contracts law is based on common law principles derived from case law, the provisions of the Uniform Commercial Code (UCC)—particularly Articles 1 and 2—apply directly to transactions for the sale of goods. The UCC may also be cited by analogy in other contract situations. In addition, provisions of the first Restatement of Contracts and the second Restatement of Contracts are often cited by a court as authority in its analysis of contract issues, often referring to such provisions in the same way it might refer to case law. Other state and federal statutory law—*e.g.*, consumer protection statutes and disclosure requirements—will apply to certain transactions specified by those statutes. Hence, effective analysis of a contract problem requires that one be aware of the possible impact of a range of sources. Ignoring sources other than case law often leads to incomplete or inadequate answers to contract law issues.

II. MUTUAL ASSENT—OFFER AND ACCEPTANCE

A. MUTUAL ASSENT

1. Objective Theory of Contracts

Mutual assent is ordinarily arrived at by an offer and acceptance. Under the objective theory, whether there is assent is determined by asking whether a reasonable person in the position of one party would believe that the words and conduct of the other party constituted assent. This is usually a question of fact for the trier of fact. However, if a reasonable person could reach only one reasonable conclusion, it is a question of law for the court.

2. Intending Legal Consequence

The parties need not intend to be legally bound, but if the objective evidence makes it clear that they do not intend to be bound, then there is no contract.

3. Intent to Formalize Agreement

If the parties reach basic agreement on a transaction but agree that they will not be bound unless and until they sign a formal agreement, they will not be bound until that time. If they intend the future writing merely to be a convenient memorial of their prior agreement, they are bound whether or not such a writing is executed. Intent is often a question of fact.

B. OFFER

1. What Constitutes an Offer?

An offer is a promise to do or to refrain from doing some specified thing in the future if the offeree will do something in exchange. To amount to an offer, the promise must justify the other party, as a reasonable person, in concluding that his or her assent is invited and will conclude the process of offer and acceptance. It is possible, but very unusual, to have a non-promissory offer. (*See* Capsule Summary II.C.8., *infra*.)

2. What Is a Promise?

A promise is a manifestation of intent that gives an assurance (commitment) that a thing will or will not be done.

3. Offer Distinguished from Preliminary Negotiations

Preliminary negotiations are any communications prior to an operative offer. Expressions of opinion, statements of intention, hope or desire, inquiries or invitations to make offers, catalogs, circular letters, invitations to make bids, and price quotations are not offers. An advertisement for the sale of goods is ordinarily not an offer. In an auction sale, the bidder is deemed to be the offeror. The situation is more complex in an auction without reserve. (*See* text, Chapter II.B.f., *infra*.)

4. Distinction Between Offers to Unilateral and Bilateral Contracts

An offer to a unilateral contract asks for a performance; an offer looking to a bilateral contract invites a promise. The promise may be expressed in words or communicated by conduct. An offer to a unilateral contract may not be accepted by a promise. Conversely, an offer to a bilateral contract may not, except under an unimportant exception, be accepted by performance. The offeree does not become bound when starting to perform the act requested by an offer looking to a unilateral contract, but the offeror is bound by an option contract (i.e., an irrevocable offer).

5. UCC § 2–206

This section de-emphasizes the common law distinction between a unilateral and a bilateral contract. Under UCC § 2–206(1)(b), "an order or other offer to buy goods for prompt or current shipment shall be construed as inviting acceptance either by a prompt promise to ship or by the prompt or current shipment of conforming or non-conforming goods. . . ." The buyer or seller can alter this presumption. The section also has made changes in the mailbox rule (Capsule Summary, II.C.11, *infra*) by allowing acceptance of the offer "by any manner reasonable in the circumstances" and in the rules on the effect of part performance. This provision of the UCC has become general law, finding its way into the Restatement (Second) and the case law. Finally, under UCC § 2–206, where the beginning of performance is a reasonable way to accept an offer, the offeree is bound when they start to perform, provided that the beginning of performance unambiguously expresses the offeree's intention to engage. Even though the offeree is bound, the offeror is not bound to perform unless notice of beginning performance is given within a reasonable time. If timely notice is not given, the offeror, even though not bound to perform, may waive the lack of notice and hold the offeree to the contract. The basic notion is that the offeror is not bound unless notified, but the offeree is bound on beginning performance.

C. ACCEPTANCE

1. Relationship to Offer

The offer creates a power of acceptance. The acceptance creates a contract and terminates the power of revocation that the offeror ordinarily has. The acceptance must be a voluntary act.

2. Acceptance by Authorized Party

An offer may be accepted only by the person or persons to whom it is made. Thus, the offeree may not transfer (assign) the power of acceptance to another. But an irrevocable offer may be transferred if the transfer is consistent with the rules governing the assignment of contracts.

3. Knowledge of Offer

If an offer looks to a unilateral contract, the offeree must know of the offer in order to accept. If the offer looks to a bilateral contract, the rule that the offeree must know of the offer may come into conflict with the objective theory of contracts. If so, the objective theory prevails.

4. Intent to Accept

For a unilateral contract to arise, the traditional rule is that the offeree must subjectively intend to accept. The offer need not, however, be the principal inducement for performing the act. The Restatement (Second) has substituted a more objective test; an intent to accept is presumed unless the offeree disclaims an intent to accept. An offeree to a bilateral contract can accept even if he or she has no subjective intent to accept; all that is required is an outward manifestation of intent to contract.

5. Necessity for Communication of Acceptance

To create a bilateral contract, the offeree's promise must be communicated to the offeror or the offeror's agent. However, the offeror may dispense with the need for communication by manifesting such an intent. At times, a reasonable attempt to communicate is sufficient. (*See* 11, *infra*.)

6. Necessity of Notice in Unilateral Contract

There are three views on the issue of whether the offeree must give notice of performance to the offeror. (1) Notice is not required unless requested by the offer. (2) If the offeree has reason to know that the offeror has no adequate means of learning of performance with reasonable promptness and certitude, failure to exercise reasonable diligence in giving notice discharges the offeror from liability, unless the offeror otherwise learns of performance within a reasonable time or the offeror expressly or by implication indicates that notification is not necessary. (3) The third view is the same as the second view except that no contract is consummated unless and until notice of performance has been sent. The second view is the prevailing view and is the view of both the first and second Restatements.

7. Acceptance of an Offer Looking to a Series of Contracts

If an offer looks to a series of contracts, a contract arises each time the offeree accepts. As to the future, the offer is revocable unless the offer is irrevocable. Whether an offer looks to one or a series of acceptances is a question to be determined under the reasonable person test. Care must be taken to distinguish an offer looking to a series of acceptances from an offer looking to *one* acceptance with a series of performances.

8. Acceptance by Silence

The general rule is that silence ordinarily does not give rise to an acceptance of an offer or a counteroffer. This rule does not apply: (1) Where the offeror has given the offeree reason to believe silence will act as an acceptance and the offeree intends by silence to accept; (2) Where the parties have mutually agreed that silence will operate as consent; (3) Where there is a course of dealing between the parties so that silence has come to mean assent; (4) Where the offeree accepts services with reasonable opportunity to reject them, and should reasonably understand that they are offered with expectation of payment. This illustrates a non-promissory offer.

9. Acceptance by Act of Dominion

At times, an offeree takes possession of offered goods but indicates that the offered terms are not acceptable. This conduct constitutes the tort of conversion—the wrongful act of dominion over the personal property of another. Because the conduct could have been rightful and referable to the offered terms, the offeror has the option to treat the conduct as rightful, suing on a contract theory and estopping the offeree from claiming to be a wrongdoer. There is some authority, however, to the effect that this option is not available if the offered terms are manifestly unreasonable.

10. Unsolicited Sending of Goods

An exception exists to the exercise-of-dominion rule under legislation providing that a person who receives unsolicited goods may treat them as a gift.

11. When Is an Acceptance in a Bilateral Contract Effective (Mailbox Rule)?

When the parties are at a distance from one another, is an acceptance effective when put out of the possession of the offeree or when it is received? This depends upon whether the method of acceptance is appropriate or not. If the medium of communication is reasonable, the acceptance will be effective when sent and *even if it is lost or delayed.* It is likely to be reasonable if it is the same medium used by the offeror (unless the offeror specified otherwise) or it is customary in similar transactions at the time and place the offer is received. However, a communication will not be effective when sent if proper care has not been taken in transmitting it (e.g., incorrectly addressed). Under the Restatement (Second), even if an unreasonable means is used or care is not taken in transmission, the acceptance nonetheless will be effective when sent, provided it is received within the time a seasonably dispatched acceptance sent in a reasonable manner would normally have arrived.

12. Prescribed Method of Acceptance

If the offer prescribes an exclusive method of acceptance, no contract arises if the offeree utilizes another means of acceptance even if the acceptance comes to the attention of the offeror. This is a qualification of the rules stated above.

13. Parties in the Presence of One Another

Contrary to the rule for parties at a distance, when the parties are in the presence of one another, an acceptance is inoperative unless the offeror hears or is at fault in not hearing. Even if the offeror is at fault in not hearing, there is no contract if the offeree knows or has reason to know that the offeror has not heard.

14. Offeror's Power to Negate Mailbox Rule

An offeror may negate the mailbox rule by providing in the offer that the acceptance will be effective only when and if received.

15. Withdrawal of Acceptance

Even if the offeree is able to regain possession of the letter pursuant to postal regulations, the letter of acceptance is effective.

16. When Offeree Sends a Rejection First and Then an Acceptance

An acceptance dispatched after a rejection has been sent is not effective until received and then only if received prior to the rejection.

17. When Offeree Sends Acceptance First but Rejection Is Received Before Acceptance

The usual holding is that a contract is formed, but if the offeror relies on the rejection before receiving the acceptance, the offeree will be estopped from enforcing the agreement.

18. Risk of Mistake in Transmission by an Intermediary

The mistake discussed here is not made by a party or an agent, but by an intermediary, e.g., a telegraph company. Lost messages are governed by the mailbox rule and the present discussion has nothing to do with them. The topic has to do with a message that is received but is garbled or otherwise incorrectly transmitted. The majority view is that the message as transmitted is operative unless the other party knows or has reason to know of the mistake. The minority view is to the effect that there is no contract if the offer or acceptance is not the message authorized by the party.

D. TERMINATION OF REVOCABLE OFFERS

A revocable offer may be terminated in a variety of ways.

1. Lapse of Time

An offer is terminated after the lapse of time specified in the offer. Usually, this time is measured from the time the offer is received. If no time is specified, the offer is open for a reasonable time.

a. Face to Face Offer

Where an offer is made in any situation where there are direct negotiations (e.g., face to face, telephone) the offer is deemed, in the absence of a manifestation of a contrary intention, to be open only while the parties are conversing.

b. Termination upon Happening of a Particular Event

If the offeror stipulates that the offer shall terminate upon the happening of a certain event and the event occurs before acceptance, the power of acceptance is terminated.

c. Effect of a Late Acceptance

There are three views with respect to a late acceptance. (1) The late acceptance is an offer which in turn can be accepted only by a communicated acceptance. (2) The original offeror may treat the late acceptance as an acceptance by unilaterally waiving the lateness. (3) If the late acceptance is sent in what could plausibly be considered to be a reasonable time, the original offeror has a duty to so inform the offeree within a reasonable time. Failure to do so creates a contract by silence.

2. Death of Offeror

If the offeror dies between the making of the offer and the acceptance, the offer is terminated even if the offeree is unaware of the offeror's death. Under a minority view, death terminates the offer only if the offeror is aware of it.

3. Incapacity of Offeror

a. Adjudication of Incapacity

Where there is an adjudication of mental incapacity and the property of the offeror is placed under guardianship, any unaccepted offer made by the offeror is terminated. This is so, according to the majority view, even though the offeree is unaware of what has occurred.

b. Where There Is No Adjudication

If there is no adjudication of incompetency, the rule is that supervening mental incapacity in fact terminates the offer if the offeree is or should be aware of the incapacity.

4. Death or Incapacity of the Offeree

The death or adjudication of incapacity of the offeree terminates the offer.

5. Revocation

a. Direct Revocation

A communicated revocation terminates the offeree's power of acceptance and is effective when it is received except in a few states where statutes provide that it is effective on dispatch. At common law, even if the offer says it is irrevocable, it is still revocable unless consideration or the equivalent is given for the promise of irrevocability.

b. Equal Publication

When an offer is made to a number of persons whose identity is unknown to the offeror (e.g., a reward offer in a newspaper), the offer can be revoked by giving equal publication of the revocation as was given to the offer. Even here, if the offeror knows of the identity of a person who is taking action on the offer, the offeror must communicate the revocation to that person.

c. Indirect Revocation

Indirect revocation occurs when the offeree acquires reliable information from a third party that the offeror has engaged in conduct that would indicate to a reasonable person that the offeror no longer wishes to make the offer. Information is reliable only if it comes from a reliable source and is in fact true.

d. Special Rules Relating to the Revocation of an Offer Looking to a Unilateral Contract

There are three views with respect to the revocation of an offer looking to a unilateral contract. (1) The traditional rule is that the offer can be revoked at any time until the moment of complete performance. (2) A bilateral contract is formed upon the beginning of performance. (3) The prevailing view is that once the offeree starts to perform, the offer becomes irrevocable. (An irrevocable offer is synonymous with an option contract). This rule requires the actual beginning or tender of performance and not merely preparation. Extensive preparation for performance might, however, trigger a finding of promissory estoppel.

6. Death or Destruction

Death of a person or destruction of a thing essential for the performance of the offered contract terminates the offer.

7. Supervening Illegality

If, between the making of the offer and the acceptance, a change of law or regulations renders the proposed contract illegal, the offer is terminated.

8. Rejection or Counter-Offer

a. Common Law

An offeree's power of acceptance is terminated by a rejection or a counter-offer unless the offeror or the offeree manifests a contrary intention.

b. Nature of a Rejection or Counter-Offer

A rejection is a statement by the offeree that he or she does not wish to accept the offer. A rejection is effective when it is received. A counter-offer is a response to the offer that adds qualifications or conditions. A counter-offer acts as a rejection even if the qualification or condition relates to a trivial matter (ribbon matching, or mirror-image, rule). A counter-offer, in turn, can be accepted.

c. Counter-Offer Distinguished from Other Communications

A counter-offer must be distinguished from a counter-inquiry, a comment upon the terms, a request for a modification of the offer, an acceptance coupled with a request for a modification of the contract, a grumbling assent that falls short of dissent, an acceptance plus a separate offer, and a future acceptance. If an acceptance contains a term that is not expressly stated in the offer but is implied therein there is an acceptance and not a counter-offer.

d. UCC § 2–207

This section is designed to negate the mirror image rule in cases involving the sale of goods. Under UCC § 2–207(1), a "definite and seasonable expression of acceptance . . . operates as an acceptance even though it states terms additional to or different from those offered . . ., unless acceptance is expressly made conditional on assent to the additional or different terms." Despite the apparent simplicity of this provision, it has created quicksand-like difficulties in analysis and significant divisions of authority in the case law.

e. Additional Terms

If there is an effective acceptance under UCC § 2–207(1), under UCC § 2–207(2) additional terms in the acceptance are treated as proposals for addition to the contract. If the parties are both merchants, the additional terms become part of the contract unless (1) the offer expressly limits acceptance to the terms of the offer; (2) the additional terms would materially alter the contract; or (3) the offeror notifies the offeree in advance or within a reasonable time that he or she objects to the additional terms. If either party is a non-merchant, the additional terms are "to be construed as proposals for addition to the contract" and are otherwise discarded.

f. Different Terms

The UCC does not state a specific rule for different terms so it is difficult to know how they should be treated. A different term is one that clashes with a term of the offer. The emerging trend is to hold that different terms knock each other out.

g. Conduct of Parties

Even though a contract is not formed by the communications of the parties, a contract may arise by the conduct of the parties under subsection (3) of UCC § 2–207. In such a case, the terms of the contract are those upon which the parties agree plus terms incorporated under other UCC provisions.

E. OPTION CONTRACTS—IRREVOCABLE OFFERS

1. What Makes an Offer Irrevocable?

An offer can be made irrevocable (1) by consideration; (2) by statute; (3) under one of the special rules relating to the revocation of a unilateral contract (*see supra*); (4) under the doctrine of promissory estoppel (*see* III.I, *infra*); and (5) by virtue of a sealed instrument.

2. Statute

UCC § 2–205 empowers an offeror to create an irrevocable offer without consideration. The requisites are: (1) the offeror must be a merchant; (2) a signed writing; (3) language assuring that the offer will be held open; (4) the period of irrevocability may not exceed three months; and (5) if the language of irrevocability appears on the offeree's form, it must be separately signed by the offeror.

3. Terms Are Synonymous

For the most part, the terms "irrevocable offer" and "option contract" are synonymous. An option contract is an offer that also binds the offeror to a contract that the offer cannot be revoked. (Notice that UCC § 2–205 uses the term "firm offer" to refer to what we would otherwise call an irrevocable offer.)

4. Termination of Irrevocable Offers

Irrevocable offers *are* terminated by: (1) lapse of time; (2) death or destruction of a person or thing essential for the performance of the offered contract; or (3) supervening legal prohibition. They are *not* terminated by: (1) revocation, (2) death or supervening incapacity of the offeror or the offeree, or (3) rejection.

5. When Is the Acceptance of an Irrevocable Offer Effective?

Contrary to the mailbox rule employed for acceptances of revocable offers, an acceptance of an irrevocable offer is effective when received.

F. CERTAINTY

1. Common Law

a. Introduction

Even though the parties have gone through a process of offer and acceptance so that there is mutual assent, the agreement is unenforceable if the content of their agreement is unduly uncertain.

b. Rule

The offer must be so definite as to its *material* terms or require such definite terms in the acceptance that the promises and the performances to be rendered by each party are *reasonably* certain.

c. What Are Material Terms?

Material terms include subject matter, price, payment terms, quantity, quality, duration, and the work to be done. Given the infinite variety of contracts, it is obvious that no precise definition can be stated. Indefiniteness as to an immaterial term is not fatal.

d. Reasonable Certainty

To be reasonably certain, a term need not be set forth with optimal specificity. It is enough that the agreement is sufficiently explicit so that the court can perceive the parties' respective obligations. What is reasonably certain depends on subject matter, the purposes and relationship of the parties, and the circumstances under which the agreement was made.

e. Types of Indefiniteness Problems

(1) Where the parties have purported to agree upon a material term but have left it indefinite (not reasonably certain), there is no room for implication and the agreement is unenforceable.

(2) Where the parties are *silent* as to a material term or discuss it but do not purport to agree upon it, it is possible that the indefiniteness can be cured through the use of a gap-filler or from external sources including standard terms, usage, course of dealing and, according to some cases, by evidence of subjective intention. A gap-filler is a term supplied by the court because it thinks that the parties would have agreed upon this term if it had been brought to their attention, or because it is a term that comports with community standards of fairness.

(3) Where the parties *agree to agree* as to a material term, under the traditional rule, the agreement is fatally indefinite and the gap-filling mechanism, discussed above, may not be used. Some of the more modern cases (even without relying on the UCC and the Restatement (Second), discussed below), have abandoned this rule, and some have held that there is a duty to negotiate in good faith even though there is no such provision in the agreement. The UCC and the Restatement (Second) are generally in accord with the modern view on questions of agreement to agree.

(4) Indefiniteness may be cured by the subsequent conduct or agreement of the parties.

2. Uniform Commercial Code

a. Introduction

The provisions of the Uniform Commercial Code relating to indefiniteness are of two types. There is a very important general provision, and there are provisions relating to specific problems that can be generally categorized under the heading of gap-fillers.

b. Specific Gap-Fillers

The Code has specific provisions that supply reasonable terms in various circumstances. These include price, time for delivery, place of delivery, shipment, payment, duration of contract, and specification of assortment.

c. General Provision

Even if one or more terms are left open, a contract for sale does not fail for indefiniteness if the parties have intended to make a contract and there is a reasonably certain basis for giving an appropriate remedy. (UCC § 2–204(3)). The test is not certainty as to what the parties were to do nor as to the exact amount of damages due to the plaintiff. Rather, commercial standards on the issue of indefiniteness are to be applied.

d. Discussion of General Provision

This provision is designed to prevent, where it is at all possible, a contracting party who is dissatisfied with the bargain from taking refuge in the doctrine of indefiniteness to wriggle out of a contract. This section is designed to change the traditional common law approaches. Thus, a gap-filler would be available even though the parties purported to agree upon a term or made an agreement to agree with respect to it. But the section goes beyond gap-fillers and permits a court to use any reasonably certain basis for giving an appropriate remedy.

e. Questions of Fact and Law

Whether the parties intended to contract is a question of fact. Whether there is a reasonably certain basis for giving an appropriate remedy is a question of law.

3. Restatement (Second)

a. Compared to UCC

The Restatement is in general accord with the Uniform Commercial Code, but Article 2 of the UCC applies only to a contract for the sale of goods. (Sometimes it is applied to other types of contracts by analogy.) The Restatement (Second) applies to all types of contracts.

b. Trend

The trend is toward the rules of the UCC and the Restatement (Second).

G. DIGITAL CONTRACTS

1. Digital Contracts and Traditional Contract Law

The increasing prominence of the Internet and of digital media has had a significant effect on contract law. It has also created a tension between traditional contract law—formed and developed over centuries—and the less formal interactions between parties that can occur digitally. Two basic problems typically confront us. First, how does the electronic context of such contracts affect the application of basic principles of contract formation? Second, do unread (and, typically, unseen) terms in an electronic contract raise special problems of unfairness and unconscionability?

2. Contract Formation in an Electronic Context

The simple fact is that buyers now routinely use the Internet and other digital media to transact directly with a goods manufacturer or a service provider. Contract law emphasizes the objective intentions of the parties, and the circumstances surrounding a contract, the current and past practices of the parties and of their particular industry or trade obviously affect how those intentions are manifested. The use of digital media certainly is part of the behavior and customary practices of contracting parties. And so, one needs to be aware of how basic principles of contract law, developed over centuries, interact with these current practices of "e-commerce."

3. Electronic Contract Terms and Unfairness

In the process of digital contracting, many important terms of the contract may not be directly presented to the party accessing the other party's site. There may be links to the terms, or simply an indication that the contract will be "subject to" terms that appear on a related site. How should we handle the risk that some of these terms tend to be more favorable to the site's owner than to the other party? Beginning with a 1996 decision by the Seventh Circuit, *ProCD, Inc. v. Zeidenberg*, a majority of the case law that has addressed this issue has allowed the formation of a contract, with terms possibly realized later, unless the later terms are prohibited by some other public policy or are so unfair that they are considered "unconscionable." (On unconscionability, *see* IX.F., *infra*.) A minority position found in some of the cases only upholds "terms later" when there is conspicuous notice and an opportunity to review/reject. The majority view effectively gives the offeror the power to dictate specific terms with very passive "acceptance" by the other party.

III. CONSIDERATION AND ITS EQUIVALENTS

A. INTRODUCTION

1. What Promises Should Be Enforced

Gratuitous promises—promises not supported by consideration—are not enforced, but such promises may be enforced under the doctrine of promissory estoppel or under certain statutes. In addition, in certain instances a moral obligation may make a promise enforceable. A delivered sealed instrument is enforceable without consideration, but this rule has been changed in most states by statutes, including the UCC.

B. CONSIDERATION

1. In General

For a promise to be supported by consideration (and therefore be enforceable), two elements must concur. (a) The promisee must suffer legal detriment—that is, do or promise to do what the promisee is not legally obligated to do, or refrain from doing or promise to refrain from doing what the promisee is legally privileged to do. (b) The detriment must be bargained for.

2. Legal Benefit to Promisor

The rule above is stated in terms of legal detriment incurred by the promisee. Often, however, it is phrased in terms of either legal detriment to the promisee or legal benefit to the promisor. Because the result is invariably the same, the discussion here will be in terms of legal detriment.

3. Must Detriment Be Suffered by Promisee?

Although the rule is stated in terms of a legal detriment suffered by the promisee, it is nonetheless well settled that it does not matter from whom or to whom the detriment moves so long as it is bargained for and given in exchange for the promise.

4. Detriment Must Induce Promise

The promisor must have manifested an offering state of mind rather than a gift making state of mind. If the promisor manifests a gift making state of mind, any detriment has not induced the promise. Therefore, a promise to make a gift is not enforceable. Note that the promisor need only exchange the promise in part for the detriment to be suffered.

5. Past Consideration

Past consideration is not consideration because one does not make an exchange for something that has already occurred.

6. Motive

A promisor's motive in making a promise is not related to the question of detriment, but the motive of the promisor in making the promise is relevant on the issue of exchange.

7. Adequacy of Detriment

Any detriment no matter how small or how economically inadequate will support a promise provided that the detriment is in fact bargained for. But economic inadequacy may constitute some circumstantial evidence of fraud, duress, overreaching, undue influence, mistake or that the detriment was not in fact bargained for. Adequacy of the detriment may also be considered under the doctrine of unconscionability.

8. Sham Consideration

Where an instrument falsely recites that a consideration has been given, the consideration is *sham*. The majority view is that such a recital does not make a promise enforceable. There is a contrary view that relates only to option contracts and credit guaranties.

9. Nominal (Token) Consideration

Where the parties actually exchange or promise to exchange a peppercorn or small sum for the promise because they have learned that a gratuitous problem is not enforceable, the issue is whether *nominal* or *token* consideration will bind the promise. They have attempted to make the promise enforceable by cloaking a gratuitous promise with the form of a bargain. One view is that the promise should not be enforced because the alleged bargain is a pretense. There is also a contrary view. The overwhelming majority of the cases involve option contracts in which the use of nominal (token) consideration has generally been upheld. Where the promise is basically a promise to make a gift, it is unlikely to be upheld.

10. Invalid Claims

There are a number of views on the issue of whether the surrender of or forbearance to assert an invalid claim is detriment. (1) The earliest and now obsolete view is that the surrender of an invalid claim does not constitute detriment. (2) The surrender of the invalid claim serves as detriment if the claimant has asserted it in good faith and a reasonable person would believe that the claim was well founded. (3) Still other courts have held that the only requirement is good faith. (4) The new Restatement takes the position that either good faith or objective uncertainty as to the validity of the claim is sufficient. *Caveat*: This discussion only considers whether the surrender of an invalid claim constitutes detriment. If it does, one must still confront the question of whether this is what is bargained for. For example, in a particular case is the promisor bargaining for the surrender of an invalid claim or the surrender of a worthless piece of paper? This presents a factual question.

C. THE PRE-EXISTING DUTY RULE

1. Pre-Existing Duty and Promises

A party who does or promises to do only what the party is legally obligated to do is not suffering a legal detriment because the party is not surrendering a legal right. The problem arises in three types of fact patterns. First, the rule applies even if the duty is imposed by law rather than by contract. Second, where the parties to a contract modify an existing agreement and one party does not suffer new detriment, usually the modification is not enforced, but there are cases that, on a wide variety of theories, have enforced such a modification. For example, The Restatement (Second) upholds such a modification if it is fair and equitable in view of circumstances not anticipated when the contract is made. Third, where an outsider promises to compensate a party bound by a contract to perform a pre-existing duty under a contract, there are two views. (a) The promise is not enforceable; (b) the promise is enforceable because there is less likelihood of coercion in the three-party cases.

2. Pre-Existing Duty and Accord and Satisfaction—Foakes v. Beer

The rule of Foakes v. Beer is that part payment by the debtor of an amount here and now undisputedly due is not detriment to support a promise by the creditor to discharge the entire amount. The rule of Foakes v. Beer is another application of the pre-existing duty rule; the debtor, in making the part payment, is only performing part of a legal obligation. This rule is followed by the majority of jurisdictions with some exceptions in particular fact patterns. A minority of jurisdictions have rejected the rule completely. The rule does not apply if there is a detriment, in addition to the part payment, that is in fact bargained for.

a. Liquidated and Unliquidated Claims

The rule of Foakes v. Beer applies only to liquidated claims; that is, claims that are undisputed as to their existence and where the amount due has been agreed upon or can be precisely determined. If there is a dispute as to liability or to the amount due or some other question, the claim is unliquidated even if a party's assertion is incorrect, provided that the assertion is made in good faith and, according to some jurisdictions, if it is reasonably asserted (*see* Invalid Claims, III.B.10, *supra*).

b. Analyzing an Accord and Satisfaction

When a question of accord and satisfaction is presented, the analysis should be divided into three parts. (1) Have the parties gone through a process of offer and acceptance? The rule relating to an offer of accord is that the offeror must make it clear that the offeror seeks a total discharge, otherwise any payment made and accepted will be treated as a part payment. (2) Has the accord been carried out? (3) Is there consideration to support the accord and satisfaction?

3. UCC Inroads on Pre-Existing Duty Rule

a. UCC § 2–209(1)

Under subsection (1), a modification of a contract is binding without consideration even if it is oral, but in two instances a writing is required. A writing is required under subsection (3) if the contract as modified is within the statute of frauds provision of the UCC (discussed below). The second situation where a writing is required is under subsection (2).

b. UCC § 2–209(2)

At common law, if a contract provides that it cannot be modified or rescinded except in writing, an oral modification is nonetheless binding. Under this subsection such a provision will be honored. A modification (or rescission) will be enforced (except as stated below) only if the modifying agreement is in a signed writing. If the form containing the provision is prepared by a merchant, a non-merchant will be bound by it only if this provision is separately signed.

c. UCC § 2–209(4) & (5)

If a signed writing is required under the provisions of subsections (2) and (3), and the modifying agreement is not in a signed writing, it may nevertheless be enforced if there has been performance under the modifying agreement. Subsection (5) provides that, despite performance, a party as to the unperformed part may reinstate the original agreement unless to do so would be unjust in view of a material change of position as a result of reliance upon the modification.

d. Bad Faith and Duress

UCC § 2–209 also changes the common law rule with respect to duress. The traditional common law rule is that a threat to breach a contract does not constitute duress (*see infra*). But under this provision of the UCC the extortion of a modification without a legitimate commercial reason is ineffective as a violation of the good faith provisions of the Code. Conversely, a modification based upon a legitimate commercial reason does not constitute duress unless undue coercion is applied. Nor, under this provision, can a mere technical consideration support a modification extracted in bad faith.

e. Release (UCC § 1–107)

The pre-existing duty concept, together with the weakening of the power of the sealed instrument, led to the rule that a release of a duty is ordinarily ineffectual without consideration. UCC § 1–107 provides, however, that any claim of right arising out of an alleged breach can be discharged in whole or in part by a written waiver or renunciation signed and delivered by the aggrieved party. Under this section, a written signed and delivered release will be effective to discharge an alleged breach in whole or in part even though the release is not supported by consideration. Section 1–306 of the revision is in accord but does not require delivery.

D. SPECIAL PROBLEMS IN BILATERAL CONTRACTS

1. Is One Promise Consideration for the Other?

A promise in a bilateral contract is consideration for the counter-promise only if the performance that is promised would be consideration.

2. Mutuality of Obligation

a. Introduction

The doctrine of mutuality of obligation is commonly, but inaccurately, expressed in the phrase that in a bilateral contract both parties must be bound, or neither is bound. The doctrine is, however, really one of mutuality of consideration. The point is that if *B*'s promise is not consideration, *B* may not enforce *A*'s promise. Conversely *A* may not enforce *B*'s promise even though *A*'s promised performance is consideration.

b. Unilateral Contracts

The doctrine of mutuality does not apply to unilateral contracts.

c. Voidable and Unenforceable Promises

The doctrine of mutuality does not apply to a voidable or unenforceable promise because a voidable or unenforceable promise is consideration for a counter-promise.

d. Illusory Promises

An illusory promise is an expression cloaked in promissory terms but which, upon closer examination, reveals that the promisor has made no commitment. The modern decisional tendency is against finding a promise to be illusory and in general against defeating agreements on the technical ground of lack of mutuality. One method of circumventing the illusory promise problem is by interpolating into an agreement that otherwise seems illusory the requirement of good faith and/or reasonableness.

e. Right to Terminate in Contract

If a party reserves the right to terminate the arrangement by giving notice at any time or without giving notice at all, the older cases held that the party was not suffering detriment. The later cases lean to the view that there is detriment in giving notice. When the provision is for termination without notice, these cases ignore the provision by a process of interpretation and require reasonable notice. UCC § 2–309(3) has a provision that bears on this problem. It states, "Termination of a contract by one party except on the happening of an agreed event requires that reasonable notification be received by the other party and an agreement dispensing with notification is invalid if its operation would be unconscionable."

f. Conditional Promises

If a condition is attached to a promise, it does not render a promise illusory if the condition is outside the control of the party who makes it, or if it relates to an event that is outside of the promisor's unfettered discretion. At times, an illusory promise problem is avoided by treating the express language of condition as carrying with it an implied promise to use reasonable efforts to bring about the happening of the condition.

g. Aleatory Promises

A promise is aleatory if it is conditional on the happening of a fortuitous event, or an event supposed by the parties to be fortuitous. An aleatory promise is not illusory, because the condition is based upon an event outside of the control of either party.

h. Consideration Supplied by Implied Promise

At times, a party has made what amounts to an illusory promise, but the entire fact pattern shows that a commercially serious transaction is contemplated. In such a case a court may infer a promise (e.g., to use reasonable efforts) to eliminate the illusory promise problem. Sometimes, the promise inferred is called an implied promise. At other times, it is referred to as a constructive promise. Whichever label is attached the result is the same.

i. UCC § 2–306(2)

This section provides: a lawful agreement by either the seller or the buyer for exclusive dealing in the kind of goods concerned imposes unless otherwise agreed an obligation by the seller to use best efforts to supply the goods and by the buyer to promote their sale. While this section is about more than consideration, it imposes the kind of obligation that courts have sometimes inferred. *See* h *supra*.

j. Agreement Allowing Party to Supply Material Term

If a bilateral agreement permits a party to supply a material term, the promise at common law sometimes was deemed to be illusory and, therefore, the bilateral agreement void under the mutuality doctrine. The UCC, with its insistence on good faith, changes the common law rule relating to the right of a party to supply a term.

k. Void Contract Is Not Always a Nullity

Although a wholly executory void contract is a nullity, if there is performance under a void bilateral contract, the case should be treated as if an offer looking to a unilateral contract or a series of unilateral contracts was made. If this cannot be done, a quasi-contractual action for reasonable value may be available.

E. REQUIREMENTS AND OUTPUT CONTRACTS

1. Introduction

The quantity term may be measured by the requirements of the buyer (requirements contract), or by the output of the seller (output contract). Since the rules are basically the same in the two situations, as a matter of convenience, emphasis will be on the topic of requirements contracts.

2. Validity

Under the UCC it is clear that these contracts are binding.

3. How Much Is a Requirements Buyer Entitled to?

Under the UCC the buyer under a requirements contract is entitled to good faith needs with two exceptions. (1) If there is a stated estimate, the buyer is not entitled to any quantity disproportionately greater than the estimate. (2) If there is no estimate or maximum or minimum stated in the contract, the buyer may demand only any normal or otherwise comparable prior requirements.

4. May a Requirements Buyer Diminish or Terminate Requirements?

Under the UCC, the buyer may go out of business or change methods of doing business in good faith. This is so even if the reductions are highly disproportionate to normal prior requirements or stated estimates.

F. MUST ALL OF THE CONSIDERATION BE VALID?

1. Rule

The general rule is that all of the purported considerations need not be valid.

2. Conjunctive Promises

The rule stated above applies to conjunctive promises, e.g., a debtor promises to pay a past due debt and to perform additional services. The debtor's promise provides consideration for a counter-promise.

G. ALTERNATIVE PROMISES

1. Where the Choice of Alternatives Is in the Promisor

In this case, each alternative must be detrimental unless, according to the Restatement (Second), there is a substantial possibility that events may eliminate the alternative that is not detrimental before the promisor exercises a choice.

2. Where the Choice of Alternatives Is in the Promisee

If the choice of alternatives is in the promisee, the alternative promises supply consideration for a counter-promise if any of the alternative promises is detrimental.

H. MORAL OBLIGATION

1. Introduction

Where a promisor makes a promise because of an antecedent moral or legal obligation, it is clear that the promise is not enforceable under the doctrine of consideration because of the rule that past consideration is not consideration.

2. Rule

In most instances, a promise made in recognition of a prior moral or legal obligation is not enforceable.

3. Major Exceptions

a. Promise to Pay Fixed Amount for Services Previously Requested Where No Price Fixed

If services were rendered with the expectation on both sides that they would be paid for, and the parties agree on a fixed price, there is consideration for the new agreement. Beyond that most courts enforce a promise by a party to pay a fixed amount even though it is not accepted by the other party. Under a minority view, the promise is enforced only to the extent that it is not greatly disproportionate to the value of the services.

b. Promise to Pay When Services Not Requested

Under the majority view, a promise to pay for services not requested is not enforceable. The Restatement (Second), however, states that the promise is enforceable to the extent necessary to prevent injustice if the promisee has conferred a material benefit on the promisor.

c. Promises to Pay Debts Discharged by a Statute of Limitations

A promise to pay all or part of any antecedent contractual or quasi-contractual obligation for the payment of money causes the applicable statute of limitations to run anew. An acknowledgment is ordinarily deemed the equivalent of a promise, as is a voluntary part payment of principal or interest. In most states, the promise or the acknowledgment must be in writing. The action is limited by the terms of the new promise.

d. Promises to Perform a Voidable Duty

A promise to perform a voidable duty is enforceable despite the absence of consideration, as long as the new promise does not suffer from an infirmity that would in turn make it voidable. This rule does not generally apply to void contracts.

I. PROMISSORY ESTOPPEL

1. Introduction

The doctrine of promissory estoppel was created as a separate and specific doctrine in the Twentieth Century. Prior to that, the doctrine was employed, although not so labeled, in a limited number of cases. These included (1) family promises; (2) a promise to make a gift of land; (3) gratuitous agencies and bailments; (4) charitable subscriptions; and (5) marriage settlements. There were specific rules for each category.

2. Restatement, First

Under the formulation of the First Restatement, the elements required for the doctrine to operate are: (1) A promise is required. (2) The promise must be one which the promisor should reasonably anticipate will lead the promisee to act or forbear. The same thought could be expressed by saying that the promisee must justifiably rely on the promise. (3) The reliance must be of a substantial character. (4) The promise will be enforced only if injustice can be avoided by the enforcement of the promise. (5) Although not stated, the notion is that the promise will be enforced as made or not at all.

3. Restatement (Second)

The Restatement (Second) has made four important changes in the formulation of the doctrine. (1) In the text it has eliminated the requirement that the reliance be definite and substantial. However, a comment indicates that these are still factors to be considered except as indicated below. (2) It added a new sentence permitting flexibility of remedy. Thus, the promise need not be enforced as made but may be enforced to the extent of reasonable reliance. (3) It provides for the contingency of reliance by a third party. (4) It contains a provision that a charitable subscription or a marriage settlement is binding without proof that the promise induced action or forbearance.

4. Present Approach to Gift Promises

Although initially the courts for the most part used promissory estoppel as a substitute for consideration in the types of cases mentioned in the introduction, with the impetus given to the doctrine by the two Restatements, it is fair to say that the present tendency is to use promissory estoppel in just about any case where the necessary elements are present.

5. Doctrine Has Been Used in Business Context

The doctrine has been used in some cases: (1) to make an offer irrevocable; (2) to enforce a promise that is part of an otherwise unenforceable defective contract; and (3) to enforce a promise made during the course of preliminary negotiations.

IV. LEGAL CAPACITY

A. INFANTS

1. Who Is an Infant?

A person remains an infant until the first moment of the day preceding his or her 18th birthday and remains an infant despite emancipation and despite marriage.

2. Is Infant's Promise Void or Voidable?

A contract made by an infant is voidable at the option of the infant. However, the infant may not disaffirm certain contracts because public policy or a statute so provides or because the infant has done something or promised to do something which the law would compel even in the absence of contract (e.g., support his out-of-wedlock child).

3. Tort Liability

An infant may avoid a contract but is liable for torts. At times, it is difficult to distinguish tort liability from contractual liability, such as in the area of fraud and warranty.

4. Avoidance and Ratification

a. Avoidance

The infant may avoid (disaffirm) the contract at any time prior to ratification. The avoidance may be made during the period of infancy and once made is irrevocable. In the case of real property, however, the majority rule is that the infant's promise may be avoided only after majority.

b. Ratification

The infant may ratify (affirm) the contract after reaching majority. This may take place in three ways: (a) express ratification, (b) conduct manifesting an intent to ratify (retention and enjoyment of benefits and services), and (c) failure to disaffirm within a reasonable time after majority.

c. Ignorance of Law and Fact

A ratification is ineffective if the former infant is unaware of the facts upon which the ratification depends. There is a split of authority as to whether the infant must know that the law gives a power of avoidance.

5. Effect of Misrepresentation of Age

According to the majority view, infants may disaffirm even if they misrepresented their ages. The authorities are about evenly split on the question of whether infants are liable in tort for misrepresenting their ages.

6. Infants and Subsequent Purchasers for Value

If a minor disaffirms a conveyance of real property, the land may be reclaimed from a subsequent good faith purchaser for value without notice. The rule is different in the case of a sale of goods and a sale of securities.

7. Restitution After Disaffirmance

a. Infant as Defendant

Upon disaffirmance, the infant is liable for the return (or the value) of any tangible benefits the infant has received and still has.

b. Infant as Plaintiff

If upon disaffirmance an infant sues for the return of the consideration the infant has supplied, under the now prevailing view the infant's recovery is offset by the value of use and depreciation of any property obtained from defendant. The more traditional view is that only property the infant still has need be returned.

c. Necessaries

An infant is liable in quasi-contract for the reasonable value of necessaries the infant has received.

B. MENTAL INCOMPETENTS

1. Tests of Mental Incompetency

Where there is no prior adjudication of incompetence, the great majority of the cases utilize the test of whether the party was able to understand the nature, purpose, and consequences of the act at the time of the transaction. The more modern view adopts *in addition* the test of whether by reason of mental illness or defect a person is unable to act in a reasonable manner in relation to the transaction, and the other party has reason to know of this condition. Under either test, the promise of the incompetent is voidable. If, however, the party had been adjudicated as incompetent prior to the transaction and a guardian had been appointed, the transaction is void.

2. Restrictions on Power of Avoidance

The promise of an unadjudicated incompetent that is still executory is voidable; but executed transactions are not voidable (contrary to infancy cases) unless the incompetent can restore the other party to the status quo ante. If the incompetence was obvious, however, the incompetent must make restitution only to the extent that tangible benefits remain.

3. Necessaries

As in the case of infants, incompetents are liable for the reasonable value of necessaries furnished them.

V. INTERPRETATION AND PROPER FORM (WRITING REQUIREMENT)

A. PAROL EVIDENCE RULE

1. Rule

A total integration (a writing that the parties intend to be final and complete) cannot be contradicted or supplemented. A partial integration (a writing that the parties intend to be final but not complete) cannot be contradicted but may be supplemented by consistent additional terms.

2. Focus of Rule

If applicable, the rule excludes prior written or oral agreements entered into by the parties and contemporaneous oral agreements, but contemporaneous writings are normally held to be part of the integration.

3. How to Determine Finality

Any relevant evidence is admissible on the question of finality. There are not many disputes about finality. The basic question is, did both parties assent to the written terms?

4. How to Determine Completeness

There are many disputes about completeness and a wide variety of views as to how completeness should be determined. These include: (1) The Four Corner's Rule; (2) The Collateral Contract Concept; (3) Williston's Rules; (4) Corbin's

View; (5) The UCC (§ 2–202) Approach; and (6) That of the Restatement (Second).

5. Subsequent Agreement

The parol evidence rule never excludes subsequent agreements.

6. Rule of Substantive Law or Procedure?

The rule has both a procedural and a substantive aspect. It is procedural because it excludes evidence; it is substantive because it determines the terms of the contract.

7. Is the Offered Term Contradictory or Consistent?

Under the modern view, to be contradictory the offered term must contradict an express term of the integration. It is not enough that it may contradict an implied or inferred term.

8. Undercutting the Integration

The parol evidence rule is not applicable unless there is a contract. Thus, the rule permits evidence offered to show that the agreement is void or voidable. For example, a party may show sham, illegality, mistake, duress, or the existence of a condition precedent to the formation of the contract.

B. INTERPRETATION

1. What Is Interpretation?

Interpretation is the ascertainment of the meaning of a communication or a document. In interpreting, there are two fundamental questions: (1) Whose meaning is to be given to the communication—in technical language, what standard of interpretation is to be used? (2) What evidence may be taken into account?

2. Variety of Views

As in the case of the parol evidence rule there are a wide variety of views on these two questions. These include (1) The Plain Meaning Rule; (2) Williston's Rules; (3) Corbin's View; (4) The UCC Rule.

3. Rules of Construction

A rule of construction is an aid in interpreting contracts. For example, specific terms are given greater weight than general terms.

4. Course of Dealing

A course of dealing is based upon a sequence of conduct in *previous* contracts between the parties. Under the UCC, this as well as the evidence discussed in 5 and 6 below may always be shown unless negated by the contract.

5. Course of Performance

A course of performance relates to conduct of the parties in the performance of the agreement.

6. Usage of Trade

A usage of trade is any practice or method of dealing having such regularity of observance in a place, vocation, or trade as to justify an expectation that it will be observed with respect to the transaction in question.

7. Relationship Between Parol Evidence Rule and Interpretation

Again, there are various views. For example, Corbin takes the position that the parol evidence rule does not apply to a question of interpretation. Williston, however, in general follows the notion that an integrated writing may not be contradicted under the guise of interpretation.

C. STATUTES OF FRAUDS

Major Classes of Cases Covered by Writing Requirements. These include: (1) a promise to answer for the debt, default or miscarriage of another; (2) a contract to transfer an interest in real property or an actual transfer of real property; (3) a promise which by its terms is not to be performed within one year from the making thereof; (4) a promise in consideration of marriage; and (5) contracts for the sale of goods (UCC).

1. Suretyship Agreements

a. Where There Is No Prior Obligation Owing from the Third Party (*TP*) to the Creditor (*C*) to Which *D*'s Promise Relates

Here, *D* stands for Defendant—the party who has allegedly made a promise to answer for the liability of another, here, the *TP*. The promise of *D* is original (*i.e.*, not within this subsection of the statute so that the statute is not a defense) unless (1) there is a principal-surety relationship between *TP* and *D*, and *C* knows that; (2) the promise is *not* joint; and (3) the main purpose rule does *not* apply. If all of these elements are present, *D*'s promise is collateral (the statute of frauds is a defense).

b. Cases Where There Is a Prior Obligation Owing from *TP* to *C* to Which *D*'s Promise Relates

Here, the promise is collateral (and the statute is a defense). Exceptions: (1) where there is a novation; (2) where *D*'s promise is made to *TP*; (3) where the main purpose rule applies.

(1) Main Purpose Rule

Where the promisor (*D*) has for an object a benefit which *D* did not enjoy before the promise, which benefit accrues immediately to *D*, *D*'s promise is original (enforceable) whether or not *TP* was obligated at the time of the promise, and even though the effect of the promise is to answer for the debt, default or miscarriage of another.

(2) Promise of *Del Credere* Agent

A *del credere* (Italian, "of belief") agency is an arrangement in which an agent takes possession and agrees to sell goods for his or her principal and consents for an additional fee to guarantee that the purchaser, to whom credit has been extended, is financially solvent and will perform the contract. An oral promise of a del credere agent is enforceable (original). *D* is a del credere agent if *D* receives possession of *C*'s goods for sale upon commission and guarantees to *C* that those to whom sales are made (*TP*) will perform.

(3) Promise of Assignor

The oral promise of an assignor to an assignee guaranteeing performance by the obligor is original (enforceable).

(4) Promise to Buy a Claim

If *TP* owes C $100 and *C* assigns this right to payment to *D* and *D* promises to pay a price for the assignment, *D*'s promise is enforceable because *D*'s promise is a promise to buy a claim and not a promise to answer for the debt, default or miscarriage of another.

(5) Promise by Executor or Administrator

The statute applies only where the executor or administrator promises to pay out of *his or her own* pocket a debt of the deceased. Thus, this provision is merely a particular application of the suretyship statute of frauds.

2. Real Property

a. In General

A conveyance of land or of an estate in land, or a promise to transfer an interest in land, or a promise to pay for an interest in land are all required to be evidenced by a writing.

b. Interest in Land

This includes the creation, transfer or assignment of a lease (except for a lease of short duration). It also includes an easement, rent and, according to the majority rule, a restriction on land. Also covered are equitable interests in lands such as an assignment of a right to purchase land. An option to buy realty is also included. But the statute does not apply to an interest in land that arises by operation of law.

c. Liens

A promise to give a mortgage or other lien as security is within the statute. However, an assignment of a mortgage is not within the statute; it is connected to the debt it secures. The debt (sometimes referred to as a chose in action) is regarded as the core of the rights transferred.

d. Products of the Soil—Timber—Unborn Animals

Products of the soil such as timber and annual crops obtained through labor or borne on perennial trunks (*e.g.*, apples) are not interests in land. These products (as well as unborn animals) are goods.

e. Other Things Attached to Land

A contract for the sale of minerals or a building attached to land is the sale of an interest in land if they are to be severed by the buyer but not if they are to be severed by the seller.

f. Contracts Indirectly Relating to Land

Contracts that indirectly relate to land are not within this statute. For example, a contract to build a building is not within this statute of frauds.

g. Performance

If the *vendor* of the property conveys it to the vendee, an oral promise by the vendee to pay is enforceable. Payment by the *vendee* does not make the promise of the vendor enforceable unless there is other conduct that is unequivocally referable to the agreement, for example, taking possession of the land and making improvements.

3. Contracts Not Performable Within a Year

a. In General

The statute applies only to a promise which *by its terms* does not admit of *performance* within one year from the *making* thereof. If, by its terms, performance is possible within one year, however unlikely or improbable that may be, the promise is not within this statute of frauds provision.

b. Promises of Uncertain Duration

Promises of uncertain duration are not within the one-year provision.

c. Contracts for Alternative Performances

Where a contracting party promises one of two or more alternative performances, the promises as a unit are not within the one-year section if any of the alternatives can be performed within one year from the time of the making thereof. It does not matter which party has the right to name the alternative.

d. Agreement with Option to Terminate

If a contract calls for a performance of more than a year, but one or both of the parties has an option to terminate within a year, the majority view is that the statute applies because termination is not performance. The minority view is contrary, on the theory that alternative promises exist: (a) performance for more than one year *or* (b) performance within a year. The same two views exist in the case of a contract for less than a year where one or both parties have an option to extend or renew it beyond a year.

e. Effect of Performance Under One-Year Section

Under the majority view, full performance by one party makes the promise of the other party enforceable. A minority of jurisdictions restrict the performing party to a quasi-contractual remedy. Part performance does not generally permit a party to enforce the contract.

f. Measuring the Year

If *A* contracts to work for *B* for one year, but the work is to begin more than one day after making the agreement, the contract is within the one-year provision. If the work is to begin the very next day, however, the contract is not within the statute, on the theory that the law disregards fractions of a day.

g. Restatement of Contract at Beginning of Performance

A subsequent restatement of the terms of the contract starts the one-year period running again if the manifestation of mutual assent would be sufficient in the absence of prior agreement.

h. Unilateral Contracts

There is substantial authority that unilateral contracts do not fall within this statute of frauds provision, because full performance by one party in any event takes the case out of the one-year statute of frauds. In jurisdictions where this is not true, it must be noted that a contract does not arise until there has been performance. Therefore, the year should be measured from that time.

i. Scope of One-Year Provision

The one-year provision applies to all contracts no matter what the subject matter, except for a short-term lease and a sale of goods. However, it does not prevent specific performance of a land contract under the rules governing specific performance set forth below.

j. Is a Promise or a Contract Within the One-Year Provision?

Where any of the promises on either side of a bilateral contract (except for alternative promises) cannot be performed within a year from the formation of the contract, the entire contract is within the statute. This means that none of the promises in the contract may be enforced in the absence of a sufficient memorandum, or performance, or the application of the doctrine of estoppel (*see infra*).

4. Contracts in Consideration of Marriage

a. Consideration of Marriage

The statute applies to any agreement made in consideration of marriage except mutual promises to marry. It applies to marriage settlements and prenuptial agreements even if the promise is made by a third party.

b. Not in Consideration of Marriage

If the promise is made in contemplation, but not in consideration, of marriage, this subsection of the statute does not apply. The same is true if the marriage is merely an incident of the contract and not an end to be attained.

c. Performance

A marriage ceremony does not take the case out of the statute of frauds, but additional performance may be sufficient to make the contract enforceable.

5. Contracts for the Sale of Goods (UCC § 2–201)

a. Rule

A contract for the sale of goods for a price of $500 or more is within the statute.

b. Exceptions

(1) A contract for the sale of goods to be manufactured is not within the statute "if the goods are to be specially manufactured for the buyer and are not suitable for sale to others in the ordinary course of the seller's business and the seller, before notice of repudiation is received and under circumstances which reasonably indicate that the goods are for the buyer, has made either a substantial beginning or commitments for their procurement." (UCC § 2–201(3)(a).) The seller need not be the manufacturer.

(2) A contract is enforceable if the party against whom enforcement is sought admits that a contract for sale was made, but the contract is not enforceable beyond the quantity of goods admitted. (UCC § 2–201(3)(b).)

(3) No writing is necessary as to items which have been received and accepted. (UCC §§ 2–201(3)(c), 2–606.)

(4) The writing requirement is also eliminated with respect to goods for which payment has been made and accepted. (UCC § 2–201(3)(c).)

c. What Is Covered?

This section relates to a contract to sell or a sale of goods. It does not apply to choses in action.

6. Sufficiency of Memorandum

a. Introduction

If the contract is within the statute, a sufficient writing is required. The writing need not be formal or integrated. A note or a memorandum is sufficient.

b. Contents of Writing

The writing should (1) indicate that a contract has been made or that the signer made an offer; (2) state with reasonable certainty (a) the identity of the contracting parties, (b) the subject matter, and (c) the essential terms in contrast to details or particulars; and (3) be signed by the party to be charged.

c. What Is a Signature?

A signature is any mark, written, stamped or engraved, which is placed with intent to assent to and adopt (authenticate) the writing as one's own.

d. Who Is the Party to Be Charged?

The party to be charged is the one against whom the claim is being made.

e. Agency

A memorandum is sufficient if it is signed by an authorized agent of the party to be charged. The authority of the agent need not be expressed in writing, except in many jurisdictions under the real property provision.

f. Oral Evidence Offered by Defendant to Defeat Claim

The party sued may show that the memorandum does not reflect the true agreement and thus defeat the claim, except to the extent that the parol evidence rule excludes such evidence.

g. Oral Evidence Offered by Plaintiff

Evidence of an *essential* term orally agreed to is not admissible on behalf of the party seeking to contradict or supplement the writing, and this is true whether or not the writing is an integration.

h. Interpretation

Oral evidence is admissible in aid of interpretation unless it is excluded under the rules of interpretation set forth above.

i. Consideration

If the plaintiff has fully performed, the plaintiff's consideration need not be stated in the writing. Any essential promise that is executory must be stated.

j. Form

The memorandum may be in any form.

k. Time

It may be made at any time.

l. Purpose

It need not be prepared with the purpose of satisfying the statute, except in the case of a contract in consideration of marriage.

m. Delivery

It need not be delivered.

n. More than One Writing

If the essential terms are in two writings, and only one is signed by the party to be charged, the statute is satisfied if the unsigned document is physically attached to the signed document at the time it is signed, or if one of the documents by its terms expressly refers to the other, or if the documents by internal evidence refer to the same subject matter or transaction. Extrinsic evidence is admissible to help show the connection between the documents and the assent of the party to be charged.

7. Memorandum Provision of the UCC

a. Contents of Memorandum

Under the UCC, there are only three requirements: (1) the writing must evidence a contract for the sale of goods; (2) it must be signed by the party to be charged; and (3) it must specify a quantity.

b. Written Confirmation Between Merchants

If a merchant sends a signed memorandum to another merchant in confirmation of the agreement, and if the memorandum is sufficient against the sender, it is also sufficient against the receiver provided it is received, and the party receiving it has reason to know of its contents and fails to give notice of objection to its contents within 10 days after it is received.

c. Auction Sales

The auctioneer is authorized to sign a memorandum on behalf of both parties for a limited period of time after the sale.

8. Other Problems Under Statutes of Frauds

a. Purpose of Statute

The statute is designed to prevent perjury and to promote deliberation and seriousness.

b. Effect of Noncompliance

Under the majority view, failure to comply with the statute renders the contract unenforceable. The minority view regards the contract as void. Under the majority rule, the oral promises are valid, but they may not be sued upon at law.

c. Promissory Estoppel

Many recent cases allow recovery despite a statute of frauds when the plaintiff injuriously relied on an oral promise. The phrase that is often used is "unconscionable injury."

d. Estoppel in Pais

If a party falsely represents that a memorandum of the contract has been signed and the other party injuriously relies on the representation, the party so representing will be estopped from relying upon a statute of frauds.

e. Effect of Some Promises Within and Others Outside Statute

The general rule, subject to limited exceptions, is that where one or more of the promises in a contract are within the statute and others are not, no part of the contract is enforceable.

f. Rescission of Contract Within Statute

The parties may orally rescind a written executory contract within the statute. They cannot orally rescind a transfer of property.

9. Modification of a Contract Within the Statute

a. If the new agreement is not within the statute of frauds, it is not only enforceable without a writing but also serves to discharge the prior agreement.

b. If the new agreement is within the statute and is not evidenced by a sufficient writing, the former written contract remains enforceable unless the new agreement is enforced because of waiver or estoppel.

10. Relationship of Various Subsections

A promise may contravene one or more statute of frauds and not the others. If it falls within even one provision, a writing is required unless the case is taken out of the statute under the theory of performance or estoppel. For example, a contract for the sale of real property that by its terms cannot be performed within one year must satisfy both the one-year and real property provisions. However, the UCC statute of frauds stands alone. If the UCC is satisfied no other provision applies.

VI. CONDITIONS, PERFORMANCE, AND BREACH

A. CONDITIONS DEFINED

A condition is an act or event, other than a lapse of time which, unless the condition is excused, must occur before a performance under a contract becomes due, or which discharges a duty of immediate performance.

1. Classifications of Conditions

Conditions are either precedent, concurrent, or subsequent to the time when the other party's duty of performance becomes absolute. Any of these conditions can be created by agreement (express and implied-in-fact conditions) or imposed by the court (constructive condition).

2. Conditions Versus Promises

Failure of a condition imposes no liability on any party. A breach of promise creates a duty to pay damages. Note, however, that the same act may be both a condition and a promised event. In other words, a party may have promised that the event would occur and have conditioned his or her rights on the occurrence of the event. If the event does not occur, there is both a breach of promise and a failure of condition.

B. CONDITIONS, SUBSTANTIAL PERFORMANCE, AND MATERIAL BREACH

1. Performance of Express and Constructive Conditions

Express conditions must be fully performed. Constructive conditions are satisfied by substantial performance. If a party has substantially performed, any breach is immaterial. A party who has materially breached cannot have rendered substantial performance.

2. Measuring the Materiality of Breach

The following factors help determine materiality: willfulness, the degree of harm, curability of the breach by a monetary allowance, hardship on the breaching party, and the type of transaction. The same and similar factors are used to determine the substantiality of the performance. There are times when a breach is immaterial but substantial performance has not been rendered, e.g., a delay in conveying land may be immaterial, but substantial performance has not been rendered.

3. Effect of Delay

A reasonable delay is not a material breach unless the contract expressly makes time of the essence, or the contract is for the sale of goods or the payment of a debt and there is a day or period certain for performance.

4. Effect of a Condition of Satisfaction

Where the contract expressly conditions performance upon the satisfaction or certification of a third person (e.g., an architect), the condition is treated as any other condition. If it is conditioned on the satisfaction of a contracting party, the same rule is applied if the performance is designed to gratify the taste or fancy of the party. However, if the performance is a matter of mechanical fitness, utility or marketability, the condition of satisfaction of a *party* is fulfilled if the performance is objectively satisfactory even if the party is not personally satisfied. In all cases, an expression of dissatisfaction must be made in good faith.

C. RECOVERY DESPITE MATERIAL BREACH

1. Divisibility

A contract is divisible if the performances of each party are divided into two or more parts and the performance of each part by one party is the agreed exchange for a corresponding part by the other party. If a divisible portion is substantially performed, recovery may be had for that portion despite a material breach of the overall contract.

2. Independent Promises

A promise is unconditional (independent) if it is unqualified or if nothing but a lapse of time is necessary to make the promise presently enforceable. The promisee may enforce an independent promise without rendering substantial performance.

3. Quasi-Contractual Recovery

Although the orthodox and still prevailing view is that a party who has materially breached may not recover from the other party in contract or quasi contract, the modern trend permits such recovery in quasi contract for benefits conferred in excess of damages caused by the breach.

4. Statutory Relief

A number of statutes permit recovery despite a material breach. Laborers, mechanics, and clerical workers must be paid their wages despite the non-fulfillment of agreed conditions. The UCC has a formula that permits a buyer in default to get partial restitution of a down payment.

D. EXCUSE OF CONDITIONS

1. Prevention

A condition is excused by prevention, hindrance, or failure to cooperate, provided the conduct is wrongful. When a condition is excused, recovery is permitted despite the non-occurrence of the condition.

2. Estoppel, Waiver, and Election

A waiver is often defined as an intentional relinquishment of a known right. It is important to know that this definition is nonsense. Conditions, not rights, can be waived. Waivers are often unintentional. Not all waivers, however defined, are effective.

a. Waiver Before Failure of Condition

(1) A waiver of a condition that constitutes a material part of an agreed exchange is ineffective in the absence of consideration, its equivalent, or an estoppel.

(2) A waiver of a condition that is not a material part of the agreed exchange is effective, but it may be reinstated by notice prior to any material change of position by the other party.

(3) An effective waiver disables the party from canceling the contract but does not discharge the waiving party's right to damages.

b. Waiver After Failure of Condition

A waiver after an express or constructive condition has failed is an election. An election may take place by conduct or by promise. No consideration is needed for an election and, according to the majority rule, an election once made cannot be withdrawn.

3. Excuse of Conditions Involving Forfeitures

A condition may be excused if it involves an extreme forfeiture, its occurrence is not a material part of the agreed exchange, and if one of the foundations for equitable jurisdiction exists.

4. Excuse of Condition Because of Impossibility

Impossibility excuses a condition, if the condition is not a material part of the agreed exchange and if a forfeiture would otherwise occur.

E. PROSPECTIVE UNWILLINGNESS AND INABILITY TO PERFORM: REPUDIATION

1. Repudiation

A repudiation is a material breach whether or not performance is due now or in the future. A party's unjustified statement positively indicating an inability or unwillingness to substantially perform is a repudiation. A voluntary act that renders one's own performance impossible or apparently impossible is another kind of repudiation.

2. Prospective Failure of Condition

If a party repudiates or appears unwilling or unable to perform, the other party may possibly (1) continue performance; (2) suspend or withhold performance; (3) change position or cancel the contract. Which of the responses is permissible depends upon the degree of the prospective failure of condition.

3. Retraction

A repudiation may be retracted and a prospective unwillingness or inability to perform can be cured unless the aggrieved party has canceled or materially changed position or otherwise indicated the contract is canceled.

4. Urging Retraction

Rights are not prejudiced by the mere fact the aggrieved party has urged the other party to retract a repudiation.

5. Effect of Impossibility on a Prior Repudiation

Subsequent impossibility will discharge an anticipatory breach and partial impossibility will limit damages for the breach.

6. Failure to Give Assurances as a Repudiation

Under UCC § 2–609, a party who has reasonable grounds for insecurity may suspend performance and demand adequate assurance of the other's performance. Failure to give adequate assurance within a reasonable time, not exceeding 30 days, operates as a repudiation. The Restatement (Second) is in substantial accord.

7. Insolvency

When a seller discovers that a buyer is insolvent the seller may: (a) refuse delivery except for cash, including payment for all goods previously delivered under the same contract; (b) stop delivery of goods in transit; (c) reclaim goods delivered on credit to a party while insolvent, provided that demand for their reclamation is made within ten days of receipt by the buyer; (d) reclaim goods delivered on credit to a party while insolvent irrespective of the ten day period, if the buyer has made a representation of solvency to the particular seller within three months before delivery.

8. Repudiation of a Debt

There is one important exception to the general rule that a repudiation operates as a total breach. No action lies for repudiation of a unilateral obligation to pay a sum of money at a fixed time or times in the future.

9. Repudiation and Right to Elect

As a general rule, the aggrieved party may elect to continue the obligations of the contract despite a material breach. Where, however, there is a repudiation, anticipatory or otherwise, the aggrieved party usually cannot elect to continue the contract. Except in the rare case where continuation of performance would minimize damages, the aggrieved party has no right to continue performance after a repudiation.

F. PERFORMANCE OF THE SALES CONTRACT

1. Obligations of the Seller

The seller must make a tender conforming in every respect to the contract. If the tender is not perfect, the buyer may reject the whole, accept the whole, or accept any commercial unit or units and reject the rest. This drastic rule is eroded by the following qualifications.

a. Unless Otherwise Agreed

The contract may expressly limit the perfect tender rule, or the rule may tacitly be limited by a trade usage, course of dealing or course of performance.

b. Cure Within the Contract Time

If a non-conforming tender is made and the time for performance has not yet expired, the seller may seasonably notify the buyer of an intention to cure and may within the contract time make a conforming tender.

c. Cure After the Contract Period

When the buyer rejects a non-conforming tender that the seller had reasonable grounds to believe would be acceptable with or without a money allowance, the seller may, upon reasonable notification to the buyer, have a further reasonable time to substitute a conforming tender.

d. Acceptance

Once the goods have been accepted, rejection is no longer possible, although revocation of acceptance may be an available alternative. An acceptance may be express, or it may result from a failure to reject or to demand cure before a reasonable time to inspect the goods has passed.

e. Revocation of Acceptance

The buyer may revoke acceptance of a lot or commercial unit whose non-conformity substantially impairs its value to the buyer, provided (a) acceptance was on the reasonable assumption that seller would cure and has not seasonably cured; or (b) acceptance was reasonably induced by the difficulty of discovery or by the seller's assurances. Revocation must be made within a reasonable time after the buyer discovers or should have discovered the ground for it and before any substantial change in the condition of the goods that is not caused by their own defects. Note that the rule is one of substantial performance.

f. Installment Contracts

The perfect tender rule does not apply to installment contracts. An installment can be rejected only if its value to the buyer is substantially impaired. The buyer may cancel the contract only if the non-conformity substantially impairs the value of the contract to the buyer.

g. Improper Shipment

The perfect tender rule does not apply to breach of the duty of proper shipment. Failure to give prompt notice of shipment or to make a reasonable contract (in a shipment contract) with the carrier is grounds for rejection only if material delay or loss ensues.

2. Obligation of the Buyer

a. Payment

Absent an agreement to the contrary, receipt of the goods and tender of payment are concurrent conditions. Thus, even in a shipment contract (where the seller delivers the goods by placing them on board a carrier) payment is not due until the goods are received at their destination.

b. Proper Tender of Payment

Unless credit has been extended, the buyer must tender the entire amount. Tender need not be legal tender unless the seller demands it and grants the buyer sufficient additional time to procure cash.

c. Acceptance of Conforming Goods

Failure to accept conforming goods or wrongful revocation of acceptance constitutes a breach. Unless otherwise agreed, however, the buyer's duty to accept and pay for tendered goods is subject to a right to inspect them at any reasonable time and manner.

d. Reasonable Care

If the buyer properly rejects (or revokes acceptance of) goods in the buyer's possession, a duty is imposed to refrain from any acts of ownership over the goods, and to hold them with reasonable care at the seller's disposition for a time sufficient to permit a seller to remove them. A merchant buyer has additional responsibilities.

G. WARRANTIES IN THE SALES CONTRACT

1. Express Warranties

An express warranty is an affirmation of fact or promise with respect to the quality or future performance of goods that becomes part of the basis of the bargain. The affirmation may be in words or by sample or model. An affirmation merely of the value of the goods or merely of the seller's opinion of the goods is not a warranty.

2. Implied Warranties

a. Merchantability

If a seller is a merchant with respect to the kinds of goods contracted for, unless effectively disclaimed, there is an implied warranty that the goods be such as pass in the trade under the contract description and are fit for the ordinary purposes for which such goods are used.

b. Fitness for Particular Purpose

If the seller has reason to know that the buyer wants the goods for a particular purpose and knows that the buyer is relying on the seller's skill and judgment, unless effectively disclaimed, there is an implied warranty that the goods shall be fit for that purpose.

c. Free and Clear Title

Unless effectively disclaimed, a seller impliedly warrants that the title conveyed is good, transfer is rightful, and the goods are free from any security interest or lien of which the buyer was unaware at the time of contracting. Note that this warranty applies also to nonmerchant sellers.

d. Infringement

A merchant who regularly deals in the kind of goods in question warrants, unless effectively disclaimed, that no patent or trademark is being infringed, but if the buyer furnishes the specifications, the buyer must hold the seller harmless against any third-party claim if infringement arises out of the use of the specifications.

3. Disclaimer of Warranties

a. Express Warranties

If a contract contains express warranties as defined above, as well as a provision that states no express warranties are made, an attempt must be made to reconcile the two provisions. If consistency cannot be attained, the disclaimer is inoperative.

b. Implied Warranties

All implied warranties, except free and clear title, are disclaimed by language such as "as is." If other language is employed, the warranty of merchantability is the most difficult to exclude. If the exclusion is written, the language of exclusion must use the word "merchantability" and must be conspicuous. The warranty of fitness can be excluded only in writing and only if the exclusion is conspicuous.

c. Implied Warranty of Free and Clear Title

This warranty can be excluded only by specific language or circumstances that give the buyer reason to know that the seller does not claim title or is only purporting to sell such right as the seller has.

d. Limitation on Remedies

Even if there is no disclaimer, remedies for breach of warranty may be limited pursuant to the provisions of UCC §§ 2–718 and 2–719.

VII. DEFENSES

A. IMPRACTICABILITY

1. Impracticability Is Not Necessarily a Defense

The general rule is that the promisor must perform or pay damages for failure to perform no matter how burdensome performance has become even if unforeseen changes have created the burden.

2. When Impracticability Is a Defense

When a performance becomes impracticable because of an event, the non-occurrence of which was a basic assumption on which the contract was made, the duty is discharged, unless the language or situation points to a contrary result.

3. What Assumptions Are Basic

There are certain understood risks assumed by the parties. These include market shifts, interruption of supplies (unless caused by war, embargo, or the like), and financial capability. Where, however, the difficulty in performing is caused by certain supervening events, it is sometimes held that a basic assumption is violated. These events include (1) destruction of the subject matter or of the tangible means of performance; (2) death or illness of a person essential for performance; (3) supervening illegality or prevention by law; (4) reasonable apprehension of danger to life, health or property.

4. Temporary and Partial Impracticability

When the impracticability is temporary or partial, the general notion is that the promisor is obligated to perform to the extent practicable unless the burden of performance would be substantially increased. However, the promisee may reject any delayed or partial performance if the tendered performance is less than substantial.

a. Temporary Impracticability Under the UCC

If the seller expects to be late in tendering delivery and if the lateness is excusable because of impracticability, the seller must timely notify the buyer of the expected delay. The buyer may then cancel any non-installment contract. The buyer may cancel any installment delivery or installment contract under the criteria for cancellation discussed in connection with exceptions to the perfect tender rule. On the other hand, the buyer may within a reasonable time, not exceeding 30 days, agree to accept the delayed delivery or deliveries.

b. Partial Impossibility Under the UCC

Allocation is the key concept when the seller, on grounds of impracticability, can deliver only part of the promised goods. The seller must seasonably notify the buyer of the shortfall, and inform the buyer of the estimated quota allocated. The buyer has a reasonable time, not exceeding 30 days, to accept the allocation. If the buyer does not accept, the seller's duties are discharged. If the contract is an installment contract, the buyer's right to cancel is subject to the criteria for canceling installment contracts discussed in connection with exceptions to the perfect tender rule.

5. Impracticability of Means of Delivery or Payment

a. Delivery

The UCC provision that deals with unavailability of an agreed type of carrier, docking facility, or manner of delivery focuses on the use of commercially reasonable substitutes. Although delivery modalities may be of serious concern, they are not usually at the core of the bargain. Consequently, if available, a commercially reasonable substitute must be employed and accepted.

b. Payment

If the agreed manner of payment becomes unavailable, the seller's obligation to deliver is discharged but, if a commercially reasonable substitute manner of payment is available, the buyer has the option to use the substitute, thereby reinstating the seller's duty to deliver.

c. Payment After Delivery

If the agreed manner of payment fails because of governmental regulations after the goods are delivered, the buyer may pay in the manner provided in the regulation. Even if this is not a commercially reasonable equivalent, the buyer is discharged unless the regulation is discriminatory, oppressive or predatory.

B. FRUSTRATION

1. In General

Where the object of one of the parties is the basis upon which both parties contract, the duties of performance are constructively conditioned upon the attainment of the object. Performance is practicable, but the performance one party contracted for has become valueless (or nearly so).

2. Elements

There must be: (1) an event that frustrates the purpose of one of the parties and the non-occurrence of this event must be the basis on which both parties entered into the contract; (2) the frustration must be total or nearly total; (3) the party who asserts the defense must not, expressly or impliedly, have assumed the risk of this occurrence nor be guilty of contributory fault.

3. Restitution After Discharge for Impracticability or Frustration

When a contract is discharged for impracticability or frustration, the executory duties are at an end. Compensation for part performance is available in the restitutionary action of quasi contract.

C. RISK OF CASUALTY LOSS

1. Perspective

When goods or real property are in the process of being sold or are under lease or bailment, the question frequently is, which of the parties must bear the risk of damage or destruction of the subject matter? For example, if Vendor and Purchaser enter into a contract for the purchase and sale of real property, which party should bear the loss caused by a fire that occurs after the contract was entered into and before closing of title?

2. Real Property

The majority rule places the risk of loss on the purchaser. This result is based on the theory of equitable conversion; once the contract is made, the purchaser is regarded by a court of equity as the owner. The minority view places the risk of loss on the seller until title closes. A third view, embodied in the Uniform Vendor and Purchaser Risk Act, enacted in about ten states, places the risk of loss upon a purchaser only if the purchaser is in possession or has legal title.

3. Leases

The orthodox common law rule placed the risk of loss on the lessee. Today, this view seems to have been largely abandoned in favor of the concepts of constructive eviction and implied warranties.

4. Sale of Goods

a. Effect of Risk of Loss

Assume goods have been damaged without fault of either party. If the risk of loss had shifted to the buyer, the buyer must pay the price. If the risk of loss is on the seller, the seller will be liable for breach of contract unless the breach is cured by tender of replacement conforming goods. In two limited situations the seller may have the risk of loss (seller will not be paid) but will not be liable for damages. These are situations (1) where impracticability can be invoked; and (2) where the contract expressly provides, No Arrival No Sale. (UCC § 2–324).

b. Shipment Versus Destination Contracts (Where Carrier Is Contemplated)

Most risk of loss cases involve injury to goods in transit. The Code seeks to provide clear and certain rules that usually work in tandem with normal insurance practices in commerce. Merchants have long thought in terms of contracts whereby the seller is responsible for shipping the goods—getting them aboard a common carrier in the seller's city, as opposed to the much less usual destination contract whereby the seller undertakes the responsibility of getting the goods to the buyer's city or plant. Under a shipment contract, the risk of loss passes to the buyer when the goods are delivered to the carrier, even if the seller reserves a security interest in the goods. Under a destination contract, risk of loss shifts when the goods are duly tendered to the buyer at destination.

c. Distinguishing Shipment from Destination Contracts

If the contract is unclear whether it is a shipment or destination contract, it is a shipment contract. It is not a destination contract unless it explicitly so provides. There are certain terms, entrenched in commercial usage, which are frequently used to indicate the parties' intent. These are: F.O.B., F.A.S., C.I.F., and Ex-ship.

d. Delivery by Seller's Own Truck or on Seller's Premises

Where a carrier is not used, as where the seller transports the goods in the seller's own vehicle or the buyer is to pick up the goods, the seller is in control of the goods and is likely to carry insurance on them. If the seller is a *merchant,* risk of loss shifts only if and when the buyer takes possession of the goods. If the seller is a *nonmerchant,* the risk shifts when the seller tenders delivery.

e. Goods Held by a Bailee

At times goods in the hands of a bailee, such as a warehouse manager, are sold with no expectation of a prompt transfer of possession. Risk of loss passes to the buyer in either of three eventualities. First, if the buyer receives a negotiable document of title that covers the goods; second, if the bailee acknowledges the buyer's ownership; third, if the seller gives the buyer a non-negotiable document of title or a written direction to the bailee, risk of loss passes after the buyer has had a reasonable time to present the document or direction to the bailee. If the buyer presents the document or direction to the bailee, risk of loss does not shift if the bailee refuses to honor it.

f. The Effect of Seller's Breach on Risk of Loss

The rules on risk of loss are suddenly made murky if it can be proved that the seller is in breach by tendering non-conforming goods. If the non-conformity is such that the buyer may reject (under the perfect tender rule or the installment contract rules), the risk of loss remains on the seller until the tender is cured or the buyer accepts the non-conforming goods. If the buyer revokes acceptance of the goods the seller is liable for any casualty to the goods to the extent that the buyer's insurance coverage is inadequate. The buyer, however, must have revoked prior to the casualty for this rule to apply.

g. The Effect of the Buyer's Breach on Risk of Loss

If the buyer breaches prior to the shift of the risk of loss, the breach will itself shift the risk to the buyer provided that (a) the goods are conforming; (b) they have been identified to the contract; and (c) the loss occurs within a commercially reasonable time from the breach. However, the risk of loss passes to the buyer only to the extent that the seller's insurance is inadequate to cover the loss.

5. Risk of Loss and Impracticability

The mere fact that the particular goods the seller intends to deliver are destroyed does not give the seller the defense of impracticability. The seller must offer replacement goods or be liable, although under appropriate circumstances the seller may be excused for any unavoidable delay under the doctrine of temporary impracticability. Under the provisions of UCC § 2–613, however, if the contract dealt with identified goods (e.g., particular pieces of furniture rather than particular types), the seller is excused if the goods are totally destroyed, without the seller's fault, prior to the risk being shifted to the buyer. If the loss is partial, the buyer has the option to reject the goods or accept them with an allowance.

6. Two Special Situations: Sale on Approval and Sale or Return

a. Sale on Approval

In a "sale on approval," the goods are sent to the buyer for the buyer's use with the understanding that the buyer may return the goods if they do not meet the standard of satisfaction. (*See* the material on conditions of satisfaction, VI.B.4, *supra*). The risk of loss remains with the seller until the buyer accepts the goods. Failure to notify the seller of a rejection within a reasonable time is an acceptance. The expense of return is also thrust on the seller.

b. Sale or Return

In a "sale or return" (consignment) sale, the goods are sent to the buyer primarily for resale. Although the buyer may return conforming goods, the risk of loss passes to the buyer under the ordinary rules that govern the shifting of risk of loss. The risk remains with the buyer until the goods are returned to the seller at the buyer's expense.

7. The Omnipotence of the Contract

All the rules governing risk of loss are gap fillers based in large part on the probable intention of the parties. The parties are perfectly at liberty, subject to the rule of conscionability, to provide for the allocation of risk of loss in any way they wish.

D. ILLEGALITY

1. In General

A bargain is illegal if either its formation or its performance is criminal, tortious, or contrary to public policy. The difficult cases are those where the illegality is somewhat remote from the agreement. Remoteness will be illustrated by four kinds of situations: bribery, license violations, depositary cases, and instances where one party has knowledge of the illegal purpose of the other.

2. Bribery Cases

An agreement is illegal if it calls for the payment of a bribe, is procured by a bribe or is performed by bribery.

3. Licensing Cases

If a license is designed to control the skill or moral quality of persons engaged in a trade or profession, an agreement to practice that trade or profession by an unlicensed person is illegal. If the license is solely a revenue raising measure, the agreement is not illegal. If the license is required for other purposes, the courts will decide on a case-by-case basis.

4. Depositaries

A depositary of the fruits of a crime may not refuse to return the money or goods deposited, unless the depositary is a party to the illegal transaction.

5. Knowledge of Illegal Purpose

Knowledge by the seller of goods or services of the illegal purpose of the buyer taints the contract with illegality only if the intended purpose involves serious moral turpitude or if the seller does something to further the illegal purpose of the other. Some states, however, make criminal facilitation a crime. Under such a statute, knowledge of the illegal purpose would make the contract criminally illegal.

6. Effect of Illegal Executory Agreements

An illegal executory bargain is void so that neither party to the agreement can enforce it.

7. Exceptions

a. If a party is justifiably ignorant of the facts creating the illegality and the other is not, the ignorant party may recover damages for breach.

b. If the illegality is minor and the party who is ignorant of the illegality justifiably relies upon an assumed special knowledge of the requirements of law by the other party, the contract may be enforced in an action for damages by the innocent party.

c. Certain statutes, enacted to protect a certain class, make only one party the wrongdoer. Contracts in violation of such statutes are enforceable by the protected party.

d. If an illegal provision does not involve serious moral turpitude and if the parties would have entered into the contract irrespective of the offending provision, the illegal portion of the agreement is disregarded, and the balance of the agreement is enforceable. The illegal provision must not be central to the party's agreement.

e. If an agreement can be interpreted so that either a legal or illegal meaning can be attributed to it, the interpretation giving the agreement a legal meaning will be preferred. An illegal contract can also be reformed to make it legal.

8. Illegal Bargains Executed in Whole or in Part

Where there has been performance under an illegal bargain, the court will not aid either party and will leave the parties where it finds them.

9. Exceptions

a. Reprise

The exceptions under Illegal Executory Agreements also apply to actions for restitution.

b. Divisibility

If a performance is illegal, but other performances are legal, recovery may be had for the legal performances provided that the illegal performance does not involve serious moral turpitude. Divisibility is not used in this context in the same sense as it is used in the chapter on performance. Divisibility is not determined according to fixed rules but by the judicial instinct for justice.

c. Not *in Pari Delicto*

A party who has performed under an illegal bargain is entitled to a quasi-contractual recovery if this party is not guilty of serious moral turpitude and, although blameworthy, is not equally as guilty as the other party to the illegal bargain.

d. *Locus Poenitentiae* (Place for Repentance)

Even if a plaintiff is *in pari delicto* and therefore as blameworthy or more blameworthy than the defendant, the plaintiff is entitled to avoid the bargain and obtain restitution if the attempted avoidance is in time to prevent the attainment of the illegal purpose for which the bargain was made, unless the mere making of the bargain involves serious moral turpitude. The plaintiff is generally not permitted to withdraw if any part of the illegal performance is consummated. Repentance comes too late if it comes only after the other party to the bargain has breached the illegal agreement or after attainment of the unlawful purpose is seen to be impossible.

10. Change of Law

a. Legalization of the Activity

If a contract is illegal when made and subsequently becomes legal because the law is changed, the change does not validate the contract except where the repealing statute so provides.

b. Supervening Illegality

If a contract is lawful when made, but the performance is outlawed prior to full performance, the case is governed by the doctrine of impracticability of performance.

c. Supervening Illegality of an Offer

If a lawful offer is made, but the making or performance of the proposed contract is subsequently outlawed, the power of acceptance is terminated.

11. Change of Facts

Where the bargain is illegal and a change of facts removes the cause of the illegality, the contract remains illegal. However, the parties, with full knowledge of the facts, may subsequently ratify the agreement.

E. DISCHARGE OF CONTRACTUAL DUTIES

1. Perspective

Many methods of discharging a contractual duty are discussed elsewhere; for example, non-fulfillment of a condition, anticipatory repudiation, impossibility of performance, disaffirmance for lack of capacity, etc. In this chapter several kinds of consensual discharge will be discussed.

2. Mutual Rescission

Within limits, parties to a contract are free to end the obligations of the contract by agreement. The limits are imposed by the doctrine of consideration. One must distinguish three situations: (1) the rescission occurs before any performance; (2) the rescission occurs after part performance by one or both parties; (3) the rescission occurs after full performance by one party. In the first two situations, consideration is found in the surrender of rights under the original agreement by each party. In the third situation the rescission is void for want of consideration.

3. Implied Rescission

While rescissions are ordinarily expressed in words, they can be implied from conduct. Some courts call an implied rescission an abandonment.

4. Cancellation Versus Rescission

In the face of a material breach the injured party may properly cancel the contract. In canceling, this party may inartfully use an expression such as "I rescind." According to UCC § 2–720, which restates the sounder common law cases, unless the contrary intention clearly appears, expressions of cancellation or 'rescission' of the contract or the like shall not be construed as a renunciation or discharge of any claim for damages for an antecedent breach.

5. Executory Bilateral Accord

An agreement, either express or implied, to render in the future a stipulated performance that will be accepted in satisfaction or discharge of a present claim is known as an executory accord. At common law, executory accords were unenforceable. Today, the executory accord is a binding contract. Prior to performance or breach, the existing claim is suspended. Upon performance, there is an accord and satisfaction that discharges the claim. If, however, the debtor breaches, the prior obligation revives, and the creditor has the option of enforcing the original claim or the executory accord. If the creditor breaches, the debtor may ordinarily obtain specific performance of the accord. New York requires executory accords to be in writing.

6. Unilateral Accord

An offer by a creditor or claimant to accept a performance in satisfaction of a credit or claim is known as a unilateral accord. At early common law, the offeror could, with impunity, refuse the tender of performance. Under modern law, the debtor may, upon refusal of the tender, sue for damages for breach of the accord, or, in a proper case, for specific performance. New York requires that the offer be in writing.

7. Accord and Satisfaction

An accord and satisfaction is formed either by (1) performance of an executory bilateral accord or by acceptance of an offer to a unilateral accord, or (2) creation of a substituted contract.

8. Substituted Contract

A substituted contract resembles an executory bilateral accord. The distinction is that the claimant or creditor agrees that the claim or credit is immediately discharged in exchange for the promise of a future performance. The prior claim or credit is merged into the substituted contract. Consequently, in the event of its breach, it alone determines the rights of the parties. There would be no right to enforce the prior claim, unless the new agreement is void, voidable, or unenforceable.

9. Novation

A contract is a novation if it does three things: (a) discharges immediately a previous contractual duty or a duty to make compensation; (b) creates a new contractual duty; and (c) includes as a party one who neither owed the previous duty nor was entitled to its performance. It is necessary to distinguish a three-party executory accord from a novation. A novation is a substituted contract that operates immediately to discharge an obligation. If the discharge is to take place upon performance, the tripartite agreement is merely an executory accord.

10. Account Stated

An account stated arises where there have been transactions between debtor and creditor resulting in the creation of matured debts and the parties by agreement compute a balance that the debtor promises to pay and the creditor promises to accept in full payment of the items of the account.

11. Release

A release is a writing manifesting an intention to discharge another from an existing or asserted duty. A release supported by consideration discharges the duty. At common law, a release without consideration, under seal, also effectively discharged a duty. Today, the effectiveness of a release, without consideration, is largely dependent upon local statutes. UCC § 1–107 provides that: "Any claim or right arising out of an alleged breach can be discharged in whole or part without consideration by written waiver or renunciation signed and delivered by the aggrieved party." Section 1–306 of the revision is to the same effect but delivery is not required.

12. Covenant Not to Sue

A covenant not to sue is a promise not to sue, supported by consideration, either permanently, or for a limited period of time. A release is an executed transaction, while a covenant not to sue is executory. The latter is sometimes used to circumvent the common law rule that the release of one joint obligor releases all of them.

13. Acquisition by the Debtor of the Correlative Right

Acquisition by the debtor of the correlative right in the same capacity in which the debtor owes the duty discharges it.

14. Alteration

A fraudulent alteration of a written contract, by one who asserts a right under it, extinguishes the right and discharges the other party's obligation. The aggrieved party may forgive the alteration, thus reinstating the contract according to its original tenor. A holder in due course of an instrument altered by a prior holder may enforce it according to its original tenor.

15. Performance—to Which Debt Should Payment Be Applied?

Where a person owes several debts to a creditor, payments are to be applied in the following sequence:

(a) in the manner manifested by the debtor, unless the manifestation violates a duty to a third person such as a surety; but

(b) if the debtor manifests no intention, the payment may be applied at the discretion of the creditor, provided it is not applied to a disputed, unmatured, or illegal claim and also provided it is not applied so as to violate a duty of the debtor to a third person of which the creditor is aware, and is not applied as to cause a forfeiture; but

(c) if the creditor manifests no intent on receipt of payment, the law will allocate payment in the manner deemed most equitable.

VIII. REMEDIES

A. DAMAGES

1. Goal and Measurement of Damages

The basic goal of contract damages is to compensate the aggrieved party with enough money to attain the same economic position that would have been attained if the contract had been fully performed. The aggrieved party is entitled to the benefit of the bargain, receiving gains prevented (expectancy interest) plus losses sustained (reliance and restitutionary interests), subject to the limitations imposed by the doctrines of foreseeability, certainty, and mitigation.

2. Foreseeability—General and Consequential Damages

Contract damages cannot be recovered unless they were foreseeable to the parties at the time of contracting. General Damages are those foreseeable to reasonable persons similarly situated and are calculated by the standardized rules discussed below. Special or consequential damages are those that are foreseeable because, at the time of contracting, the party in breach knows that in the event of breach no substitute performance will be available.

a. Sale of Goods

(1) Seller's Non-Delivery

Purchaser recovers difference between market price and contract price or between cover price (price reasonably paid even if in excess of the market) and contract price.

(2) Seller's Breach of Warranty

Purchaser can recover the difference between the value the goods would have had if they had been as warranted and their actual value. Value is determined as of the time and place of acceptance.

(3) Buyer's Breach

For total breach by the buyer as to goods that have not been accepted, the seller may recover the difference between the contract price and the market or resale price. If the seller has an unlimited supply of the goods involved, however, the seller has lost the profits on the sale, so the seller may instead recover the profit (including reasonable overhead) that would have been made from full performance. UCC § 2–708(2).

(4) Buyer's Liability for the Price

If the buyer has accepted the goods, or if the goods are destroyed after risk of loss has passed to the buyer, the seller can recover the price. A price action is also available if the goods are identified to the contract and the seller cannot reasonably resell the goods.

(5) Consequential and Incidental Damages in Sales Cases

Consequential damages are available to a buyer if the foreseeability test is met. The UCC consequential damages test is different from the common law test. If the seller has reason to know at the time of contracting *or at the time of breach* that the buyer will not be able to cover, the seller is liable for the ensuing damages. Sellers cannot claim consequential damages, but frequently can get incidental damages. Buyers can also claim incidental damages. These include brokerage commissions, storage charges, advertising costs, auctioneer's fees, etc., made necessary by the other's breach.

b. Employment Contracts

(1) Employer's Breach

An employee who has been discharged in breach of contract may recover the wages or salary that would have been payable during the contract term minus the income that the employee has earned, will earn, or could with reasonable diligence earn during the contract term. In the case of a long-term contract, the present worth doctrine will be applied.

(2) Employee's Breach

If an employee wrongfully quits, the employer recovers the difference between the market value of the employee's service minus the contract price.

c. Construction Contracts

(1) Contractor's Delay

Damages for delay are measured by the rental value of the completed premises for the period of delay.

(2) Contractor's Failure to Complete

Failure to complete is compensated by the additional cost of completion plus delay damages.

(3) Defect in Construction

If the breach consists of a defect in construction, the damages are the cost of remedying the defect, unless this would constitute unreasonable economic waste. In that case, damages are measured by the difference between the value the structure should have had and its value as defectively constructed.

(4) Owner's Breach

If no work has been done, the contractor recovers the anticipated profit, that is, the contract price minus the projected cost of performance. If the work has been started, the contractor recovers the anticipated profit plus the cost of labor and supplies actually expended.

(5) Consequential Damages in Construction Cases

If foreseeability is shown, consequential damages are available against a breaching contractor. If an owner's breach is a failure to pay or a repudiation, consequential damages are *never* available to the contractor. (*See* Failure to Pay *infra*).

d. Contracts to Sell Realty

(1) Vendee's Breach

If a contract vendee totally breaches, the vendor may recover the difference between the contract price and the value of the realty.

(2) Vendor's Total Breach: Two Competing Rules

(a) English Rule

For total breach, the vendee may recover only the down payment plus reasonable expenses of a survey and examination of title, unless the vendor was aware of the defects in title or refuses to convey.

(b) American Rule

Under the American Rule, followed in a bare majority of jurisdictions, no matter what the reason for the breach, the vendor is liable for the difference between market value and contract price. This is the same as the primary rule of damages applicable where a seller of goods totally breaches.

(3) Consequential Damages

Consequential damages against a vendor in default is a strong possibility under both the American rule and the exceptions to the English rule.

(4) Vendor's Delay

If the breach consists of a delay in conveying, the vendee may recover the rental value of the premises during the period of delay.

e. Failure to Pay

If the breach consists in the failure to pay a debt, consequential damages are not available. The aggrieved party is entitled only to recover the debt plus interest.

3. Certainty

a. In General

The fact of loss and its amount must be proved with certainty. The standard of certainty requires a higher quality of proof on the issue of damages than on other issues in a lawsuit. It is rarely applied with stringency except as to lost profits, particularly lost profits as consequential damages.

b. Alternatives Where Expectancy Is Uncertain

(1) Protection of Reliance Interest

Where the aggrieved party cannot establish the lost expectancy interest with sufficient certainty, recovery is allowed for the expenses of preparation for and of part performance, as well as other foreseeable expenses incurred in reliance upon the contract. If it can be shown by the defendant that the contract was a losing proposition for the plaintiff, an appropriate deduction will be made for the loss that was not incurred.

(2) Rental Value of Profit-Making Property

If the breach disables the aggrieved party from utilizing profit-making property, recovery of the rental value of the property is permitted.

(3) Value of an Opportunity

If a duty is conditioned upon a fortuitous event, and because of the breach it is uncertain whether the event would have occurred, the aggrieved party may recover the value of the chance that the event would have occurred.

4. Mitigation

a. In General

Damages that could have been avoided by reasonable efforts cannot be recovered. Conversely, the aggrieved party may recover reasonable costs incurred in an effort to minimize damages.

b. Exception

One is not required to enter into another contract with the breaching party even if the offered contract would have minimized damages.

c. Non-Exclusive

The principle of mitigation is not necessarily applicable in cases where the relationship between the parties is not exclusive. If the aggrieved party is free to enter into other similar contracts, entry into such a contract after breach does not reduce the damages that may be recovered.

5. Present Worth Doctrine

Where damages include payments that were required to be made in the future, the value of the payments must be discounted to their present worth.

6. Liquidated Damages

a. Penalties Distinguished

Penalty clauses are designed to deter breaches by the prospect of punishment. Penalty clauses are void. Liquidated damages clauses are valid. Such clauses are designed to avoid or simplify litigation by liquidating the aggrieved party's damages in advance. A clause will be deemed a liquidated damages clause rather than a penalty if it is a reasonable, bona fide attempt to pre-estimate the economic injury that would flow from the breach.

b. Formulas Are Acceptable

Valid liquidated damages clauses are often expressed in formulas rather than in exact dollar amounts. Such an expression does not affect the validity of the clause.

c. Shotgun Clauses Are Dangerous

A clause providing that $50,000 will be paid for breach of this contract will be deemed a penalty because it does not proportion the damages to any particular kind of breach.

d. Can't Have It Both Ways

The courts will strike down a clause that attempts to fix damages in the event of breach while giving the aggrieved party the right to obtain judgment for additional actual damages that may be established. Such clauses do not involve a reasonable attempt definitively to pre-estimate the loss.

e. Specific Performance Not Excluded

A valid liquidated damages clause does not give a party an option to pay liquidated damages or perform. Therefore, the presence of such a clause does not preclude a decree for specific performance. The aggrieved party, however, cannot normally have both remedies, but if specific performance is decreed, such actual damages as may have been sustained between the time of the breach and the time of the decree are also recoverable.

f. Additional Agreed Damages—Attorney's Fees

The award of damages does not ordinarily include attorney's fees, but a clause providing for reasonable attorney's fees will be enforced.

7. Limitations on Damages

The UCC and the common law permit the parties to limit damages, as by limiting the buyer's remedies to return of the goods and repayment of the price or to repair and replacement of non-conforming goods or parts. UCC § 2–719(1)(a). The UCC further provides that: "Consequential damages may be limited or excluded unless the limitation or exclusion is unconscionable. Limitation of consequential damages for injury to the person in the case of consumer goods is prima facie unconscionable[,] but limitation of damages where the loss is commercial is not." UCC § 2–719(3).

8. Failure of Essential Purpose

If circumstances cause an exclusive or limited remedy to fail of its essential purpose, a remedy may be had as provided in the UCC. UCC § 2–719(2). This rule is statutory and does not exist at common law. It is far less broad than an initial reading might convey. The issue is not the conscionability of a limitation clause. Rather, the issue is the purpose of the limitation clause.

9. Punitive Damages

According to the majority view, punitive damages are not available in a contract action, unless the breach involves an independent tort.

10. Mental Distress

The law does not compensate for mental distress caused by a contractual breach in most contractual contexts. In a few non-commercial cases, *e.g.*, breach of contract for funeral arrangements, such compensation has been allowed.

11. Nominal Damages

Every breach of contract creates a cause of action. If the aggrieved party suffers no economic harm or cannot prove such harm with sufficient certainty, nominal damages, e.g., six cents, are recoverable.

B. RESTITUTION

1. Goal of Restitution

The basic goal of actions at law or in equity for restitution is to place the aggrieved party in the same economic position that existed prior to entering into the contract. This is accomplished by requiring restoration to the plaintiff what defendant has received from the plaintiff. Such restoration will not fully recapture the status quo ante if the plaintiff has incurred expenses in reliance upon the contract that have not benefited the defendant. A modern, but unorthodox, trend permits recovery of such expenditures in a restitution action.

2. When Is Restitution Available?

Restitution is available in six principal kinds of contractual situations.

a. Restitution is available as a remedy for total breach; that is, where the breach is material and the aggrieved party has canceled. Notice of cancellation must be given if the other party has not ceased performance or repudiated, or if the aggrieved party fails to offer return of returnable property in accordance with the rules stated in 3, below.

b. The contract is avoided for incapacity, duress, misrepresentation, and the like.

c. The agreement is not a contract because of indefiniteness, lack of an agent's authority, or the like.

d. The agreement is unenforceable because of a statute of frauds provision or certain kinds of illegality.

e. The agreement is discharged because of impracticability or frustration.

f. A defaulting plaintiff seeks recovery for part performance.

3. The Plaintiff Must Offer to Return Property

A party who seeks restitution must first offer to return any property received pursuant to the contract. The offer may be conditioned on the other party's restitution of what that party has received. Exceptions and qualifications of this rule are discussed below. Exceptions:

a. Equitable Action

Specific restitution may be decreed in an equitable action despite the plaintiff's failure to offer to make restitution. The decree in equity can be conditioned upon the plaintiff's restoration.

b. Worthlessness

If the property received was worthless or became worthless because of its defects, failure to offer its return will not defeat the plaintiff's action.

c. Consumption or Loss of Possession

If services have been received, they, of course, cannot be returned. If part of goods received has been consumed or disposed of, return is not possible. Consequently, the requirement of an offer to return is dispensed with. Instead, the value of the services or goods will be offset from the plaintiff's recovery.

d. Divisibility

If the contract is divisible into several agreed exchanges and the grievance does not relate to all of them, the plaintiff need not offer to return those things received pursuant to a divisible portion about which plaintiff has no grievance.

4. Defendant's Refusal to Accept an Offered Return

If a defendant improperly refuses an offer of return, the plaintiff may assert a lien on the goods and may sell them. The price will be debited against the restitution claim.

5. Measure of Recovery

Unjust enrichment, the principal philosophical underpinning of the restitution remedy, does not provide the measure of recovery. The plaintiff receives the reasonable value of services rendered, goods delivered, or property conveyed, less the reasonable value of any counter-performance received, irrespective of any enrichment and usually irrespective of the contract rate.

6. No Restitution After Complete Performance

Restitution is not available if a debt has been created.

7. Election of Remedies

In the absence of statute, a plaintiff cannot recover both restitution and damages. Under the UCC, recovery may be had under both headings.

8. Specific Restitution

a. In General

The typical restitution action at law for the reasonable value of one's performance is a quasi-contractual action. In equity, through various devices, such as a decree canceling a deed, or the imposition of a constructive trust, specific restitution of property transferred or wrongfully acquired may be compelled. Specific restitution will be ordered where the legal remedy is inadequate.

b. Inadequacy of the Legal Remedy

The remedy at law is deemed inadequate where property is transferred in exchange for the promise of something other than a sum certain and the exchange will not be forthcoming, and also where the contract breacher has acquired money or property in violation of a relationship of trust and confidence.

C. EQUITABLE ENFORCEMENT

1. Inadequacy of the Legal Remedy

Equity will enforce a contract by decreeing specific performance or by a restraining order only if the legal remedy of damages or restitution is inadequate.

a. Uniqueness

Equity will order specific performance to a contract purchaser if the subject matter of a contract of sale is unique. The legal remedy is inadequate because the disappointed purchaser cannot replace the subject matter on the market. Land is always deemed unique, as are heirlooms, works of art, and other one-of-a-kind objects, as well as patents, copyrights, closely held stock, and other intangibles not readily available on the market.

b. Affirmative Rule of Mutuality

If a purchaser could have obtained a decree of specific performance in the event of the seller's breach because the purchaser's legal remedy would have been inadequate, the seller can obtain a decree of specific performance in the event of the purchaser's breach.

c. Conjectural Damages

The legal remedy is inadequate if damages are conjectural and restitution does not carry out the ends of the contract.

2. Defenses to Specific Performance

a. Validity of the Contract and Value

Equity will not enforce a contract that is invalid. Moreover, it requires that the contract be for value. Nominal consideration will not suffice, and a contract under seal without consideration will not suffice.

b. Exception

An option contract for a nominal (unbargained-for) consideration or under seal (in those jurisdictions where the seal is still viable) will be specifically enforced provided that it looks to further performances for a fair exchange.

c. Certainty of the Contract

Equity requires that the parties' performances be described in the contract with greater precision than is the case in an action at law. Because the penalty for non-compliance with a decree is punishment for contempt, the parties must know what to do with reasonable certainty.

d. Impossibility

Equity will not order a defendant to render a performance that is impossible even where impossibility will not excuse the breaching party in an action for damages.

3. Judicial Discretion as to Equitable Remedies

Specific performance is never a matter of pure entitlement. The court has wide powers of discretion in determining whether or not to grant the remedy. The factors to determine when the discretion will be exercised against enforcement are reducible to certain doctrines, such as difficulty of supervision, discussed below.

a. Difficulty of Supervision

Equity, in its discretion, will refuse to order specific performance of contracts where supervision of performance by the court will be unduly burdensome.

b. Personal Service Contract

Employment contracts are not specifically enforced against the employee. Such decrees would reek of involuntary servitude and possibly would run afoul of the Constitution. At times, however, an employee may be enjoined against working for another, resulting in indirect enforcement (*see infra*). Enforcement against an employer is normally denied because of the difficulty of supervision, or because of the adequacy of the legal remedy, but arbitration awards of reinstatement have been enforced.

c. Undue Risk

If performance of the contract would impose an undue risk that the counter-performance will not be received, specific performance will be denied.

d. Unconscionability

Under the doctrine of unconscionability, equity has refused to enforce contracts that are valid at law. Inadequacy of consideration coupled with any sharp practice, non-disclosure, overreaching, abuse of confidential relationship, etc., will result in a refusal of specific performance even where the inequitable conduct would not enable the party to avoid the contract.

e. Unclean Hands

Specific performance will be denied if the plaintiff is guilty of any inequitable conduct with respect to the transaction, even if in concert with the defendant so that no unconscionability exists.

f. Laches

Even if the statute of limitations has not run, specific performance will be denied if the plaintiff's failure promptly to pursue the remedy prejudices the defendant as by causing the defendant to change position or where the plaintiff has remained inactive until the subject matter has risen in value.

g. Balancing Hardships

Specific performance will be denied where the hardship to the defendant or to the public will be greatly in excess of any benefit to the plaintiff.

4. Specific Performance with an Abatement

When a vendor's title to real property is encumbered so that there is an inability to convey the interest contracted to be conveyed, or a structure has been damaged by a supervening fire or the like, the vendee may obtain a decree of specific performance with an abatement in price. In rare cases, specific performance would be refused if only a radically different kind of estate can be conveyed from that contracted for.

5. Relationship Between Specific Performance and Damages

a. Specific Performance Plus Damages

A decree for specific performance is often accompanied by an award of damages. Often, this will be an award of damages for delay in performing, say, a contract to convey real property. In other cases, it may be an award of damages for partial breach of, say, an output contract.

b. Specific Performance and Liquidated Damages

The presence of a liquidated damages clause does not preclude an award of specific performance.

c. Effect of Denial of Specific Performance

If specific performance is denied because of the adequacy of the legal remedy or because of the exercise of equitable discretion, the plaintiff may thereafter commence an action for damages or restitution at law. The denial of specific performance on equitable grounds does not deprive the plaintiff of any legal remedy. Under modern practice, in many jurisdictions, a plaintiff may join an equitable action with a law action in one suit. In such a suit, if the equitable remedy is denied, the legal remedy may be granted.

6. Restraining Orders

Specific relief is sometimes obtained by a restraining order. While these are most often sought in personal service contracts, they are not limited to such contracts.

a. Employment Contracts with Affirmative and Negative Duties

Where an employee promises to work exclusively for an employer for a given period, although equity will not compel the employee to work, it will enjoin the employee from working for another if the employer can show irreparable harm from breach of the express or implied negative covenant not to work for another.

b. Trade Secrets

A covenant not to divulge trade secrets will be enforced by injunction. Even in the absence of such a covenant, a duty not to divulge will be implied and enforced by injunction.

c. Covenants Not to Compete

An agreement not to compete, unconnected with another transaction, is void. An ancillary covenant connected with the sale of a business, an employment contract, a lease, and certain other transactions may be valid, if reasonable. If unreasonable, the orthodox view was that the entire covenant fell. The modern cases allow partial enforcement, limiting the injunction to a reasonable time and area.

(1) Ancillary to Sale of Business

Reasonableness is judged by whether the duration and territorial area of the restraint is in excess of the area in which the seller enjoyed goodwill or of the period of time the goodwill can reasonably be expected to continue.

(2) Ancillary to Employment

Covenants of this kind are tested by stricter criteria. Equity will enforce such a covenant to the extent necessary to prevent an employee's use of trade secrets or confidential customer lists. In rare cases such covenants will also be enforced where the employee's services are special, unique and extraordinary. An injunction will be limited to the area and time necessary to protect the employer's interests.

IX. AVOIDANCE OR REFORMATION FOR MISCONDUCT OR MISTAKE

A. DURESS

1. In General

Any wrongful act or threat that is the inducing cause of a contract constitutes duress and is grounds for avoiding the contract so formed. Where the coercion involves economic pressure, as in a. (3), (4), (5) below, rather than a threat of personal injury or the like, however, duress is usually not present unless the party coerced can show that there was no reasonable alternative but to assent.

a. What Constitutes Wrongful Conduct?

1) Violence or Threats of Violence
2) Wrongful Imprisonment or Threat of Imprisonment
3) Wrongful Seizure or Withholding of Property, Including the Abuse of Liens or Attachments
4) The Abuse of Legal Rights or the Threat Thereof
5) Breach or Threat to Breach a Contract

b. Coercion by a Third Party

If the wrongful pressure is applied by a third person, the transaction can be avoided only if the other contracting party knows of the coercion, or does not give value. If the other party gives value without notice of the wrongful conduct, the coerced party cannot avoid the contract.

2. Voidable or Void?

We have been presupposing a valid transaction and its possible avoidance. The general run of duress cases involve voidable transactions. There is one situation where duress renders a transaction void. A transaction is void if it is in no sense the consensual act of the party. A contract signed because a shotgun is pointed at one's head is consented to if one has a general idea of what one is signing. The contract is voidable. If one does not have any idea of the contents of the writing, one is in no sense consenting, the document is void. These cases are rare; almost non-existent.

B. UNDUE INFLUENCE

The gist of undue influence is unfair *persuasion* rather than coercion. Persuasion is unfair in two classes of cases. First, where a person uses a position of *trust and confidence* to convince the other to enter into a transaction that is not in the best interests of the persuaded party. Second, undue influence is exerted where a person uses a *position of dominance* to influence a transaction against the best interests of the subservient party. The foremost indicator of undue influence is an unnatural transaction resulting in the enrichment of one of the parties at the expense of the other.

C. MISREPRESENTATION

If a misrepresentation constitutes an actionable tort, avoidance is allowed, but all of the elements of tortious misrepresentation are not required for avoidance.

1. Scienter Is Not a Requirement

A misrepresentation is an assertion that is not in accord with existing facts. Avoidance may be based on a negligent or even an innocent misrepresentation. However, an *intentional* misrepresentation *need not be material,* while an *unintentional* misrepresentation *must be material*. A representation is material if (a) it would influence the conduct of a reasonable person; or (b) the person using the words knows that it would likely influence the conduct of the other party.

2. Deception

The party must have been deceived. If the party did not believe the representation, it cannot later be used as a basis for avoidance.

3. Reliance

The party must have relied upon the representation in the sense that the party regarded the representation as an important fact and that it influenced the decision to enter into the transaction.

4. Justification

The old idea that a party could not avoid a contract for fraud unless there was a right to rely has largely been superseded by the idea that avoidance will be allowed even to the simple and credulous. The law is in flux on the question, but if the representation is purely factual (as opposed to a misrepresentation of fact and opinion or fact and intention), the modern law regards reliance as justified in almost every case. A party is justified in relying even if negligent in investigating or not investigating the facts. Generally, however, if the subject matter is a corporate acquisition, the acquiring company is expected to conduct an in-depth investigation.

5. Injury Not Usually a Requisite

Even if a party gets something as valuable as, or more valuable than, the performance promised, the party may avoid the contract. The reason is that the party's autonomy has been tinkered with when presented with untrue information that prevents the exercise of good judgment. A major exception is that most cases hold that where a purchaser of land misrepresents the purpose for which the purchase is made, avoidance is not permitted unless the seller owns adjacent land, the value of which will decrease because of the intended use.

6. The Misrepresentation Must Be of Fact and Not Opinion or Law

A party is not justified in relying on a statement merely of opinion. Nonetheless, many statements of opinion also imply factual assertions. "It's uncomfortably hot and muggy today" expresses an opinion but does imply certain facts about the temperature and humidity. An assertion of law is sometimes a statement of fact; *e.g.*, "Iowa has adopted the UCC," but usually it is a statement of opinion, as when the person making an assertion prognosticates how the Iowa courts will solve a battle of the forms case. Although one may not rely on what is merely an opinion, one may rely on the implied facts contained in an opinion if it is reasonable to do so. The following are categories of cases in which such reasonableness is likely to exist. In each case it is assumed that the other elements of avoidance (deception, reliance and justification) exist.

a) The representer is or claims to be an expert.

b) The representer has superior access to the facts upon which the opinion is based.

c) There is a relationship of trust and confidence between the parties.

d) The opinion intentionally varies radically from reality.

e) The representation is of the law of another jurisdiction.

7. Promissory Fraud and Untrue Statements of Intention

The making of a promise without an intention to carry it out is a misrepresentation of fact, as is a statement of intention when one has no intention to carry it out.

8. Non-Disclosure

We start with a general rule that there is no duty to disclose facts that would tend to discourage the other party from entering into a proposed deal. This general rule is being eroded by a group of exceptions.

Exceptions:

a) Statutory disclosure rules, such as S.E.C., Truth-in-Lending, etc.

b) Concealment (positive action to hide) is the equivalent of a misrepresentation.

c) Where partial disclosure is misleading.

d) Where changing circumstances cause an assertion to no longer be true or if the representer discovers that a representation made innocently is incorrect.

e) Where one party becomes aware that the other is operating under a mistake as to a vital fact.

f) Where there is a confidential relationship.

g) In cases of suretyship, marine insurance, partnership, or joint venture.

h) Where specific performance is sought.

9. Misrepresentation by a Third Party

If a party, prior to contracting, has received false or otherwise incorrect information from a third person who is not an agent of the other party, the deceived party cannot avoid a contract induced by that information unless the other party learned of the misrepresentation prior to contracting. This is a variant of the bona fide purchaser for value principle.

10. Cure of a Misrepresentation

If, after a misrepresentation is made, the facts are brought into line with the representation before the deceived party has avoided the contract, the contract is no longer voidable.

11. Merger Clauses

Despite a merger clause or a no representations clause, parol evidence is admissible to show that a misrepresentation was made. An "as is" clause excludes warranties but does not exclude evidence of representations.

12. Election of Remedies

If the misrepresentation and ensuing deception, reliance and injury constitute a tort, the deceived party must elect between either a tort action or the exercise of the power of avoidance followed by a restitutionary action. Under the UCC both remedies are available, but items of recovery cannot be duplicated.

13. Restoration of *Status Quo Ante*

Where restitution is sought at law in a quasi-contractual action, the plaintiff must, before suing, offer to restore any tangible benefits received under the contract, but not if what has been received has perished because of its defects, is worthless, or consists of money that may be offset. However, in an equitable action no prior offer to restore is required, but the equitable decree can be conditioned upon such restoration. An equity action is available if something other than, or in addition to, a money judgment is sought; e.g., cancellation of a deed.

14. Fraud-in-the-Factum

Where a party signs a document that is radically different from that which was represented and the circumstances are such that a reasonable person similarly situated would have signed it, the document is *void*.

D. MISTAKE

1. Perspective

Certain kinds of mistakes may prevent the formation of contracts. These include misunderstandings and mistakes in transmission. Here, however, the discussion centers on mistake as a ground for *avoiding* a transaction.

2. Mistake of Fact Versus Mistake in Judgment

For avoidance, the mistake must relate to a basic assumption as to a *vital existing fact*. Risks as to *changing facts* are governed by the rules of *impracticability* and *frustration*. Risks of mistakes in judgment such as to the profitability of a stock purchase, or as to the number of labor hours required to complete a task, are quintessential contractual risks from which the court will not relieve a party.

3. Mutual Mistake

Where the parties are mistaken about a basic assumption upon which they base their bargain, the transaction can be avoided if, because of the mistake, a quite different exchange of values occurs from the contemplated exchange of values, provided, however, the risk is not otherwise allocated by agreement of the parties, or by the court because such other allocation is reasonable.

4. Mistake Versus Uncertainty

Where the parties are uncertain or consciously ignorant of a vital fact there is no right of avoidance.

5. Mutual Mistake as to Injuries

The orthodox view is that a release of a personal injury claim can be avoided if there are unknown injuries but not if there are unforeseen consequences of known injuries. Diagnosis is distinguished from prognosis. Some jurisdictions also allow avoidance if there is a vital mistake as to the nature and effect of known injuries.

6. Mutual Mistake as to Acreage

a. Avoidance

If the number of acres contracted to be conveyed or actually conveyed are discovered to be materially different from what the parties believed, the aggrieved party may avoid the contract or conveyance. Avoidance is permitted whether the sale is on a per acre basis or in gross.

b. Restitution

If the contract or conveyance is on a per acre basis, the purchaser may have restitution of the purchase price for any shortage of acres, and the seller has a restitution action for payment for additional acres. If the purchaser has not paid, an abatement in price rather than restitution is the appropriate remedy.

c. Perspective

These cases are treated under mistake, despite the fact that the vendor may have made a misrepresentation of fact. The reasons are historical.

7. Unilateral Palpable Mistake

A mistake by one party of which the other is, or ought to be, aware is grounds for avoidance. Cases of this kind are cases of fraudulent non-disclosure.

8. Unilateral Impalpable Mistake

Avoidance is allowed for unilateral mistake if (a) the mistake is computational, clerical or something of that sort, rather than a mistake in judgment; (b) enforcement of the contract would be oppressive, resulting in an unconscionably unequal exchange of values; and (c) avoidance would impose no substantial hardship on the other.

9. Mistake of Law

The orthodox view is that a mistake of law (except for mistake of the law of another jurisdiction) is not grounds for avoidance, but the modern trend and the Restatements take the position that relief will not be denied merely because the mistake is one of law. Mistake of law is not in all respects treated as mistake of fact. If the mistake relates to something other than the legal consequences of their words or conduct, the mistake, if vital, may be grounds for avoidance. Generally, a person is bound by the legal consequences of his or her acts, such as making an offer, an acceptance, a waiver, etc., whether or not the person knows the legal consequences.

10. Mistake in Performance

Recovery may be had for payments, overpayments, deliveries of returnable goods, and conveyances of excessive land made in the mistaken belief that the performance was owed under a contract, even if the mistake is negligent and unilateral.

a. Exception

If the party who mistakenly pays has a moral obligation to do so, restitution is not allowed. *E.g.*, *X* pays a debt, not remembering that the statute of limitations has run. *X* cannot obtain restitution.

b. Perspective

The rule stated for mistake in performance refers to money, returnable goods, and land and makes no reference to services. Services rendered by mistake cannot be returned. Consequently, there is no duty to pay for such services unless the receiver had a reasonable opportunity to reject them.

11. Defenses to Avoidance or Recovery for Mistake

a. Change of Position

A contract cannot be avoided, or the value of a performance recovered, for mistake, if the other party has detrimentally changed position in reliance upon the contract.

b. Affirmance of the Transaction After Discovery of the Mistake

c. Failure to Avoid the Contract with Reasonable Promptness After Discovery of the Mistake

E. REFORMATION FOR MISTAKE, MISREPRESENTATION, OR DURESS

1. Reformation for Mistake

Reformation of a writing for mistake is available if three requisites are met. (1) There must be a written agreement. (2) There must have been a prior agreement to put the agreement in writing. (3) There is a variance between the prior agreement and the writing caused by mistake.

a. The Prior Agreement

The prior agreement may have been oral or written. An indefinite or tentative agreement suffices. If by error, rather than by modification, clauses earlier agreed upon are misstated or omitted, the writing may be reformed.

b. The Agreement to Reduce to Writing

Reformation is not available if the parties mutually intended to omit or misstate the term. Reformation is available on grounds of misrepresentation, if one party, without the consent of the other, intentionally omits a term that has been agreed upon.

c. The Variance

Frequently, the variance is an arithmetical error. Sometimes, it is a misdescription of the subject matter, as a typist's error in a metes and bounds description of real property. At times, the parties mistake the legal effect of their writing. Reformation is available in each of these circumstances.

2. Reformation for Misrepresentation

If one party misrepresents the content or legal effect of a writing to the other, the other may elect to avoid the contract or to have it reformed to express what was represented.

3. Reformation for Duress

Cases of reformation for duress are few. The remedy requires (1) a binding contract preliminary to entering into a more formal contract, and (2) coercion into agreeing to a more formal contract that is at variance with the original agreement.

4. Reformation and the Parol Evidence Rule

The parol evidence rule is inapplicable in an action for reformation. However, a decree for reformation must be based on clear and convincing evidence, a higher standard than is normally required in a civil suit.

5. Defenses to Reformation

a. Bona Fide Purchasers for Value

Reformation will not be granted if the effect of the decree would infringe on the rights of a bona fide purchaser for value or other third persons who have justifiably relied upon the document as written.

b. Equitable Defenses

Reformation is an equitable action. Consequently, it is subject to equitable defenses such as unclean hands and laches. A decree for reformation may be withheld in the sound discretion of the court.

c. The Effect of Negligence

Negligence is no bar to reformation. It is important to note, however, that reformation is not available if one party carelessly believes that a writing will contain a particular provision. Unless this belief was shared or induced by the other, no proper case of reformation is made out. This is not because of negligence. Rather, it is because the writing is not at variance with the agreement.

F. UNCONSCIONABILITY

1. Unconscionability in Equity

For centuries, equity has refused to grant specific performance of contracts that were unconscionably obtained or unconscionable in content. Such decisions do not necessarily invalidate contracts but often leave the parties to their legal remedies, if any.

2. Unconscionability at Law

Since enactment of UCC § 2–302, courts in sales cases and in non-sales cases have exercised the power to strike down or limit contracts or contract clauses on grounds of unconscionability. Prior to enactment of the UCC, courts sometimes reached similar results by indirection, particularly by spurious interpretation. Only rarely did they directly apply a doctrine of unconscionability.

3. What Constitutes Unconscionability

A UCC comment indicates that there are two kinds of unconscionability. First, unfair surprise, often termed procedural unconscionability. Second, oppression, termed substantive unconscionability.

a. Unfair Surprise (Procedural Unconscionability)

A burdensome clause that does not come to the attention of a party adhering to a contract will be struck down if a reasonable person would not expect to find it in the contract and the reason it was not noticed was its burial in small print, or the inability of the adhering party to comprehend the language.

b. Oppression (Substantive Unconscionability)

Provisions of a contract that are assented to but are grossly one-sided may be invalidated or modified by the court. A contract that suffers from total overall imbalance, that is, one that is grossly one-sided, may be invalidated.

c. The Hybrid—Surprise and Oppression

Although analytically the surprise and oppression cases can be distinguished, in general, where unconscionability has been found, the facts contain a mixture of lack of knowledgeable assent and a clause or contract that unduly benefits the party who has drafted it.

4. Judge Versus Jury

Unconscionability is a question of law for the court, not for the trier of fact. The court must allow evidence of the commercial setting and purpose of a provision prior to ruling on the question. Consequently, it is almost always impossible to read a contract and decide that it, or any part of it, is unconscionable. Extrinsic evidence is necessary prior to deciding.

5. The Irrelevance of Supervening Events

Unconscionability must be judged by looking at the circumstances existing at the time of contracting without reference to future events. Supervening oppressiveness is governed by the doctrine of impracticability.

6. Consumer Protection

In the great majority of cases in which unconscionability has been found, the party protected by the finding has been a consumer. Generally, business people and business organizations are expected to protect themselves. There have been a few cases protecting a small business against a corporate giant.

7. Termination Clauses and Sales of Goods

Under § 2–309(1) of the UCC, a contract for the sale of goods that is indefinite in duration is not terminable except on reasonable notice. The Code's focus is on retail franchises and wholesale distributorships that envisage continuing, often exclusive, relationships. But other relational contracts are also included; e.g., a requirements contract of indefinite duration. UCC § 2–309(3) goes on to provide that an agreement dispensing with a reasonable period of notice is invalid if its operation would be unconscionable.

8. Limitation on Consequential Damages—Personal Injuries

Although the Code permits limitations on damages and permits the exclusion of consequential damages, it indicates that the exclusion is subject to the rule of conscionability. Limitation of consequential damages for injury to the person in the case of consumer goods is prima facie unconscionable, but limitation of damages where the loss is commercial is not. UCC § 2–719(3). It is, of course, possible to have a finding of unconscionability in the case of commercial losses based on the general doctrine of unconscionability. This would be most unusual, however.

G. AFFIRMANCE OR RATIFICATION

1. Discussion

Affirmance and ratification are equivalent terms. Upon discovering a misrepresentation or mistake, and on escaping duress or undue influence, a party has choices. One of these choices is to continue to accept the obligations of the contract. A manifestation of intent to continue with the transaction is an affirmance. No consideration is required for an affirmance. After affirmance, the power of avoidance and the right to seek reformation are lost.

2. Affirmance by Conduct

a. Exercise of Dominion

After a party's power to choose between affirmance and avoidance ripens, the continued exercise of dominion over property received under the contract or the continued acceptance of benefits under the contract affirms the contract.

b. Delay

An affirmance occurs if a party fails within a reasonable time to avoid the contract after the power to do so has ripened. What is a reasonable time is normally a question of fact. Three factors dominate the determination of reasonableness of time to avoid: (1) reliance by the other, (2) speculative benefit gained by stalling, and (3) fault.

3. The Party Avoiding Must Offer to Return Property Received

This requisite and its exceptions are discussed in connection with the remedy of restitution.

X. THIRD PARTY BENEFICIARIES

A. TYPES OF BENEFICIARIES

1. In General

An intended beneficiary may recover on a contract. This is one of several exceptions to the privity requirement.

2. Intended Beneficiaries

A third person to whom a promisee intends the benefits of a promisor's promise to run is an intended beneficiary. There are a number of tests to determine who is an intended beneficiary. The most commonly used tests are: (1) to whom is the performance to run (if it is to run directly to the third person, this person is an intended beneficiary); and (2) whether the promisor reasonably understood that the promisee intended to benefit the beneficiary; that is, whether the beneficiary was an ultimate intended beneficiary of the promisor's performance.

3. Incidental Beneficiary

A party who receives benefits from a promisor's performance but who was not intended to be a beneficiary, and therefore has no rights, is an incidental beneficiary.

4. Creditor Beneficiary

If a promisee extracts from another a promise to render a performance to a third party because the promisee is indebted to the third party, the third party is a creditor beneficiary.

5. Donee Beneficiary

If the promisee's purpose in extracting the promise is to confer a gift upon the third party, the third party is a donee beneficiary. The distinction between donee and creditor beneficiaries is not ordinarily important on the issue of intent to benefit but may be important on other issues, such as when rights vest.

6. Promises of Indemnity

A promise to indemnify against loss does not create a third party beneficiary. Performance runs to the promisee. A promise to indemnify against liability often creates third party beneficiaries. This is especially true in municipality cases. However, the typical automobile insurance policy does not because the language of the policy bars third party actions.

7. The Municipality Cases

Municipal contracts that create enforceable rights in third persons are of three types. These are: (1) where a contractor agrees to perform a duty that the municipality owes to individual members of the public and the breach of which would create tort liability against the municipality; (2) where the contractor promises the governmental body to *compensate* members of the public for injuries to them despite the absence of a governmental duty; and (3) where the governmental body enters into a contract to gain advantages for individual members of the public.

8. The Surety Bond Cases

Laborers, suppliers, and subcontractors are not third party beneficiaries of a performance bond because the purpose of this type of bond is to assure payment of damages to an owner in the event of a contractor's non-performance. They are generally held to be third party beneficiaries of a payment bond—a bond that promises to pay laborers, etc., if the employer fails to pay. While the motive of a promisee in procuring a payment bond is self-protection, the intent is also to benefit the laborers, suppliers, and subcontractors. It is presumed that these third parties are not intended beneficiaries of a joint performance-payment bond because the bond might be dissipated in paying third party beneficiaries without paying the promisee.

B. PROMISOR'S DEFENSES

1. In General

In the absence of agreement to the contrary, the promisor can assert against the beneficiary any defense the promisor has against the promisee.

2. Exceptions

a. Where the parties agree that the beneficiary will have enforceable rights despite any defense that the promisor might be able to assert against the promisee;

b. Where the rights of the beneficiary have vested, the rights may not be varied by subsequent arrangement between the promisor and the promisee.

3. When Rights Vest

a. Omnipotence of the Contract

The parties may provide as they wish with respect to vesting. For example, the contract may validly provide that rights of third parties are always divestable or that they vest immediately.

b. Creditor Beneficiaries

The rights of a creditor beneficiary vest, at the latest, when the beneficiary brings an action to enforce the contract or otherwise materially changes position in reliance on it. The tendency today is to hold that the rights vest as soon as the beneficiary learns of the promise and assents to it.

c. Donee Beneficiaries

According to the original Restatement, the rights of a donee beneficiary vest immediately upon making the contract, but the Restatement (Second) and much case law has indicated that the rule that applies to creditor beneficiaries should be applied to donees.

d. Perspective

Vesting has a very limited role. It does not give the beneficiary the equivalent of a fee simple absolute in the promise. It only insulates the beneficiary from a curtailment of rights by mutual agreement of the promisor and promisee. It does not insulate the beneficiary from defenses such as failure of a constructive condition.

4. Counterclaim

The promisor can effectively raise against the beneficiary a counterclaim that the promisor has against the promisee only if it is in the nature of a recoupment; that is, if it arises out of the same transaction upon which the promisor is being sued. The recoupment may be used only as a subtraction from the beneficiary's claim and not for affirmative relief.

5. Promisee's Defense Against the Beneficiary

Suppose the promisor, *A*, makes the promise to *B* for the benefit of *C*, a supposed creditor of *B*. Afterwards, *A* discovers that *C* is not a creditor because *B* has a valid defense against *C*. The availability of this defense to *A* depends upon the interpretation of the contract. If the promisor promises to pay irrespective of any such defense, it cannot be raised. If *A* promises merely to perform to the extent *B* is obligated, the defense may be raised. If the promise is to pay a specific debt, it is interpreted to mean that the promise is to pay irrespective of such a defense.

C. CUMULATIVE RIGHTS OF THE BENEFICIARY

1. Creditor Beneficiary

A creditor beneficiary has rights against both the promisor and the promisee. Judgment may be had against both, but only one satisfaction may be obtained.

2. Novation Contrasted

No novation occurs in a normal third party beneficiary contract because the beneficiary does not impliedly release the debtor when the beneficiary assents to, or even attempts to enforce, the promisor's assumption.

3. Donee Beneficiary

A donee beneficiary has rights against the promisor, but has no rights against the promisee, unless, after the rights have vested, the promisee has received a consideration to discharge the promisor. The beneficiary's remedial rights are limited to the value of the consideration.

D. RIGHTS OF THE PROMISEE AGAINST THE PROMISOR

1. In General

In addition to liability to the beneficiary, the promisor is under an obligation to the promisee for performance of the contract.

2. Discussion

It should not be forgotten that the promisor's contract is with the promisee. In the case of a donee beneficiary contract, the promisee usually suffers no damage by a promisor's breach and restitution may not be a satisfactory remedy. Thus, the legal remedy may be inadequate and, if so, the promisee's action for specific performance will be entertained. In a creditor beneficiary contract, breach by the promisor can cause substantial harm to the promisee. If such damages occur, they are recoverable.

XI. ASSIGNMENT AND DELEGATION

A. ASSIGNMENT OF RIGHTS

1. What Is an Assignment?

An assignment is a manifestation of intent by the owner of a right to the assignee to effectuate its present transfer.

2. Perspective

An assignment's closest relatives are sales of goods and conveyances of land. It is an executed transaction. Consequently, words of promise do not create an assignment. An order communicated to the debtor alone is not an assignment.

3. UCC Coverage

Although, in its simplest form, an assignment is an outright transfer, frequently an assignment is made as a security device. It is similar to a mortgage of real property rather than the conveyance of a fee simple. Although Article 9 of the UCC focuses primarily upon security devices, it governs the assignment of rights to payment whether the assignment is an outright transfer or the creation of a security device.

4. UCC Exclusions

Although Article 9 of the UCC governs assignments of rights to payment regardless of the purpose of the assignment, specific exceptions are enumerated in the Code. These include: (a) Wage assignments; (b) Assignments of accounts in connection with the sale of a business from which they arose; (c) An assignment of rights under a contract coupled with the delegation of the assignor's duties to the assignee; (d) If the right to payment is evidenced by chattel paper.

Where the transaction is not governed by Article 9, the common law rules apply, or, in some instances, other legislation. For example, most states have statutes regulating or outlawing wage assignments; the FTC has banned them in consumer credit transactions. Article 2 of the Code has several provisions that govern the assignment of rights in contracts for the sale of goods.

5. Deviations from the Norm

There are three types of assignments that deviate from the norm and have problems that ordinary assignments do not have.

a. Gratuitous Assignment

The fact that the assignor makes a gift of a right against the obligor is not a defense to the obligor. An assignment, as an executed transaction, requires no consideration. But, as between the assignor and the assignee, the gift must be complete; otherwise, the assignee's rights can be terminated by the death of the assignor, by a subsequent assignment of the same right or by a notice of revocation communicated to the assignee or to the obligor. Since a right cannot be physically delivered, the gift can be completed by other substitute delivery methods such as: the assignee's receipt of payment, delivery of a symbolic writing to the assignee, or the application of promissory estoppel. An assignment given for a pre-existing debt is for value and is not deemed to be gratuitous.

b. Voidable Assignment

An assignment may also be voidable by the assignor because of infancy, insanity, fraud, duress, etc. The same rules that apply for avoiding a contract apply.

c. Assignment of Future Rights

An assignment of a future right is the assignment of a right to arise under a contract that has not yet been made. The generally accepted common law rule is that an assignment for value of a future right is an equitable assignment. At common law, such rights were generally superior to those of the assignor but inferior to those of a subsequent assignee of the same right for value without notice and to the rights of a subsequent attaching creditor of the assignor who is without notice of the claim of the assignee provided the attachment occurs before the right comes into being. Under the UCC, generally speaking, if the assignee of future rights complies with the perfection requirements of the Code, the assignee will prevail.

6. Formalities

In the absence of statute, an assignment may be oral. Under Article 9, a writing is required unless the assignee is in possession of the collateral involved. Possession of a right to payment is not possible; consequently, if the assignment of the account is governed by Article 9, a writing is required. If there is no writing, the assignment is not enforceable against anyone.

7. Attachment of Security Interests in Accounts

Attachment relates to the relative rights of the assignor and assignee. Once the rights of an assignee attach, the assignee's rights are superior to those of the assignor. Unless there is an agreement to the contrary, the rights of the assignee attach as soon as (1) there is an agreement that the rights attach; (2) value has been given; and (3) the account in which the assignee has rights is identified. It is important to remember that if Article 9 governs, the assignment must be in writing for the assignee's rights to attach.

8. Perfection of Security Interests in Accounts

Perfection relates to the rights of the assignee against third parties. Perfection cannot occur until the assignment attaches. Perfection, under Article 9, generally occurs when the assignee takes possession of the collateral, but in the case of accounts, since possession is not possible, filing of a notice (financing statement) of assignment in a public record office is the normal method of perfection. Filing is not required to perfect a security interest in an account where the assignment (either by itself or in conjunction with others) does not constitute a significant part of the accounts of the assignor. In this case, the rights of the assignee are perfected on attachment.

9. Priorities Under the UCC

Under the UCC, an assignee who has perfected a security interest in an account has priority over a party whose rights are subsequently perfected, including lien creditors, secured creditors and a trustee of the assignor's bankrupt estate. A subsequent secured creditor, and a subsequent lien creditor, will prevail over an assignee who does not have a perfected interest. A lien creditor is an unsecured creditor who has acquired a lien by attachment, levy or the like and includes a trustee of the assignor's estate in bankruptcy.

10. Priorities When the UCC Doesn't Apply

a. Assignee Versus Attaching Creditor

At common law, the priority between an assignee and a creditor who had obtained an attachment on the right assigned is governed by the rule: prior in time, prior in right. Consequently, priority depended on the relative time of the attachment and of the assignment. However, the assignee may be estopped from asserting this priority. For example, it is often held that the assignee loses priority if the *obligor* has not received notice of the assignment in sufficient time to call the assignment to the attention of the court in the attachment proceedings. The more modern view deprives the assignee of priority only if the assignee fails to give notice of assignment prior to payment by the obligor to the attaching creditor.

b. Successive Assignees

At common law, there are three competing rules to determine priority among successive assignees of the same claim:

1) New York Rule

Prior in time is prior in right.

2) English View

The first assignee to notify the obligor prevails provided this assignee gives value and has no notice of any prior assignment.

3) Four Horsemen Rule (Rule of the Restatements and the Prevailing Rule)

Prior in time is prior in right unless a subsequent assignee who pays value in good faith (1) obtains payment from the obligor; or (2) recovers judgment from; or (3) enters into a substituted contract with the obligor; or (4) receives delivery of an instrument that incorporates the debt.

c. Latent Equities

An assignment to a bona fide assignee for value without notice destroys any latent equities third persons may have in the right. The older view was to the contrary.

11. Floating Lien

The UCC expressly validates a floating lien on a shifting stock of goods or accounts.

12. Non-Assignable Rights

A right is assignable except where the assignment would: (1) materially change the duty of the other party; (2) materially vary the burden or risk of the obligor; (3) impair materially the other party's chance of obtaining return performance; or (4) be contrary to public policy.

13. Contractual Prohibition of an Assignment

a. Common Law Rule

At common law, a provision in a contract prohibiting an assignment of rights was generally sustained as valid under the general principle of freedom of contract, although several courts struck down such provisions as illegal restraints on alienation. If, however, the court was able to find that the provision was not drafted with sufficient clarity to accomplish the purpose of voiding the assignment, the anti-assignment clause was treated as a promise not to assign. An assignment would breach the promise and give the obligor an action for breach, but the assignment was valid. Because damages for breach of the provision are ordinarily nominal, the anti-assignment clause was frequently of no practical value.

b. The UCC Rule

Under UCC Article 9 an anti-assignment clause is ineffective to prohibit the assignment of an account. Also, Article 2 permits the assignment of the right to damages for total breach or of a right arising from the assignor's total due performance, despite a clause purporting to prevent assignment.

c. Interpretation Under Article 2

UCC Article 2—and the Restatement (Second) agrees—provides that general language purporting to prohibit assignment of the contract should be construed as barring only the delegation of duties, unless the circumstances indicate the contrary. (On delegation of duties, *see* XI.B., *infra.*)

14. Option Contracts

Option contracts are offers but are also contracts. While offers are not assignable, option contracts generally are. The offeree's rights in an option contract are assignable, provided the rights are otherwise assignable and the duties otherwise delegable and any promise expected to be made by the offeree has been made.

15. Defenses of the Obligor Against the Assignor

The obligor may assert against the assignee any defense that could have been asserted against the assignor. The maxim is that the assignee stands in the shoes of the assignor.

16. Vesting

As an exception to the rule stated immediately above, when the rights of the assignee have vested they may not be discharged or curtailed by a subsequent agreement or other voluntary transaction between the obligor and assignor. Vesting occurs when the assignee notifies the obligor of the assignment. Under UCC Article 9, however, even after notice to the obligor, the assignor and obligor have a limited right to curtail the rights of the assignee. If the assigned right to payment has not yet been earned by performance, the assignor and obligor may, in good faith and in accordance with reasonable commercial standards, modify or substitute for the contract. When this occurs, the assignee has rights under the new agreement.

17. Counterclaims

To what extent may an obligor raise a counterclaim against an assignee? Under UCC Article 9, this depends in part on whether or not the counterclaim stems from the same transaction.

a. Same Transaction (Recoupment)

If the obligor's counterclaim arises out of the same contract from which the assignee's rights stem, the obligor may raise the counterclaim by way of defense. This defense, known as recoupment, cannot be used for affirmative relief against the assignee but only by way of subtraction.

b. Different Transaction (Set-Off)

If the obligor's counterclaim arose from a different transaction with the assignor, this counterclaim may be raised against the assignee only if it accrues before the obligor receives notice of the assignment. This defense, known as set-off, cannot be used for affirmative relief against the assignee but only by way of subtraction.

18. Waiver of Defenses or Counterclaims

A contractual clause that the debtor cannot raise against an assignee the defenses it has against the creditor is valid under UCC Article 9, provided the assignee takes the assignment in good faith, for value, and without notice of the claim or defense, except that such a clause cannot effectively prohibit the raising of a real defense. Real defenses are: voidability for infancy; voidness for total incapacity, illegality or fraud in the factum; and discharge in insolvency proceedings. The UCC provision validating waiver of defense clauses subordinates the rule to any statute or decision which establishes a different rule for buyers or lessees of consumer goods. . . . The FTC has invalidated such clauses in consumer transactions. The rule validating waiver of defense clauses continues to be viable only in non-consumer transactions.

19. Rights of the Assignee Against the Assignor

a. Express Warranties or Disclaimers of Implied Warranties

Within broad limits, the assignee and assignor may agree as they wish as to warranties. Thus, the assignor will be held to any express warranty made. A warranty disclaimer is similarly upheld where the obligor and assignor agreed to the disclaimer.

b. Implied Warranties

In the absence of an express agreement to the contrary, an assignor warrants that:

1) the assignor will do nothing to defeat or impair the value of the assignment;
2) the right exists and is subject to no defenses or limitations not stated or apparent; and that
3) any document delivered is genuine and what it purports to be.

B. DELEGATION OF DUTIES

1. What Is a Delegation?

A delegation occurs when an obligor (delegant) appoints another person (delegate) to render a performance that the obligor owes to a third person.

2. Liability of the Delegant

A delegant cannot obtain freedom from liability by delegating duties. This is perhaps the only immutable rule in the law of contracts. There is no way an obligor can be freed from liability other than by consent of the obligee, the decree of a bankruptcy court, or the passage of time under the statute of limitations.

3. Liability of the Delegate

The delegate becomes liable to the third party only by making a promise that is for the benefit of the third person.

4. Non-Delegable Duties

a. What Duties Are Non-Delegable?

The test is whether performance by the obligor or under the obligor's personal supervision is required by the contract. Such a requirement may be expressed in the contract. If it is not, such a requirement will be implied: (a) where the contract is predicated on the unique skills of the obligor; and (b) where the contract is predicated on the trust and confidence that the obligee has placed in the obligor.

b. Delegation in Sales Contracts

In general, the delegation rules of UCC Article 2 are the same as the common law. It will be recalled that, under the UCC, a general clause prohibiting assignment of the contract has the effect of prohibiting the delegation of duties. Also, under the UCC, unless the language or circumstances point to a contrary intention, an assignment in general terms is treated as doing three things: assigning the rights, delegating the duties, and creating an assumption of duties. The UCC also authorizes the obligee to demand assurances from the delegate whenever the other party assigns rights and delegates duties to a third person.

c. Effect of Improper Delegation

An attempted delegation of a non-delegable duty is ineffective. It is also a breach. If persisted in, the breach is material.

Perspective

APPROACH TO CONTRACTS

Contracts is a very difficult course. At the same time, it is very important. It is the foundation for many other courses in the curriculum (for example, Uniform Commercial Code courses, Real Estate Financing, Mergers and Acquisitions). It also trains students "to think like lawyers."

The course in Contracts tackles a large number of issues that at first appear to be unrelated. While some legal subjects, such as Torts, can be compared to a bowl of fruit, each topic being discrete from each other, the course in Contracts is like an onion, a many-layered subject. A large number of layers may lurk in a short fact pattern. The function of this outline is not only to state the general principles of Contract Law but to structure those principles in an orderly fashion.

You should be prepared to accept that in some areas there are a number of views. When this is so, you will be required to state all of the views and the relative merits of each one. (More later.) Although Contracts is basically a common-law course, there are a number of instances where the common law has been changed by statute. Here again, it is important to know why the common law was changed and what the statute says. The most significant statute in this area is the Uniform Commercial Code.

HOW TO STUDY

Most professors use a case method of instruction. It goes without saying that the cases should be carefully briefed and analyzed. If you do not do this, you will not be prepared for the intensive class discussion. Prepare critically! Question everything you read, especially the results reached in cases you read. Compare cases carefully. Remember that a change in one fact may change the result reached in a case that has many similar facts.

The most important skill that a lawyer needs is the ability to analyze. Innate analytical ability varies from person to person, but to some extent it can be acquired. This means that you should carefully analyze each assigned case with a passion. Get a clear understanding of the essential facts. To do this you should use your own words in the brief rather than the language of court. Try to state the precise issue in the case. Do not state a broad issue such as, "Was there a contract?" Find the precise issue that determines whether there is a contract. Find the general principle. How was it applied to the facts? Is the decision sound? Can you make a good contrary argument? Remember, the party on the losing side thought there was a good case for a contrary decision. Do not ignore dissenting opinions. The casebook editors include dissenting opinions to show another perspective on the resolution of the case.

Although preparation is important, what happens in class is much more important. Review the material prior to going to class. Get sufficient rest so that you are eager and alert. Then take the best set of class notes that is possible. How well you do this will depend on your professor's method of instruction. The most important thing you can do is to organize your notes as soon after class as possible. This Outline should help you do that. If you are still uncertain after reading this Outline, you may wish to turn to a text such as CONTRACTS IN A NUTSHELL or the CONTRACTS Hornbook, both published by West Academic. Don't go to bed until you have mastered the lecture. It is most important to put the material in outline form. Preparing this outline will help you master the material. Continuously review your outline! Do not wait until exam time to learn it.

EXAMINATION

If you have faithfully done what is stated above, you should be well prepared for the exam. This does not necessarily mean that you will get a good grade. One reason is that law school is highly competitive, and grades are relative. Another is that you may have a bad day, and still a third is that you may not do a good job of analyzing one or more issues in a question.

There are, however, exam techniques that can help. One part of these may be termed mechanical. Bring a working watch. Budget your time. Do not spend it all on the first question. Follow all instructions carefully. Write legibly, otherwise your paper may not be read carefully. Use complete sentences and write grammatically.

These relatively mechanical suggestions aside, your first important job is to master the facts. Many students do poorly because they misread or misunderstood the facts. Read the facts carefully several times. As you do, jot down the issues you see—you must get the overall picture. If the facts are complicated, use a diagram. (Do not supply additional facts, but you are free to indicate that important facts may be missing.) You must also look at each word in the question carefully. Do not lightly assume that any word is superfluous. Do not repeat the facts, but as indicated below, work them into your answer where they are relevant. Also, make sure you understand *precisely* what the question is asking for.

When you have listed all of the issues, try to put them in logical order. For example, the question of whether a contract was formed should precede any discussion of breach of the contract.

Let us assume that the first issue in the question relates to the existence of an offer. Identify the issue and then state the general principle involved. For example, would a reasonable person in the position of the plaintiff conclude that an offer has been made? Now the facts that relate to this issue must be analyzed. Some of the facts may lead to an affirmative answer, others to a negative one. Both sides should be explored and then you should reach a conclusion. Your conclusion is not nearly as important as your analysis.

If you conclude that there was no offer, then as a matter of *logic* you could conclude that no further discussion of any problem is required. *However*, discretion in this instance is more important than logic. You must go on to discuss all of the other issues. You should go on to say, "Assuming that there was an offer, the next question is one of acceptance."

The important thing is to raise each issue, state the general principle that governs, and then apply that principle to the facts showing how the facts fit the principle. If there is more than one view, apply all of the views to the facts. If there is a relevant statute, discuss it and apply it to the facts. Cover all of the possibilities. If your professor has mentioned policy considerations, it would be a good idea to bring them into the discussion. If you conclude that certain facts are "red herrings"—irrelevant to the decision—it is always a good idea to state briefly *why* you so concluded. Your answer should reflect your mental operations. Do not bury an issue because you are unsure of the answer. Even if your answer is wrong and indefensible, you will get credit for identifying the issue. After all this is done, you should state your ultimate conclusion. When you have finished your answer, reread it carefully to check for any inadvertent mistakes.

Chapter I

Introduction: Sources of Law

■ ANALYSIS

A. Introduction

One of the important features of *Contracts* as a course of study in law school is that it gives law students an opportunity to examine a broad range of sources of law, and to understand how these sources may interact in any particular dispute involving a contract. These sources include cases, scholarly texts, state statutes based on the Uniform Commercial Code, and other more general state and federal statutes that may apply to contracts.

B. The Common Law

In deciding a contracts case, a judge will often rely on commonly accepted rules or principles found in prior cases and applied to disputes like the one in the case now before the judge. Contract law is a basic part of the "common law" that the United States inherited ("received") from England. U.S. courts have continued to develop the common law of contracts by adapting the law to evolving economic and social developments. We typically refer to this source of law as *case law*.

C. The First Restatement of Contracts

In the early Twentieth Century, a private, not-for-profit organization known as the American Law Institute (ALI) was founded. One of its goals was to help the courts to reach sound and uniform decisions when applying the common law. To this end it commissioned "Restatements," carefully numbered code-like documents that lay out "the law" in black letter form. The black-letter rules are fleshed out with comments and illustrations. The first Restatement of Contracts was published in 1932. Strictly speaking, the Restatement does not have the force of law; it is a scholarly text that draws on case law and tries to organize common law rules in an orderly and logical fashion. Nonetheless, courts found it quite persuasive, and its provisions have been the basis of many court decisions. Indeed, some provisions of the Restatement (like § 90 on promises "reasonably inducing definite and substantial action") are often cited and applied by courts as if they *were* binding case law rules.

D. The Uniform Commercial Code

Although ten states have codified general contract law in statutes, the most important statutory source of state contract law is the Uniform Commercial Code (UCC). The ALI and the National Conference of Commissioners on Uniform State Laws (NCCUSL), now known as the Uniform Law Commission (ULC), a not-for-profit organization that is a consortium of the fifty states, worked together for decades putting together a draft statute codifying a good portion of the commercial laws of the states. The result was the Uniform Commercial Code (UCC).

Of particular importance for the course in *Contracts* is UCC Article 2, which covers rules applicable to the sale of goods (*i.e.*, movable tangible things, generally things other than real estate and services). Article 2 was enacted with only slight variations by all of the states except Louisiana. These enactments occurred mainly in the 1960's. The importance of the UCC is that every state that enacted it now has basically the exact same rules to apply to all contracts for the sale of goods—rules that, at least on paper, are more *uniform* than the common law rules that depend upon what a particular state's courts have developed for contract disputes generally. Although a revision of Article 2 was approved by the ALI and by the ULC in 2003, no state has enacted it, and it appears to be dead on arrival. In July 2022, the ULC approved a package of UCC amendments to address matters relating to emerging technologies. (The draft, approved by the ALI in May 2022, was officially promulgated later in 2022 after final review by the ULC style committee.) Much of the package addresses matters relating to digital assets referred to as "controllable electronic records" and payment obligations that are "tethered" to them. Coverage of matters governed by UCC Article 2 will be amended to conform to these changes. The definition of "conspicuous" in Article 1 will be changed, and Article 2 will provide statutory guidance as to whether, and the extent to which, the Article applies to "hybrid transactions" involving not only a sale of goods but also the provision of services or the transfer of other property.

As of this writing, it is not clear whether states will generally embrace the latest UCC revisions. (Note, however, that in June 2022, New Hampshire enacted a draft version of the 2022 revisions, effective January 1, 2023. In addition, Arkansas, Indiana, Iowa, and Texas have enacted a draft version of new Article 12, governing transfer of property rights in virtual currency and nonfungible tokens (NFTs)). As a result of current and possible future variations in state responses to official versions of the UCC, throughout this book the text will rely on the pre-2022 Official Text of the UCC.

E. The Second Restatement

In 1964, work was begun on a revised Restatement of Contracts, to reflect developments in case law since the publication of the first Restatement. The Restatement (Second) of Contracts, published in 1981, in general followed more flexible notions of Professor Corbin's treatise, while the first Restatement had favored Professor Williston's more rigid "classical" approach to contract law. A second very significant influence on the Restatement (Second) was the more flexible approach taken by UCC Article 2. Hence, the Restatement (Second) includes rules that are derived not only from modern case law developments but also from the more or less uniform state statutes that adopted the UCC as enacted state law.

F. Other State and Federal Law

Contracts casebooks concentrate on the common law of contracts, the UCC, and the Restatements of Contracts. However, there are other state and federal statutes that may also apply to a contract situation. You will occasionally see references to these other statutes in the casebooks, and in your law practice they may be a crucial part of an argument that you are making in a particular case. One important example would be state and federal statutes providing special rules or procedures intended to protect consumers who become involved in a commercial transaction. In most law school programs, such specialized statutes are the subject of separate, elective courses, and may not receive much if any coverage in the required *Contracts* course. However, one group of such specialized statutes has been a traditional part of the required *Contracts* course—so-called "statutes of frauds," which require specific, written formalities to make a transaction enforceable. (*See* III.C.f,, IV.C, *infra* (discussing statutes of frauds).) Most casebooks refer to these as "the Statute of Frauds," but this is misleading. Every state, as well as the federal government, has at least *two* statutes of frauds, and often more than that, each applicable to a specified type of transaction.

Chapter II

Mutual Assent—Offer and Acceptance

■ ANALYSIS

- b. Acceptance by Authorized Party
  - 1) Options
  - 2) Undisclosed Principal
- c. Knowledge of the Offer and Intent to Accept
  - 1) Knowledge of the Offer
  - 2) Intent to Accept
- d. Necessity for Communication to Create a Bilateral Contract
  - 1) Theory
  - 2) Exception
- e. Necessity for Notice of Performance of a Unilateral Contract
  - 1) Introduction
  - 2) Three Views
  - 3) Discussion of View (b)
- f. Acceptance of an Offer Looking to a Series of Contracts

2. Acceptance of a Bilateral Contract
   - a. Acceptance by Silence
   - b. Acceptance by Conduct
     - 1) Discussion
     - 2) Statutory Exceptions
   - c. When Is an Acceptance Effective?
     - 1) Introduction
     - 2) Prescribed Method of Acceptance
     - 3) Parties at a Distance
       - a) Reasonable Means of Acceptance (Mailbox Rule)
       - b) Unreasonable Means of Acceptance
   - d. Offeror's Power to Negate the Mailbox Rule
   - e. When Offeree Sends Both Acceptance and Rejection
     - 1) When a Rejection Is Sent First
     - 2) When an Acceptance Is Sent First
   - f. Lost or Delayed Acceptance
   - g. Parties in the Presence of One Another

D. Termination of Revocable Offers

1. Introduction
   - a. Lapse of Time
     - 1) Time Specified in the Offer
     - 2) Time Not Specified in Offer
       - a) Face to Face Offer
     - 3) Termination on the Occurrence of a Particular Event
     - 4) Effect of Late Acceptance
   - b. Death or Lack of Capacity
     - 1) Death of Offeror
     - 2) Incapacity of Offeror
       - a) Adjudication of Incapacity
       - b) No Adjudication of Incapacity
     - 3) Death or Incapacity of the Offeree
   - c. Revocation
     - 1) Direct Revocation

- 2) Where the Parties Are Silent as to a Material Term
- 3) Where the Parties Agree to Agree
- a) Traditional Rule
- b) Modern View

2. Uniform Commercial Code
   - a) Introduction
   - b) General Provision
   - c) Specific Provisions
     - 1) Place of Delivery
     - 2) Time for Shipment or Delivery
     - 3) Time for Payment
     - 4) Failure to Specify Assortment

G. Digital Contracts
1. Introduction
2. Digital Contracts Under the UCC
   - a. Introduction
   - b. Other Provisions
     - 1) Statute of Frauds Writing Requirement
     - 2) 2022 Revision of the Writing Requirement
   - c. Other Statutes
   - d. Judicial Approaches
     - 1) In General
     - 2) Judicial Battle over the "Battle of the Forms"
       - a) Hidden Terms

A. Mutual Assent

1. Nature of Mutual Assent

Mutual assent, with few exceptions, is required for the formation of a contract. Mutual assent is ordinarily arrived at by offer and acceptance. At times, however, mutual assent exists even though it is impossible to identify the offer and the acceptance.

Examples: (1) *A* makes an offer to sell *B* a vintage Aston-Martin automobile for $200,000, specifying all necessary terms. *B*, in turn, states that he accepts the offer. Mutual assent has arisen through a process of offer and acceptance.

(2) *A* and *B* reach general agreement on a complex deal. They then ask their lawyers to draw up a binding contract. Numerous drafts are shuttled back and forth between the lawyers after many consultations with their clients. At a closing, *A* and *B* sign and exchange a final draft. Neither the offer nor the acceptance can be identified, but the parties have manifested mutual assent.

2. Objective Theory of Contracts

With certain exceptions discussed later, the existence of mutual assent is determined under the objective theory of contracts rather than under a subjective approach.

a. Discussion

The objective theory of contracts states that mutual assent should be determined solely from objective manifestations of assent—what the parties do and say rather than what either party subjectively intends, believes, or assumes. This objective approach is designed to protect the parties' reasonable expectations. Another aspect of this theory is that objective manifestations of intent should be viewed from the vantage point of a reasonable person in the position of the addressee of the communication. The addressee is charged not only with the knowledge of a reasonable person but also with any special knowledge that the addressee has or should have.

There are other approaches, both objective and subjective, which will be discussed below. In the meantime, the objective approach will be employed as an acceptable tentative test. The United Nations Convention for the International Sale of Goods follows the same basic objective approach.

Examples: (1) *A*, laughing, makes an "offer" to sell his new truck to *B* for the chocolate-chip cookie in B's lunch box. *A* is joking, and *B* knows that *A* is joking. *B* cannot create a contract by accepting because *B* knows that *A* is not serious.

(2) *A* tells *B* that he will trade *A*'s truck for *B*'s land. *A* is joking, but he appears serious. Because *B*, as a reasonable person, would believe that *A* was serious, *A* has made an offer.

(3) Assume the facts in (2) above, except that while a reasonable person would conclude that *A* made an offer, *B*, because of previous dealings with *A*, knew or should have known that *A* was joking. Because of *B*'s special knowledge about *A*'s intent, there is

no offer. Whether *B* knows or should know *A*'s intention will often be a question of fact.

b. Law and Fact

What a reasonable person in the position of *B* would understand is ordinarily a question of fact. But, as in any civil proceeding, if a reasonable fact finder—jury or trial judge sitting without a jury—could reach only one reasonable conclusion, the question is one of law. The key difference is this. If it is a question of law, it will be decided by the trial judge, and it is subject to appellate review. If it is a question of fact, however, it will be decided by the trier of fact, and that determination is ordinarily not subject to appeal. Appellate courts ordinarily review only questions of law.

3. Must the Parties Intend Legal Consequences?

Parties are bound by contracts without manifesting an intent to be bound or consciously considering the legal consequences of their words and actions. They may, however, expressly or impliedly agree to exclude legal consequences.

Discussion: This is a sound rule because the parties at the time of contracting rarely consider these matters, much less discuss them. However, if from their statements and conduct, or the surrounding circumstances, it appears that the parties did *not* intend legal consequences, then there is no contract. If the parties act under such an agreement, legal consequences sometimes attach. The purpose is to achieve a just result.

Examples: (1) *A* and *B* are two ignorant persons who are unaware that society offers a remedy for the enforcement of contracts. They agree to exchange a horse for a cow. The agreement is enforceable; their ignorance of legal sanctions does not prevent the formation of a contract. This result is consistent with the rule that a mistake as to a rule of law does not necessarily deprive an agreement of legal effect.

(2) *A* and *B* enter into an agreement regulating their commercial relations, but further agree that their agreement is to create no legal obligations. The agreement is not enforceable because the parties did not intend legal obligations. There are, however, cases that have upheld such agreements where the parties have *acted under the agreement* and it would be unfair not to enforce the agreement. Most of these cases have involved pension and employee benefit plans and bonuses. These cases are supported by the doctrine of promissory estoppel. (*See* III.D., *infra.*) There may also be the possibility of "quasi-contractual recovery," if one party received a benefit that justly should be paid for. (*See* Glossary for "quasi contract.")

(3) *A* invites *B* to dinner. *B* accepts the invitation and arrives at *A*'s house at the appointed time and *A* is not there. *B* would not have a cause of action, because it is a reasonable factual presumption that the parties intended that the dinner invitation created a social rather than a legal obligation.

(4) *A* wants *B*, a celebrity, to come to *A*'s dinner party to add glamour to the occasion. *B* agrees to come if *A* promises to pay $5,000. *A* promises. Both parties are bound by a contract. The agreement as to

the payment rebuts any presumption that the agreement has merely social consequences.

(5) Husband and wife, while living together amicably, make an agreement with respect to the household budget. This agreement is not a contract, because there is a reasonable factual presumption that the parties did not intend legal consequences but rather a working arrangement. This reasonable factual presumption would be overcome if the parties manifested a contrary intention. (However, this type of agreement would raise questions of public policy.) If the parties were separated so that they were not living "in amity," the separation agreement would be binding.

4. Intention That the Agreement Be Memorialized

If the parties agree that they are not to be bound unless and until they sign a formal agreement, they will not be bound until that time. If they intend the future writing to be merely a convenient memorial, they are bound when they reach agreement, whether or not such a writing is prepared or signed.

Discussion: During negotiations, parties often manifest an intention that when an agreement is reached it will be reduced to writing. When they so indicate, there are three possibilities. (1) They want the writing as evidence of their prior agreement; that is, as a convenient memorial. (2) They do not intend to be bound unless and until the agreement is reduced to writing. Under the first scenario, it is clear that there was a contract from the time they agreed, and a refusal to execute the writing would constitute a breach of that contract. Under the second scenario, there is no contract until the writing is prepared and signed. (3) The parties have not expressly manifested their intention. This third scenario is difficult to resolve. There are many factors to be considered in determining whether or not the parties intended to be bound. Among them are: (1) the language of the agreement, (2) the context of the negotiation, (3) the existence of open terms, (4) partial performance, and (5) the custom in this kind of transaction. Very often the question is one of fact as to the intention of the parties, objectively viewed.

During negotiations, the parties may sign a "letter of intent." Although such documents are usually understood to be non-committal statements, there is no magic attached to the name of the document. A court may decide that the document, whatever its title, has created a contract.

B. Offer

1. Meaning of Offer

An offer, with minor exceptions, is a promise to do or refrain from doing some specified thing in the future.

Discussion: An offer empowers the offeree to create a contract by acceptance. For a promise to be an offer, the promise must justify the other party, as a reasonable person, to conclude that his or her assent is invited and will create a contract. It is possible, however, to have an offer without a promise. Such is the case of an offer to a reverse unilateral contract, a relative rarity, discussed later.

2. Meaning of Promise

A promise is a manifestation of intent that gives an assurance that a thing will be done or will not be done.

Examples: (1) *A* says to *B,* "I will sell you my black Mercedes for $51,000." *B* says, "I accept." Even though *A* does not use the word "promise," *A* has made a promise. The language justifies *B*, as a reasonable person, to conclude that *A* has invited an acceptance and that this acceptance will conclude the deal.

(2) *A* decides to rent a car for the weekend. She goes to a local rental outlet and describes the kind of car she wants. The rental clerk determines that such a car is in stock and fills out some printed forms with information about the car and about *A,* who signs the form without reading it. The form contains promissory language attributed to the customer. By signing the form, *A* has adopted those promises as her own.

(3) *A,* a house owner, pays $1,000 to an insurance company in connection with an application that asks for the company's promise to pay *A* up to $250,000 if *A*'s house is damaged by fire. *A* is the offeror but has made no promise. Rather, *A* has requested a promise from *B.* When *B* makes the promise there is a contract. Later, this fact pattern will be reviewed, and explained as a "reverse unilateral contract."

3. Offers Distinguished from Statements That Are Not Offers

a. Expressions of Opinions and Words of Reassurance

Expressions of opinion and words of reassurance are not promises and, therefore, not offers.

Discussion: This distinction is important in all cases, but it's especially crucial in the doctor-patient relationship, because the courts recognize that a doctor sometimes makes an *express* promise to cure or to obtain a specific result or to use a particular treatment. Such an express promise would be enforceable. The difficult question that courts must resolve, using the reasonable person test, is whether the doctor has made such a promise or has only stated an opinion or given a therapeutic reassurance. This analysis is not limited to the doctor-patient relationship. For example, an estimate given by a contractor is generally held not to be an offer. It is a statement of opinion.

Examples: (1) Doctor says to patient, "Don't worry, you'll be back to work in three or four days." As a matter of law, there is no promise. A reasonable patient would conclude that this is an expression of opinion or words of reassurance.

(2) Doctor says, "Electroshock treatments are 100% safe," or "I promise to perform a Caesarean section," or "I guarantee that you

will have perfect vision." A reasonable person could conclude that a promise was being made in each of these instances.

(3) Patient (*P*) came to doctor (*D*) for treatment. *D* makes no express promise, but does not use requisite skill in treating *P*. In the doctor-patient relationship, *P* is limited to an action in malpractice—the tort of negligence—except in those exceptional cases where (as in example (2)) the doctor makes an express promise.

(4) *A* asks *B* for an estimate on certain work to be done. *B* estimates the work can be done for $5,000. *B*'s statement is a statement of opinion and not a promise; therefore, it is not an offer.

b. Statements of Intention, Hopes or Desires

A mere statement of intention or of hopes and desires does not constitute an offer.

Example: *A* says to *B*, "I am going to sell my car for $500." This is not an offer but a statement of intention.

c. Inquiries or Invitations

A mere inquiry or an invitation to the other party to make an offer does not constitute an offer.

Examples: (1) *A* writes to *B*, "Will you sell me your property on Rockledge Drive for $50,000?" This is not an offer but an inquiry. *A* is not making a promise but is simply seeking information.

(2) In reply to an inquiry from *B* as to whether *A* would sell certain property for $6,000, *A* answered "it would not be possible for me to sell it unless I was to receive $16,000 cash." *A* was not making an offer. *A* made no promise to *B*.

d. Ads, Catalogs and Circular Letters

Advertisements, catalogs, and circular letters for the sale of goods are not ordinarily offers because they do not contain express language of promise and do not spell out the quantity term. Quantity, unlike terms such as price, can never be filled in by a court. Rarely, a quantity term can be implied from the facts; e.g., where there has been a course of dealing.

Examples: (1) *A* advertised computer scanners for sale at $79, specifying the make and model. The ad is not an offer because there is no language of promise or commitment to any definable persons or for any definable quantity.

(2) A newspaper advertisement stated: "1 Black Lapin Stole, Beautiful, Worth $139.50 . . . $1 First Come First Served." This was an offer because the ad contained language of commitment to an identifiable person ("First Come First Served"), and the ad stated a quantity (one). "One" is also a quantity per person. If the ad had said "10 stoles" instead of "1," it is not clear whether it would have been held to be an offer because, although it states a quantity, it does not state a quantity per person.

(3) *A* sends a catalog to its customers listing the types of items to be sold and the price. The catalog is not an offer because there is no language of promise and no quantity is stated.

(4) *A* wrote to *B*, "I have 18,000 bushels of millet seed of which I am mailing you a sample. I want $2.25 per bushel for this seed." The letter indicated that it was being sent to other potential buyers. This does not constitute an offer; it is a circular letter. The circular indicates a fixed quantity, but the language used is not language of commitment. *B*, as a reasonable person, would conclude that *A* was not manifesting an intent to make offers to all of the individuals to whom the letter was sent because this would expose *A* to multiple acceptances and therefore multiple breaches of contract. This case is similar to cases involving real property where the seller has only one piece of property to sell. Courts are more reluctant to find offers in such cases than where a seller communicates that it is willing to sell stock in trade.

(5) *X*, a supermarket, has a large display of bottled soda on its shelf with a sign stating that the price is six cans for $5. The cases are in disagreement on the question of whether an offer has been made. The older view is that this is not an offer, because there is no language of commitment and no quantity stated or at least no quantity per person. Some modern cases, however, hold that it *is* an offer because there is an implied language of promise to sell the goods on display. These courts do not consider the question of quantity per person.

e. Price Quotations

A price quotation is usually a statement of intention to sell at a given unit price. Under this definition the quantity term is not specified, and there is no offer. Even if a quantity term is stated in a communication addressed to an individual, and the word "quote" is used in this communication, it is commonly understood to mean that an offer is invited. But this is not a hard and fast rule; the word "quote" in context may mean "offer." Conversely, the word "offer" may mean "quote." An important factor is whether the terms, especially the quantity terms, are sufficiently definite.

Examples: (1) *S* sends a fax to *B* stating, "We quote you Hungarian flour $35.40 per barrel, car lots only. We would suggest your using fax to order as prices are rapidly advancing that they may be beyond reach before a letter would reach us." *S* is not making an offer because, even if the word "quote" can be interpreted to mean "offer," there is still no statement of quantity.

(2) *P* asked for *D*'s price on 1,000 gross of Mason Green Jars (quarts). *D* answered, stating a price and other detailed terms and using the word "quote" but also stating that the reply was "for immediate acceptance." *D*'s answer is an offer, despite the use of the word "quote." The court stressed three factors: (a) *D*'s communication came in response to an inquiry that obviously sought an offer; (b) It contained detailed terms and by implication the quantity of 1,000 gross inquired about by *P*; (c) *D* used the

term, "for immediate acceptance," which is language of commitment.

(3) *S* sends a letter to *B* saying, "We quote you two cars Hungarian flour at $35.40 per barrel." There is no clear answer to this hypothetical. Williston indicates that *S*'s statement is an offer, but the Restatement (Second) indicates that it should be considered an offer only if it contains detailed terms. Also, the alleged offer did not come in response to an inquiry seeking an offer as in example (2) and did not contain language of commitment.

f. The Offer at Auction

An auction is "with reserve" unless it is stated to be "without reserve."

Discussion: "With reserve" means that the seller reserves the right to set a minimum price on the property to be sold. The reserve price may be secret. In an auction "with reserve," each bid is an offer, and the auctioneer is free to reject offers. In an auction "without reserve," however, the auctioneer may withdraw the goods only until the first bid is made, provided it is made within a reasonable time. Thereafter, the auctioneer must sell to the highest bidder. However, in either case, a bidder is free to withdraw a bid before the fall of the hammer. A bid terminates all prior bids, but a bidder's retraction does not revive any prior bids.

g. Offers Distinguished from Preliminary Negotiations

The term "preliminary negotiations" covers any communication prior to an operative offer. Under this definition, the types of communications already discussed that were not offers amount to preliminary negotiations.

4. Distinction Between Unilateral and Bilateral Contracts

a. Basis of Distinction

An offer looking to a bilateral contract looks to a promise on the part of the offeree. An offer looking to a unilateral contract looks to an acceptance by performance, except in the unusual case of a reverse unilateral contract.

While all contracts involve at least two contracting parties, two parties need not make a promise to form a contract. Contracts where only one party makes a promise are "unilateral." Contracts where there is an exchange of promises are "bilateral." Another way of looking at bilateral contracts is to note that two parties are under obligations to each other.

b. Acceptance of Offer Looking to a Bilateral Contract

An offer looking to a bilateral contract may be accepted by an express promise or an implied promise. In addition, an offer may designate an act that will serve as a promise; e.g., "Blink your eyes three times."

c. Acceptance of an Offer Looking to a Unilateral Contract

An offer looking to a unilateral contract may be accepted by performance, except in the case of a reverse unilateral contract. The most important difference between any unilateral contract and a bilateral contract is that in the unilateral contract only one party comes under an obligation.

d. Indifferent Offer

Where the offeror does not make it clear how the offeree must accept, the offer is indifferent, and the offer can be accepted by promise or by commencing performance. In either case, a bilateral contract is formed.

Examples: (1) *A* says to *B*, "If you enter the New York Marathon and finish the race, I will pay you $1,000." *A* has made an offer looking to a unilateral contract. *B* can accept only by performing. *B* cannot accept by making a promise.

(2) *A* says to *B*, "If you promise to walk across Brooklyn Bridge, I will pay you $100." *A* has made an offer looking to a bilateral contract. If *B* makes the promise, there is an acceptance. There would also be an acceptance if *B* started to walk in *A*'s presence, for in this situation *B*'s promise could be inferred.

(3) *A* says to *B*, "I will pay you $12,000 if you pave my driveway with asphalt." The offer is unclear and therefore indifferent as to the manner of acceptance. Therefore, *B* may accept by any reasonable means, such as by promising to perform or commencing to perform. If *B* commences performance, *B*'s rights are in jeopardy if the notice of performance requirements discussed in II.C.1.e., *infra*, are not complied with.

(4) *A*, a house owner, pays $1,000 to an insurance carrier. The payment is attached to an application that asks for the company's promise to pay up to $250,000 if the house is damaged by fire. The insurance company agrees. *A* has made an offer looking to a reverse unilateral contract. The offeror, the house owner, makes no promise. The only promise is made by the offeree. The contract is unilateral because only one party—the insurance carrier—ever comes under an obligation. Note that, aside from standard contracts in certain industries—like the insurance contract in this example—reverse unilateral contracts are rare.

(5) *A*, a house owner, *promises* to pay $1,000 to *B*, an insurance carrier, asking for the company's promise to pay up to $250,000 if *A*'s house is damaged by fire. *B* makes the promise, and the house is destroyed by fire. When *B* makes the promise, a bilateral contract is made. Note that damage to the house by fire does not affect the formation of the contract; it only acts as a condition to the company's duty to pay *A*'s loss. Thus, a contract exists even if no loss ever occurs.

C. Acceptance

1. General Requirements

a. Introduction

An offer creates a power of acceptance in the offeree. The exercise of this power creates the set of legal relations called a contract and terminates the power of revocation that the offeror ordinarily has.

b. Acceptance by Authorized Party

An offer may be accepted only by the person or persons to whom it is made.

The offeror is master of the offer, and thus controls who has the power of acceptance. Since the power of acceptance is personal to the offeree, it follows that the offeree may not transfer the power of acceptance to another.

Examples: (1) *A* makes a revocable offer to sell his car to *B* at a set price. *C*, a longtime admirer of the car, may not accept even though *B* makes an assignment of rights to *C*.

(2) *A* makes an offer jointly to *B* and *C* for them to pave her driveway. *B* or *C* alone cannot accept.

(3) *A* individually is doing business under the trade name of "Acme Supply Company" and *B* sends an order (offer) to "Acme Supply Company." *C*, who has bought out *A*, including the name, fills the order. The issue is whether a reasonable person would conclude that *B* manifested an intention to make the offer to "Acme Supply Company" irrespective of who owned it. If so, *C* may accept. Contrariwise, *C* may not accept if a reasonable person would conclude *B*'s manifested intention was to make an offer to Acme only so long as *A* was the proprietor. This could be a question of fact. If the offer is not made to *C*, there may still be a quasi-contractual recovery where *B* has received and kept valuable goods.

Exceptions:

1) Options

If *A* makes an irrevocable offer (also known as an option contract) to *B*, *B* may assign the rights to *C* consistent with the rules governing assignments, discussed in Chapter XI.

2) Undisclosed Principal

If the offeror has indicated a refusal to deal with a specific person, an offeree who obtains an offer as an undisclosed agent for that person may not accept the offer.

c. Knowledge of the Offer and Intent to Accept

The offeree must know of the offer and manifest an intent to accept.

1) Knowledge of the Offer

If the offer looks to a unilateral contract, the rule that the offeree must know of the offer invariably applies. There is some conflict as to when knowledge of the offer must exist. If the offer looks to a bilateral contract, however, the requirement that the offeree must know of the offer may sometimes conflict with the objective theory of contracts. In such conflict, the objective theory prevails.

The rule that an offeree must know of the offer gives rise to the rule that identical cross offers do not create a contract.

Examples: (1) *A* publishes an ad to the effect that she would pay $20,000 to anyone who provides information to the police leading to the arrest and conviction of the murderer of her husband. *B* provides information to the police leading to the arrest and conviction of the murderer. *A* made an offer to a unilateral contract. Unless *B* knew of the offer, *B* would not recover.

(2) *A* mails *B* an offer looking to a bilateral contract. *B* receives the letter, but without opening it and without suspecting that it is an offer, decides to confuse *A* by sending a letter which states, "I accept." *B* does not know of the existence of the offer, but under the objective theory of contracts, *A* could reasonably conclude that *B* had accepted. Here the rule that the offeree must know of the offer conflicts with the objective theory of contracts and the objective theory prevails. This problem cannot arise in the case of an offer looking to a unilateral contract.

(3) *A* mails *B* an offer to sell a rare edition of Hamlet at a certain price. *B,* in ignorance of this offer, mails an offer to buy the same edition at the same price. These are identical cross offers. There is no acceptance because neither party knows of the other's offer. The Restatement (Second) attempts a partial subversion of this rule when it asserts that two offerors could assent in advance to cross offers and suggests that such assent may be inferred when both parties think a contract has been made.

(4) *A* offers a reward of $100 to anyone who finds and returns a lost watch. *B* finds the watch, learns of the reward and returns the watch to *A*. The traditional rule is that *B* may not recover because *B* did not know of the offer at the start of performance. The more modern view is that it is sufficient that the offeree completes performance with knowledge of the offer.

2) Intent to Accept

If the offer looks to a unilateral contract, the offeree must intend to accept. Where the offer looks to a bilateral contract, it is quite possible to have a contract without an intent to accept because of the objective theory of contracts.

Examples: (1) *A* makes an offer to *B* looking to a bilateral contract. *B*, does not intend to accept, but carelessly mails an acceptance. There is a contract under the objective theory of contracts even though *B* did not intend to accept.

(2) *A* says to *B*, "I will pay you $100 if you walk across Brooklyn Bridge." *B* walks. *B*'s walking is ambiguous on the issue of intent to accept. *B* may have walked to gain the $100 or to get exercise or from a combination of these two motives. Under the traditional view, *B* may testify that the walking was done with the intent to accept and, if believed, *B* will prevail. *B* will also prevail if the trier of fact concludes that *B* performed for many reasons so long as one of the reasons was to earn the $100. A more modern view is that *B* may not testify to subjective intention. Under this view, intent to accept is presumed in the absence of words or conduct to the contrary. Since the intent to accept is merely a presumption, if the offeree manifests an intent not to accept before the *offeror* performs, a disclaimer is effective.

d. Necessity for Communication to Create a Bilateral Contract

To create a bilateral contract, the offeree's promise must be communicated to the offeror.

1) Theory

The offeree as a reasonable person should understand that the offeror expects to know that the offeree has made the requested return promise so that the offeror's conduct may be guided accordingly.

2) Exception

Since the offeror is the master of the offer, the offeror may dispense with the communication requirement.

Examples: (1) *A* makes an offer to *B*. *B* tells *C*, a friend, that "I accept." There is no contract. Of course, if *C* were *A*'s agent, the result would be different.

(2) The requisite for communication may be dispensed with. *A*, an agent for *B* Corp., presents *C* with a document that states the terms of a bilateral arrangement but adds that "this will become a contract when approved by an executive officer of *B*." *C* signs the document. *B* Corp. has not made an offer, because *B* did not commit itself to anything. *C* became the offeror by signing the document. *C*'s offer includes the term relating to approval by an executive officer. This offer is accepted by *B* when the offer is approved by *B's* executive officer even though acceptance is not communicated. The

language used in the offer—"this will become a contract"—dispenses with the necessity of communication.

e. Necessity for Notice of Performance of a Unilateral Contract

1) Introduction

Performance creates a unilateral contract. Must the offeree notify the offeror that performance has occurred? There are three views.

2) Three Views

(a) The first and simplest view is that notice is not required unless requested by the offer. This is a minority view, little followed.

(b) The second view is the majority view and the view of both restatements. It is exactly the same as the first view but contains a major exception. The offeror's obligation will come to an end ("be discharged") if notice of performance is not given within a reasonable time in a limited set of circumstances. If the offeree has reason to know that the offeror has no adequate means of learning of performance with reasonable promptness, the duty of the offeror is discharged unless the offeree exercises reasonable diligence to notify the offeror, or the offeror otherwise learns of performance within a reasonable time, or the offeror expressly or by implication indicates that notice is not necessary.

(c) Same as (b) above, except that, if notice is required, no contract is consummated until notice of performance has been sent. This is a small minority view, little followed.

3) Discussion of View (b)

The rule, adopted by both Restatements, is designed to balance two factors. The offeror may wish to know that performance has occurred to avoid entering into other contracts concerning the same subject matter or for other planning reasons. On the other hand, if the offeror is in a position to learn of performance, notice should not be required. It is an exceptional case in which the offeror does not have the means of finding out what happened.

Examples: (1) *A* makes an offer looking to a unilateral contract on November 1. The offeree performs on November 2. *A* purports to revoke the offer on November 3 and *B* sends notice of performance on November 4. According to the first and second rules stated above, the revocation would not be effective because the acceptance had already taken place. Assuming that notice is required under the second (majority) rule, the requisite is satisfied because the offeree has exercised reasonable diligence to give timely notice to the offeror. Under the third view, the revocation would be effective, unless the offer was irrevocable.

(2) Assume the same facts as above, except that notice of performance was not given in a timely manner. Under

majority rule (b) the contract that arose upon performance is discharged by the failure to give timely notice. Stated another way, failure to give timely notice is a condition subsequent discharging *A*'s obligation to perform. Under rule (c) there is no contract. Again, there is no problem under rule (a).

(3) *G,* a guarantor, makes an offer to *C,* who lives in a foreign country, that if *C* delivers certain merchandise to *G*'s brother *X,* if *X* doesn't pay *G* will pay. According to the Restatement, *C* is obliged to give notice of performance, otherwise *G*'s duty will be discharged.

f. Acceptance of an Offer Looking to a Series of Contracts

Typically, an offer looks to a single contract. But an offer may instead look to the formation of a number (series) of contracts, unilateral or bilateral. Such an offer continues after the first contract is formed. Other contracts can also be formed by accepting the continuing offer. However, as to those potential subsequent contracts, the offer is as revocable as any other offer.

Care must be taken to distinguish an offer looking to a series of contracts from an offer looking to *one* contract with a series of performances. The distinction is crucial in determining whether an offeror can revoke the offer. This distinction hinges on a question of the intention of the parties and is often one of fact.

Examples: (1) *A,* on January 1, writes to *B,* "in consideration of your advancing money from time to time over the next twelve months up to $5,000, to *X,* at *X*'s request, at your option, I hereby undertake to make good any losses you may sustain in consequence." *B* lends $1,000 to *X* on February 1, and another $1,000 on March 1. *A* then revokes the offer. *B* makes an additional loan of $1,000 on March 15. *A*'s offer looked to a series of unilateral contracts. The advance made on February 1 created a unilateral contract. The advance made on March 1 created a second unilateral contract. The offer continued into the future, but it was terminated by revocation. Thus, the third attempted acceptance on March 15 was preceded by a revocation and was therefore ineffective. If this were a case where notice of performance was required, one notice would probably suffice.

(2) *A* offers *B* stated quantities of certain goods as *B* may order from time to time during the next year at fixed prices. *A* has made an offer looking to a series of bilateral contracts. The series is bilateral because each time *B* places an order *B* impliedly promises to pay.

(3) *A* offers to sell *B* 6,000 tons of coal, deliveries to be made in equal monthly installments during the months of May, June, July and August. *B* accepts. One bilateral contract has been created. However, there will be a series of performances under the contract.

2. Acceptance of a Bilateral Contract

a. Acceptance by Silence

Silence ordinarily does not give rise to an acceptance of an offer or a counter-offer, but there are exceptions. When silence would be deceptive, there is a duty to speak.

Discussion: The question is whether silence may amount to a promise. The issue is whether the offeror has a justified expectation of a reply.

(1) Silence acts as acceptance where:

(a) the offeror has given the offeree reason to believe that silence will act as an acceptance and the offeree intends by silence to accept, (*see* example 1);

(b) the parties have mutually agreed that silence will operate as assent;

(c) there is a course of dealing whereby silence has come to mean assent;

(d) someone takes offered services with a reasonable opportunity to reject them, and it is reasonable for the person to understand that the services are offered with expectation of payment.

Examples: (1) *A* makes an unsolicited offer to *B* by mail in which *A* states, "If I do not hear from you by next Tuesday, I shall assume you accept." *B* has no intention of accepting but remains silent. *B* has no duty to reply and may freely discard the offer. But suppose that *B* likes the offer and intends to accept. Because *A* has led *B* to believe that a contract will be formed by *B's* remaining silent, there is a contract. Because of the ambiguity, *B* may testify as to his or her subjective intention to accept. If the trier of fact believes *B*, the court will enforce the contract.

(2) *A* says to *B*, "I offer to sell you my old computer for $200." *B* replies, "If you don't hear from me by next Tuesday, you may assume that I accept." *A* agrees. By agreement of both parties, B's silence will be acceptance.

(3) *A* asks *B* to send certain goods on approval. *B* sends the merchandise. *A* fails to return the goods within a reasonable time. *A*'s acceptance is implied.

(4) On several past occasions, *A*, the offeror, has sent unsolicited goods to *B* who has always paid for the goods. *A* makes an additional shipment of similar goods, and *B* retains the goods for an unreasonable period of time without notifying *A* that this time the goods are not wanted. *A*, as a reasonable person, could conclude that the offer was accepted because of *B*'s retention of the goods in the light of the prior course of dealing. The question may be one of fact. In this case, evidence of subjective intention is not admissible.

(5) *A*, through a sales representative, has frequently solicited orders from *B*, the contract to arise when approved by *A* at *A*'s

home office. *A* has always shipped the goods to *B* without prior notification and has billed for them after shipment. *A*'s sales representative solicits and receives another order from *B*. *A* remains silent for a long period of time. The issue is whether the offeror (*B*) would reasonably conclude that *A*'s silence indicated assent. Again, the question may be one of fact, and again evidence of subjective intention is inadmissible.

(6) *I*'s agent seeks to sell *A* insurance. *A* fills out the application and gives it to the agent together with a check for the premium. The application makes it clear that *I* must approve the application before there is a binding agreement. Acceptance may be implied from the retention of the check and failure to reject within a reasonable time.

(7) *B*, the owner of property, sees *A*, a stranger, cutting *B*'s lawn and does nothing to stop *A*. *B* is liable for the reasonable value of the services because *B* has the opportunity to reject the services and should reasonably understand that *A* expects to be compensated.

(8) Assume the same facts as in example (7), above, except that the grass is being cut by *S*, *B*'s son. Although *B* has an opportunity to reject the services, there is a rebuttable presumption that the son rendered the services gratuitously—without expectation of payment. A family relationship gives rise to the presumption and can arise through blood, marriage, or by living together as a family.

b. Acceptance by Conduct

Just as an offer may be accepted by silence, it may also be accepted by conduct. In addition, an acceptance may arise as a result of an offeree's act of dominion—the offeree's exercise of power over offered property as if the offeree were the owner.

1) Discussion

There are times when a reasonable person would understand by the offeree's conduct that the offeree has accepted the offer. (Example 1, *infra*). There is also a line of cases holding that the offeree's exercise of dominion over offered property constitutes an acceptance even if the offeree disavows an intention to accept. If the exercise of dominion is wrongful, as where the offeree takes offered goods while stating that the offer is rejected, the offeror could proceed on a tort theory, but offeror has the alternative of asserting that the offeree's dominion over the goods and that the offeree should be estopped from asserting that the conduct was tortious not contractual. This is an old common law doctrine that is also enacted by UCC § 2–606(1)(c).

Examples: (1) *A*, passing by a market, picks up an apple from a box marked "50 cents ea." and holds it up so that the clerk sees it and nods at *A*. *A* has made an offer by conduct, and the clerk has accepted in the same way. A contract that arises by such conduct is often referred to as an implied-in-fact contract.

(2) *A* sends a book to *B* saying, "If you wish to buy this book send me $26.50 within one week after receipt, otherwise notify me, and I will forward postage for return." *B,* without replying, makes a gift of it to her husband. *B*'s act is an act of dominion referable to the offer. *B* has accepted the offer.

(3) Instead, *B* writes to *A* stating that she has taken the book but that it is worth only $15.00 and that she will pay no more. Here *B's* act of dominion is wrongful, because it is not justified by the terms of *A*'s offer. *B's* letter shows that *B* does not intend to accept the offered price. Nonetheless, the offeror may sue either on a theory of contract or conversion. A fictitious contract is created by preventing *B* from testifying that *B*'s own conduct is wrongful when it could be referable to a lawful intent. But *A* may not sue on a contract theory if the offered terms are manifestly unreasonable.

(4) *S* (seller) sends a freezer unit on approval to *B. B* uses the freezer unit to operate an air conditioner. *B* denies any intention to accept and claims the exercise of dominion was wrongful. Here *S* has the option of suing in tort or contract. The measure of damages will be different depending on the theory (contract or tort) selected. Note that, in cases where persons claim their own conduct is wrongful, they are usually trying to escape contract prices higher than the value of the goods.

2) Statutory Exceptions

In order to discourage the unsolicited sending of goods to unwary customers, several states have enacted legislation making it unlawful to offer merchandise for sale by the unsolicited sending of goods. Generally, these statutes also provide that a person who receives such goods has a complete defense to an action by the offeror. At the federal level, the Postal Reorganization Act of 1970 provides that, with certain narrow exceptions, one who receives "unordered merchandise" by mail may treat the transaction as a gift. *See* 39 U.S.C. § 3009. State and federal consumer protection statutes may also be relevant. Examples 2 and 3 above are now changed by these statutes. However, the principle behind the examples is alive in a number of contexts that will be discussed below.

c. When Is an Acceptance Effective?

1) Introduction

Ordinarily, an acceptance in a bilateral contract must be communicated. Communication is generally understood to be necessary to the definition of the word "promise." Is the offeree's acceptance effective when it is sent or when it is received?

2) Prescribed Method of Acceptance

If the offeror prescribes an exclusive method of acceptance—and courts are reluctant to interpret an offer in that way—a contract does not arise if the offeree uses another means of acceptance even if it comes to the attention of the offeror. The defective acceptance is treated as an offer.

Examples: (1) *A* offers to buy computer software from *B* on certain terms. The offer also states, "You must accept this, if at all, in person, in my office at ten o'clock tomorrow." *B* sends a messenger who is on time and "accepts" the offer. The words make it clear that "in person" is prescribed as an exclusive method of acceptance. Thus, the attempted acceptance by the messenger is ineffective. This defective acceptance is treated as an offer that *A* may in turn accept.

(2) *A* makes an offer to *B* stating, "This offer shall be accepted by signing in the appropriate place and returning to me." According to some cases (probably a majority) signing and returning is not prescribed. Students may think *A* has made a strict demand but again, courts are reluctant to find that an exclusive means of acceptance has been prescribed. If a method of acceptance is not prescribed, the rules stated in 3 below will apply.

3) Parties at a Distance

a) Reasonable Means of Acceptance (Mailbox Rule)

An acceptance dispatched by a reasonable means of communication is effective on dispatch.

Discussion: Under current law expressed in the UCC and the Restatement (Second), the means of communication needs to be "reasonable" to trigger this "mailbox rule." The concept of reasonableness is intended to be flexible and to enlarge on the older concept of "authorized." Moreover, under the Restatement (Second), even if an unreasonable means is used, the acceptance will nevertheless be effective when dispatched provided it is seasonably dispatched and provided it is received within the time a seasonably dispatched acceptance sent in a reasonable manner would normally have arrived. The Restatement (Second) has a similar rule where an authorized means is carelessly used. It states that the acceptance is effective when sent provided that it is seasonably dispatched and provided that it is received within the time a seasonably dispatched properly stamped and addressed acceptance would normally have arrived. Otherwise, it is effective on receipt if the offer is still open. The UCC (§ 1–201(38), revised § 1–201(36)) has a similar rule with respect to carelessness. But the unrevised provision does not state any rule to cover an unreasonable means of acceptance, although the revised provision does.

Whether an acceptance is effective on dispatch or on receipt is a crucial question when the offeror attempts to revoke the offer. This is because once there is an acceptance, a contract is created, thereby extinguishing the offeror's power to revoke.

b) Unreasonable Means of Acceptance

If an unreasonable means of acceptance is used, or an authorized means is carelessly used (e.g., improper addressing, insufficient postage, etc.) and the acceptance is late, it will be effective on receipt, provided the offer is still open on its receipt.

d. Offeror's Power to Negate the Mailbox Rule

An offeror may negate the mailbox rule by providing in the offer that the acceptance will be effective only when and if received. Remember, the offeror is master of the offer.

Examples: (1) *A* made an offer to *B*. The offer stated: "Email me 'yes' or 'no.' If I do not hear from you by the 20th, I shall conclude 'no'." *B* immediately emailed an "acceptance" which was never received by *A* because *A*'s e-mail software failed. There is no contract because the language, "If I do not hear from you," etc. negates the mailbox rule.

(2) *A* sent an offer to *B* by mail. The last sentence of the offer read: "As soon as acceptance is received we shall send harvesters amongst the farmers and secure the first lots." *B* promptly sent a letter of acceptance, but it was lost and never received. Here, there is a contract. The language does not negate the mailbox rule because it can be interpreted to mean that the offeror will act promptly once the acceptance is received, rather than that the acceptance is contingent on receipt.

e. When Offeree Sends Both Acceptance and Rejection

The rule that an acceptance is effective when sent is troublesome when the offeree sends both an acceptance and a rejection. A rejection is effective when received.

1) When a Rejection Is Sent First

An acceptance dispatched after a rejection has been sent can be effective if and only if the acceptance is received prior to the rejection; such an acceptance is not governed by the mailbox rule and is effective on receipt if it arrives prior to the rejection.

Examples: (1) Rejection sent, acceptance sent, rejection received, acceptance received. There is no contract, and the "acceptance" is regarded as a new offer.

(2) Rejection sent, acceptance sent, acceptance received, rejection received. There is a contract on the receipt of the acceptance.

2) When an Acceptance Is Sent First

Example: Acceptance sent, rejection sent, rejection received, acceptance received. A contract was formed on dispatch of the acceptance. Otherwise, the offeree could speculate at the offeror's expense by seeing how the market went. However, if the offeror relies on the rejection before receiving the acceptance, the offeree may be estopped from enforcing the agreement. The overtaking rejection can be looked on as an offer to rescind the contract or as a repudiation.

f. Lost or Delayed Acceptance

The mailbox rule also applies to a lost or delayed acceptance. But the offeror will not be guilty of a breach of contract unless the offeror receives notice that the contract has been formed.

Example: *A* offers to buy cattle for *B* from a third party on the understanding that if *B* communicates "yes," *A* will notify *B* of the amount of money needed, and *B* will supply the money. *B*'s "yes" message is duly dispatched but does not arrive within a reasonable time. According to the Restatement (Second), the contract formed by the dispatch of the message is discharged. The theory is that a condition of receipt of the acceptance should normally be implied where notice of acceptance is essential to enable the offeror to perform. If the offeree sends an acceptance that is effective when sent but retrieves the acceptance in conformity with postal regulations, it is generally agreed that the withdrawal is ineffective. There is a contract. It may be, as a practical matter, that the acceptance will rarely come to the attention of the offeror, but there are reported cases that have found these facts and applied this rule.

g. Parties in the Presence of One Another

The mailbox rule does not apply when the parties are in the presence of each other. Here, an acceptance is inoperative unless the offeror hears it or was at fault in not hearing it. Even if the offeror is at fault in not hearing, there is still no contract if the offeree knows or has reason to know the offeror has not heard.

D. Termination of Revocable Offers

1. Introduction

To become a contract, a revocable offer must be accepted before the power of acceptance created by the offeror is terminated.

a. Lapse of Time

An offer expires after the lapse of time specified in the offer or, if no time is specified, after a reasonable time has elapsed.

1) Time Specified in the Offer

Example: A mails an offer to *B*, dated January 29, that states "Will give you eight days to accept or reject." *B* receives the offer on February 2 and on February 8 sends a letter of acceptance which is received on February 9. By its terms, the offer lapses after eight days, but should the eight days be measured from January 29 or February 2? The generally accepted rule is that, in the absence of countervailing indications, the eight days should be measured from the day the offer is received. Therefore, the acceptance is timely.

If the offer were delayed in the course of the post, the question becomes whether the eight days should be measured from the date it was received or when it should have been received. If the offeree knows, or has reason to know, of the delay, the eight days should be measured from the date it should have been received. This is so even if the delay is due to the fault of the offeror.

2) Time Not Specified in Offer

If the duration of the power of acceptance is not stated, the offer is open for a reasonable time.

What constitutes a reasonable time is ordinarily a question of fact depending on the circumstances of the case. These circumstances include whether the transaction is speculative and the manifest purpose of the offeror. The Restatement (Second) adds to these considerations the question of whether the offeree is acting in good faith.

a) Face to Face Offer

In the absence of a manifestation to the contrary, where the offer is made in a face-to-face conversation, the offer is open only while the parties are conversing.

3) Termination on the Occurrence of a Particular Event

The offer may stipulate that the power of acceptance will terminate on the occurrence of a given event. If the event happens before the acceptance, the power of acceptance terminates regardless of whether the offeree knows that the event has occurred.

Example: *A* offers to sell Greenacre to *B* on specified terms. The offer states: "This offer is made subject to prior sale." *C* makes an offer to *A* to purchase Greenacre that *A* accepts. *A*'s offer to *B* automatically terminates.

4) Effect of Late Acceptance

If an offer lapses before an acceptance becomes effective, it would seem to follow that the late acceptance is an offer which in turn can be accepted only by a communicated acceptance. But this rule reflects only the classical view; there are two others. Another view states that the offeror may treat the late acceptance as an acceptance by waiving the lateness without communicating this fact to the offeree at any particular time. Under the third and intermediate view, if the acceptance is late but sent in what could plausibly be argued to be a reasonable time, the original offeror has the burden of replying within a reasonable time. Otherwise, silence creates a contract. The offeror has "a duty to speak" because it is not clear to the offeree that the original acceptance is late.

Example: *A* mails an offer to *B*. A week after receiving the offer, *B* mails an acceptance. A jury would conclude that a week is beyond a reasonable time. *A* does not reply to the late acceptance. Under the classical view there is no contract; it doesn't matter whether *A* is happy with the purported acceptance or not. Under the second view, the existence of a contract depends on *A's* subjective intention. If *A* is pleased by the letter of acceptance, there is a contract; otherwise, there is no contract. Under the third view, which is held by the Restatement (Second) and which accords with modern notions of contract, there is a contract unless *A* notifies *B* within a reasonable time that the acceptance is too late.

b. Death or Lack of Capacity

1) Death of Offeror

If the offeror dies after the making the offer but before the acceptance, the offer is terminated even if the offeree was unaware of the offeror's death. A minority view states that the death terminates the offer only if the offeree is aware of it.

Examples: (1) *A* makes an offer to *B* looking to a bilateral contract. Before *B* accepts, *A* dies. *B* is not aware of *A*'s death. Under the majority view, *A*'s death terminates the offer. Under the minority view, there is a contract if *B* accepts in an otherwise timely fashion.

(2) *A* makes an offer to *B* looking to a bilateral contract. *B* accepts, *A* dies. The rule does not apply, because the death occurred after the acceptance. The issue now is whether there is impossibility of performance of an existing contract. This topic is discussed in VII.A., *infra*.

2) Incapacity of Offeror

a) Adjudication of Incapacity

Where there is a prior adjudication of mental illness or defect of the offeror, and, as a result, the property of the offeror has been placed under guardianship, any of the offeror's outstanding offers are terminated. This is so even though the offeree is unaware of what has occurred. The adjudication is treated as the equivalent of the offeror's death. There is a small minority view to the contrary.

b) No Adjudication of Incapacity

If the offeror has not previously been declared mentally incompetent, supervening mental incapacity terminates the offer only if the offeree is or should be aware of the incapacity. (What constitutes mental incapacity is discussed in IV.B., *infra.*)

3) Death or Incapacity of the Offeree

The supervening death or adjudication of incapacity of the offeree will prevent the offeree's representative from accepting the offer.

c. Revocation

1) Direct Revocation

If an offer has not been accepted, it may be terminated by a communicated revocation. Under the majority view, a revocation is effective not on dispatch but when received. (By statute, in some states, however, a revocation is effective on dispatch.)

A written communication is received when the writing comes into the possession of the person addressed or of a person authorized to receive it, or when it is deposited in some place authorized by the person addressed as the place for this or similar communications to be deposited.

Example: *A* mails an offer to *B* in the morning. At 1:00 P.M. the same day, *A* mails a letter of revocation that is received the next morning. At 2:00 P.M., one hour after *A* deposited the revocation, *B* mails an acceptance. Two rules are involved here. Under the mailbox rule, the acceptance is effective at 2:00 P.M. Under the majority view, the revocation is effective only when received. Therefore, there is a contract. Under the statutes mentioned, there is no contract because the revocation is effective when dispatched.

2) Equal Publication

When an offer is made to a number of persons whose identity is unknown to the offeror, as for example a reward offer in a newspaper, the offer may be revoked by equal publication of the revocation.

But even here, if the offeror knows of the identity of persons who are taking action on the offer, the offeror must make reasonable efforts to communicate the revocation directly to them.

3) Indirect Revocation

Indirect revocation occurs when the offeree acquires reliable information that the offeror has engaged in conduct that would indicate to a reasonable offeree that the offeror no longer wishes to make the offer.

a) Reliable Information

Information is reliable if it is both objectively and subjectively reliable. Objectively reliable means that the information must be true.

Subjectively reliable means that the information must come from a reliable source. If the source is not reliable, it may be ignored: if it is subjectively reliable, the offeree should inquire into its accuracy.

Examples: (1) *D* is the owner of real property. *D* made an offer to sell the property to *P*. Later, while the offer to *P* was still open, *D* contracted to sell the same property to *A*. After *P* had received reliable information of *D*'s contract with *A*, *P* attempted to accept. The doctrine of indirect revocation applies, because there was reliable information about conduct—the contract of sale—that reasonably indicated to *P* that *D* no longer wished to keep the offer alive. *D* would not wish to be under an obligation to sell the same property twice when only one sale could be made.

(2) Assume, instead, that *P* hears that *D* has made an offer to sell the same property to *A*. Would a reasonable person in *P*'s position conclude that the offeror no longer wished to keep open the offer to *P*? It could be argued that *P* should conclude that *D* did not wish exposure to double liability, but it could also be concluded that because *D* did not bother to communicate a revocation, *D* is willing to run the risk of making two offers.

4) Revoking an Offer to a Unilateral Contract

The classical, but almost obsolete, rule is that the offer to a unilateral contract may be revoked at any time up until the moment of complete performance. The rationale is that there is no contract until the offeree has completely performed. This was an unfair approach. A second view is that a bilateral contract is formed with the beginning of performance. This is an illogical approach. The third—the modern and prevailing view—is that once the offeree starts to perform, or tenders performance, the offer becomes irrevocable. (An irrevocable offer is another term for an option contract.) Under this view, the offeree who has commenced or tendered performance is never obligated to complete the performance, but cannot claim the offeror's promised performance without completing performance within the time allowable. If the offeror repudiates after the beginning of performance, the offeree has a contractual cause of action because the failure to complete performance is excused by the repudiation.

Examples: (1) *A*, a manufacturer of racing cars, says to *B*, a race car driver: "If you enter every race on this list, driving our new super-model that we have sold you, we will pay you a fee of $200,000." After *B* has raced in half the races on the list, *A* says, "We have changed our minds. The offer no longer holds." Under the first view, this is an effective revocation, but *B* is entitled to quasi-contractual relief for the value of his performance up to the revocation. Under the second view, the beginning of performance creates a bilateral contract and there is no longer any possibility of revocation. Under the third view, the offer became irrevocable when *B* began to perform. *A* may not revoke. Nonetheless, under the second and third views, *B* should quit entering the races if such quitting would mitigate damages. If *B* continues racing, *B* cannot claim any compensation for activities after the repudiation, but can claim damages for total breach.

(2) *A* makes an offer to *B* looking to a unilateral contract. *B* starts to perform and *A* dies. Under the first view, the offer is terminated. Under the second view, there is a bilateral contract. Under the third view, the offer is irrevocable and not terminated.

a) Additional Problems Under Third View

(1) Preparation v. Performance

Under the third view, the offer becomes irrevocable only if the offeree has actually started to perform or has tendered part performance. Mere preparation is not enough. This distinction also applies to the second view.

(2) Promissory Estoppel

Preparation for performance by an offeree may create a right to relief under the doctrine of promissory estoppel, a doctrine discussed in III.D., *infra*.

d. Death or Destruction

Death of a person or destruction of a thing essential for the performance of the offered contract terminates the offer if it occurs before acceptance whether or not the offeree is aware of the death or destruction.

e. Supervening Illegality

If between the time of the making of the offer and the acceptance, a change of law or regulation renders the proposed contract illegal, the offer is terminated whether or not the offeree is aware of the change.

f. Rejection or Counter-Offer by Offeree

1) Common Law

A rejection or counter-offer terminates an offeree's power of acceptance, unless the offeror or the offeree manifests a contrary intention.

A rejection is a statement by the offeree declining to accept the offer. A rejection is effective when it is received.

A counter-offer, in contrast, is a response to an offer that adds qualifications or conditions. Nevertheless, a counter-offer acts as a rejection even if the qualification or condition relates to a trivial matter. This is the "ribbon matching" or "mirror image" rule.

If *A* makes an offer that *B* rejects with a counter-offer, and then the parties perform without ever reaching any further agreement on the terms, whatever is in the last communication exchanged between the parties is the final binding contract. At common law, under the "last shot principle," in these circumstances *A* (intentionally or unintentionally) accepted *B*'s counter-offer.

Examples: (1) *B* writes purporting to accept an offer from *A* but adds: "Prompt acknowledgment must be made of receipt of this letter." Under the mirror image rule, this is a counter-offer because the alleged acceptance states a qualification or condition. Therefore, it operates as a rejection.

(2) In reply to an offer from *A*, *B* states, "for the present, I reject your offer, but I am keeping it under advisement." Although this is a rejection, it does not terminate the offer, because the offeree manifests a contrary intention by using the words "keeping it under advisement."

a) Counter-Offer Distinguished from Other Communications

A counter-offer must be distinguished from a counter inquiry, a comment on the terms, a request for the modification of an offer, a request for a modification of the contract, a grumbling assent, an acceptance plus a separate offer, and a future acceptance. Additionally, if an acceptance contains a term that is not expressly stated in the offer, but is implied in it, the acceptance is good and is not a counter-offer.

Examples: (1) *A* makes an offer to *B* to paint *B*'s fence for $1,000.

(a) B replies: "I'll pay $800." This is a counter-offer that operates as a rejection and terminates the offer. Any later attempted acceptance is ineffective.

(b) *B* replies: "Will you take $800?" This is a counter-inquiry and does not terminate the offer.

(c) *B* replies: "Your price is extremely high." This is a comment on the terms and does not terminate the offer.

(d) *B* replies: "Send lowest cash price." This is a request for a modification of the offer; the offer is still open for acceptance.

(e) *B* replies: "I accept, but I would appreciate it if you give me the benefit of a 5% discount." This is an acceptance. The 5% clause is not a qualification or condition. It merely requests or suggests the addition of this term and is a request for modification of the contract.

(f) *B* replies: "Do the work but I wish you would give me a better price." This has been described as a "grumbling assent."

(g) *B* replies, "I accept your offer; please paint the barn as well for $5,000." This is an acceptance. *B* has made a separate offer, not a counter-offer.

(2) *G*, a general contractor, is about to bid on a project. *G* receives a bid (offer) from *S*, a subcontractor. *G* accepts the offer on the condition that *G*'s bid is successful. *S*, either expressly or impliedly, agrees to the condition. The parties are not currently bound. But once the future event (the award of the general contract to *G*) occurs, neither party is free to withdraw. There is no further necessity for any additional manifestation of intention. But it may be necessary for the offeror to give the offeree notice that the event has occurred. This situation is referred to as a future acceptance.

(3) *A* makes a written offer to *B* to sell Bleak House. *B* replies: "I accept your offer, if you can convey me a good title." Because good title is already implicit in the offer, *B* has accepted.

2) UCC Section 2–207

a) Introduction

This section is designed to negate the "mirror image" rule in cases involving the sale of goods. It is also designed to change the "last shot" principle of the common law. The first two subsections relate to the mirror image rule and the third relates to the "last shot" principle. As Professor Gilmore has noted, this section is "a miserable, bungled, patched-up job."

b) The Framework of the Statute

(1) Subsection (1)

This subsection provides that, even though the alleged acceptance contains "additional" or "different" terms (so that at common law there would be a counter-offer), there is an acceptance provided the alleged acceptance amounts to a "definite and seasonable expression of acceptance" and the acceptance "is not expressly made conditional on assent to the additional or different terms."

(a) Definite Expression of Acceptance

What constitutes a definite expression of acceptance under the UCC is not precisely clear. It is clear that the alleged acceptance must purport to be an acceptance. It is also clear that the existence of an additional or a different term does not prevent the communication from being an acceptance. But according to the majority of cases, if the acceptance diverges significantly from the offer as to a dickered term, it is not a "definite expression of acceptance." Dickered terms certainly include the description of the goods, price, quantity and delivery terms.

Examples: (1) *A* makes an offer to buy a drum of emulsion from *B*. *B* immediately sends an acknowledgment and an invoice repeating the dickered terms but negating implied warranties, and ships the emulsion. This combination (acknowledgment, invoice and shipment) is a definite and seasonable expression of acceptance. Warranties are not generally considered to be dickered terms. There is a contract. (What the warranty terms are is determined by subsection (2), discussed below.)

(2) *A* makes an offer to sell *B* 10 drums of emulsion. *B* sends a communication purporting to accept 5 drums. The communication is not a definite and seasonable expression of acceptance. Quantity, above all other terms, is a dickered term. There is no contract.

(b) Not Conditional on Assent

According to the vast majority of the cases, the statutory words "unless acceptance is expressly made conditional on assent to the additional or different terms" are to be taken literally.

Examples: (1) *A* makes an offer to *B*. *B* sends what appears to be an acceptance but adds, "This acceptance is expressly made conditional on assent to the new terms contained herein." Here the acceptance *is* conditional on assent to the additional terms and no contract is created.

(2) *A* makes an offer to buy widgets from *B*. *B* sends an acknowledgment and invoice that repeats the dickered terms of the offer and adds: "All goods sold without warranties express or implied. Seller's liability hereunder shall be limited to the replacement of any goods that materially differ from the seller's sample." The acceptance is not expressly made conditional on assent to the additional or different terms, because the words used are not conditional on the *assent* of *A* to the additional terms.

(c) Structure Reemphasized

If the offeree makes "a definite and seasonable expression of acceptance," that is not "expressly made conditional on assent to the additional or different terms," a contract is made by the communications of the parties.

At this point, subsection (2) dictates whether the additional or different terms incorporated into the acceptance become part of the contract.

(2) Subsection (2)

(a) Introduction

This subsection makes a distinction between merchants and non-merchants. It also distinguishes "additional" from "different" terms.

(b) Additional Terms—Non-Merchants

If either of the parties is *not* a merchant, the statute states that "additional terms are to be construed as proposals for addition to the contract." This means that any additional term in the acceptance does not become part of the contract unless accepted by the offeror.

Example: *A*, a non-merchant, makes an offer to *B*, a merchant. *B* accepts under the provision of Subsection (1), but includes an additional term—an arbitration clause—in the acceptance. Because one of the parties is not a merchant, the part of Subsection (2) quoted above applies; the arbitration clause does not become part of the contract unless *A* assents to it. *A* has not assented. *A*'s silence is not normally an acceptance. The arbitration clause does not become part of the contract.

(c) Additional Terms—Merchants

If both parties are merchants, additional terms become part of the contract unless: (a) the offer expressly limits acceptance to its terms; or, (b) the additional terms materially alter it, or, (c) notification of objection to them has already been given or is given within a reasonable time after notice of them is received.

Example: *A*, a merchant, makes an offer to *B*, another merchant. *B's* acceptance includes an arbitration clause as an additional term. The issue is whether the arbitration clause is a material alteration. According to the majority view, it is. Therefore, this term does not become part of the contract. Do not confuse this question with the question of whether the parties have made a contract. What is or is not a material alteration is often a question of fact.

(d) Different Terms

(A) What Is a Different Term?

A different term is one that contradicts a term of the offer. An additional term is one that introduces a new term.

Example: *A* makes an offer to *B* to buy a certain item and insists that the sale include a warranty of fitness for purpose. *B* accepts the offer, but states that there is to be no warranty of fitness for purpose. The term in the acceptance negating a warranty of fitness is a different term.

(B) Rules for Different Terms

Essentially there are two views relating to the effect of a different term. (1) Comment 3 to UCC § 2–207 indicates that different terms should be treated as additional terms. Prof. Summers concludes that, as a practical matter, this means that different terms do not become part of the agreement unless accepted by the offeror. This is certainly true in the case of a non-merchant. As between merchants, he argues that a different term would automatically be ejected under the provisions of 2(c) because notification of objection to the different term would already have been given. In any event, his conclusion (as opposed to his reasoning) is in accord with a number of cases that ignore this comment and conclude that different terms do not become part of the agreement unless in turn accepted by the offeror. This approach is clearly in accord with the plain meaning of the statute (as opposed to the comment). (2) Prof. White concludes that different terms cancel each other out. The canceled term is to be replaced by any gap-filler that is available under the UCC. This approach has been labeled the "neutrality" principle and is gaining ground.

(3) Subsection (3)

This subsection governs acceptance by conduct where the communications of the parties do not result in a contract. The subsection changes the "last shot" principle of the common law. If the communications of the parties do not produce a contract, but the conduct of the parties recognizes the existence of a contract, there is a contract. The terms of the contract are those on which the writings of the parties agree "together with any supplementary terms incorporated under any other provisions of this Act."

Examples: (1) *B* (Buyer) makes an offer to *S* that includes a warranty of merchantability. *S*'s reply is expressly conditioned on *B*'s assent to a no-warranty provision. No contract is formed by the communications of the parties, because *S* expressly conditioned acceptance on *B*'s assent to the no-warranty clause. Therefore, *S* has not made an acceptance and no contract exists. Suppose, thereafter, *B* does not reply, and *S* sends the goods. *B* takes and uses them; that is, *B* exercises dominion over them. The goods are defective, and *B* sues for breach of warranty of merchantability. At common law, under "the last shot principle," *S*'s sending of the goods was looked on as a performance of the counter-offer. *B,* in turn, accepted by the exercise of dominion over the goods, thereby (intentionally or unintentionally) accepting *S*'s offer, including the no-warranty provision. Under subsection (3) of § 2–207, however, there is a contract but on a different theory. The terms of the contract are those on which the parties agree "plus any supplementary terms incorporated under any other provision of [the UCC]." Thus, the question is, does the UCC contain a provision creating warranties of merchantability? It does, and therefore a warranty of merchantability based on the provisions of the UCC would be a term of the contract.

(2) If *B* had expressly conditioned acceptance on an arbitration clause, the analysis would be the same, except that the arbitration clause would not be in the contract, because the UCC does not have a provision relating to arbitration clauses.

c) Confirmation

(1) Language of Statute

UCC § 2–207(1) also governs confirmations. It provides that "A written confirmation which is sent within a reasonable time operates as an acceptance even though it states terms additional to or different from those agreed upon." It appears strange to say that a written confirmation may operate as an acceptance, because a confirmation confirms a contract that has already been formed. This is just one of the bungled aspects of the statute.

This provision applies where an agreement has been reached either orally or by informal correspondence, and one or both of the parties later sends a formal acknowledgment or memorandum and additional terms are introduced in the memorandum.

(2) Application of Rule

Where there are additional terms in memoranda that conflict, the conflicting terms knock each other out. The contract consists of the terms originally agreed on, terms on which the confirmations agree, and terms supplied by the Act, including UCC § 2–207(2). The last phrase includes additional or different terms that sometimes become part of the contract under the rules stated in UCC § 2–207(2).

Examples: (1) *X* and *Y* exchange correspondence and enter into a contract containing terms "A, B and C." *X* sends a written confirmation listing terms "A, B, C, and D." "D" is an additional term. Whether "D" becomes part of the contract depends on the rules for additional terms stated above.

(2) In Example (1), assume that both parties send memos. *X*'s memo lists terms "A, B, C, and D." And *Y*'s memo sets forth terms, "A, B, C" and specifically states "not D." Since "D" and "not D" are conflicting terms, neither term becomes part of the contract.

(3) In Example (1), assume that *X*'s memo mentions terms "A and B" but does not mention term "C." *Y* should be able to show the existence of term "C" even though it is not in the memorandum. The problem involves the parol evidence rule. (*See* V.A., *infra.*)

d) Restatement (Second)

UCC § 2–207 applies only to contracts for the sale of goods. Courts sometimes decide to apply it to other contracts by analogy. The Restatement (Second) has borrowed the UCC rule and applied it to other contracts. However, at this point it is clear that the mirror image rule is still the common law rule, and the courts have not followed the Restatement on this point.

E. Option Contracts—Irrevocable Offers

1. Introduction

The terms "irrevocable offer" and "option contract" are generally interchangeable. Note also that UCC § 2–205 uses the term "firm offer" for what we would generally call an irrevocable offer.

2. What Makes an Offer Irrevocable?

An offer can be made irrevocable a) by consideration; b) by statute; c) by part performance or tender of performance under an offer to a unilateral contract; d) under the doctrine of promissory estoppel (to be discussed later); and e) in some jurisdictions, by a sealed instrument.

Examples: (1) *A* makes an offer to sell specific real property to *B* and states that the offer is open for 10 days. This is a revocable offer.

(2) In example (1), *A* states that the offer is irrevocable for 10 days. This is still a revocable offer.

(3) In example (1), *A* states to *B* that the offer is irrevocable for 10 days provided that *B* pays $100 for this privilege. *B* pays *A* $100. The offer is irrevocable because *B* has given consideration to make the offer irrevocable.

(4) *A* says to *B*, "If you run the marathon and finish, I promise to pay you $1,000." *B* starts to run the race. *A* attempts to revoke the offer. Under the prevailing view relating to the termination of an offer looking to a unilateral contract, *B's commencement of performance* makes the offer irrevocable.

3. By Statute

UCC § 2–205 empowers an offeror to make an irrevocable offer for sale of goods, without consideration. The requisites are:

(a) the offeror must be a merchant;

(b) the offer must be in a signed writing or other record;

(c) if the language of irrevocability is on a form supplied by the offeree, the offeror must sign twice—once to make the offer and must separately sign the clause providing for irrevocability;

(d) the writing must contain language of irrevocability;

(e) the period of irrevocability may not exceed three months.

There are other local statutes with similar provisions that are not limited to offers for the sale of goods (*e.g.*, Michigan and New York).

Examples: (1) *A*, a merchant, makes an offer to sell goods to *B*, stating in a signed writing that "this is a firm offer for 10 days." Under the UCC, this is an irrevocable offer. If no time had been stated in the offer, it would have been irrevocable for a reasonable time.

(2) *A*, a merchant, makes an offer to sell goods to *B*, stating in a signed writing that "this is a firm offer for six months." *B* pays $500 to *A* for this promise of irrevocability. This is an irrevocable offer. The UCC's three-month limitation only applies to irrevocable offers formed without consideration.

4. The Nature of an Option Contract—Irrevocable Offer

Discussion: An option contract is not only a contract; it is also an offer. The contract is the binding promise that makes the offer irrevocable for a period of time. Nevertheless, it is also an offer that the offeree has the option of accepting during that period of time.

Example: A makes an offer to sell Bleak House to *B* for $250,000 and states that the offer is open for 10 days, provided *B* pays $100 for this privilege. *B* pays *A* $100. This is an option contract that makes the offer irrevocable for 10 days. *B* has the option of buying or not buying the property. Acceptance of the underlying offer—the offer to sell the property—is, except as indicated below, governed by the rules of acceptance for revocable offers.

5. Termination of Irrevocable Offers

Irrevocable offers are terminated by:

(a) *lapse of time;*

(b) *death of a person or destruction of a thing essential for the performance of the offered contract;*

(c) *supervening legal prohibition.*

Irrevocable offers are not terminated by:

(a) *revocation;*

(b) *death or supervening incapacity of the offeror or offeree (except where that person is essential for the performance);*

(c) *rejection (modern view).*

Examples: (1) *A* makes an offer to sell Bleak House to *B* for $250,000 and states that the offer is open for 10 days, provided that *B* pays $100 for this privilege. *B* pays $100. *B* attempts to accept the underlying offer 12 days later. Although the offer was made irrevocable by the payment of $100, the attempted acceptance is too late. The offer by its own terms terminated by lapse of time.

(2) In example (1), if *A* dies after *B* paid the $100, the offer would still be irrevocable, and *A*'s death would not terminate the offer. If *B* had accepted within the 10-day period, the issue would be impossibility of performance (discussed later).

(3) In example (1), *B* rejects the offer but later, within the ten-day period, attempts to accept. *A* relies on the rejection and sells to another party. The offer is irrevocable. Under the older view, the irrevocable offer would be terminated by the rejection. Under the more modern view, it would not. There would be a contract, except that *B* would be estopped from asserting the existence of the contract, because *A* justifiably relied on the rejection.

6. When Is the Acceptance of an Irrevocable Offer Effective?

Discussion: The acceptance of a revocable offer is usually effective, under the "mailbox rule," when it is sent. But if the offer is irrevocable, the weight of authority is that the acceptance is effective when received by the offeror. The "mailbox rule" is often justified on the theory that it protects the offeree against revocation. When dealing with an irrevocable offer, the offeree does not require the protection of this rule.

F. Certainty

1. Common Law

a. Introduction

The offer (whether revocable or irrevocable) must be so definite as to its material terms, or require such definite terms in the acceptance, that the performances to be rendered by each party are reasonably certain.

Comment: Even though the parties have reached agreement, the agreement is unenforceable if the content of their agreement is unduly uncertain. Indefiniteness as to an immaterial term is not fatal. However, the more terms that are indefinite the less likely it is that the parties intended to contract. Nonetheless, uncertainty and lack of contractual intent are analytically distinct concepts.

b. What Are Material Terms?

Material terms include subject matter, price, payment terms, quantity, quality, duration and the work to be done. Given the infinite variety of contracts, it is obvious that no precise and comprehensive definition can be formulated.

Example: In a construction contract involving $1,000,000, an item involving $9,300 was left open. This was held to be an immaterial term, because in proportion to the contract price, $9,300 is not very significant.

c. When Is a Material Term Reasonably Certain?

What constitutes "reasonable" certainty depends on subject matter, the purposes and relationship of the parties, and the circumstances under which the agreement is made. A term need not be set forth with the utmost specificity. It is enough that the agreement is sufficiently clear for the court to determine the respective obligations of the parties.

Example: A makes an offer to sell from 1 to 10 copies of a specified book at a certain price and adds: "State the number in your acceptance." *B* replies, "I'll take five." Although the offer, standing alone, does not state a precise quantity, the contract itself is definite. It is the contract and not the offer that must be definite. (An incidental point might be made here. Once *B* accepts by stating the number he wants, he cannot then accept again. The offer terminates by the first acceptance.)

d. Cure of Indefiniteness

Indefiniteness may be cured by the subsequent conduct of the parties or by the subsequent agreement of the parties.

Examples: (1) *A* promises to make a tailor-made suit for *B* for $600, without specifying the material. *A* commences to make the suit with cotton cloth and *B* acquiesces. At the outset, the agreement was too vague and indefinite to be enforced, but the conduct of the parties cured the indefiniteness. Therefore, *A* is entitled to the agreed contract price—$600.

(2) *A* promises to pay *B* "well and enough" on retirement. When *B* retired, *A* promised to pay *B* $200 per week. *B* agreed. The initial indefiniteness was cured by the subsequent agreement of the parties.

e. Types of Indefiniteness

Indefiniteness problems arise in three situations: (a) where the parties have purported to agree on a material term but have left it indefinite; (b) where the parties are silent as to a material term; and (c) where the parties have agreed to agree on a material term.

1) Where the Parties Have Purported to Agree on a Material Term but Have Left It Indefinite

Where this occurs, at common law there is no room for implication or gap-fillers (*see infra*) and, therefore, the agreement is unenforceable.

Examples: (1) *A* says to *B,* "If you work for me for one year as a foreman of my plant I will pay you a fair share of the profits." According to a majority of the cases, the agreement is unduly uncertain, limiting *B* to a quasi-contractual recovery measured by the difference between what *B* received in salary and the reasonable value of *B's* services.

(2) *P* sold real property to *D* for a price that was paid. In addition, *D* had promised to build "a first class theater" on the site. *P,* as *D* knew, desired the theater to enhance the value of *P's* other properties in the area. But *D* sold the property to a third party without having built the theater. *P* sued for damages. *D* argued indefiniteness. The court, expounding the more modern view, said that the agreement was sufficiently definite and made the following points: (a) The law leans against destruction of an agreement because of uncertainty. (b) This is especially true where, as here, there has been performance under the contract. (c) Evidence of subjective intention was properly admitted and helped to resolve the meaning of the words. (d) Since *P's* purpose was to enhance the value of *P's* other property, that purpose could be served by the erection of any theater that fits the definition of a first class theater. (e) Less certainty is required in an action for damages than where specific performance is sought.

(3 & 4) Examples (1) and (2) under the heading of Cure of Indefiniteness (II.F.1.d., *supra*) illustrate agreements that initially were too uncertain because the parties' original provision was too vague.

2) Where the Parties Are Silent as to a Material Term

If the parties are silent as to a material term, or discuss it but do not purport to agree on it, there is the possibility that the term may be implied from the surrounding circumstances or supplied by a court using a gap-filler. A gap-filler is a term that a court supplies because it thinks that the parties would have agreed on this term if it had been brought to their attention, or because it is a term "which comports with community standards of fairness." The intent of the parties is a primary factor. Also, courts will sometimes refuse to supply a gap-filler where no objective standard can be found for the missing term.

Other external circumstances that may supply a missing term include course of performance, course of dealing and trade usage.

Examples: (1) *A* hires a plumber to do certain work. No price is set. The court supplies a gap-filler that a reasonable price is to be paid or, according to some courts, that the plumber is to be paid what the plumber usually receives for the work, provided it is not unreasonable.

(2) In a sale of goods where no price is set, courts assume that the parties contracted on the basis of a reasonable price. The UCC has continued this rule in § 2–305.

(3) If no time is stated for the delivery of goods, the completion of a building or other performance, a reasonable time is assumed.

(4) If the parties are silent as to the kind or quantity of goods or the specifications in a building contract, the court will *not* ordinarily supply a gap-filler because no objective standard can be found in such cases.

(5) *A* and *B* agree that *A* will work for *B* for $52,000 per year. The majority view is that this is a hiring at will. The minority view is that the reference to "per year" creates an inference that the hiring is a binding contract for one year. A corollary of the hiring-at-will doctrine is that such an agreement may be terminated for good cause, for no cause or even for an immoral cause. There is, however, a growing list of exceptions. Aside from statutes setting up civil rights or other grounds for job protection, case law grounds for job protection include a discharge that is against public policy (e.g., an employee is discharged for filing a Worker's Compensation claim), or in violation of the implied covenant of good faith and fair dealing (e.g., where a female employee is discharged for resisting the advances of a foreman, or where an employee is discharged to prevent a pension from vesting), and cases where the doctrine of promissory estoppel would apply (e.g., where the employee left existing employment in reliance on the defendant's promise of employment). Wrongful discharge of an employee whose hiring is at will is usually treated as a tort.

(6) Where an employer promises *permanent employment,* the majority of courts have held that the hiring is at will because the duration term is too vague. Under the minority view, however, the employee is entitled to work at least until retirement age, so long as the employee is able to do the work properly, and the employer continues in the business in which the employee was hired. Even under the majority view, if a consideration over and above the employee's services is given, courts have indicated that the hiring will not be considered to be at will. As an example, assume an individual has a tort claim against a company. To settle the claim, the company offers the claimant a "permanent job," and the claimant accepts the offer and drops the tort claim. Courts hold that

the company has committed itself for the claimant's working lifetime.

(7) If the promise is "lifetime employment," there are again two views. Some cases hold that such a promise amounts to a hiring at will, but others take the position that the term should be taken literally.

(8) In most non-employment cases, where no duration is specified in the agreement, the court will imply that the contract will last for a reasonable time. But some courts still conclude that the arrangement is at will, especially where there is no way to determine what is a reasonable time.

(9) Suppose that a service contract is made for a one-year term. After the expiration of the term, the parties continue to perform. In the absence of contrary agreement, the contract has been renewed for another one-year term.

3) Where the Parties Agree to Agree

a) Traditional Rule

The traditional common law rule is that an agreement to agree as to a material term results in an unenforceable agreement. Because the parties are not silent, the parties have manifested an intention to fill the gap themselves. The gap-filler mechanism may not be used. But an agreement to agree must be distinguished from a case where the parties have agreed to use reasonable efforts to reach an agreement. In such cases, there is a duty to negotiate in good faith.

b) Modern View

Some of the more modern cases (even without relying on the UCC and the Restatement (Second), discussed below), have recognized that an agreement to agree serves a valuable commercial purpose and that the traditional rule may operate unfairly where one party uses the rule to defeat an agreement that the parties intended to be binding. Some courts have applied a gap-filler where there is an agreement to agree. Other courts have held that there is a duty to negotiate in good faith even though there is no such provision in the agreement.

Examples: (1) *A* agrees to sell and *B* agrees to buy 1,000 widgets. All of the material items are agreed upon except that the parties agree to agree on the price at a later date. Under the traditional view, the agreement to agree as to a material term would result in fatal indefiniteness. Under the more modern common law, a court could use a reasonable price as a gap-filler. Under the UCC, which governs the case, the price would be a reasonable price at the time of delivery. But, if the parties did not intend to be bound unless agreement were reached on price, there still would be no contract. (UCC § 2–305(4).)

(2) *A* and *B* negotiate an oral agreement that they intend to be binding, but are aware that they have not reached an agreement on price. They later reaffirm their agreement and agree that they shall make every effort to reach an agreement on price. Before any further negotiations take place, *A*, because of a change in market conditions, refuses to negotiate the price. *A* has breached a duty to negotiate in good faith. This problem does not involve an agreement to agree.

(3) *P* obtained an option to buy a parcel of real property for the sum of $23,500 "on payments and terms to be negotiated provided the same is exercised by June 1." On May 15, *P* sought to exercise the option. *P* offered to pay $5,300 in cash and to assume two mortgages in the combined amount of $18,200. *D* changed his mind about selling and refused to negotiate. This is not a case, as in Example 2, where the parties agreed to make every effort to reach an agreement. Under the traditional common law rule, the agreement would be too vague and indefinite. The court, however, held that the parties were obliged to negotiate in good faith and that *D*'s refusal amounted to a breach. The court decreed specific performance on the proposal set forth by *P*, because the proposal would satisfy a reasonable person. This is an advanced case that goes beyond most of the precedents.

2. Uniform Commercial Code

a) Introduction

The UCC's provisions on indefiniteness are of two kinds. Some provisions relate to specific issues. There is also a very important general provision. Section 2–305 is an example of a provision relating to a specific issue. It applies to open price terms and has already been mentioned. These specific provisions all assume that there has been no contrary agreement.

b) General Provision

Even if one or more terms are left open, a contract for sale of goods does not fail for indefiniteness if the parties have intended to make a contract and there is a reasonably certain basis for giving an appropriate remedy. (UCC § 2–204(3)).

Discussion: The test is not certainty as to what the parties were to do nor as to the exact amount of damages due to the plaintiff. Rather, commercial standards on the issue of indefiniteness are to be applied. This provision is designed to prevent, if at all possible, a contracting party, who is dissatisfied with his bargain, from taking refuge in the doctrine of indefiniteness to wriggle out of an agreement. This section governs all three categories of cases discussed above.

Thus, a gap-filler can be used not only where the parties are silent but also where the parties purported to agree on the term in a vague manner, or made an agreement to agree with respect to it. But the section goes beyond gap-fillers and permits a court to use any reasonably certain basis for giving an appropriate remedy whether or not a gap-filler exists. Whether the parties intended to contract is normally a question of fact. Whether there is a reasonably certain basis for giving an appropriate remedy is a question of law.

Example: A agrees to sell, and *B* to buy widgets, "the quantity to be agreed on from time to time." Under the traditional common law rule, the agreement to agree as to quantity would be fatally indefinite. At common law and under the UCC, the fact that price, duration, etc. are missing is not necessarily fatal because gap-fillers can be used. Under the UCC, an agreement to agree is not necessarily fatal. The first question under UCC § 2–204(3) is whether the parties intended to contract. This is a question of fact. The second question is whether there is a reasonably certain basis for giving an appropriate remedy. Where, as here, the quantity term is not set, it would be an unusual case where there is a reasonably certain basis for giving an appropriate remedy.

c) Specific Provisions

1) Place of Delivery

If the place of delivery is not stated, it is the seller's place of business or if the seller has none, at the seller's residence. If the goods are identified, and the parties know that the goods are elsewhere, that location is the place of delivery.

2) Time for Shipment or Delivery

If the time for shipment or delivery is not specified, "reasonable time" is the gap-filler.

3) Time for Payment

If the time for payment is not specified, payment is due at the time and place where the buyer is to receive the goods.

4) Failure to Specify Assortment

Example: S agrees to sell and *B* agrees to buy 5,000 gallons of W Brand Motor Oil, SAE 10–70. This last term designates seven weights of oil. The price for each weight is definite. Before any weight specifications were submitted, *B* repudiated the agreement. Under UCC § 2–311, there is a contract. The buyer is bound to specify, and the seller is bound to permit the buyer to specify. The specifications are to be made in "good faith and within limits set by commercial reasonableness." When the party who has the duty fails to specify, the other may proceed in any reasonable manner, such as by making the specification and treating the breach as total.

G. Digital Contracts

1. Introduction

The rise of the Internet and of digital media generally has had a significant effect on all aspects of life, including Contracts law. The simple fact is that buyers now routinely use the Internet to transact directly with goods manufacturers or service providers. Contract law emphasizes the objective intentions of the parties, and the circumstances surrounding a contract, the current and past practices of the parties and of their particular industry or trade obviously affect how those intentions are manifested. The use of digital media obviously is part of the behavior and customary practices of contracting parties. And so, one needs to be aware of how basic principles of Contracts law, developed over centuries, interact with these current practices of "e-commerce."

One issue that often remains in the background is whether we should think of "digital contract" as a different and distinct *type* of contract, requiring its own set of legal rules, or whether "digital contracting" is just a different context in which *any* contract might be formed. In some respects, the issue of understanding the impact of digital practices is similar to an earlier problem of understanding the impact of statutes like the UCC on what otherwise seems to be the classic common law of Contracts.

This may be a useful analogy; after all, aren't *sale of goods* contracts different from "other" contracts? Perhaps, but in one important respect, a sale of goods is basically the same as any other transaction involving a contract. Revised UCC § 1–103(b) provides that, except where they are displaced by particular provisions of the UCC, the principles of law and equity continue to apply, to "supplement" UCC provisions. On the other hand, "commercial law" is certainly distinct enough to be a specialized area of study beyond the generally applicable law of Contracts. Similarly, there are specialized areas of the law—and specialized statutes—that apply to digital contracts, but general Contract law also applies to these contracts.

2. Digital Contracts Under the UCC

a. Introduction

The fact that in contemporary practice many contracts are formed in a digital setting has had an impact on the UCC. For example, revised UCC § 1–201(10) defines "conspicuous" as to mean "with reference to a term, . . . so written, *displayed, or presented* that a reasonable person against which it is to operate ought to have noticed it. Whether a term is 'conspicuous' or not is a decision for the court." (Emphasis added.) This would include the various ways in which links are highlighted on a webpage. (The 2022 revision of UCC § 1–201(10) goes further, by adding "based on the totality of the circumstances" after "written, displayed, or presented" in the definition.)

b. Other Provisions

In addition to the definition of "conspicuous," other provisions of the UCC are of significance in considering the legal implications of a digital transaction.

1) Statute of Frauds Writing Requirement

For contracts with a price of $500 or more, UCC § 2–201 requires a "writing" indicating that a contract has been made, "signed" by the party against whom the contract is being charged. UCC § 1–201(43) defines "writing" to mean "printing, typewriting, or any other intentional reduction to tangible form." This raises the abstract question of whether a digital exchange—via email or text, for example—would count as a "writing."

(On statutes of frauds generally, *see* IV.C., *infra.*)

2) 2022 Revision of the Writing Requirement

The 2022 revision of UCC § 2–201 would change the "writing" requirement to a requirement that there be a "record," which is defined in the revised UCC § 1–201(31) to mean "information that is inscribed on a tangible medium or that is stored in an electronic or other medium and is retrievable in perceivable form." This would clearly include any digital record, eliminating the question of whether that would be a "writing."

c. Other Statutes

There are statutes that focus specifically on the issue of the legal significance and effects of digital transactions. These include the Uniform Electronic Transactions Act (UETA), approved in 1999, and the federal Electronic Signature in Global & National Commerce Act (e-Sign Act), 15 U.S.C. § 7001, enacted in June 2000. Here, for example, it is no longer open to question that a signature, contract, or transactional record can legally be in electronic form, at least in interstate transactions. Lingering concerns persist, however, involving authentication of messages and errors in transmission, problems addressed in UETA §§ 9 and 10. However, although the UETA has been enacted in all states except Illinois and New York, and in the District of Columbia and the Virgin Islands, it is rarely cited or applied in cases.

d. Judicial Approaches

1) In General

Despite these specialized statutes dealing with electronic transactions, federal and state courts typically analyze contracts formed online or by other digital media by invoking generally applicable state law contract principles. Adaptation and analogy are often required to reconcile relatively new ways of transacting with traditional Contract law. People who communicate with each other by electronic means may have an established pattern of conduct in which the communications occur. They may have worked this out between themselves previously (which will create a course of dealing) or it may have been established by some network or group within which the parties operate (which will create a usage of trade). This course of dealing or usage of trade will be binding upon them unless specific language in the current communication indicates a different intention.

2) Judicial Battle over the "Battle of the Forms"

The common law requirement that, to create a contract, the terms of an acceptance must be the "mirror image" of the offer (*see* II.D.f., *supra*) sometimes leads to a "battle of the forms," in which one party's communication of terms is countered by the other party's competing terms, back and forth with the last terms standing become the contract. By contrast, UCC § 2–207 generally prefers to find a contract even when the common law requirement of a "mirror image" between offer and acceptance is not met. Is there a viable role for UCC § 2–207 in electronic transactions, such as an Internet sale of goods? With the rise of digital contracting, courts have been faced with the necessity of deciding how mirror image requirements work in the digital context.

a) Hidden Terms

Ironically, much of the case law on formation of contracts in e-commerce stems from a 1996 decision by the Seventh Circuit involving the purchase of a *physical* product in a *face-to-face* situation in an *actual* store. The only thing "digital" about the actual decision, *ProCD, Inc. v. Zeidenberg,* was that it involved the purchase of a software disk that came in a sealed box with "shrink wrap" terms (i.e., additional terms inside the box you unwrap). The Seventh Circuit rejected the application of UCC § 2–207 to the shrink wrap terms, because the case involved "only one form." Since nothing in UCC § 2–207 requires two forms—or any forms at all—this position may seem obviously incorrect, but it has influenced the approach of the majority of cases treating digital contracting. Countering that approach, The Third Circuit in a 1991 case, *Step-Saver Data Systems, Inc. v. Wyse Technology*, held that "box top" terms (i.e., (i.e., additional terms stamped or printed on the box you just bought) were material alterations to terms of a previously formed contract, and thus were not part of the contract, absent express agreement of the purchaser under UCC § 2–207(2)(b)).

These two cases established a basic split in the case law authority that has developed around contracts formed online. Such contracts routinely involve potential formation issues as to "shrink wrap" terms, "click wrap" terms (*i.e.*, additional terms assented to by clicking the screen, with or without reading the terms), and "browse wrap" terms (*i.e.*, terms on a separate webpage accepted by continuing to browse the website). The Seventh Circuit and other jurisdictions routinely uphold the "contract first, more terms later" approach, at least so long as the later terms are not prohibited by other public policy or are so unfair that they are considered "unconscionable." (On unconscionability, *see* IX.F., *infra*.)

In contrast, the Second Circuit the Third Circuit, and the Ninth Circuit and others require compliance with the UCC, including UCC § 2–207 or equivalent statutory provisions, and will only uphold "terms later" when there is conspicuous notice and an opportunity to review/reject. Some circuits (e.g., the Fourth and Fifth Circuits) and many state courts have not addressed this issue definitively. The holdings in *ProCD* and its progeny represent the majority view currently, and they effectively give the offeror the power to dictate specific terms as to acceptance of the goods. As a practical matter, most courts are not requiring the seller to "unambiguously indicate" the process of acceptance required to form the contract on the website.

Before attempting to test yourself by answering these Review Questions, it would be a good idea to take a look at HOW TO STUDY and EXAMINATION in the *Perspective* section, *supra*.

Review Questions *(Answers are in Appendix A)*

1. T or F *A* owned a $55 harness that was stolen from him. While in a state of wrath and in a boastful and blustering manner, *A* in the presence of a crowd, including *P*, promised to pay $1,000 to anyone who recovered the harness. *P* finds and returns the harness and sues for the reward. *P*, in fact, believed that *A* was serious, but a reasonable person in *P*'s position would conclude otherwise. *P* cannot recover.

2. T or F *P* was in the business of manufacturing automobile parts. *P*'s customers were major auto manufacturers. *P* wished to sell to other buyers such as Midas Muffler but believed that this would displease the auto manufacturers. To achieve secrecy, *P* set up a subsidiary to distribute its products. *P* and *E*, a trusted employee, signed a document which stated that *E* had bought the business of the subsidiary for $250,000. It was orally agreed between the parties that, despite the document, *E* was acting as an agent of *P*. *E* sues on the written agreement to compel *P* to transfer the business. *E* may not recover.

3. T or F Mrs. Stewart conceived at the age of 37. After two previous stillbirths, she was convinced that she could not have a normal delivery. Consequently, when she and her husband consulted with *D*, a doctor, they demanded that a Caesarean section be performed. *D* agreed. *D*'s medical opinion was that a Caesarean would not be necessary, and so *D* later refused to perform a Caesarean when Mrs. Stewart had labor pains. The birth was stillborn. Mrs. Stewart does not have a cause of action for breach of contract against *D*.

4. T or F The Chicago Tribune, a daily newspaper, publishes a booklet called "General Advertising Rates," which lists its charges for advertisements, and another booklet called "The Chicago Tribune Advertising Guide" which indicates that the Tribune will refuse advertising that is dishonest, indecent or illegal. *P*, a labor union, tendered to the Tribune an advertisement urging readers not to patronize a certain department store because of its policy of featuring imported clothing made by low wage foreign labor. It was conceded that the tendered advertisement was not dishonest, indecent or illegal. The union also tendered sufficient funds to pay for the advertisements in accordance with the "General Advertising Rates." The Tribune refused to print the advertisement. *P* has a cause of action for breach of contract against the Tribune.

5. T or F *D* caused circulars to be distributed to dealers throughout the country announcing that an auction would be conducted without reserve of the famous Smith collection of antiques. *P* flew from California to New York, the announced site of the auction. On arrival *P* discovered that the auction had been canceled because of a recession in the antiques market. *P* does not have an action for breach of contract against *D*.

6. T or F *P* asked *D* whether *D* would consider selling certain property. *D* stated that, if *P* made an offer, *D* would consider it. *P* named a sum and *D* refused. *P*

then stated, "Will you accept $49,000?" *D* answered, "I will not sell it for less than $56,000." *P* said, "I accept." There was a contract.

7. T or F *A* offered a $100 reward to anyone who finds and returns *A*'s lost watch. *B* never learned of the reward offer but returned the watch knowing it belonged to *A* because of engraved material on the back. *B* may not recover for the sole reason that B was legally bound to return the watch.

8. T or F In problem 7, assume that *B* knew of the offer before *B* found and returned the watch and that *B* had no legal duty to return the watch. Assume further that, when *B* returned the watch, *B* did not mention the reward. *B* offers testimony that *B* intended to accept and did not say anything about the reward because of embarrassment. As a matter of law, *B* may not recover the reward.

9. T or F *A*, a newspaper, requests *B* to discontinue distribution of a rival newspaper, and offers to pay $100 per week as long as *B* abstains from such distribution. One must conclude that *A* had made an offer looking to a series of contracts.

10. T or F *A*, the owner of an unimproved piece of realty, spent the summer in Europe. When *A* returned there was a beautiful house where the empty lot had been. As *A* was about to enter, *B* informed *A* that *B* had caused the structure to be built and that, if *A* used the house, *A* would be contractually obligated to pay for it. *B* is correct.

11. T or F *A* was seriously injured in an accident. *B*, a doctor, came on the scene and treated *A* while *A* was unconscious. *B* is entitled to a contractual recovery from *A*.

12. T or F *A* invited a number of brokers to submit proposals for fire and theft insurance. Later, on *A*'s request, *B*, one of the brokers, revised the bid several times. *A* then awarded the contract to another. *B* sues to recover the cost incurred in preparing the bid and its various revisions. *B* may recover.

13. T or F Under a claim of right made in error but in good faith, *A* digs a well on *B*'s unused land and takes water therefrom which has no market value and no value to *B*, doing no injury to the value of the land. *B* notifies *A* that *B* will charge $500 a day for every day on which *A* takes water from the land. If *A* takes water, *A* is bound to pay $500 per day.

14. T or F *A* sends an offer by mail to *B*, who promptly sends what amounts to a counter-offer the next day. This letter is lost. The following day, *B* at 2:00 P.M. sends a letter of acceptance which was also lost. On the same day, at 1:00 P.M., *A* hands a notice of revocation to an independent messenger service. This notice is hand delivered to *B* at 5:00 P.M. Under the majority view there is a contract.

15. T or F *A* sent to *B* an offer to sell certain realty stating all material terms and added, "this offer is not subject to revocation for thirty days." *B* immediately rejected the offer, and *A* then stated that *A* withdrew the offer. At this point, the offer had been effectively terminated.

16. T or F *A* sends an offer by e-mail to sell oil at a fixed price which at the time is subject to rapid fluctuations in price. The offer is received near the close of business hours, and an e-mail acceptance is sent the next day after the offeree has learned of a sharp price rise. There is a contract.

17. T or F *D* offered a reward of $200 for information leading to the conviction of the person who set a specific fire. Three years and two months later, the culprit was convicted as a result of information supplied by *P* three months before the trial. *P* may not recover because the offer has lapsed.

18. T or F *A* makes an offer to *B* saying that it is to remain open for two weeks but is to end at once if *A*'s factory is destroyed by fire. If the factory burns down two days later and *B* accepts the next day, not knowing that the factory burned down, there is a contract.

19. T or F *A* in a telephone conversation makes an offer to *B* to which *B* did not reply. After the conversation ends, *B* sends a letter of acceptance. There is no contract.

20. T or F *A* made an offer to *B* looking to a series of unilateral contracts pursuant to which *A* guarantied payment of the *B*'s deliveries of building supplies to Apex Construction Co. After *B* made the first delivery, *A* was adjudicated an incompetent and a guardian of *A*'s property was appointed. *B* had no knowledge of this fact and continued to make deliveries. Under the majority view, *B* may recover contractually for all deliveries.

21. T or F *A,* a newspaper, publishes an offer of prizes to persons who procure the largest number of subscriptions as evidenced by cash or checks received by a specified time. *B* completes and mails an entry blank giving *B*'s name and address, which is received by *A*. Thereafter during the contest, *A* publishes a notice that personal checks will not be counted. *B* does not see the notice. Assume that the offer continued to be revocable. *B* is bound by the notice.

22. T or F *A* makes an offer to *B* to sell Bleak House for $100,000. *B,* at *A*'s request, pays *A* $100 to keep the offer open for one week. Two days later, *B* tells *A* that *B* will purchase but at a price of $85,000. *A* declines. The next day *B* manifests an intent to buy at the original price and tenders $100,000. Under the modern view, there is a contract.

23. T or F *A* makes a written and signed offer to sell goods to *B* which states, "This offer is for one week." The letter was dated and sent on Jan. 2. It was received on Jan. 3. *B* sent a letter of acceptance on Jan. 9. This letter was received on Jan. 12. There is a contract.

24. T or F *A,* a manufacturer, agrees to sell to *B,* a retailer, 5,000 widgets. *A*'s offer stated prices which varied according to the size of the widgets. *B* accepted. Before anything else happened, *A* "withdrew the offer." There is no contract.

25. T or F *A* and *B* enter into an employment arrangement for a period of one year. They agree that the salary to be paid should be determined by them "in a cooperative effort" at the end of each month. There is no contract.

26. T or F *A* publishes an offer of a reward of $10,000 for information leading to the arrest and conviction of the murderer of her child. *B* had such information but made no effort to accept the offer until he was stricken with a disease that appeared to be fatal. At which point *B* gave such information to the authorities, and disclaimed any intention to collect the reward. When he recovered from his illness and after the information he supplied resulted in the arrest and conviction of the murderer, he claimed the reward. *B* is entitled to recover.

27. Essay

Case owned a tractor located in the woods some miles from Case's home. On February 16, Thompson called Case and asked whether the tractor was for sale. Case said: "I will sell the tractor to you, or to anybody else for that matter, for $450. Upon an agreement, you may take possession of the tractor." On March 1, Thompson picked up the tractor and brought it home and so informed Case on March 15. On March 1, Peterson, who had learned of the offer from Thompson, sent in a notice of acceptance.

(a) Discuss the rights of the parties.

(b) Would the result be different if Case had not said, "Upon an agreement, you may make take possession of the tractor."

(c) What would be the result if instead of picking up the tractor on March 1, Thompson had sent a letter stating: "This letter is sent to confirm that I am purchasing the tractor of which we spoke on the terms indicated. Naturally I expect that an arbitration clause is part of our deal?"

28. Essay

Prior to February 20 the plaintiff and defendant had engaged in conferences and negotiations respecting the purchase by the plaintiff of all of the property and assets of the defendant, Anchor, whose president, Conroy, owned 93% of the Anchor stock.

On February 20 plaintiff wrote a letter setting forth a detailed agreement, numbered 1 through 20, which if signed by the defendant would give the plaintiff a 60-day option to purchase Anchor's business and assets. The letter contained a line for the defendant's signature. The defendant did not sign but instead sent its own letter signed by Conroy on February 28 which read as follows:

> . . . "We are unwilling to enter into a formal option with your company as proposed in your letter of February 20. We would be willing to sell the assets of our company to you for $4,025,000 in accordance with paragraphs 3, 5, 6, 7, 8, 9, 11, 13, 14 and 17 of your letter of February 20, if such an offer were made today without the reservations elsewhere contained in that letter, and subject to the exceptions noted below. You may consider this as a letter of intent authorizing you to make the survey you deem necessary to make your offer a firm and binding one; and we assure you of our full cooperation in making it. We suggest that it be completed as quickly as possible."
>
> . . . You are assured that should you make a firm offer within 50 days from this date, we will enter into a contract with you on the basis of the terms of the above numbered paragraphs of your letter of February 20 with the following exceptions:
>
> (a) That suitable assurances are given for the retention of lower level executive personnel;
>
> (b) That mutually satisfactory arrangements are made for the continued employment of Charles L. Conroy.

Plaintiff spent large sums of money in making the survey, and on April 1, wrote to the defendant saying that the plaintiff had decided to proceed with the acquisition of Anchor's assets. This letter in addition read in part as follows: "Please consider this our formal offer, therefore, to enter into agreement in accordance with our previous correspondence. You have already indicated that this offer will be accepted by you.

We trust that you will have your General Counsel contact our General Counsel in order that the formal agreement between us can be prepared promptly."

Discuss all of the contract problems involved in determining whether or not the parties are bound by a contract.

29. Short Essay

An advertising circular was sent by *Time* to Joshua, a three-year-old boy. The front of the envelope contained two see-through windows partially revealing the envelope's contents. One showed the boy's name and address. The other revealed the following words: "JOSHUA A GNAIZDA, I'LL GIVE YOU THIS VERSATILE NEW CALCULATOR WATCH FREE Just for Opening this Envelope Before February 15." On February 1, Joshua's mother opened the envelope and noticed that the sentence partly revealed through the window continued as follows ". . . AND MAILING THIS CERTIFICATE TODAY!"

The terms of the certificate clearly required that Joshua purchase a subscription to *Fortune* magazine (published by *Time*) in order to get the calculator watch. Joshua's father, an attorney, demanded that *Time* give Joshua a free calculator watch without requiring the purchase of a subscription. When *Time* refused, he instituted a class action on behalf of Joshua and others similarly situated, seeking damages. Joining in the class action were two other clients who received messages that were identical (other than their names) to that received by Joshua. However, they had made no demand on *Time* for watches. Raise and discuss the issues of contract law raised by this set of facts.

Discuss the rights of the parties including theories available, probable defenses, and your estimate of the likely result of the lawsuit.

Chapter III

Consideration and Its Equivalents

■ ANALYSIS

A. Introduction

Not all promises are enforceable. Generally, an enforceable promise must be supported by consideration. Gratuitous promises are not so supported. Thus, gratuitous promises are only enforceable if they meet the requisites of promissory estoppel or, in certain limited instances, arise from a moral obligation. Even a gratuitous promise that does not meet the requirements of promissory estoppel or the moral obligation doctrine may still be enforceable in some jurisdictions if it meets the requisites of certain statutes or if the promise was made under seal.

B. Consideration

1. Elements of Consideration

A promise that is not supported by consideration or its equivalent is not enforceable. For a promise to be supported by consideration, two elements must co-exist. When they co-exist, there is an enforceable contract.

(a) *The promisee (or a third party on the promisee's behalf) must incur legal detriment, that is, do what the promisee (or the third party) is not legally obligated to do; or refrain from doing what the promisee (or the third party) is legally privileged to do.*

(b) *The detriment must have been given in exchange for the promise. This means that the promisor must have bargained for the detriment which must have been given in exchange for the promise.*

a. The Promisee Must Incur Legal Detriment

Discussion: Two additional points need to be made. First, although we state the rule in terms of legal detriment, the rule is often phrased in terms of either legal detriment to the promisee or legal benefit to the promisor. The result is invariably the same. If the promisee incurs legal detriment, the promisor obtains a legal benefit.

Second, someone other than the promisee may incur the detriment. Although the rule is often stated in terms of legal detriment incurred by the *promisee,* it does not matter from whom or to whom the detriment moves so long as it is bargained for and given in exchange for the promise.

b. The Detriment Must Have Been Bargained for by the Promisor and Given by the Promisee in Exchange for the Promise

This means that the promisor must make the promise in exchange for the promisee's conduct. Otherwise, any detriment incurred by the promisee involved no element of exchange. In other words, a promise to make a gift is not enforceable. But note that the promisor need only exchange the promise in part for the detriment. Exchange may coexist with other motives such as friendship or the creation of goodwill.

Examples: (1) *A* says to *B,* "If you paint my house, I promise to pay you $10,000." *B* paints the house. *A* is the promisor and *B* is the promisee-offeree. The promisee, *B,* has incurred legal detriment by doing an act (painting) that *B* was not legally obligated to do. It is a reasonable conclusion that *A,* the promisor, was exchanging the promise to pay $10,000 for the act of painting. It is also a reasonable conclusion that the promisee, *B,* painted with knowledge of the offer and an intent to accept. Thus, *A*'s promise is supported by consideration.

The arrangement in example (1) was unilateral. There was only one promisor—*A,* who asked for performance, not a promise to perform. In a bilateral contract there are two promisors and additional issues are presented. These are discussed below.

(2) *A* writes to his sister-in-law, "If you will come down and see me, I promise you a place on my plantation to raise your family." Although moving from one place to another is a detriment, the court held that *A* made a promise to make a gift. Moving was simply a condition of the gift. A promise to make a gift is not enforceable. In other words, the moving was not bargained for in exchange for the promise. (Today, this case might come out differently by application of promissory estoppel, discussed below in III.D.)

The result undoubtedly would be different if *A* had asked his sister-in-law to come to his plantation to act as housekeeper, because selfish benefit to the promisor is an indication of a bargaining state of mind. Whether the detriment is bargained for is often a question of fact.

(3) Uncle promised his nephew $5,000 if the nephew refrained from drinking, smoking and gambling until he was 21. Refraining from doing what one is legally privileged to do is a detriment. Here, in contrast with example 2, the court held that the detriment was bargained for. The cases are based on different findings on the issue of whether an exchange was intended. Again, we are dealing with a question of fact.

(4) Landlord (*L*) offered to extend *T*'s lease for an additional four years if *T* promised to make improvements that would cost approximately $10,000. At *L*'s suggestion, *T* hired an architect to check figures on the proposed improvements. When *L* decided not to renew the lease, *T* argued that the offer became irrevocable, claiming that the consideration of hiring the architect made the offer irrevocable. The court sustained the finding of fact made by the trial court that the hiring of the architect was not consideration, because it was merely suggested and not bargained for.

(5) *A* is moved by friendship to promise to sell a motorcycle, worth $3,000, for $500 to *B*. Because bargained-for detriment—$500—need not be the sole or even the predominant inducement, there was in fact a bargained-for exchange.

(6) *A* promises *B* to pay *B* $5,000 if *B*'s son, C, paints *A*'s house. Although the detriment comes from *C, B* may enforce *A*'s promise.

2. Motive and Past Consideration

Past consideration and motive are not consideration.

Discussion: The term "past consideration" is a contradiction in terms. Consideration is a bargained-for exchange and parties cannot make an exchange involving something that has already occurred.

However, if the promisee incurs detriment, the promisor's motive in entering into the transaction is relevant, because it throws light on the issue of whether there is an exchange. Ordinarily the promisor's motive must be to induce action on the part of the promisee and conversely the promisee's motive must be, or objectively appear to be, to gain what is offered by the promisor.

Examples: (1) *F* says to *S*, "in consideration of the fact that you have named your child after me, I promise to pay you $5,000." The promise did not induce the detriment, because at the time when the child was named *S* did not know of the offer, if, indeed, there was one, or intend to accept.

(2) *F* says to *S*, "in consideration of the fact that you are not as wealthy as your brothers, I promise to pay you $5,000." Although *F* has stated the motive for the promise, there is no detriment.

3. Adequacy

a. The General Rule

Subject to the exceptions below, any detriment, no matter how economically insignificant, will support a promise provided that the detriment is in fact bargained for.

Discussion: Although for most purposes courts do not review the adequacy of the consideration, economic inadequacy of the detriment is one of the factors to be considered in determining whether the detriment was in fact bargained for. In other words, a small detriment will support a promise as consideration, but if a court is looking at a dubious bargain, it will consider the small size of the detriment.

b. The Exceptions

(1) The court will review the equivalence of the exchange under the doctrine of unconscionability. (*See* IX.F., *infra*).

(2) The court can always review the fairness of a lawyer's fee agreement, or other agreement with a client.

(3) When equitable relief such as specific performance is sought, the detriment's inadequacy may be considered.

(4) Inadequacy of consideration may be an indication that the detriment was not truly bargained for (*see* Nominal Consideration, discussed in III.B.4. *infra*), or it may be some evidence that fraud or other vitiating factor induced the transaction.

Examples: (1) *A* promises to pay *B* $10,000 for the surrender of a piece of paper that is in fact worthless. Because surrendering the paper constituted detriment, and the surrender of the papers is bargained for, *A*'s promise is enforceable.

(2) *A,* an impoverished person with a limited command of the local language, promises to pay $1,145 for a $348 appliance. Despite the general rule and the existence of consideration, the contract is unconscionable and therefore unenforceable.

4. Sham and Nominal Consideration

The question here is whether a pretense of consideration will suffice as consideration. The problem arises in two recurring, but analytically distinct, fact patterns. The first involves a lie: a purported contract in writing says that a consideration has been given when it has not. This is *sham* consideration.

The second arises where the parties, knowing that a gratuitous promise is unenforceable, attempt to make the promise enforceable by exchanging a small token sum to create the form of a bargain; this is known as *nominal* or *token* consideration. Here, the $1.00 or other small detriment is actually paid, but it does not in any way induce the promise. There are different views on these issues; they are set forth in connection with the illustrations below.

Examples: (1) A writing states: "I promise to sell you Greenacre for $50,000. In consideration of $100 in hand, paid receipt of which is acknowledged, this offer is irrevocable for 30 days." The $100 was not paid. Because the alleged consideration is a *sham,* the promise is not supported by consideration. The parol evidence rule (discussed in IV.B., *infra*) does not exclude the contradiction of statements of fact.

(2) But there is a minority view that applies mostly in the cases of guaranties and option contracts. Cases supporting this view hold that the option contract is binding, either (1) upon a theory that the parties are estopped from contradicting the writing, or (2) upon the theory that the recital gives rise to an implied promise to pay. The Restatement (Second) synthesizes these two views stating that "an offer is binding as an option contract if it is in writing and signed by the offeror, recites a purported consideration for the making of the offer, and proposes an exchange on fair terms within a reasonable time."

Again, these views also apply in the case of an offer of guaranty of the credit of another where there is a sham recital of consideration. Typically, this minority view applies to a situation where the creditor has already extended credit so that the consideration is past. In the case of a guaranty, the Restatement (Second) does not require the exchange be "on fair terms," etc.

(3) *A* wishes to make a binding contract to convey a Ford Explorer worth $10,000 to his son, *B,* one year later. *A* intends the car as a gift, but being aware of the doctrine of consideration, drafts an instrument in which *A* promises to convey in return for *B*'s payment of $10. *B* makes the payment. Nevertheless, *B* knows or should know that the $10 is merely a token, that is, *nominal* consideration. There are two views.

The Restatement (Second) takes the position that the promise should not be enforced because the alleged consideration is not truly bargained for. It argues that to hold otherwise destroys the doctrine of consideration. The original Restatement, and some other authorities, supported the contrary view. They argue that there ought to be a way of making a gratuitous promise binding especially in a jurisdiction where this cannot be done through the mechanism of a seal. Although this topic is much written about, there is very little case law on token consideration besides the option and guaranty cases.

5. Invalid Claims

Discussion: A promise to surrender a *valid* claim constitutes detriment and, if bargained for, constitutes consideration. But there are a number of views as to whether the bargained-for surrender of, or forbearance to assert, an *invalid* claim is detriment.

(1) The earliest view is that the surrender of an invalid claim does not constitute detriment. This view has generally been abandoned.

(2) Many courts hold that the surrender of an invalid claim serves as a detriment if the claimant has asserted it in good faith, and a reasonable person would believe that the claim is well founded.

(3) Still other courts have held that the only requirement is good faith. But some of these courts require that the invalidity of the claim not be patently obvious.

(4) The Restatement (Second) takes the position that either good faith or objective uncertainty as to the validity of an invalid claim is sufficient.

These rules do not apply in a quit-claim type case. (*See* example **2** *infra*). It should be emphasized that even if surrender of the claim constitutes detriment, one must still confront the question of what is bargained for. For example, did the promisor bargain for the surrender of a worthless piece of paper or the surrender of a supposed but invalid claim?

Examples: (1) *D* guaranteed in writing an obligation of a third party to *P*. The guaranty was not enforceable under the existing law, because a stamp tax had not been paid. *D* promised *P* that *D* would pay the amount stated in the writing if *P* returned the written document of guaranty. The return of the paper is detriment, and the court held that this is what *D* bargained for. Therefore, the promise was binding. But the court could have as easily discussed the case under the heading of invalid claims. In that event the rules stated above would have applied. If the case had been analyzed from that perspective, the good faith of the promisee would be in issue.

(2) *A*, an insurance company, requests *B*, who had been at the scene of an accident, to execute a release in exchange for $200 because it wishes to close its file. Although *B* made no claim and in fact believes that no valid claim exists, the execution of the release constitutes detriment. *A* sought the release for its own purposes and with knowledge that *B* made no claim. This is similar to a situation involving a quit-claim deed. *A* bargained for a document.

6. The Pre-Existing Duty Rule

a. Introduction

If parties do what they are legally obligated to do, or refrain from doing what they are not legally privileged to do, they have not incurred detriment, because performing a legal obligation is not detriment. No legal right is surrendered.

Discussion: This rule has been much criticized, and as a result, exceptions exist that are illogical or tenuous at best. The criticism of the rule is based upon the notion that it is unreasonable for the law to prevent competent parties from modifying their legal obligations, absent duress, even if there is no consideration for the modification. The trend in law is moving slowly toward enforcement of modifications that lack consideration. At the same time, the law of duress is evolving to make it easier to set aside a modification on the ground of duress.

b. Duties Imposed by Law

The pre-existing duty rule applies not only to a duty that exists under a contract, but also to a duty that is imposed by law.

Discussion: The duties imposed by law that are the subject of this rule include not only official duties but also duties imposed on a person as a member of the public or as a member of a family, such as caring for a child.

Example: A reward is offered for the apprehension of *X*, a violent escaped prisoner. *B*, a deputy sheriff, at great risk to life and limb, makes the arrest and claims the reward. *B* is not entitled to the reward if making such an arrest is in the general scope of the deputy's duties.

c. Modification in a Two-Party Case

Discussion: The vast majority of the cases in which the pre-existing duty rule is invoked involve the modification of a contract. The rule in the context of modifications is supported by the overwhelming weight of authority. But, on a number of theories, some jurisdictions do not apply the pre-existing duty rule. These theories include:

(1) A party incurs a legal detriment by giving up the right to breach the contract.

(2) The Wisconsin rule, instead, employs the fiction that the original consideration is imported into the new agreement.

(3) Still other cases have looked upon the modification as an attempt to mitigate damages.

(4) A few jurisdictions have even held that no consideration is required for modifying an agreement.

(5) Finally, some cases have enforced modifications that lacked consideration on a theory of promissory estoppel. But, for our purposes, these minority theories may be ignored. The minority

position that is adopted by the Restatement (Second) is important to know as it is the probable law of the future. It is presented in example 4, below. However, for now, the vast majority of jurisdictions continue to follow the pre-existing duty rule. But limited exceptions have been introduced even in these majority jurisdictions. It is clearly a doctrine in a state of decay and reformulation. The rule and the exceptions can best be explained by a series of illustrations.

Examples:

(1) In August, *B* hires *A* at $900 per week for a one-year term to commence in November. In October, the parties modify the agreement, raising the salary to $1,000 per week. *B*'s promise to pay the additional $100 per week is not enforceable, because *A* has incurred no fresh detriment. *A* is merely doing what *A* is already obligated to do. However, if *A* assumed even a slight additional duty, and this detriment was bargained for, there would be consideration for the modification.

(2) In example 1, if the parties rescinded their original agreement in early October, and entered into a new agreement for $1,000 in late October, there would not be any pre-existing duty problem, because the original agreement had been rescinded. This rescission is supported by consideration on both sides, each party surrendering all rights under the contract. It terminated all duties under the initial agreement. Thus, when the late October agreement was entered into, there could be no question of pre-existing duty. Note that in this case there are three separate agreements, each supported by consideration.

(3) Assume the facts in example 2, except that the rescission and the agreement to pay $1,000 are simultaneous, so that there are only two agreements. In this case, courts should conclude that the pre-existing duty rule is violated, because the parties clearly intend that the rescission be contingent on the new contract, which in turn is contingent on the rescission. However, some courts have reached the opposite conclusion. The Restatement (Second) rejects these cases.

(4) *A* agrees to do excavation work for *B* for a stated price. When solid rock is unexpectedly encountered, *A* notifies *B*. They agree that *A* will complete the job, but *B* will pay double the price, which is reasonable in relation to the work to be done. *A* does not have the defense of impossibility of performance and therefore has a legal duty to continue performance. Thus, in completing the work, *A* is only doing what the contract requires, and *B* is not obligated to pay the agreed additional sum. This is the classical view, reflecting the pre-existing duty rule. A more modern view is that the modification will be upheld if it's made after unforeseen difficulties, even if it is without consideration. The Restatement (Second) adopts this approach, upholding the modification "if the modification is fair and equitable in view of the circumstances not anticipated when the contract was made."

d. The Three-Party Cases

The situation and the competing views can best be explained by two illustrations.

Examples: (1) *A,* a jockey, enters into a bilateral contract with *B,* the owner of a horse, to ride in a race for $1,000. *C,* an outsider, who does not have the right to performance under the contract, owns the dam (mother) of *B*'s horse and would receive a prize if *B*'s horse wins. *C* promises to pay a bonus of $500 to *A* if *B*'s horse wins. The horse wins. There are two views. According to the classical rule, *A* may not recover the $500 because *A* was only performing an obligation owed under the contract with *B*. Another view, adopted by both Restatements, and most modern cases, is that *C*'s promise is enforceable. However, the Restatement (Second) refuses to apply this rule if the pre-existing duty is owed to the public; *e.g.*, where a police officer is promised a reward for doing something within the scope of the officer's duties. In that type of case, the promise is not enforceable.

One of the reasons given for the modern view is that there is less likelihood of duress in the three-party cases than in the two-party cases. Another rationale is that *A* owed no pre-existing duty to *C*.

(2) *A* and *B* enter into a binding bilateral contract to build a golf course. In time, they consider rescinding the agreement as they have the power to do. *C,* who has an interest in seeing the contract performed (he owns nearby land that he thinks will rise in value), promises to pay X dollars to *A* and *B* if they refrain from rescinding their agreement. Because *A* and *B* have the legal power to rescind, refraining from rescinding constitutes detriment for *C*'s promise even under the traditional view.

(3) Suppose *F* promises his son, *S*, that if *S* enters the New York Marathon and finishes the race, *F* will give him $1,000. Suppose further that *S's* uncle later makes him an identical promise. If *S* enters the race and finishes, there would be no pre-existing duty problem. *S* was never under a duty with respect to the race. *S* therefore can claim both rewards.

e. Agreement to Accept Part Payment in Satisfaction of a Debt

Part payment by a debtor of an amount here and now undisputedly due is not detriment to support a promise by the creditor to discharge the entire amount. The same is true even if there is a purported discharge.

Discussion: If the creditor purported to accept part payment in exchange for a discharge, the debtor has incurred no detriment and no discharge takes place. This is another application of the pre-existing duty rule; the debtor, in making the part payment, is only paying part of what is legally owed. This rule is sometimes referred to as the rule of *Foakes v. Beer*. The majority of jurisdictions follow it, but a small minority have rejected the rule. Even in jurisdictions that follow the rule, some do make exceptions. The rule does not apply if, in addition to the part payment, there is a detriment that is in fact bargained for.

Examples: (1) A lease called for the payment of $1,250 per quarter. The lessor subsequently agreed to accept, and has accepted, $875 per quarter. An action brought by the lessor to recover $375 per quarter would be successful since the lessee performed only part of the legal obligation by paying $875. But there are a number of jurisdictions holding that, when a person is entitled to money payable in installments, as for example under a lease, acceptance of a lesser sum in full payment discharges the debtor as to that installment despite the absence of detriment. That is the minority rule. In this illustration, if the lessee received in each case a receipt marked "payment in full" there could be a completed gift if one assumes a donative intent.

There are even cases holding that part payment is sufficient if unforeseen hardships make full payment more burdensome than anticipated. The Restatement (Second) adopts this position.

(2) *D* owes *C* $5,000 here and now undisputedly due. *D* is in financial difficulty, and *C* agrees to accept $2,500 in full payment. *C*'s promise is not enforceable in the majority of jurisdictions; *D* is liable for the full $5,000. The result would be different if *C* bargains for *D* to refrain from bankruptcy proceedings, in which *D* conceivably could obtain a full discharge of the debt.

(3) *D* owes *C* $5,000 here and now undisputedly due. *C* agrees to take $1,000 plus a horse, hawk or robe. The giving of "a horse, hawk or robe" is obviously detriment but the question is whether it is bargained for. If it is merely a token, and therefore not bargained for, it is not consideration according to the Restatement (Second).

7. Accord and Satisfaction

a. Liquidated and Unliquidated Claims

The rule of Foakes v. Beer (discussed supra) applies only to liquidated claims, that is, claims that are undisputed as to their existence and amount. If the claim is unliquidated, it can be discharged by any amount of money the parties can agree on.

Discussion: Unliquidated claims are those about which there is a dispute with the requisite degree of good faith and reasonableness required by the jurisdiction. The dispute could be as to liability, the amount due, or some other question, for example, the method of payment.

b. Definition of "Accord"

An accord is an agreement to give or to accept a stipulated performance ***in the future*** *in satisfaction or discharge of the obligor's existing duty.*

Discussion: The performance of this accord is the satisfaction. If the agreement is not performed, it is an "executory accord." Some special rules that depart from standard contract rules apply. (*See* VII.D.2., *infra.*)

c. Problems Presented

Discussion: When a question of accord and satisfaction is presented, three questions need to be asked.

1) Have the parties reached an accord?

Normally this is done by the process of offer and acceptance. The rule governing an offer of accord is that the offeror must make it clear that the offeror seeks a total discharge. If it is not made clear, any payment made and accepted will be treated as a partial payment.

2) Is the accord supported by consideration?

3) Is there a satisfaction? Stated another way, has the accord been carried out? The emphasis here will be on the majority view. The problems can best be explained through a number of illustrations that involve a check-cashing situation. How the rules of accord and satisfaction apply in a different kind of fact pattern is discussed later. (*See* VII.D.2., *infra.*)

Examples: (1) *D* (debtor) owes *C* (creditor) $1,000 here and now undisputedly due—a liquidated debt. *D* mails a check for $500, conspicuously marked "payment in full," and *C* cashes it.

(a) According to the majority, by using the words "payment in full," *D* has made it clear that *D* seeks a total discharge. Other courts want language that makes it clearer that if *C* accepts the check, *C* is *agreeing* that he or she accepts it as full payment.

(b) Most cases hold that the cashing of the check is an acceptance by *C*. (Many cases hold that the retention of the check for an unreasonable period of time amounts to an acceptance. Typically, however, such holdings involve certified checks or cashiers' checks, which, unlike personal checks, are cash equivalents.) The cashing of the check operates not only as acceptance; it also amounts to the accord's performance.

(c) But the accord and satisfaction is not supported by consideration, because there is no consideration to support *C*'s promise to take (or actual taking of) a lesser sum. Thus, *C* is entitled to recover the additional $500.

(2) Assume the same facts as in example 1, except that there is a good faith dispute. *C* tells *D* that *C* is entitled to $1,000 and *D* tells *C* that *C* is only entitled to $500. *D* sends a check for $750, marked "payment in full" and *C* cashes it. The issues of offer, acceptance and performance are the same as in example 1. Here, however, it is clear that there is consideration to support the accord and satisfaction, because of the existence of the good faith dispute and a settlement which involved the incurrence of detriment by both parties.

Here, *C*'s claim was unliquidated. *C* is not entitled to recover the additional $250 because the accord and satisfaction was supported by consideration.

(3) Assume the same facts as in example 2, except that *D* sends a check for $500, not $750. *C* cashes it. As above, there is offer, acceptance, and performance. But there is some division on the question of consideration. The majority of the courts have held that since the claim is unliquidated, there is consideration to support the accord and satisfaction. The minority view disagrees arguing that *D* is only doing what *D* acknowledges being legally obligated for.

(4) Assume the facts in example 3, except that *C*, before cashing the check, strikes out the words "payment in full" written on the check or notifies *D* that the check is accepted only in part payment. At common law, *C's* action is of no avail—by cashing the check in violation of the conditions upon which it was tendered the creditor is held to assent to its terms. This is analogous to cases where an offeree exercises dominion over unordered goods. (*See* II.D.1.f.2.b.3, *supra*.) Some cases have held that the UCC changed this result. But amendments to Articles 1 and 3 of the UCC have overruled these cases. New York now stands alone in allowing the creditor successfully to cash the check under protest and thereby reserving its rights.

(5) *P* and *D* enter into an agreement where *P* agrees to build a split-level tree house for *D*, and *D* promises to pay $16,000. *P* does the work, and there is a dispute as to whether the work was done properly. The parties settle the controversy at a figure of $15,000. As in example 2, the claim is unliquidated because there is a good faith dispute as to the amount due. The difference is that the accord (offer and acceptance) arose prior to any check being sent. Thus, in this case, the cashing of the check that is sent afterwards involves only the agreement's performance, not its creation.

(6) *P* owned a quantity of apples and requested *D* to obtain a purchaser. *D* did so and collected the price. *P* claims that the service rendered by *D* was gratuitous. *D* claims there was an agreement to pay a 10% commission. After collecting from the buyer, *D* sent a "full-payment" check for the proceeds less 10%. *P* cashed it. This is like example 3, and the expected holding there is that there is a binding accord and satisfaction. But the cases are different, because in example 3 the relationship was debtor-creditor; here the relationship is principal and agent, a fiduciary relationship. The importance of this distinction can be stated in two ways. A debtor who pays with the debtor's money may attach the condition that the check is sent in full payment, but an agent who is accounting for money belonging to the principal may not lawfully impose such a condition. In addition, to allow a

fiduciary to proceed in this way is a "flagrant abuse of the opportunities and powers of a fiduciary position." The apple agent cannot withhold the 10%.

(7) *D,* in exchange for *P*'s promise to do certain work, promised *P* among other things that *P* would receive ½ of the receipts from the products of *D*'s dairy. Prior to this arrangement, *P* had been working for *D* on a daily (per diem) basis and, the sum of $17.15 was concededly due to *P* on this per diem arrangement After a long delay, *P* received $17.15 from *D* and signed and delivered a receipt stating that $17.15 was received "in full payment of all accounts and demands to date." *P* brought an action for payment of amounts due under the second arrangement—the agreement for ½ of receipts. The court assumed that the situation was similar to example 3 above, but held that there was no accord and satisfaction, because payment of a liquidated obligation is not consideration to support the surrender of a second claim that is wholly distinct.

8. UCC Inroads on Pre-Existing Duty Rule and Foakes v. Beer

a. UCC § 2–209(1)

This subsection provides: "An agreement to modify a contract within this article needs no consideration to be binding."

b. UCC §§ 2–209(2) and (3)

The statute says that, for the modification (with or without consideration) to be effective, it must be in writing in two situations. It must be in writing if the agreement as modified is required to be in writing under the UCC statute of frauds, § 2–201. (We shall discuss this in V.C.2.e., *infra*, but the key thrust for our purposes is that contracts of sale for the price of $500 or more require a writing or some other specified kinds of proof). The second situation in which a writing is required is under Subsection (2) which is discussed immediately below.

c. UCC § 2–209(2)

This Subsection provides: "A signed writing which excludes modification or rescission except by a signed writing cannot be otherwise modified or rescinded, but except as between merchants such a requirement on a form supplied by the merchant must be separately signed by the other party."

Discussion: A clause in a signed contract that states that it cannot be modified or rescinded except by a signed writing, contrary to the common law, will be honored. (But *see* **d**, *infra.*) The clause that starts with the words "except as between merchants" describes a situation where a merchant presents a form that contains the provision excluding oral or unsigned modifications or rescissions. A non-merchant who signs the form at the bottom is not bound by this provision unless, in addition, the non-merchant signs the clause separately immediately below the clause or alongside it. If the case involves two merchants, no separate signature is required.

d. UCC § 2–209(4)

This Subsection provides, "Although an attempt at modification or rescission does not satisfy the requirements of Subsection 2 . . . it can operate as a waiver."

Discussion: Thus, even if the modification is not in a signed writing it can still operate as a waiver. The normal rule with respect to a waiver is that a waiver is retractable unless there is an estoppel—justifiable reliance on the promise made in the modification (*See* Subsection 5 immediately below.)

e. UCC § 2–209(5)

This Subsection states: "A party who has made a waiver affecting an executory portion of the contract may retract the waiver by reasonable notification received by the other party that strict performance will be required of any term waived, unless the retraction would be unjust in view of a material change of position in reliance on the waiver."

Discussion: Despite some performance under the modification agreement, a party, as to the unperformed part, may reinstate the original agreement, unless doing so would be unjust in view of a material change of position by the other party as a result of reliance on the modification.

Example: S and *B*, both merchants, entered into a signed contract for the purchase and sale of goods over a two-year period. The contract had a provision excluding modification except by a signed writing. The agreement also contained a provision that merchandise could not be returned for credit unless returned within 5 days of receipt. After one year, the parties orally agreed to drop the 5-day limitation; thereafter *B* received credit for goods returned later than after 5 days of receipt. The contract still had 6 months to go. As to the 6 months that the parties operated under the modification agreement, *S* is estopped from insisting upon the 5-day limit on returns. As to the remaining 6 months, *S* may insist upon the 5-day return period unless there was a material change of position by *B* that would make it unjust not to enforce the modification agreement as to the future.

f. Duress

(*See* IX.A., *infra*)

g. UCC § 1–107

Until recent times, a release was a formal document under seal, and no consideration was necessary. This was unlike other kinds of discharges such as accord and satisfaction that required consideration. Because the UCC gives no effect to the seal, § 1–107 was enacted to substitute for prior law. It provides that "any claim of right arising out of an alleged breach can be discharged in whole or in part by a written waiver or renunciation signed and delivered by the aggrieved party." Under this section, a release that is written, signed, and delivered will be effective to discharge an alleged breach in whole or in part even though the discharge is not supported by consideration. The section applies to all transactions that are covered by the UCC. The revised version of UCC Article 1 continues the rule in § 1–306 but has dropped the delivery requirement.

h. UCC § 3–303

This section, formerly § 3–408, deals with negotiable instruments (commercial paper). It provides that no consideration is necessary for an instrument given in payment of or as security for payment of an antecedent obligation of any kind.

9. Bilateral Contracts

A promise in a bilateral contract is consideration for the counter-promise only if the promised performance would be consideration.

Example: B says to *A*, "if you promise to pay me the $50 that you owe me, I promise to give you a baseball cap worth $10." *A* promises. *B*'s promise is not supported by consideration because (1) the mere utterance of *A*'s promise does not constitute legal detriment, and (2) the performance called for (payment of a debt here and now due) would not be detrimental because *A* would only be doing what *A* is legally obligated to do.

10. Mutuality of Obligation

a. Introduction

The doctrine of mutuality of obligation is commonly expressed as "both parties must be bound or neither is bound" in a bilateral contract. But this phrase is an over-generalization. The case law does not support a doctrine of mutuality of *obligation;* rather it supports mutuality of *consideration*. A bilateral contract is void if there is no mutuality of consideration. In essence, this means if one party to a bilateral contract has not made a promise, the performance of which would be detrimental, neither party is required to perform. If *B*'s promised performance is not consideration, *B* may not enforce *A*'s promise. Conversely, *A* may not enforce *B*'s promise even though *A* has incurred detriment.

Example: B here and now owes *A* $1,000. *A* promises not to collect the debt for six months, and *B* promises to pay the debt without interest at the end of six months. We might conclude that *A*'s promise would not be enforceable because *B* is promising only what *B* is legally obligated to do, but that *B*'s promise would be enforceable because *A*, in promising to forbear, is incurring a detriment which acts as consideration to support *B*'s promise. This conclusion is wrong. Neither promise is enforceable. Under the rule of mutuality of consideration, *A* may not enforce *B*'s promise since both parties must have supplied consideration. Otherwise, the contract is void and neither party is bound.

b. Unilateral Contracts

There is never mutuality of obligation in a unilateral contract because at no point is the offeree bound to perform.

Discussion: In a typical unilateral contract when the offeree performs, and the performance is detrimental, the offeree has provided consideration. The offeree's performance is both the acceptance and the consideration. In a unilateral arrangement, it is immaterial whether the offeror is promising only what he or she is legally obligated to do; the offeror's promise need not be detrimental.

Example: A owes *B* $1,000. *A* promises to pay *B* the $1,000 if *B* paints *A*'s fence. *B* performs. *B* could sue on the original $1,000 debt, or on the unilateral contract, but there would be only one recovery. The fact that *A* is promising to do only what *A* is legally obligated to do is not important because B, in painting the fence, has incurred detriment. The fact that *A*'s promise was not detrimental is immaterial because the doctrine of mutuality of consideration does not apply to unilateral contracts.

c. Voidable and Unenforceable Promises

Discussion: A contract infected with fraud, duress, undue influence, mistake, or lack of capacity is generally voidable. A promise is *unenforceable* when its enforcement is subject to the defense of a statute of frauds or a statute of limitations. Thus, there are a number of contracts where a party cannot be compelled to perform because the contract is voidable or unenforceable. Would that render the contract as *void* under the mutuality doctrine? No, because the real issue is mutuality of consideration, and it is well settled that a voidable or unenforceable promise is consideration. Thus, there is no problem in these situations with the contract's validity.

Example: *A*, a minor, enters into a contract with *B*, an adult. *A* has the power to avoid the contract because of infancy. But even though *A*'s promise is voidable, it nevertheless is consideration for *B*'s promise and there is no mutuality problem. If *A*'s promise were not deemed to be consideration, minors would lose the right to enforce contracts.

d. Illusory Promises

An illusory promise is an expression cloaked in promissory terms but which upon closer examination, reveals that the promisor has made no commitment.

Discussion: Where the promise of one of the parties is illusory, a mutuality of consideration problem exists. The modern tendency is against finding a promise to be illusory and, in general, against defeating contracts on the technical grounds of lack of mutuality. One method of circumventing the illusory promise problem is to interpolate into an agreement the requirements of good faith and reasonableness. Consequently, the nature of the performance is not left to the promisor's whim and caprice, which means it is not illusory.

Example: *A* makes a promise "to spend such time as I personally see fit in developing the business." Under the older view, this promise would be called illusory. Under the modern approach, a court would hold that *A* must exercise good faith in determining the time to be spent developing the business. This puts a brake on *A's* unfettered discretion. Thus, the promise is not illusory.

e. Termination Clauses

Discussion: The new approaches towards the illusory promise problem are also applied to contracts containing a provision permitting one or both parties to terminate. Such contracts are generally treated as involving alternative performances. The usual rule is that in order to have consideration each alternative must be detrimental (*see* examples, *infra*). UCC § 2–309(3) speaks to the issue and states: "Termination of a contract by one party except on the happening of an agreed event requires that reasonable notification be received by the other party and an agreement dispensing with notification is invalid if its operation would be unconscionable." (If the term is unconscionable, it should be stricken and a reasonable time substituted.) But unlike UCC § 2–302, which provides that unconscionability must be judged as of the time of the making of the contract, unconscionability under § 2–309 should be judged at the time of termination, according to a UCC comment and the plain meaning of the provision. Also, the exercise of the power of termination is subject to the rule of good faith inherent in every contract.

Examples: (1) *A* agrees to work as a computer programmer for one year, and *B* promises to pay a set salary. The contract provides that *B* has the power to terminate the agreement by giving 30 days notice. *B* has promised alternative performances—to pay wages for at least 30 days and up to one year. Because both alternatives are detrimental, and the exchange element is satisfied, there is no consideration problem. If UCC § 2–309(2) were applicable, there might be a question of unconscionability. But the section is not applicable because the case does not involve a sale of goods.

(2) In example 1, if *B* reserved the right to terminate simply by giving notice at any time, the older cases held that giving notice at any time is not detrimental. This is because *B*'s performance is at *B*'s unfettered discretion and therefore one of *B*'s alternative performances does not constitute consideration. But later decisions lean to the view that each alternative is detrimental because even the act of giving notice is detrimental. The question that would remain is whether notice is a bargained-for alternative, but this question seems to be ignored in an effort to make the agreement enforceable. Under the UCC, which is not applicable here, reasonable notice would ordinarily be required.

(3) In example 1, above, if *B* reserved the right to terminate the agreement without notice at any time, the older cases agree that the promise is illusory. According to the UCC, which is not

applicable, the issue is unconscionability. Some of the modern cases, irrespective of the UCC, have placed the case on a different footing by a process of interpretation. These cases have ignored the words "at any time" and interpolated words requiring notice of termination within a reasonable time after the contract's formation. Once this is done, the consideration problem disappears.

(4) In example 1, above, assume *B* reserved the power to terminate at any time, and nothing is said with respect to notice. Some courts have interpreted the contract as requiring notice, and others have reached the opposite conclusion. Once this problem of interpretation is resolved, the fact pattern fits either example 2 or 3 above. The UCC, which is not applicable, states specifically that in this case reasonable notice is required. Thus, under the modern view, one can usually conclude that a promise is not rendered insufficient as consideration if the promisor retains a power of termination.

f. Conditional Promises

A conditional promise is not illusory if the happening of the condition is outside the promisor's control and unfettered discretion. At times, an illusory promise problem is avoided by implying a promise that limits the promisor's control or discretion.

Examples: (1) *A* promises to pay *B* $500 "if I feel like it." The promise is illusory.

(2) *A* promises to perform "if war does not break out." The promise is not illusory because the condition is outside the promisor's control.

(3) *A* promises to buy real property "if *A* is able to obtain a mortgage loan." The promise seems illusory because *A* has not expressly promised to seek a loan. But it is routinely held that the buyer has made an implied promise to use reasonable efforts to bring about the condition. Thus, the conditional promise is not illusory.

(4) *Lucy* promised to give *Wood* an exclusive agency and *Wood* promised to pay *Lucy* one-half of the profits. *Wood* already had an organization in place that was adapted to carrying out the agency. *Wood*'s promise would be illusory if *Wood* were not required to do anything to bring about profits. A promise by *Wood* to use reasonable efforts was inferred. The rule is codified in UCC § 2–306(2). The UCC provides: "A lawful agreement by either the seller or the buyer for exclusive dealing in the kind of goods concerned imposes unless otherwise agreed an obligation by the seller to use best efforts to supply the goods and by the buyer to use best efforts to promote their sale."

g. Aleatory Promises

An aleatory promise is conditional on the happening of a fortuitous event or an event supposed by the parties to be fortuitous. Like other conditional promises, an aleatory promise is not illusory, because the condition is based upon an event that is wholly or partly outside of either party's control.

Examples: (1) In consideration of a payment of $1,000, *A* makes a promise to repay $10,000 "if I recover my gold mine." The promise is aleatory because it is conditional on a fortuitous event and is not illusory.

(2) *F* has two sons, *A* and *B*. *A* says to *B*, "You know how eccentric our father is. Let us agree that no matter what his Will contains, we will divide equally whatever he leaves to either of us." *B* agrees. *F's* Will left all of his assets to *A*. Although *B* incurred no actual detriment, *B* may enforce *A's* promise because *A* bargained against the possibility that *B* would be favored. Because the parties believed that the event was fortuitous, the promise is binding even if the Will in favor of *A* had already been drawn.

h. Agreements Allowing a Party to Supply a Material Term

If a bilateral agreement permits a party to supply a material term, that party's promise, at earlier common law, was deemed to be illusory and the bilateral agreement void under the mutuality doctrine. Modern cases focus on the duty to exercise good faith and have concluded that the power to modify a term is not fatal to the contract. The UCC, with its insistence on good faith, is clearly on the side of the modern cases. Thus, for example, a term permitting a seller to change prices from time to time to reflect market conditions is permissible.

i. A Void Contract Is Not Necessarily a Nullity

Although a void contract starts out as a nullity, performance may breathe life into it.

Discussion: If there is performance under a void bilateral contract, courts treat the promises as if they were offers to unilateral contracts. The party who performed is treated as an offeree. Two requirements are essential for the application of this doctrine of forging a good unilateral contract from a bad bilateral. 1) All of the requisites of the law of offer and acceptance must be fulfilled. 2) The performance by the party seeking to enforce the contract must have been detrimental. The same approach can be applied to a series of contracts. That is, a series of good unilateral contracts can be forged out of a bad bilateral contract.

Examples: (1) *D* had an undisputed obligation to pay *C* a liquidated debt. The parties agreed that *C* would forbear from suing on the obligation for six months, and *D* promised to pay the debt at the end of six months without interest. *C* did forbear for six months and then brought an action, not on the original debt, but on *D's* promise to pay the debt. It is clear that the agreement was void for want of mutuality of consideration, since *D* had a pre-existing duty to pay. But it is equally clear that the performance engages the doctrine of forging a good unilateral contract out of a bad bilateral contract.

(2) In a sale of goods case, if the parties fail to agree on the quality of the goods, but the seller sends a particular quality that the buyer accepts, a good unilateral contract has been forged out of a bad bilateral contract. Here, the forging doctrine is a cure for indefiniteness.

(3) *D* agreed to appoint *P* as exclusive agent within a certain territory in exchange for *P*'s promise to develop a market for *D*'s products. *P* was to be paid a commission for each sale made. No duration was stated. The court concluded the arrangement was indefinite and therefore void. Because *P* had performed under the agreement, *P* was entitled to be paid a commission for all sales *P* made, thus forging a series of good unilateral contracts out of a bad bilateral contract. The more recent cases would conclude that a valid bilateral contract existed at the outset. The arrangement would last for a reasonable time.

11. Requirements and Output Contracts

a. Introduction

Scope: This topic involves contracts where the quantity term is measured by the buyer's requirements (requirements contract) or seller's output (output contract). Because the rules relating to output and requirements contracts are basically the same, as a matter of convenience, emphasis will be on requirements contracts.

b. Validity of Requirements Contracts

At one time, requirements contracts were not enforced. They were deemed illusory because the buyer could refrain from having requirements. Later, they were generally upheld upon the theory that consideration could be found in the surrender of the buyer's privilege to buy elsewhere. But there was a view that refused to enforce the agreement when the buyer was entering into a new business or was an intermediary, apparently because such businesses had no predictable needs. Under modern law and UCC § 2–306, requirements and output contracts are clearly valid even for a new business or an intermediary.

c. UCC § 2–306

"A term which measures the quantity by the output of the seller or the requirements of the buyer means such actual output or requirements as may occur in good faith except that no quantity unreasonably disproportionate to any stated estimate or in the absence of a stated estimate to any normal or otherwise comparable prior output or requirements may be tendered or demanded."

d. How Much Is a Requirements Buyer Entitled to Demand?

Under the UCC, the buyer is entitled to good faith requirements. But two limitations are placed on the rule of good faith. (1) If there is a stated estimate, the buyer is not entitled to a quantity that's excessively and unreasonably *more* than the estimate. (2) If there is no estimate or maximum stated in the contract, the buyer may demand only "any normal or otherwise comparable prior requirements." In essence, this means that a buyer cannot demand an amount disproportionately more than the quantity reasonably foreseeable at the time of contracting.

e. May a Requirements Buyer Diminish or Terminate Requirements?

Discussion: Essentially the question here is whether a requirements buyer may go out of business and have no requirements or change the method of doing business so that the requirements are fewer or even zero. Under the UCC, the buyer may go out of business or change business methods if this is done in good faith. This is so even if the quantities are disproportionately fewer than normal prior requirements or stated estimates. There is some conflict as to whether a buyer acts in good faith if the shutdown is to curtail losses. Comment 2 to § 2–306 seems to indicate that the buyer is not free to do so, but some cases indicate that the buyer may do so if the losses are "more than trivial."

f. Does a Requirements Buyer Have a Duty to Promote the Goods?

Confusion Reigns: UCC § 2–306(2) states that, in an exclusive dealing contract, the buyer has the obligation "to use the best efforts to promote" the sale of the goods. A requirements contract is ordinarily an exclusive dealing contract. Is the requirements buyer obliged to promote the sale of goods? The question arises only if the goods are purchased for resale. But Comment 5 to § 2–306 suggests that this duty exists only if the buyer is an agent with an "exclusive territory."

g. Can a Requirements Contract Be Non-Exclusive?

UCC § 2–306 has also been applied to a non-exclusive contract.

Example: As part of a complex commercial relationship, *D* had contracted with *P* to market computer products that *P* had developed. The contract lacked a quantity term. Also, it did not provide for exclusivity on either side; both parties were free to contract with other companies. Nevertheless, the court held the contract to be enforceable as a "non-exclusive requirements contract." The probable reason for this holding is that otherwise the agreement, lacking a quantity term, would have been too indefinite, and the reasonable expectations of the parties would have been dashed.

12. Must All of the Consideration Be Valid?

All of the consideration need not be valid.

Example: Uncle tells nephew that, in exchange for the nephew's promise to refrain for smoking for one year, "in consideration of your past good conduct and in consideration of your promise to refrain from smoking for one more year, I will pay you $5,000." The fact that part of the recited consideration is past does not prevent the valid part from serving as consideration.

13. Consideration and Multiple Promisors

One consideration will also support the promises of more than one promisor.

Example: Landlord promises to lease space in exchange for *X* Corporation's promise to pay rent and the promise of *X's* principal shareholder to guaranty payment of the rent. The promises of both *X* and of the principal shareholder are binding.

14. Conjunctive and Alternative Promises

a. Conjunctive Promises

If one of the conjunctive promises is consideration, it is sufficient to support a counter-promise.

Example: B says to A, "I will paint your fence and pay you the liquidated sum of $50 that I owe you if you promise to give me your motorcycle." *A* accepts the offer. Although, in promising to pay the debt, *B* is only promising to perform a legal obligation, *B's* promise to paint is detrimental. Therefore, *B* is supplying consideration for *A*'s counter-promise. For *B* to recover, *B* must paint and pay the debt. Even though the payment is not consideration, it is still a condition that must be performed.

b. Alternative Promises

1) Where the Promisor Has the Choice of Alternatives

We have already seen that where the choice of alternatives is in the promisor, the rule is that each alternative promise must be detrimental. The Restatement (Second) says that the rule does not apply if there is a substantial possibility that events may eliminate the alternative that is not detrimental before the promisor makes a choice.

Example: *A* promises to paint for *B*. In exchange, *B* promises to do certain masonry work for *A*, or to pay *A* the liquidated debt of $500 that *B* owes *A*. *B* has made alternative promises. Because one of the alternative promises is not detrimental (paying the debt), *B*'s promises are not consideration for *A*'s promise. Therefore, under the mutuality doctrine there is no contract.

2) Where the Promisee Has the Choice of Alternatives

If the promisee has the choice of alternatives, the alternative promises supply consideration if any of the alternatives is detrimental.

C. Moral Obligation

1. Introduction

Subject to several exceptions, a promise made in recognition of a prior moral or legal obligation is not enforceable.

Scope: This section addresses promises that are enforceable despite the absence of consideration or injurious reliance. The discussion centers on two kinds of promises 1) promises made because the promisor is under a prior legal obligation to the promisee, and 2) promises made because the promisor has received a benefit that places the promisor under a moral obligation to the promisee. The promise relates to the fulfillment of the antecedent legal or moral obligation.

In these cases, consideration in the sense of a bargained-for exchange is absent because the promise is based solely upon past events and no detriment was incurred in exchange to support the promise. Nevertheless, there are a number of exceptions to the general rule of non-enforcement. For the most part, the exceptions are explained not by logic but by history.

2. Exceptions

a. Promises to Pay a Liquidated Debt

At early common law, a promise to pay an existing debt was enforceable despite the fact that the consideration for the promise was past. Today, most authorities agree that the promise is enforceable provided it is co-extensive with the pre-existing liquidated debt. "Co-extensive" means substantially the same amount. The continued existence of the rule is academic if suit may still be brought on the original claim. The effect that the promise would have on the statute of limitations is discussed below. The UCC makes it clear that the promise is enforceable if the promise is made in an instrument, such as a note or a check governed by Article 3 of the Code. This Article 3 rule is not merely academic, because several substantive and procedural advantages accrue to the holder of a negotiable note, check, or other negotiable instrument that other creditors do not enjoy.

Example: C lends *D* $1,000 which is to be repaid by *D* on January 2, 2003. *D* fails to repay but again promises to repay on March 1, 2009. There is no consideration to support the March promise. However, the promise is enforceable. *C* may prefer to sue on the March promise because it was made in the presence of many reliable witnesses, or was made in writing.

If the March 1 promise was in the form of a negotiable promissory note it would be enforceable under Article 3 of the UCC and would be given the special substantive and procedural advantages given to negotiable instruments.

b. Promises to Pay Fixed Amounts for Services Previously Requested

A promise to pay a fixed amount for an unliquidated debt is enforceable without fresh consideration or even mutual assent.

Discussion and Example: *A* requests *B* to perform services for *A*. *B* performs. Since there was no agreed upon price prior to performance, *A* is liable for the reasonable value of the services rendered. If *A* offers to pay a fixed amount in discharge of the obligation, one would think that under general contract principles that the promise would be unenforceable unless it is accepted by *B*. In addition, without *B*'s acceptance there is no consideration for *A*'s promise. Nevertheless, for reasons rooted in history, it is generally held that the promise is enforceable without new consideration and without mutual assent. The promise is enforced only to the extent that it is not grossly disproportionate to the value of the services.

However, if the services were rendered without expectation of payment, and therefore created no legal obligation, the promise is not enforceable.

c. Promises to Pay a Fixed Amount for Services Not Requested

1) Where Promisee Is Entitled to a Quasi-Contractual Recovery

If *B* confers a benefit on *A* without *A's* request, *B* is entitled to a quasi-contractual recovery in limited situations, *e.g.*, furnishing emergency medical care to *A's* minor child. If *A* subsequently promises to pay a fixed amount, the rule stated above with respect unliquidated debts applies.

2) Where Promisee Is Not Entitled to a Quasi-Contractual Recovery

Under the majority rule, where the promisee is not entitled to quasi-contractual relief, a promise to pay for a benefit conferred without request is not enforceable. There is a contrary minority view which has been adopted by the Restatement (Second). The Restatement (Second) states that the promise is enforceable if the promisor has received an economic benefit and only "to the extent necessary to prevent injustice." Also, there will be no recovery, even under the minority view, if the benefit was conferred as a gift or under a contract. Recovery is limited to the extent of the benefit received by the promisor.

Examples: (1) *D*'s adult son, *S*, falls ill while he is away from home. Without any request from *D*, *B* takes care of *S*. Later, *D* promised to reimburse *B* for the expenses of *S*'s care. Under the majority view, it is clear that *D*'s promise is not enforceable. Nor is it enforceable under the minority view, because *D* did not receive any economic benefit. However, *B* could recover under a New York statute that requires that the promise be made in a writing that describes the nature of the benefit or detriment.

(2) *P* is crippled as a result of saving *D*'s life. In gratitude, *D* promises to send *P* $500 a week for the rest of *P*'s life. *D* kept the promise until his death. The estate refused to continue

the payments. Under the view of the Restatement the promise is enforceable because *D* had received a material benefit. Under the classical view, the promise is not binding.

d. Promises to Pay Debts Discharged or Rendered Unenforceable by Operation of Law

If a claim is discharged or rendered unenforceable by operation of law, a subsequent promise to pay that obligation is enforceable despite the absence of consideration. The new promise that revives a debt discharged by the statute of limitations must be made by the debtor or the debtor's agent to the creditor or the creditor's agent.

1) Discharge in Bankruptcy

At one time, a promise to pay a debt discharged in bankruptcy was enforceable despite the absence of consideration for the promise. The federal Bankruptcy Act, however, has made it impossible to make a binding promise to pay a debt discharged or to be discharged in bankruptcy, except those made in the bankruptcy proceeding itself.

2) Statute of Limitations

A promise to pay all or part of any prior contractual or quasi-contractual obligation for the payment of money, whether liquidated or not, causes the statute of limitations to run anew.

Discussion: An acknowledgment of the obligation is treated as an implied promise to pay unless there is an indication of a contrary intention. In most states the promise or acknowledgment must be in writing. A voluntary part payment of principal or interest or the giving of collateral may have the same effect as an acknowledgment and be treated as the equivalent of a writing.

The action is limited by the terms of the new promise, including any conditions therein. A promise not to plead the statute of limitations generally has the same effect as a promise to pay the debt. But in most jurisdictions, if the promise is made in the original contract or before maturity of the debt, it is void as contrary to public policy. The UCC, like most common law decisions, invalidates attempts to provide in a contract for a longer period of limitations than provided for by statute.

The general rule applies after maturity of the debt, whether the new promise is made before or after the statute of limitations has run out.

The rule does not apply to a promise to pay damages for breach of contract or for a tort. The rule is limited to debts.

Examples: (1) *A* lends *B* $1,000 on January 2, 1999, the money to be repaid on January 2, 2000. No payment is made. On January 2, 2003, *B* promises to pay. Assume a six-year statute of limitations. The six-year statute of limitations would start running anew on January 2, 2003, so that the debt would be barred in 2009. If instead, in 2007, after the statute had run, *B* promised to pay, the statute would start to run again so that the statute would expire in 2013.

(2) *D* owes *C* $10,000, but the debt is barred by the statute of limitations. *D* acknowledges the debt in writing but adds, "I will never pay it." Although there is an acknowledgment of the debt and this is normally sufficient, the quoted language manifests an intention not to pay and therefore the promise that normally would be implied from an acknowledgment is not implied.

(3) *D* owes *C* $10,000, but the debt is barred by the statute of limitations. *D* promises to pay "when I am able." Because *C* is limited by the promise, *C* may not bring an action until *D* is able to pay.

(4) *D*, a painter, breached a bilateral contract to paint *P's* house. Ten years later, after the statute of limitations on an action for breach of contract has run out, *D* promises (without new consideration) to pay *P's* damages. *P* may not recover since *D's* promise to pay damages for breach of contract (except to pay a debt) has no effect on the statute of limitations.

e. Promises to Perform a Voidable Duty

A promise to perform a voidable duty is enforceable despite the absence of consideration as long as the new promise itself does not suffer from an infirmity that would in turn make it voidable.

Discussion: A party whose promise is voidable may either avoid the contract or ratify it. An effective ratification terminates the right to avoid the contract. Void contracts generally cannot be ratified.

Examples: (1) *A* is induced by fraud to promise to pay $100,000 in exchange for Greenacre. As a result of the fraud the promise is voidable. Upon discovering the fraud, *A* again promises to pay $100,000 for the property. The promise is enforceable without consideration because the party who has a right to avoid the contract may also elect to continue it. The result would be different if *A* did not know of the fraud at the time *A* made a new promise to purchase.

(2) *A*, a minor, enters into a contract that is voidable because of infancy. Before reaching majority, *A* again promises to perform the contract. The promise to ratify the agreement is voidable, because *A* is still an infant. *A* can still avoid the promise.

f. Statutes of Frauds

A contract within a statute of frauds not evidenced by a writing is unenforceable, but a sufficient memorandum made at any time makes the original contract enforceable. If a party who has the defense of the statute of frauds subsequently orally promises to perform, failing to satisfy the statute of frauds, two problems arise. One problem relates to consideration, and the other involves the statute of frauds itself. Most cases hold that consideration is not a problem and make an analogy to **e.** above. As to the statute of frauds, it is generally held that the subsequent oral promise is not enforceable because to enforce it would defeat the policy of the statute. However, a written promise has at times been enforced even though it is in a writing that does not state the terms sufficiently to satisfy the statute of frauds.

Example: In a jurisdiction that includes a promise to pay a commission to a real estate broker within the statute of frauds, *A*, a real estate broker, without any written agreement, procures *P*, a purchaser for *B*'s land. *P* enters into a signed written contract of sale with *B*. In that instrument, *B* promises to pay *A* $2,000 for services rendered. Despite consideration doctrine and the statute of frauds, there are cases holding that the promise is enforceable, even if the writing does not state the terms sufficiently to satisfy the statute of frauds.

g. Miscellaneous Promises Supported by Antecedent Events

These include (a) a subsequent promise by a surety who has been discharged on technical grounds; (b) a promise to repay sums collected by the force of an erroneous but valid judgment; (c) a promise to pay for benefits received under an illegal bargain where the illegality does not involve moral turpitude.

h. To Whom the Promise Must Be Made

A new promise to pay an antecedent obligation, to be enforceable, must be made to an obligee or the obligee's agent. Under a small minority view, an admission or promise to any third person is sufficient. Even under the majority view, the promise to any third person is enforceable, if it can be anticipated that this person will communicate the promise to the obligee.

D. Promissory Estoppel

1. Introduction

A promise that foreseeably induces substantial and definite acts of injurious reliance by the promisee or a third party is enforceable.

Discussion: This statement identifies a number of elements required by the doctrine.

(1) A promise is required. Thus, an estimate or a statement of intention is not sufficient.

(2) The reliance must be of a kind that the promisor could definitely have expected; that is, it must be foreseeable and reasonable. The same thought could be expressed by saying that the promisee must justifiably rely upon the promise.

(3) The reliance must be of a substantial character and must be *injurious* rather than detrimental in the consideration sense.

(4) The promise will not be enforced unless injustice can be avoided only by the promise's enforcement. Generally, the remedy is the same

as for breach of any other kind of contract, but enforcement may be limited to reliance losses if justice so indicates.

We saw in the consideration discussion that a donative promise is not supported by consideration even though the promisee relied upon it. Cases that rigidly applied this approach created injustices in the application of contract law; to rectify these injustices, promissory estoppel has been created as a separate and specific doctrine. Note, however, that not all gift promises will be enforced even where the promisee has relied on them.

Example: Uncle (*U*) promises Junior (*J*), $20,000 to be given to him on his 21st birthday. On his 21st birthday, *J* buys a used sports car for $20,000, mostly on credit. *U* telephones *J* wishing him a happy birthday, and is appalled to learn that *J* had splurged because of *U*'s promised gift. *U* refuses to make the gift. *J* sues. Williston would dismiss *J's* lawsuit. He would require that the promisor be able to foresee the nature of the definite and substantial action that the promisee would take. Corbin would probably make the foreseeability of *J's* conduct a jury question. He would not require that the promisor be able to foresee the precise nature of the promisee's action in reliance.

2. The Roots of Promissory Estoppel

The roots of promissory estoppel can be found in a number of cases that enforced promises not supported by consideration on various theories but had the common element of injurious reliance. In these cases, the courts did not use the term "promissory estoppel," but either stretched the doctrine of consideration or formulated narrow specialized doctrines. The cases for the most part involved family promises, promises to make gifts of land, gratuitous agencies and bailments, charitable subscriptions, and marriage settlements. These precedents are still good law, whether treated as applications of specialized doctrines or as promissory estoppel exemplars.

Examples: (1) *Estoppel in pais. A* gave his granddaughter a promissory note indicating that it was for the purpose of freeing her from the necessity of working. It was clear that he was not requesting that she cease work in exchange for the note. There was no consideration, because *A* made a gift promise. He did not bargain for anything. Enforcing the note, the court stated that it was applying the doctrine of "estoppel *in pais*," but really was creating a new doctrine. Estoppel *in pais* had been based upon misrepresentations of fact, not upon breaches of promise.

(2) *Intra-family promises. U* promised *P*, his nephew, that if *P* would take a trip to Europe he would reimburse *P*'s expenses. The nephew made the trip. The court held that *U*'s promise was supported by consideration. Although it is true that *P* incurred detriment, it is not likely that the detriment was bargained-for in exchange for the promise.

(3) *Equity rule for gifts of land. A* promises to make a gift of land to *B*, his son-in-law. *B*, with knowledge and assent of *A*, takes possession of the land and makes improvements. *B* is entitled to specific performance or other equitable remedies. The modern basis of the action is promissory estoppel.

(4) *Old rule of bailee's misfeasance as consideration. A,* a carter, agreed with *B* to transport a keg of brandy free of charge. The keg of brandy was damaged by the carter's negligence. An action lies for the breach of the implied promise by *A* to use due care—misfeasance. Although there is in reality no consideration for *A*'s promise as it was gratuitous, *B* relied on the promise and incurred injury. If *A* had refused or neglected to take possession of the keg, *A* would not be liable for the nonfeasance. The distinction made was between misfeasance and nonfeasance. In other words, if the gratuitous bailee (promisor) takes possession of the goods and fails to carry out the implied promise to use requisite care, liability exists. If, however, the promisor fails to take possession, traditionally there is no liability for subsequent damage to the keg because there is only nonfeasance. The modern approach is to find promissory estoppel in both cases.

(5) *Old rule of agent's misfeasance. Mrs. Wilson* told *B,* an agent of the life insurance company that insured her husband's life, that she did not have ready cash to pay a particular premium, but she would have it in the summer, as she ran a seasonal business. *B* assured *Mrs. Wilson* that the payment would be taken care of. In reliance on *B*'s promise, *Mrs. Wilson* did not obtain a loan to pay the premium. The insurance policy lapsed and the husband died. The doctrine of promissory estoppel was applied to this gratuitous agency situation. Notice that in this situation nonfeasance is involved. Nevertheless, *B's* promise is enforced. Consistent with the approach of both Restatements, courts have abandoned the distinction between nonfeasance and misfeasance in such cases. However, the older cases, based upon the distinction between misfeasance and nonfeasance, refused to enforce such a promise. If *B* attempted to take care of the payment and did it negligently, this would have amounted to misfeasance and a basis for liability. (*See* example 4 *supra.*)

(6) *Charitable subscriptions. A* promises to give *B,* a college, $50,000 in four annual installments in connection with *B*'s general fund-raising campaign. Two annual installments are paid before *A* dies. There is no consideration to support *A*'s promise, because *A* did not bargain for anything. Nor is *B* able to show that there was injurious reliance on *A*'s promise. But *A*'s promise has been enforced under a wide variety of theories including promissory estoppel. The Restatement (Second) recognizing the theoretical problem, states that charitable subscriptions are enforceable for public policy reasons despite the absence of either consideration or injurious reliance.

(7) *Marriage settlements. A* and *B* are engaged to be married. In some jurisdictions an engagement to marry is a binding contract. In contemplation of the marriage, *F, B*'s Father, and *A* enter into a formal agreement in which *F* promises to make certain payments to *A* "in consideration of the marriage." The marriage occurs. If *A,* in marrying, is doing something that he is not legally obligated to do, there is consideration. If *A* is legally bound to marry *B,* then the only theory of recovery is promissory estoppel. But if the engaged couple would have married regardless of *F*'s promise, *A* would not be able to show injurious reliance. Because of the policy in favor of marriage

settlements, the Restatement (Second) provides that such promises are enforceable "without proof that the promise induced action or forbearance."

3. Present Approach to a Gift Promise

Initially the courts used promissory estoppel as a substitute for consideration mostly in cases of gift promises, mainly the kinds of cases listed in 2 above. There is now a trend toward using promissory estoppel in just about any gift promise case where all of the necessary elements are present. But again, note that to enforce charitable subscriptions or marriage settlements under promissory estoppel, reliance is not necessary.

4. Doctrine Not Limited to Donative Promises

Discussion: Initially there was some authority that promissory estoppel should be limited to donative promises and should not be applied to bargain transactions. However, the trend today is in the other direction. Thus, the doctrine has been used:

1) to make an offer irrevocable;

2) to enforce a promise that is part of an otherwise unenforceable or defective contract; and

3) to enforce a promise made during the course of preliminary negotiations.

Examples: (1) *A,* a subcontractor, submits a bid (offer) to *B,* a general contractor, who uses the bid in calculating *B*'s bid on a large construction project. *A* attempts to withdraw the offer prior to acceptance by *B*. Under the traditional rules of offer and acceptance, the revocation would be effective. But under the doctrine of promissory estoppel, the offer is irrevocable, *B* justifiably relied on *A*'s offer. It is irrevocable until *B* learns that it has been awarded the contract and has a reasonable opportunity to notify *A* that *A*'s offer has been accepted. (*B* cannot reopen the bargaining with *A* or others and claim a continuing power to accept the original offer.)

Comment: It is unusual to invoke promissory estoppel in the context of an offer to a bilateral contract. Ordinarily, the offeree would not be justified in relying on the offer. Normally, the offeree must accept the offer prior to relying. And again, note that the reliance must be justifiable. Reliance on an estimate or on a mistaken bid so palpably low as to indicate a mistake would not be justifiable.

(2) *B* sent a letter to *S* stating that *B* would buy poultry raised by *S* at prevailing market prices. Upon receiving the letter *S* purchased and began raising 7,000 chicks for future delivery. At this point, *B* attempted to withdraw the offer. Under the Restatement (Second) and some decisions, the offer is made irrevocable under the doctrine of promissory estoppel even though the acts performed are merely acts of preparation. Applying the notion of flexibility of remedy, damages might be limited to reliance damages.

(3) *A* has been employed by *B* for 40 years. In consideration of *A*'s previous service, *B* promises to pay *A* $200 per month when *A* retires.

In reliance on the promise *A* retires and forbears to work elsewhere for several years. *B* pays the pension during this time and then repudiates. Because past consideration is not consideration, *B's* promise is not binding. The promise, however, is enforceable under the doctrine of promissory estoppel because of *A*'s injurious reliance on the promise. Instead of continuing to work or seeking other employment, *A* retired in reliance on the pension.

(4) *P* owned a lot and desired to construct a commercial building there. *P* entered into an agreement with *D* under which *D* was to obtain a loan in the sum of $70,000 for *P* from a third party or provide it himself. *D* in turn was to be paid $5,000 plus 5% of the rent of tenants procured by *D*. After the agreement was signed, *D* assured *P* that the money would be available and urged *P* to demolish the buildings presently on the site. *P* complied. But when the loan arrangement was held to be too vague and indefinite to be enforceable, the doctrine of promissory estoppel was applied because of *P*'s injurious reliance. Damages were limited to a reliance measure.

(5) *A* was the lessee of an apartment house under a 99-year lease given by *B* for a rent of $100,000 per year. Because of war conditions, many of the apartments became vacant. To enable *A* to stay in business, *B* agreed to reduce the rent to $50,000. The reduced rent was paid for five years. When the war was over and the apartments were finally fully rented, *B* demanded that the rent be restored to $100,000, and that *A* pay the balance, $50,000 per year, for the five wartime years. Under the traditional rule, the modification was void for lack of consideration. But it was enforced for the five-year period because of injurious reliance by *A*. As to the future, *B* was allowed to reinstate the full rent. There was injurious reliance because *A* lost a large amount of money by staying in business and should not be punished further.

(6) *A* was assured by *B* that if *A* took certain steps and raised $18,000 worth of capital, *B* would grant *A* a supermarket franchise. In compliance with the recommendation of *B, A* sold a bakery, purchased a grocery to gain experience and resold it, acquired an option on land for building a franchised outlet and moved nearer to where the franchise was to be. *A* raised the necessary capital by borrowing from a relative. At first, *B* approved this plan, but later withdrew approval of this method of financing and demanded that *A* procure from the relative a statement that the loan was a gift. *A* refused and sued. At the time of the rupture the parties had not come to any agreement as to size, cost, design, layout or the terms of the lease. The agreement was not only too vague and indefinite to be enforced, but the parties did not intend to be bound until a later date; up to the point of the rupture there had been nothing but preliminary negotiations. Nevertheless, under the theory of promissory estoppel, *A* was permitted to recover the amounts expended in reliance upon the negotiations.

(7) The parties were negotiating for a sale of *D's* business to *P*. Although agreement had been reached on most of the contract's important terms, *D* demanded a dramatic improvement in the terms

at a time when the market for *D's* product had abruptly improved. Although their preliminary agreement referred to the possibility of the failure of negotiations, certain events had occurred subsequently; *P* had occupied offices in *D's* premises and *D* had introduced *P's* principals to others as the owners of the business. The court held that there was no contract but found that *D* had breached an implied obligation to negotiate in good faith; thus, the court entered a judgment for *P's* reliance damages.

5. Approach to a Problem

Before reaching for the doctrine of promissory estoppel, one should determine whether a conventional contract argument exists. If the issue is consideration, and there is consideration, the applicability of promissory estoppel will ordinarily be an academic question. But if there is no consideration, or if its existence is doubtful under some or all views, the promissory estoppel approach should be considered. The question then is, does the fact pattern present all of the elements required for the doctrine of promissory estoppel? The only remaining question is does that jurisdiction accept promissory estoppel in the particular kind of case? As we have seen, the tendency is to employ it in any case to which the elements are present because the doctrine is "an attempt by the court to keep remedies abreast of increased moral consciousness of honesty and fair representations in all business dealings. . . ."

If the issue is some alleged defect in the contract other than an alleged lack of consideration—indefiniteness, lack of intent to be bound, lack of a required writing, etc.—one should first search out more traditional doctrines to salvage the contract before attempting to apply the doctrine of promissory estoppel.

E. Sealed Instruments

At common law, any promise contained in a delivered sealed instrument was held to be enforceable despite the absence of consideration. The rule still holds true in some jurisdictions. However, many states have enacted statutes that either abolish the binding effect of a seal or provide that a seal raises a presumption of consideration. The presumption is refutable, but the burden of proof on the issue of the absence of consideration is on the promisor. The UCC eliminates the effect of a seal in sales transactions.

Review Questions (*Answers in Appendix A*)

We suggest you first review HOW TO STUDY and EXAMINATION in the *Perspective* section, *supra*.

1. T or F The putative father of an illegitimate child promised the mother that if she named the child Wallace if it were a boy or include the name Wallace if it were a girl, he would pay $100 per week for the support of the child until the child reached the age of 21. The child was so named. The mother has a cause of action if the putative father fails to make the payments.

2. T or F *D* promised *P* that if *P* delivered specified merchandise to *D's* brother, *D* would pay for items previously delivered and for items to be delivered. *P* performed. *P* is not entitled to enforce the promise to pay for the past deliveries.

3. T or F *D* was the legal guardian of *P*, a 12-year-old boy. *P* left the home of *D* and went to live with a relative. *D* promised *P* that if *P* would return and live with him, *D* would not charge *P* board and would send him to school without charge. (Under the law of Guardian and Ward, the Ward is liable to the Guardian for these expenses.) *P* returned. *P* is entitled to enforce *D*'s promise.

4. T or F *P* and *D* entered into a contract for *P* to do certain work in exchange for *D*'s payment of $8,000. The first payment of $5,000 was to be made by the assignment of a bond and mortgage held by *D*. *P* performed, and when *D* offered to assign the bond and mortgage, *P* refused to take it unless *D* guarantied payment. *D* was not obligated to do so. *D* then executed the assignment with a guaranty of payment. The guaranty is not supported by consideration.

5. T or F Plaintiffs were sailors on *D*'s vessel and agreed to work for a certain sum for a particular voyage. Midway through the voyage, the plaintiffs demanded an increase in wages and *D* promised to pay a specified additional amount. Under the majority view, *D*'s promise is not supported by consideration.

6. T or F *P* and *D* entered into a contract for the sale and delivery (in installments) of 4,000 wooden display stands at a price of 65 cents each. After 2,000 stands had been delivered and paid for, *P* truthfully told *D* that increased costs had made the contract unprofitable. *D* agreed to pay 75 cents for each stand delivered in the future. *P* is entitled to 75 cents for each stand delivered in the future.

7. T or F *P* entered into a contract with *D* to paint a shopping center. The contract provided that the agreement could not be modified except by a signed written agreement. The parties orally modified the agreement. The oral modification was supported by consideration. The oral modification is not binding.

8. T or F *A* promises to work for *B* for one year in return for *B*'s promise to pay *A* a fair share of the profits. *A* performs. *A* is entitled to a contractual recovery.

9. T or F *P* and *D* entered into an agreement by the terms of which *D* was to sell and *P* was to buy 1,500,000 gallons of a specified grade of oil, shipments to be made equally in February, March and April. The agreement also provided as follows: "Seller may cancel any unshipped portion of this order on five days notice." *D* has incurred detriment.

10. T or F *S* and *B* entered into an agreement by the terms of which *S* agreed to sell and *B* agreed to buy 12 carloads. A clause in the agreement provided: "It is agreed that Buyer may have the privilege of increasing quantity by an additional 13 carloads during the period covered by the agreement." *B* is not entitled to receive the additional 13 carloads, since there is no consideration for the privilege of increasing quantity.

11. T or F *A* asked *B*, a builder, to build a stable. *B* agreed to do the job. The parties did not discuss price. *B* did a fine job and upon seeing the stable for the first time, *A* promised *B* $8,000. The reasonable value of the work was $7,200. Before *B* assented to the promise, *A* withdrew the promise. *B* is not entitled to recover $8,000.

12. T or F Father (*F*) promised to give his daughter (*D*) $17,000 for the purpose of enabling her to purchase a house. In reliance on the promise, *D* entered into an option contract for the purchase of the property and expended $2,000 of her own money for this purpose. *F* declines to furnish the $17,000 promised. *D* is entitled to recover at least $2,000 from *F*.

13. T or F *P* was away from home on an extended trip and had parked a car in his driveway. *P* heard a weather forecast predicting an early and heavy frost. Fearing for the possible damage to the car, *P* telephoned *D*, a neighbor, who agreed to take *P*'s car to a service station that very day to have anti-freeze placed in the cooling system. *D* failed to do anything, and the predicted frost severely damaged *P*'s car. Under the traditional view, *P* does not have a cause of action against *D*.

The following essay questions may involve issues from Chapter 1 as well as this Chapter 2.

14. **Essay** *A* and *B* were boyhood chums in Poland. At one point *B* had saved *A*'s life and as a result *B* had suffered a permanent injury to his leg. *A* came to the United States and prospered. *B* remained in Poland and informed *A* that he was having troubles with the authorities. *A* then sent the following letter to *B*: "In view of our success and our friendship and your previous kindnesses to me, I am willing to send you enough money to come to the United States and when you get here I will be glad to give you permanent employment in my business." *B* answered that he was delighted. *A* sent the money. *B* sold his farm in Poland and came to the United States. *A* gave *B* a job as a truck driver. One day, during a vodka drinking contest, they had an argument and *A* fired *B*. Does *B* have any claim against *A*?

15. **Essay** Plaintiff was interested in getting the contract from the Air Force to construct a missile installation. The Air Force had solicited bids and had provided detailed specifications. Defendant submitted a bid to Plaintiff for the piping subcontract. The bid was for "all mechanical piping with the following exclusions: 1. Cafeteria & Kitchen equipment; 2. Painting of Elevated Tank; 3. Barricades, signs, flags, lights, power, water, heat—which is to be furnished by you. Total amount of proposal $3,463,000." Later that day, Defendant agreed to lower its bid by $50,000. Plaintiff agreed to use Defendant's bid in calculating its bid, and did use the figure in its calculations. After Plaintiff was awarded the general contract by the Air Force, Plaintiff sent Defendant a letter, stating, in part:

> "Your proposal for piping work in the sum of $3,413,000, including a performance and payment bond is hereby accepted. This excludes the following items: 1. Cafeteria and Kitchen equipment (only the Cafeteria and Kitchen Equipment items specified to be furnished and installed by others are covered by this exclusion. All rough-in work required therefore is your responsibility.) 2. Painting of Elevated Tank. Please signify your acceptance of this award by signing in the space allocated for your signature below."

After some discussions, defendant withdrew its bid and refused to do any of the work on the project. Raise and resolve the contracts issues in this fact pattern.

16. **Essay** On January 1, 2003, Lessor and Lessee signed a lease of real property which by its terms was to terminate on December 31, 2008. The lease contained all of the necessary terms. It also provided as follows: "In addition the Lessor grants to Lessee an option to renew the within described lease for an additional five years. The monthly rental for the extended term is to be agreed upon between the Lessor and

the Lessee. In the event we are unable to agree on this matter, the Lessor shall appoint one arbitrator, the Lessee shall appoint one arbitrator, and the two arbitrators so appointed shall appoint a third arbitrator and the decision of the majority shall be binding upon both the Lessor and the Lessee."

In January 2008, the parties began negotiating the new lease. Initially the Lessee stated that it was willing to continue as Lessee only if Lessor financed stated improvements. Later, Lessee sought to relate the amount of the rent to be paid to an extension of the term. In time, Lessee made it clear that he intended to exercise the option. Negotiations continued until November 2008 when the parties agreed that the only course available was arbitration. Lessor agreed to notify the Lessee of the name of his arbitrator "within a couple of days." A month passed and Lessee heard nothing, and his calls were not returned.

By this time, the January 2009 rent was due, and Lessee sent a rent check that included $100.00 over and above the rent previously paid. Along with the check Lessee sent a letter which stated, "since I have not heard from you I assume that you do not wish to go to arbitration. I thought that this was the right amount to send at this time." Lessor cashed the check but marked it "Under Protest." Before the next rental payment became due the Lessor informed the Lessee that "the lease was at an end." Lessee replied that he disagreed and added that he was deprived of an opportunity to make other arrangements because of Lessor's conduct.

Discuss all of the contracts problems presented.

Chapter IV

Legal Capacity

■ ANALYSIS

A. Infants

1. Who Is an Infant?

At common law, a person remained an infant until the age of twenty-one. Today, we call such persons "minors" but legal digests and cases continue using the archaic word "infants." By legislation enacted mostly in the 1970's, the age of majority is now eighteen almost everywhere. To be more precise, persons remain infants until the first moment of the day preceding their 18th birthdays because "the law disregards fractions of a day." Infancy continues despite emancipation from parents and, in most jurisdictions, despite marriage.

2. Is an Infant's Promise Void or Voidable?

An infant's contract is voidable rather than void. Executed transactions, such as sales, conveyances and releases are also voidable.

Discussion: The power of avoidance resides only in the infant or the infant's guardian, heirs, administrators, or executors. The power does not reside in the adult party. This means that the infant may enforce his or her contract with an adult.

Exception: However, the infant may not disaffirm certain contracts if they are contrary to public policy or because the infant has done or promised to do something that the law would compel even in the absence of a contract; e.g., to support a child born out of wedlock. Despite the common law rules, most jurisdictions have enacted statutes that limit the power of avoidance. These include insurance and banking laws, educational loan statutes, and military enlistment law.

Effect on Bona Fide Purchasers

After an infant has exercised the power to avoid the contract, the transaction is treated for many purposes as if it were void from the beginning. Thus, by disaffirming a conveyance, the infant may reclaim *real property* from a subsequent purchaser who purchased in good faith without notice of the fact that an infant had preceded the vendor in the chain of title. As to a *sale of goods*, however, the Uniform Commercial Code provides that a subsequent *bona fide* purchaser for value obtains goods free from an infant's power of disaffirmance.

3. Avoidance or Ratification

a. Avoidance

An infant may disaffirm a contract during minority and thereafter at any time prior to ratification.

Discussion: The exercise of the power of avoidance is often called disaffirmance. The effective surrender of this power is known as ratification. The infant cannot pick selected provisions to disaffirm. If at all, the entire contract must be avoided.

Disaffirmance may effectively be made during infancy and once made is irrevocable. In the case of real property, however, the majority rule is that the infant's conveyance may be avoided only after reaching the age of majority.

b. Ratification

An effective ratification cannot take place prior to the attainment of majority.

Discussion: Any purported ratification prior to the age of majority suffers from the same infirmity as the contract itself—the minor is not deemed old enough (with all its implications of hard-earned wisdom and the like) to make such a decision. After majority, the infant may ratify in three ways.

1) *Express ratification.* As to contracts not yet performed by the former infant, a mere acknowledgment of the contract is not enough—nothing less than a promise will suffice. If the contract is fully performed, an acknowledgment or other words consistent with an intention to stand on the contract is sufficient to constitute ratification.

2) *Ratification by conduct.* When a party retains and uses property for more than a reasonable time after attaining majority, it ordinarily amounts to ratification. Receipt of performance from the other party after attaining majority will also normally be considered to be ratification by the infant. On the other hand, part payment or other performance by the infant, without more, will not ordinarily be deemed a ratification.

3) *Failure to make a timely disaffirmance.* An infant may disaffirm contracts until a reasonable time after reaching the age of majority. What is a reasonable time is often a question of fact dependent upon such circumstances as whether or not there has been any performance by either party, the nature of the transaction and the extent to which the other party has been prejudiced by any extensive delay in disaffirming. Where it has been performed by the adult or both parties, it would ordinarily be inequitable to permit the infant to retain the benefits of the contract for a long period of time and then disaffirm. Ordinarily, however, if the infant has obtained no benefits under the contract, as will usually be the case where the adult has not performed, there is no reason to bar the infant from disaffirming at any time up until the statute of limitations has run.

Under the majority view, the rules stated above also apply to conveyances of real property, but many cases hold that in the absence of estoppel, the former infant has the right to avoid a conveyance until the statute of limitations has run.

c. Ignorance of Fact or Law

There can be no effective ratification if the former infant does not know the facts on which liability depends.

Discussion: However, the cases disagree whether the former infant had to know that the law granted the power to avoid the original contract. A majority of cases have held that ignorance of the law is immaterial. A significant minority disagree.

4. Restitution After Disaffirmance

a. Infant as Plaintiff

If, upon disaffirmance the infant sues for the return of the consideration, under the modern view recovery will be allowed, but minus the value of the use and depreciation of any property obtained from the defendant.

Discussion: The maxim is that infancy may be raised as a shield and not a sword. The more traditional rule still in effect in some places is that the infant need not account for use and depreciation but only return the consideration the infant has received.

b. Infant as Defendant

Upon disaffirming, the infant is liable for the return (or the value) of any tangible benefits received and retained.

Discussion: This rule is subject to one extension. If the infant has exchanged or sold the property, and the proceeds of the exchange or sale can be traced, the infant will be liable to the extent of the traceable assets. Note that the general rule applies to tangible benefits; there is no obligation to return or account for services received.

5. Necessaries

An infant is liable for the reasonable value of necessaries he or she has received. This liability is quasi-contractual rather than contractual. Therefore, the infant is liable only for the reasonable value of the necessaries, not the contract rate.

Discussion: The concept of "necessaries" is relative to the infant's status in life. Thus, it is a fruitless quest to analyze the cases to determine, for example, whether an automobile is a necessary. Food, shelter, clothing and medical services are generally considered to be necessaries but the kind of food, etc. is another question. Education is also a necessary but to what level is again another question. Business and employment expenses have received variable treatment. If an infant borrows money for the purpose of purchasing necessaries and so uses it, the infant is liable to the lender.

The liability of the infant also depends upon whether or not the infant has an existing supply of necessaries, or parents or guardians who are willing and able to supply the infant with the necessities of life.

In addition, the goods and services must have been supplied on the credit of the infant and not of the parent, guardian or a third person. Thus, the liability, although quasi-contractual, requires that there be a contract with the infant.

6. Infant's Liability for Benefits Received

Many jurisdictions now require an infant who seeks to disaffirm a contract and obtain restitution to return or account for benefits received under the contract. If, however, the infant is a defendant and sets up a defense of infancy, the infant is liable only for necessaries or the value of tangible consideration still retained. (This is a restatement of some of the rules identified in IV.A.4., *supra*.)

Several recent cases have taken the position that it is immaterial whether the infant is the plaintiff or defendant, holding that if the infant has received benefits, whether necessaries or not, the infant is liable in an action for restitution of their value.

7. Torts Connected with Contracts

Although infants are not generally liable on contracts, they are liable for torts.

Comment: Very often tort liability is intimately connected with a contractual relation. At least three kinds of problems arise from the interplay of tort and contract liability in cases involving infants.

a. Infant's Torts Stemming from Contracts

The other party to a contractual relation may not sue the infant for tort if the tort is in essence a breach of contract.

Example: An infant carelessly destroys personal property in the infant's possession that belongs to another (a bailment); it is possible to frame a cause of action sounding in negligence or in contract. Neither a tort nor a contract action will be sustained, because the action is ultimately rooted in the contract. The infant, however, would be liable for conversion of a chattel because this type of wrong is deemed to be independent of the contract.

b. Effect of Misrepresentation of Age

The majority view is that infants may exercise the power of avoidance even if they have misrepresented their age. The minority view is that infants who misrepresent their age and who wish to disaffirm must restore the adult parties to their original position.

Discussion: A separate question is whether the infants are liable in tort for willful misrepresentation of age. Again, there is a split of authority. The division stems from the rule that a tort action will not be allowed against an infant if in essence it involves the enforcement of a contract. The question is whether the tort action is sufficiently independent of the contract.

It is very clear, however, that the infant's fraudulent misrepresentation of age or other material fact will permit the other party to avoid the contract on grounds of fraud.

c. Torts and Agency Relationships

According to the majority view, an infant may also avoid liability for the torts of the infant's agents, at least in so far as the tort liability stems from the doctrine of respondeat superior.

B. The Mentally Infirm

1. Is the Promise of a Mentally Infirm Person Void or Voidable?

The overwhelming weight of modern authority is that promises of the mentally infirm are voidable. However, in most jurisdictions the promise is deemed void if the person so afflicted has been adjudicated an incompetent and a guardian of property has been appointed prior to the incompetent's entering into the transaction.

2. Test of Mental Infirmity

Under the traditional rule, it must be established that the person with a mental infirmity did not understand the nature and consequences of the transaction. Under a subsidiary test, the transaction would be voidable if the person in question was rational except for "insane delusions" as to the particular transaction.

The more modern view, espoused by the Restatement (Second), reaffirms the cognitive test "of ability to understand." In addition, it adopts the rule that the contract is voidable if the party "by reason of mental illness or defect . . . is unable to act in a reasonable manner in relation to the transaction and the other party has reason to know of this condition."

Comment: These rules apply to insane persons, and to persons with other mental infirmities, such as senility, mental disability, delirium deriving from physical injuries and the side effects of medication.

3. Requirement of Restitution

If the transaction is executed, and the other party took no advantage of an unadjudicated incompetent, and had no reason to know of the infirmity, the transaction is not voidable unless the incompetent can place the other party in the status quo ante.

Discussion: If the incompetency would be obvious to a reasonable person, there is no obligation upon the incompetent to make restitution if the consideration has been consumed or dissipated.

4. Avoidance and Ratification

a. Avoidance

As in the case of an infant's contracts, there is no power of avoidance in the competent party. The power of avoidance and ratification is reserved to the incompetent or a duly appointed guardian and the incompetent's heirs or personal representative after death.

b. Ratification

The incompetent may ratify the contract after capacity is restored.

Discussion: As in the case of infants' contracts, ratification can be effected by conduct or words and, once ratified, the contract may not be avoided. After ratification, the former incompetent may have an action for damages if exploitation of the incompetent amounted to actionable fraud.

5. Liability for Necessaries

As in the case of an infant, a mental incompetent is liable in a restitutionary action for necessaries.

Comment: Roughly the same classes of goods and services considered necessaries for infants are necessaries for incompetents.

6. Intoxicated Persons and Drug Users

When a person is so drunk or under the influence of narcotics that the person does not understand the nature and consequences of the transaction, the afflicted person may avoid the transaction under circumstances similar to those available to other classes of the mentally infirm.

Discussion: Under the rule laid down in the Restatement (Second), however, contracts made by an intoxicated party are voidable only if the other party has reason to know that the intoxicated party is unable to act in a reasonable manner in relation to the transaction or lacks understanding of it.

Where the other party is aware of the intoxication, the rules alluded to in the next paragraph also come into play.

7. Exploitation of Alcoholics and Weak-Minded Persons

Mental infirmity, feebleness of intellect or intoxication may exist to a lesser degree than required by law for avoidance of a contract. The cases frequently reveal exploitation of such people. The fact patterns usually involve subtle forms of duress, fraud, undue influence, or overreaching. Some degree of infirmity, coupled with the unfairness of the bargain, will often result in a finding of fraud, undue influence, overreaching, or even mental incapacity. The recent enlargement of the doctrine of unconscionability offers another, more forthright, approach to cases of this kind.

Review Questions *(Answers in Appendix A)*

We suggest you first review HOW TO STUDY and EXAMINATION in the *Perspective* section, *supra.*

1. T or F *A,* a minor, sold a painting for $100. On reaching the age of majority, *A* received a book on French art. While perusing the book, *A* noticed that the painting was now worth $15,000. In an action to recover the painting brought promptly thereafter, *A* will succeed upon accounting for the $100 received.

2. T or F *A,* a minor, sought to purchase a $500 stereo unit. The vendor would not give *A* credit, but promised to put the unit aside if the youth would make periodic payments towards the purchase price. After having paid $300, *A* reached majority, and told the vendor that payment would soon be made. A week after this meeting, *A* disaffirmed the contract and brought suit to recover the payments that had been made. *A* will succeed.

3. T or F On March 1, Icarus went to a Rolls Royce dealer and bought a Silver Cloud with cash. The deal went smoothly and was fair. Icarus immediately attempted flight off a cliff, and the car was destroyed. Icarus' executor brought suit to recover the purchase price. The executor will recover.

4. **Essay** Janice, a 17-year-old high school senior in N.Y., has been accepted by Berkeley. Ace Airlines offers a discount flight for persons under 18 for $150, one-half of the adult fare. To attend the school, Janice, who has no money, misrepresents her age in order to obtain credit from the airline which is available only to adults. Naturally, the credit was for full fare. Upon arrival in San Francisco, Janice's grandfather gave her $200, as he had previously promised, to reimburse her for the

cost of the flight. She then disaffirmed the contract with the airline and the airline brought suit. What result? Discuss.

Chapter V

Interpretation and Proper Form (Writing Requirement)

■ ANALYSIS

A. Parol Evidence Rule
   1. The Nature and Meaning of the Rule
      a. What Type of Evidence May Be Excluded by the Rule?
      b. Theory of the Rule
   2. How to Determine Finality
   3. How to Determine Completeness
      a. Four Corners Rule
      b. The Collateral Contract Rule
      c. Williston's Rules
      d. Corbin's View
      e. The UCC Approach (UCC § 2–202)
      1) UCC § 2–202(b)
      2) UCC § 2–202(a)
      3) Confirmations
      f. The Restatement (Second)
   4. Roles of Judge and Jury
   5. Separate Consideration
   6. Subsequent Agreement
   7. Is the Rule Substantive or Procedural?
   8. Is the Term Offered Consistent or Contradictory?
   9. Undercutting the Integration
B. Interpretation
   1. Introduction
   2. Varying Views

A. Parol Evidence Rule

1. The Nature and Meaning of the Rule

A total integration (a writing that the parties intend to be final and complete) may not be contradicted or supplemented.

A partial integration (a writing that the parties intend to be final but not complete) may not be contradicted but may be supplemented by consistent additional terms.

a. What Type of Evidence May Be Excluded by the Rule?

The rule excludes evidence of certain terms agreed upon *prior* to an integrated writing, whether the terms are written or oral. According to the great majority of cases, it also excludes an oral term agreed upon contemporaneously with the writing. The rule does not exclude terms contained in a contemporaneous writing. The contemporaneous writing is deemed to be part of the integration. Contemporaneous writings are common in large-scale transactions. Even in the sale of a small business, there may be the simultaneous delivery of a bill of sale, the assignment of a lease, an employment contract hiring the seller to manage the business, etc.

b. Theory of the Rule

Two theories have been advanced to justify the rule. The first is contractual. If the parties intend the writing to be final and complete, they intend to supersede their *prior* agreements.

The second theory is evidentiary. Sound policy requires that prior and contemporaneous oral agreements are suspect and that the writing deserves a preferred status against potential perjury.

Usually, the two theories work together. However, when they conflict (*see* V.A.9., *infra*), the contract theory takes precedence.

2. How to Determine Finality

Any relevant evidence is admissible to establish finality.

Discussion: The first issue in a parol evidence problem is the parties' intent—whether the given writing represents the final embodiment of the parties' intended agreement; completeness of the writing is a second issue. The final writing need not be signed and need not be in any particular form. The crucial requirement is that the parties have regarded the writing as the final embodiment of their agreement, and any relevant evidence is admissible to determine this question of fact. The more complete and formal the instrument, the more likely it is that it is intended as an integration. Most writings that evidence a valid contract are final and therefore are at least partial integrations.

Examples of Non-Final Writings: (1) a memorandum prepared by one party and not shown to the other party. Such a document is not final because the party who has not seen it cannot possibly consider it to be the final embodiment of the agreement;

(2) a draft of a contract shown to but not assented to by the other party.

The question of finality, although actually one of fact, is often decided by the trial judge because the courts feel that unsophisticated jurors could be easily beguiled by an artful presentation and thus would not give the writing the protection it deserves. Where there is conflicting evidence as to whether a party had manifested assent to the writing, the question may be determined by the jury.

3. How to Determine Completeness

Once it is determined that a writing is *final*, the next question is whether the writing is *complete* so that it is a total integration. This is a difficult problem, since there is no unanimity on how to determine completeness. Here are the six most widely accepted approaches.

a. Four Corners Rule

If the instrument is complete on its face, the instrument is presumed to be a total integration. The court determines whether the writing is complete on its face solely by looking at the instrument.

Comment: Although the Four Corners Rule is somewhat illogical because it is impossible to tell whether an agreement is complete on its face simply by looking at the writing, many jurisdictions follow it.

b. The Collateral Contract Rule

Unfortunately, there are two versions of this rule. Fortunately, this rule is losing favor. Under one version, if the term offered does not contradict the writing, it may be received in evidence. In effect, this means that the writing is only a partial integration.

Under the other version, the important issue is whether the term offered has to do with a subject that is dealt with in the writing. If the term offered is dealt with at all in the writing, it is a total integration. If the term offered relates to a subject matter that is not mentioned in the writing, the writing is treated as a partial integration.

c. Williston's Rules

Probably more cases follow Williston's Rules than any other. Professor Williston states three rules.

(1) If the writing expressly states that it is a final expression of all the terms agreed upon and that it is a complete and exclusive statement of these terms—often referred to as a merger clause—this declaration conclusively establishes that the writing is a total integration. There are exceptions for when the document is obviously incomplete or the merger clause itself was included as a result of fraud or mistake, etc.

However, even a merger clause does not prevent enforcement of a separate agreement supported by a separate consideration on both sides. This statement is accepted under all versions of the rule.

(2) In the absence of a merger clause, the determination of whether the writing is a total integration is made by looking at the writing. If the writing is obviously incomplete on its face, consistent additional terms may be proved. In other words, the writing is a partial integration. However, even if the writing appears to be complete, the writing will still only be a partial integration when the writing expresses the undertaking of one party only, as in the case of deeds, bonds, and bills and notes.

(3) Where the writing appears to be a complete instrument expressing the rights and obligations of both parties, the writing is deemed a total integration unless reasonable persons in the position of the parties to the agreement might naturally exclude the alleged additional terms from the writing.

d. Corbin's View

Professor Corbin is determined to search out the actual intent of the parties on this issue of total integration rather than some fictional or presumed intent. He states that all relevant evidence should be taken into account in making the determination. Thus, he would admit evidence of prior negotiations. Furthermore, he states that a merger clause is only one of the factors to consider in determining whether there is a total integration. Under his view, a writing is ordinarily only a partial integration.

e. The UCC Approach (UCC § 2–202)

1) UCC § 2–202(b)

Paragraph (b) states the common law rule that a total integration may not be contradicted or supplemented, but it does not determine the existence of a total integration according to any of the rules previously discussed. Rather, the paragraph creates a presumption that a writing is only a partial integration. This presumption is overcome if the parties actually intend the writing to be a total integration (Corbin), or if it is *certain* that parties similarly situated would have included the term in the writing, a variation of Williston's third rule.

Most courts have followed the traditional rule that a merger clause is conclusive even in cases that arise under the UCC.

2) UCC § 2–202(a)

Under this paragraph, a course of dealing or a trade usage may be used to supply a consistent additional term even though the writing appears to be a total integration.

3) Confirmations

Parties often reach agreement orally and follow up by sending a written confirmation of the terms of the agreement. Also, sometimes agreement is reached by a series of letters, faxes, conversations, etc. When the parties declare that they have a deal, it is common for one party to write a confirmation summarizing its understanding of the deal. Under the common law, a confirmation often acts as a total integration if the other party makes no response to it prior to performance. It could be argued that this solution could arise under the UCC only if there were common terms in both parties' memoranda; the provision states: "Terms to which the confirmatory memoranda of the parties agree." But there are cases where one confirmatory memorandum has been held to be a total integration.

f. The Restatement (Second)

The Restatement (Second) appears to say that it is impossible to have more than a partial integration except where the parties had a real, as opposed to an objective, intention to have a total integration.

The major premise of the Restatement (Second) is Corbin's rule that the actual intent of the parties should be sought in determining whether there is a total or a partial integration. Even if this test leads to a determination of a total integration, consistent additional terms are still admissible if:

(a) the offered agreement is made for a separate consideration or

(b) the offered agreement is not within the scope of the integration or

(c) the offered terms might naturally be omitted from the writing.

4. Roles of Judge and Jury

There are a number of issues that arise under the rules stated above that would generally be treated as questions of fact. For example, would it be natural to exclude a particular term from the writing? However, under the parol evidence rule, these questions are generally decided by the trial judge as a question of law and are reviewable on appeal as questions of law. If the court decides that the parol evidence rule applies, the court excludes the offered term not because it was not agreed upon, but because it is legally immaterial. Conversely, if the court decides that the parol evidence rule does not apply, the court admits the term into evidence but then leaves to the jury the issue of fact as to whether the term was actually agreed upon.

5. Separate Consideration

The parol evidence rule does not prevent proof of a separate oral contract with a separate consideration on both sides, provided it does not contradict the written agreement.

Comment: Although there are numerous conflicts of authority in the application of the parol evidence rule, there is unanimity on this point.

Example: *A* and *B*, in a signed writing, agree to buy and sell a specific automobile. Contemporaneously, they orally agree that *B* may keep the automobile in *A*'s garage for one year in return for *B*'s promise to pay $150 per month. The contemporaneous agreement is admissible because it is supported by a separate consideration on each side, and it does not contradict the main agreement.

6. Subsequent Agreement

The parol evidence rule NEVER excludes evidence of a subsequent agreement.

Comment: Under the UCC, and some broader state statutes, it is sometimes possible to prohibit oral proof of a subsequent agreement by inserting a "no oral modification clause" into the contract. (*See* II.B.8.c., *supra.*)

7. Is the Rule Substantive or Procedural?

Although the earlier cases said the parol evidence rule was a rule of evidence, the more modern cases look upon it as a rule of substantive law. In truth, it has both a procedural and a substantive aspect. It is procedural because it excludes evidence; it is substantive because it helps to determine the terms of the contract. One consequence of the classification is whether the parol evidence can be raised for the first time on appeal. A majority of the courts conclude that if the rule is one of substantive law, the parol evidence issue may be raised for the first time upon appeal despite the failure to object at trial. Another consequence has to do with the conflict of laws question of which state's law governs. Generally, as substantive law, the parol evidence rule that is applied should be the same law as is applied to other questions having to do with the formation of the contract.

8. Is the Term Offered Consistent or Contradictory?

There is little or no consistency on the question of how to determine whether an offered term is contradictory or consistent. There are cases that have found the offered term inconsistent in the following situations: (1) where it contradicts an express term of the contract; (2) where it contradicts a merger clause; (3) where it contradicts an inference that all of the seller's obligations were listed in the contract. For example, if a contract lists a number of obligations of the seller, and the buyer offers proof that the seller assumed an additional obligation, it has been held that the term contradicts the inference that all of the seller's obligations are listed. (4) Where it contradicts an implied in fact term. But an implied in law term that becomes part of the agreement may be contradicted.

The more modern cases, including those decided under the UCC, lean to the view that to be contradictory a term must contradict an express term of the integration.

Examples: (1) *L* (Landlord) and *T* (Tenant) signed a two-year lease. Under the terms of the lease, the tenant agreed not to sell tobacco in any form but was permitted to sell soft drinks. At the trial *T* seeks to introduce into evidence an oral agreement made contemporaneously with the writing that in consideration of the promise not to sell tobacco, *L* promised an *exclusive* right to sell soft drinks on the premises, and *L* breached this promise.

The issue was whether there was a *total* integration. There would undoubtedly be a total integration under the "four corners" rule. Under the collateral contract approach, it would depend on which version of the rule the court decided to apply. Using Williston's approach, the court concluded that it would have been natural for parties similarly situated to have included this term in the writing. This means that there is a total integration, and the term is excluded even if it is a consistent additional term. The UCC does not apply because the case does not involve a sale of goods. Under the Restatement (Second) the writing would undoubtedly only be a partial integration, and the issue would be whether the term offered is a *contradictory* term or a *consistent* additional term. The term would be a consistent additional term because it does not contradict an express term of the writing. Therefore, under the Restatement approach it would be admissible.

(2) *D.M.* and his wife conveyed a ranch to *D.M.*'s sister and her husband. The deed contained an option to repurchase. *D.M.* was

adjudged a bankrupt. His trustee in bankruptcy and *D.M.*'s wife seek to exercise the right to repurchase. The grantees assert that there was a prior oral agreement that the option to repurchase was personal to the grantors and could not be invoked by the trustee in bankruptcy. The case was decided under Williston's view so we will limit our discussion to that approach. The court assumes that there is an integration, and the first question is whether the integration is total. Would it have been natural for parties situated as these parties were to have excluded this term from the deed? The court concluded that it was, because a deed has limited space, and expresses the rights and obligations of only one party. Another reason why it was natural to exclude the term was that the family relationship implies trust. Thus, the deed is only a partial integration and the issue is whether the term is contradictory.

The offered term (option personal to grantors) contradicted an implied term of the writing—namely, free assignability. The term is implied in law rather than implied in fact and therefore could be contradicted.

(3) *S* and *B* entered into a written agreement for the licensing of a computer program on September 6. On September 7, they orally agreed that *B* might try out the program for a week and if unsatisfied, *B* could return it for a refund. Because the agreement is subsequent to the writing, no parol evidence problem arises. The only issue is one of consideration for the oral modification. In most jurisdictions, as a common law proposition, *S*'s promise would not be enforceable because *B* suffered no detriment. The result would be different under UCC § 2–209(1) if it were applicable. Most courts hold that the UCC does not apply to software licensing.

(4) The parties entered into an agreement whereby *P* agreed to sell and *D* agreed to buy 31,000 tons of phosphate during the next calendar year. The contract specified a price per ton that was subject to an escalation clause. *D* took only part of the 31,000 tons. *D*'s defense was that there was a usage of the trade and course of dealing to the effect that "because of uncertain crop and weather conditions, farming practices, and government agricultural programs, express price and quantity terms in contracts for materials in the mixed fertilizer industry are merely projections to be adjusted according to market forces." Because the case involved a sale of goods, UCC § 2–202(a) applied. Under the UCC, course of dealing and trade usage are always admissible although not always controlling. The same case raised the question of the effect of a merger clause upon evidence of a usage of the trade and a course of dealing. It indicated that a merger clause should not rule out this type of evidence unless the clause makes specific reference to this kind of evidence.

9. Undercutting the Integration

Parol evidence is admissible to show that the agreement was never formed, or even if formed is void or voidable, or to show grounds for granting or denying reformation.

Discussion: A party may show, for example, that the writing had never been assented to, was a sham and not intended to be operative, was unconscionable, or illegal or subject to a condition precedent to its formation. In addition, it may be shown that the agreement is voidable because of duress, mistake, fraud, lack of capacity, or undue influence. Many cases hold that fraud includes promissory fraud; where a promise is made by a party who has no intention of performing.

Rationale: The theory behind undercutting the integration is that the parol evidence rule should not be applied until it is decided that there is a contract. Although the rule discussed here is not explicitly found in the UCC, it is generally agreed that the courts will apply all aspects of this rule to UCC cases. A number of cases that agree with the general rule, however, hold that such evidence is not admissible if the basis of the attack on the writing is a term that contradicts specific language in the writing.

Example: *P* and *D* agreed to transfer the stock of corporations that each owned to a new corporation. The new corporation agreed to issue its stock to *P* and *D*. *P* made the transfer of stock to the new corporation, but *D* refused to do so. *D*'s defense was that *P* and *D* orally agreed that the agreement was not to operate until an equity expansion fund of $672,000 had been procured. The raising of the equity expansion fund was a condition precedent to the *formation* of the contract and therefore it was held that the term could be admitted in evidence to show that there was no contract until this event occurred. Some courts would admit the evidence only if it did not contradict explicit terms of the writing. For example, if the writing provided that the parties would transfer stock in ten days, the evidence would be held to contradict this term and be inadmissible.

B. Interpretation

1. Introduction

Interpretation deals with the meaning of language. Contract interpretation raises two fundamental questions. (1) Whose meaning is to be given to the communication? (2) What evidence may be taken into account? A wide variety of views exist as to this last question. While interpretation relates to ascertaining the parties' meaning, construction relates to the legal effect of the manifestations of intent. The distinction between interpretation and construction is not a clear one, and most courts do not appear to concern themselves with it. Nor do we.

2. Varying Views

a. Plain Meaning Rule—Ambiguity

The Plain Meaning Rule states that if a writing or the relevant term has a plain meaning, that meaning must be given effect without resort to extrinsic evidence of any kind.

Discussion: In many jurisdictions, for example, New York, the plain meaning rule prevails. In many other jurisdictions, for example, New Jersey, the rule is applied sporadically. In still others, for example, California, the rule is rejected. When it is applied, whether there is plain meaning or its opposite, ambiguity, is a question of law to be determined first by the trial judge looking solely to the writing.

Some of the modern cases hold that the trial judge should consider extrinsic evidence before determining whether the meaning is plain, but these are in the minority. If the trial judge finds the term is ambiguous, extrinsic evidence is admissible for clarification. The term "extrinsic evidence" includes prior and contemporaneous statements made in negotiations, surrounding circumstances, subjective intent, what the parties said to each other about meaning, trade usage, course of performance and course of dealing. "Extrinsic evidence" may be written or oral.

Exception: Even plain-meaning courts will hear evidence of the meaning of non-ambiguous but obscure or technical terms; *e.g.*, the meaning of "Amacid Blue Black KN."

b. Williston's Rules

Williston rejects the plain meaning rule and sets up rules for interpretation that vary, depending on whether or not the writing is an integration.

1) Integration

As to integrated writings, Williston's standard of interpretation is the meaning that would be attached to the integration by a reasonably intelligent person acquainted with all operative usages and knowing all of the circumstances prior to and contemporaneous with the making of the integration. However, Williston would exclude what the parties said to each other about meaning (e.g., "buy" was to mean "sell") and what the parties subjectively believed the writing meant at the time of agreement. But when these rules are applied and the result is ambiguity, then Williston's non-integration rules will be applied.

2) Non-Integration

Where there is no integration and no ambiguity, Williston's standard is the meaning that the party making the manifestation should reasonably expect the other party to give it—the standard of reasonable expectation—a test based primarily on the objective theory of contracts. (Compare the working test under Mutual Assent, in II.A.2., *supra*, that set up the standard of reasonable understanding.) In the case of a non-integration, where there is no ambiguity, all extrinsic evidence is admissible except evidence of subjective intention. If there is an ambiguity, in the case of a non-integration, evidence of subjective intention is also admissible and, when it is introduced, Williston argues that the rules indicated in the example below apply.

Example: S agreed to sell, and *B* agreed to buy, certain cotton. Shipment was to be from Bombay on the ship Peerless. It happened that there were two ships that went by the name Peerless. One was to sail from Bombay in October, the other in December. The evidence was to the effect that *B* meant the ship Peerless that sailed in October, and *S* meant the one that sailed in December. The possible results in this type of situation are as follows.

(1) If both parties meant the same ship, Peerless, there is a contract based on that meaning.

(2) If one party knew or had reason to know of the ambiguity, and the other did not know or did not have reason to know, there is a contract based upon the meaning of the party who was not at fault.

(3) If both parties knew or should have known of the ambiguity or neither party knew nor should have known of the ambiguity, there is no contract if they meant different ships named Peerless. Notice that Williston's rule does not weigh fault—that is to say, it makes no difference whether one party knew and the other merely should have known.

c. Corbin's Rules—Restatement (Second)

Under Corbin's view, *all* relevant extrinsic evidence is admissible on the issue of meaning, even if there is an integration and there is no ambiguity. Corbin tempers his more liberal rules by stating that the trial judge must initially determine whether the asserted meaning is one the language, in the light of all of the evidence taken in context, could reasonably mean. If it is not, then the asserted meaning may not be attached to the language in question unless both parties mean the same thing. The Restatement (Second) is generally in accord with Corbin. Procedurally, the trial judge conducts a preliminary hearing or otherwise determines whether the language can reasonably mean what is contended.

Under Corbin's rule, most parties would introduce evidence of subjective intention. When this evidence is introduced, the problem is similar to the Peerless case discussed above. When Corbin's rules—which, unlike Williston's, do weigh fault—are applied in this situation the following results obtain.

(1) If both parties mean the same ship named Peerless there is a contract based on that meaning.

(2) Where the meanings do not coincide, the meaning is the meaning of the party who is less at fault. Ascertaining who is less at fault involves what a party *knows* or should know. For example, if one party knows that there are two ships named Peerless, and the other party *should know* of this fact, the meaning of the party who should know will prevail. Again, notice that Williston's rule is different on this point.

(3) If both parties are equally at fault, there is no contract where, as here, one is dealing with a material term.

d. UCC on Interpretation

UCC § 2–202 does not have a comprehensive rule in the area of interpretation, but it does contain particular rules of interpretation in the area of trade usage, course of dealing and, course of performance. These are discussed in V.B.4., *infra*.

3. The Relationship Between Parol Evidence and Interpretation

At times it has been said that a total integration may not be contradicted, *varied* or supplemented. The word "varied" is often also used in the context of interpretation.

The notion is that just as the first phase of the parol evidence rule prevents a party from introducing a term that contradicts an integration, so also the interpretation phase of the parol evidence does not permit a party to introduce evidence that varies the meaning of the language in the writing. Whether this last statement is true depends upon the court's choice of the competing rules of interpretation.

a. Plain Meaning Rule

Under the Plain Meaning Rule, if it is determined that there is a plain meaning, no contradiction is permitted because extrinsic evidence of all types is excluded.

b. Williston's Rules

Williston foresaw the possibility that the parol evidence rule could be undermined under the guise of interpretation. Therefore, he structured a rule for an integration that does not permit the integration to be contradicted by evidence of what the parties said to one another about the meaning of language in the integration or by evidence of subjective intent.

c. Corbin's Rules—Restatement, Second

Corbin's basic position is contrary to Williston's. Corbin and the Restatement (Second) take the position that the parol evidence rule should have no effect on the question of interpretation—the meaning of language. According to them, the parol evidence rule comes into play only to determine the content of the contract, not its meaning. Corbin states that, before extrinsic evidence can be excluded, the meaning of the writing must be ascertained, because one may not determine whether a writing is being contradicted or even supplemented until one knows what the writing means. Thus, all types of extrinsic evidence are admissible on the issue of meaning. The only limitation is that "the asserted meaning must be one to which the language of the writing read in context is reasonably susceptible in the light of the evidence introduced." The rules of the Restatement (Second) are basically the same.

4. Course of Dealing, Course of Performance and Trade Usage

a. Introduction

We have already mentioned course of dealing, trade usage, and course of performance in connection with the discussion of the parol evidence rule and interpretation. Here, our main purpose is to define these terms and to discuss their effects. This discussion may overlap to some extent our prior discussion of the parol evidence rule and interpretation.

b. Course of Dealing

A course of dealing is defined in the UCC as "a sequence of previous conduct between the parties to a particular transaction which is fairly to be regarded as establishing a common basis of understanding for interpreting their expressions and other conduct."

Otherwise stated, a course of dealing is how these two parties have interacted before.

c. Course of Performance

A course of performance is how these two parties have acted after the agreement in question. The UCC provides that "where the contract for sale involves repeated occasions for performance by either party with knowledge of the nature of the performance and opportunity for objection to it by the other, any course of performance accepted or acquiesced in without objection shall be relevant to determine the meaning of the agreement."

Comment: A course of dealing and a course of performance can be established by the testimony of the parties or third persons such as employees and other observers. Trade usage, however, is usually proved by expert witnesses.

d. Trade Usage

The UCC defines a trade usage as "any practice or method of dealing having such regularity of observance in a place, vocation or trade as to justify an expectation that it will be observed with respect to the transaction in question."

Discussion: Trade usage, course of dealing and course of performance are not limited to cases involving sales of goods. At early common law, in order to establish a usage, including a trade usage, it had to be (1) legal, (2) notorious, (3) ancient or immemorial and continuous, (4) reasonable, (5) certain, (6) universal and obligatory. Under the UCC, the trade usage need not be ancient or immemorial or universal or certain. Reasonableness is also eliminated and substituted is a requirement against "unconscionable contracts and clauses." Instead of being notorious, the UCC has a lower requirement that the usage have regularity of observance as to justify an expectation that it will be observed with respect to the transaction in question.

Another question is, who is bound by a usage? The general notion is that a person is bound by a trade usage if the person is aware of it or should be aware of it. Under the UCC, a party engaged in a trade is bound by its usages whether or not the party knows of them.

e. For What Purposes May They Be Used?

1) Trade Usage and Course of Dealing

Under the common law, a trade usage or a course of dealing may not be shown to contradict the plain meaning of the language. Many common law cases require that the contract be ambiguous before this kind of evidence is admissible. The UCC, which has liberalized their admissibility, will be discussed in connection with one of the examples below.

2) Course of Performance

A course of performance (also called practical construction) may be used to add a term, because it is subsequent to the writing and therefore it is not excluded under the parol evidence rule. Thus, if a course of performance is used to add a term to the writing, the issue is modification or waiver. A course of performance may add a term or subtract one. But a course of performance is also relevant on the issue of meaning. At common law it can be used in aid of interpretation if a reasonable person could attach that meaning to the manifestation. This rule has been changed under the UCC and will be discussed in connection with one of the examples below.

Examples: (1) *S* and *B* entered into a written contract for the sale and purchase of 1,000 shingles. At trial, evidence was offered that two packs constitute 1,000 shingles even though not containing that exact number. The court received this evidence on the issue of meaning and ruled that a jury could find that the parties intended the usage to take priority over the facially inconsistent express provision. This is the modern approach taken by the UCC and some non-UCC cases. Many non-UCC cases, however, continue to follow the older plain meaning rule and will not allow parol evidence of usage to contradict a plain meaning.

UCC § 2–202 expressly states that evidence of trade usage and course of dealing are ALWAYS admissible. UCC § 2–208 states that evidence of course of performance is ALWAYS admissible. Under the revision of Article 1 this is shifted to § 1–103.

Whether the evidence is controlling is another question. UCC § 1–205 establishes an order of priority. It reads: "The express terms of an agreement and an applicable course of dealing or a usage of the trade shall be construed wherever reasonable as consistent with each other; but when such construction is unreasonable express terms control both course of dealing and usage of the trade and course of dealing controls usage of trade." (Revision § 1–303 is in accord.) There is a companion provision in UCC § 2–208. Some courts have used this order of priority to exclude evidence if the term offered is facially inconsistent with an express provision. This result is based on a misreading of the UCC. It has been called a "false parol evidence approach."

(2) *M,* a manufacturer, sues *B,* an authorized distributer, for electronic equipment supplied and delivered. By the terms of the writing, *B* had no right to return conforming goods and obtain credit. *B* now asserts that the parties continually ignored the agreement and that 210 units have been returned for credit. This conduct constitutes a course of performance. UCC § 2–202 indicates that the course of performance by the parties is the best indication of what the parties meant. This would appear to be so under UCC § 2–202 even if the course of performance is carefully negated or is inconsistent with the writing. But, as above, some courts have mistakenly excluded evidence of course of performance because of the provisions of UCC §§ 1–205(4) and 2–208. The court should also consider the question of waiver and modification because a course of performance is subsequent to the integration. It has been

held in some cases that a course of performance has modified the contract.

5. Other Rules of Interpretation

There are many rules of interpretation that have not been mentioned. For purposes of this basic discussion of contract interpretation, it is sufficient to identify only a few of these rules. These include:

(1) specific terms are given greater weight than general terms;

(2) separately negotiated terms are given greater weight than standardized terms;

(3) if there is an inconsistency between typed or handwritten terms and printed terms, a typed or handwritten term prevails over a printed term;

(4) in choosing among reasonable meanings, the instrument should be construed against the party who drafted it, because that party is responsible for its lack of clarity. This simple rule tends to be given too much weight by students. It is really a rule of last resort when the attempt to determine the "real" meaning has failed.

(5) it is the policy of the law to uphold contracts and courts prefer to construe them so that they are lawful and operative rather than unlawful and inoperative.

C. Statutes of Frauds

1. Introduction

Invariably, cases and texts refer to *the* "Statute of Frauds." This is a misleading practice, because in fact there are multiple statutes of frauds in every state, each applicable to a specific type of contract or situation. To begin with, when oral promises became enforceable in England, perjury and subornation of perjury became common. In 1677 Parliament enacted an Act for the Prevention of Fraud and Perjuries that required that certain contracts be evidenced by a writing. Since then, statutes of frauds—of varying applicability and often with different requirements—have proliferated throughout the United States. A writing requirement obviates perjury and also promotes certainty by preventing faulty recollection. In addition, it promotes deliberation and seriousness. While these are desirable goals, carrying them out may frustrate honesty, fair dealing and the parties' intent. The rule may prevent oral terms, actually agreed upon, from being received in evidence. The potential of the statute to cause injustice has had a strong impact on judicial decisions. Thus, courts have given such statutes a narrow construction and have developed devices "for taking the contract outside" such statutes.

In 2000, Congress enacted the Electronic Signatures in Global and National Commerce Act, commonly called the E-Sign Act, which provides that electronic messages that can be read are the equivalent of writing for purposes of any statute of frauds. E-Sign allows the states to preempt E-Sign's provisions by adopting the Uniform Electronic Transactions Act (UETA). For purposes of statutes of frauds, E-Sign and UETA are in harmony. There is one major difference. Under UETA, an electronic message cannot satisfy the statute unless the parties have agreed to communicate electronically. These statutes do not use the term "writing." Instead, they refer to a "record," which includes writings and electronic mail.

2. Major Classes of Cases Covered by Writing (Record) Requirements

Record requirements affect five major classes of cases:

(1) a promise to answer for the debt, default or miscarriage of another, including the promise of an executor or administrator to answer for the obligations of the decedent out of the administrator's or executor's own pocket;

(2) a contract to transfer an interest in real property or an actual transfer of real property;

(3) a promise that by its terms is not to be performed within one year from the making thereof;

(4) a promise in consideration of marriage;

(5) a contract for the sale of goods.

Note: In the following discussion, the term "within" a statute of frauds means the contract must be evidenced by a writing; conversely, "not within" such a statute means an oral agreement can be enforced.

a. Suretyship Agreements

In a suretyship case, three parties are normally involved: 1) the party who has made the promise but now pleads the statute as a defense (*D*); 2) the person to whom the promise is made—ordinarily the creditor (C), who is suing *D;* and the third party on whose behalf *D* makes the promise (*TP*).

1) Cases Where There Is No Prior Obligation Owing from TP to C to Which D's Promise Relates

In this type of case, the promise of D is "original"—not within this statute so that it is not a defense—unless

(1) *there is a principal-surety relationship between TP and D to the knowledge of C, and*

(2) *the promise is not joint, and*

(3) *the main purpose rule does not apply.*

If all of these elements are present, D's promise is "collateral"—the statute of frauds is a defense.

Discussion: A principal and suretyship relation exists between *TP* and *D* if both are liable to *C* for the same obligation, but as between the two (*TP* and *D*) the principal (*TP*) rather than *D* (the surety) should ultimately pay. Therefore, if *D* (surety) pays, *D* is entitled to reimbursement from *TP* (principal).

Examples: (1) *D* says to *C*, "Deliver these goods to *TP* and I will see that you are paid." *C* delivers the goods to *TP* but manifests an intent not to treat *TP* as a debtor, relying solely on the credit of *D*. The promise of *D* is original, because *TP* never became liable to *C*. Therefore, by definition, there is no suretyship relationship between *TP* and *D*.

(2) When goods are being purchased from *C, D* orally promises to pay and *TP* orally guarantees *D*'s payment. *C* is informed that the goods are to be delivered to *D. C* delivers the goods to *D* who, in turn, according to a prior agreement, delivers them to *TP*. Credit is extended to both so that both *TP* and *D* are liable to *C*. There is a principal and suretyship relation between *TP* and *D*, and *C* knows that one party is the principal and the other is the surety. But *C* reasonably thinks *D* is the principal, therefore *D*'s promise is enforceable (original). *TP*'s promise is also enforceable because *TP* is in fact the principal.

(3) When goods are being purchased from *C, D* orally promises to act as surety for *TP. C* insists that they undertake a joint obligation, and the parties agree. Although there is a principal-suretyship relationship between *TP* and *D*, to the knowledge of *C, D*'s promise is original (not within the statute) because of the joint nature of the promise. This rule does not apply where the obligation is joint and several or several.

(4) The Main Purpose Rule is discussed below.

2) Cases Where There Is a Prior Obligation Owing from TP to C to Which D's Promise Relates

Such a promise is collateral (the statute is a defense).

Exceptions: (1) where there is a novation;

(2) where *D*'s promise is made to *TP;*

(3) where the Main Purpose Rule applies.

Examples: (1) *TP* owes *C* $1,000. For a consideration, *D* orally promises *C* to become a surety. *D*'s promise is collateral. Therefore, it is unenforceable.

(2) *TP* owes *C* $1,000. *D* says to *C*, "Release *TP* and I will pay." *C* releases *TP*. There is a novation, and therefore *D*'s promise is enforceable.

(3) *TP* owes *C* $1,000. *TP* and *D* enter into a contract by the terms of which *D*, for a consideration, agrees to assume the obligation. Although this is not a novation, *D*'s promise is enforceable because it is made to *TP* rather than to *C*. In addition, *D* is now the principal debtor.

(4) The Main Purpose Rule is discussed below.

3) Main Purpose Rule

Where the object of a promisor is a benefit that the promisor did not previously enjoy, and the benefit accrues immediately to the promisor, the promise is original (enforceable), whether or not TP was obligated at the time of the promise and even though the effect of the promise is to answer for a debt, default or miscarriage of another.

Examples: (1) *TP* owes *C* $1,000. *C* is about to levy an attachment on *TP*'s factory. *D,* who is an unsecured creditor of *TP,* orally promises that, if *C* forbears, *D* will pay *TP*'s debt if *TP* does not. *D*'s promise is original because *D*'s main purpose is to secure *D*'s own economic advantage.

(2) *TP* is indebted to *C* and, as a result, *C* has a lien upon *TP*'s property. *D* orally promises to pay the debt if *TP* does not, provided that *C* discharges the lien of the mortgage. *C* discharges the lien of the mortgage. The Main Purpose Rule does not apply because there is no benefit to *D,* and *D*'s promise is not enforceable.

4) Promises of Indemnity

Contracts of indemnity do not fall within the statute. So also, according to the majority view, a promise to indemnify against any loss suffered by one becoming a surety is one of indemnity and not of suretyship.

A contract of indemnity is a promise to pay third persons to whom the promisee may become liable or to reimburse the person against loss irrespective of the liability of third persons.

Examples: (1) *A* promises *B* that if *B* becomes liable as a result of the operation of a motor vehicle, *A* will pay any judgment obtained against *B*. *C* obtains a judgment against *B*. *B* is an indemnitor against liability, and the statute does not apply.

(2) *A* promises *B* that, in the event that *B* is compelled to pay *C*, *A* will reimburse *B*. *B* is an indemnitor against loss. Because *C* is not a third party beneficiary of *A*'s promise made to *B*, only *B* is liable to *C* and suretyship does not exist.

(3) *A* promises *B* that, in the event *B*'s car is damaged in a collision, *A* will reimburse *B* for the loss. *C* and *B* have a collision for which *C* is responsible. Here the possibility of suretyship exists, because *C* and *A* are both liable to *B* for the same loss. But *A*'s promise is considered one of indemnity, because *A*'s promise is made irrespective of whether *C* is liable or not.

(4) *A* promises *B* that in the event that *C*, *B*'s employee, steals money from *B*, *A* will reimburse *B*. Here *C* and *A* are liable to *B*, and the potential for suretyship exists. *A*'s promise is one of suretyship because *A*'s promise is not made *irrespective* of *C*'s liability but because of *C*'s liability.

(5) *D* requests *P* to become a surety on *TP*'s obligation to *C*, and *D* orally promises *P* that if *P* is compelled to pay, *D* will reimburse *P*. This is a *four*-party situation, and the majority of the cases have held that *D*'s promise made to a surety (*P*) is a promise of indemnity and therefore is enforceable.

5) Promise of the Del Credere Agent

An oral promise of a del credere agent is enforceable (original).

A del credere agent (*D*) is one who receives possession of goods for sale upon commission and who guarantees to his own principal (C) that those to whom he sells (*TP*s) will perform.

6) Promise of Assignor

The promise of an assignor to the assignee guaranteeing performance by the obligor is original (enforceable).

7) Promise to Buy a Claim

A promise to buy a claim is not within the statute.

Example: If *TP* owes *C* $100, and *C* assigns this right to payment to *D*, in exchange for *D*'s oral promise to pay a stated sum for the assignment, *D*'s promise is enforceable. It is not a promise to answer for the debt, default or miscarriage of another.

8) Promise by Executor or Administrator

The statute applies only where executors or administrators promise to pay out of *their own* funds a debt of the deceased. Thus, this provision is merely a particular application of the suretyship statute of frauds.

b. Real Property

A conveyance of land or of an estate in land or a promise to transfer an interest in land or a promise to pay for an interest in land are all required to be proved by a written or electronic record.

1) What Is a Contract for Sale of Land?

This term covers any agreement that contains a promise to create or transfer an interest in land. It also applies to an option contract, but interests created by operation of law (equitable liens, constructive trusts) are not included. It does not cover an agreement by an agent or a broker to arrange a transfer on behalf of another, but some states require brokerage contracts to be evidenced by a writing or other record under a special statute regulating brokers.

2) What Is an Interest in Land?

The law of real property determines what is an interest in land. Not only is a promise to transfer a legal estate covered, but also a promise to create or transfer a lease or assign a lease (an exception is made for a short-term lease, typically those for one year or less), an easement or rent, and, according to the majority rule, a restriction on land. Also covered is an equitable interest in lands such as an assignment of a right to purchase land. Unlike an easement, a license is not within the statute. A promise to give a mortgage or other lien as security is within the statute. However, an assignment of a mortgage is not within the statute. The mortgage is looked upon as a chose in action because it is connected with the debt it secures.

3) Real Property Distinguished from Goods

According to the Restatement (Second), real property comprises all tangible property other than goods. The UCC clarifies the area very well. It provides that a contract for sale "of growing crops and other things attached to realty and capable of severance without material harm thereto . . . or of timber to be cut" is a sale of goods. It also provides that in the case of a "contract for the sale of minerals or the like (including oil and gas) or a structure or its materials to be removed from realty" the determination depends upon who is to sever the property to be sold. If the seller is to sever, it is a contract for the sale of goods. If the buyer is to sever, it is a contract of the sale of an interest in land.

4) Effect of Performance

If the vendor of property conveys to the vendee, the vendee's oral promise to pay is enforceable.

On the other hand, payment by the vendee in whole or in part does not make the promise of the vendor enforceable unless there is other conduct that is "unequivocally referable" to the agreement. This occurs in most jurisdictions where there is (a) payment and possession by the vendee or (b) the making by the vendee of valuable improvements upon the land with the consent of the vendor. Even if acts of part performance are insufficient to take a case out of the statute, the promisor may, in a proper case of hardship, be estopped from asserting the defense. If the vendee fails to succeed in these approaches, a right of restitution exists.

c. Contracts Not to Be Performed Within a Year

1) Bilateral Contracts

The one-year provision applies only to a promise that by its terms cannot be performed within one year from its making. If by its terms performance is possible within one year, however unlikely or improbable that may be, the promise is not within this statute of frauds. The issue is not how long performance is to run but, by its terms, can it be performed within one year from its making without breaching it.

Examples: (1) *A* makes an oral promise on June 1, 2009, to make a TV appearance for one hour on July 1, 2010. The promise by its terms cannot be performed within one year from its formation. It is unenforceable unless evidenced by a record.

(2) *A* orally promises to work for *B* for two years. The promise is within this statute of frauds. Therefore, it is unenforceable.

(3) *A* orally promises to pay upon the completion of a dam. It is contemplated that the erection of the dam will take three years and it does take three years. The promise is not within the one-year section because, by its terms, the contract, however remote that possibility, can be performed within a year without breaching it. It is enforceable.

a) Promises of Uncertain Duration

Promises of uncertain duration are not generally deemed to be within the one-year provision. These include a promise conditional upon an uncertain event, and a promise of extended performance that may come to an end upon the happening of a condition that may occur within a year.

Examples: (1) *A* promises to pay *B* $10,000 when *A* sells Stoneacre. The promise is not within the one-year statute of frauds because the act of selling can be performed within a year, and it is possible that the condition will occur within a year.

(2) *A* makes a promise to pay *B* $10,000 when *A* dies. The promise is not within this statute of frauds because *A* may die within a year. In some states, by virtue of an additional statute, a promise that cannot be performed before the end of a lifetime is not enforceable. In some jurisdictions, a promise to leave a bequest by will is also subject to a statute of frauds.

(3) *A* promises to supply *B* with goods for the duration of the war. *A*'s promise is not within the statute, because the war may end within one year.

(4) *A* promises to pay for the support of a four-year old child until the child becomes 21. Since this promise, by its terms, is to last for 17 years (a definite term) it would seem that, under the general rule, the promise should be within the statute because the contract cannot be performed within one year from its formation. But the majority of the cases grimly hold that because the purpose of the contract, (support), can be completely attained within a year by the death of the child, the case is not within the one-year statute of frauds. There are some contrary cases, particularly in the area of a promise not to compete.

b) Contracts for Alternative Performances

Where a party promises alternative performances, the promises are not within the one-year statute if any of the alternatives can be performed within one year from the time of the making thereof. It does not matter which party has the right to name the alternative.

Example: *A* leases a car for a five-year term with an option to purchase it in the first year. Because one of the alternative promises of *A* may be performed within one year from the making thereof, the promises are not within the one-year statute of frauds.

c) Contracts with Options to Terminate or Renew

Where a contract contains a term in excess of one year but one or both parties have the option to terminate within a year, the majority view is that the statute applies because termination is not performance. The minority view is to the contrary, on the theory that the rule with respect to alternative promises applies. The same two views exist in the case of a contract for less than one year where one or both parties have the right to extend or renew it.

Example: *A* promises to clean *B*'s pool once a week for five years. The contract gives *A* or *B* the power to terminate within a year by giving thirty days' notice. Under the majority rule, *A*'s promise is within the statute of frauds. Under the minority rule, *A*'s promises are looked upon as alternative promises. *A* promises either to perform for five years or 30 days, or a range of possibilities that are less than one year. Because some of the alternatives (30 days, 31 days, etc.) can be performed within one year, *A*'s promise is not within the statute.

d) What if Only One of Several Promises Cannot Be Performed Within a Year?

Where any of the promises on either side of a bilateral contract (except for alternative promises) cannot be fully performed within one year from the formation of the contract, all of the promises are within the one-year statute of frauds. This means that the contract is unenforceable by either party in the absence of a sufficient memorandum or performance, or the application of the doctrine of estoppel. (See V.C.9., *infra.)*

e) Effect of Performance Under One-Year Section

Under the majority view, full performance by one party makes the promise of the other party enforceable.

Discussion: Some jurisdictions qualify this view by holding that performance must have actually taken place within one year from the making of the contract. A minority of jurisdictions, however, hold that the performance is ineffective to render the contract enforceable. These jurisdictions restrict the performing party to a quasi-contractual remedy. Part performance does not permit a party to enforce the contract, except possibly under the doctrines of divisibility and estoppel. A quasi-contractual recovery is available.

2) Unilateral Contracts

Unilateral contracts requiring the promisee to perform for more than one year are not within the statute of frauds.

One reason for this rule is that, under the majority view, full performance by one party takes the case out of the one year statute of frauds. But even in jurisdictions where this is not true, because a unilateral contract does not arise until the offeree has fully performed, it is not within the statute even if the offeree's performance is not completed within one year from the making of the offer.

Example: A says to *B*, "If you enter and complete the New York Marathon race two years from today, I promise to pay you $1,000." *A*'s promise is not within the one-year statute because the contract does not arise until *B* performs.

3) How Is the Year Measured?

If *A* contracts to work for *B* for one year, and the work is to begin the very next day, the contract is not within the statute, on the theory that the law disregards fractions of a day. If the work is to begin more than one day after making the agreement, the contract is within the one-year statute. However, if, once the employment begins, the parties restate their bargain and the restatement can be regarded as the making or remaking of the contract, the year begins to run from that time.

4) Relationship to Other Statute of Frauds Provisions

The one-year statute may apply to contracts that are governed by other statute of frauds provisions. It does not apply to a short-term lease, even if the lease begins at a distant future date. Most cases hold that it is not applicable to sales of goods. The one-year provision does not prevent specific performance of a land contract if the part-performance exception applies. According to the weight of authority, an engagement to marry (where that is still an enforceable contract), if not performable within one year is within the one-year statute, although not within the consideration of marriage provision.

d. Contracts in Consideration of Marriage

This provision applies to any agreement in consideration of marriage except mutual promises to marry. Thus, the statute applies primarily to pre-nuptial agreements. It applies even if the promise is made by a third party, such as a marriage settlement made by a parent of one of the parties to the engagement. If the marriage is not the consideration, as where a promise is made in contemplation of marriage, the statute does not apply. The same is true if the marriage is merely an incident of the contract and not an end to be attained. The fact that a marriage has taken place is not sufficient to take the contract outside of the statute. But additional performance may be sufficient to render the contract enforceable.

e. Contracts for the Sale of Goods

A contract for the sale of goods for a price of $500 or more is within the UCC statute of frauds (UCC § 2–201). There are a number of ways to satisfy the statute.

Methods of Compliance: (1) A contract for the sale of goods to be manufactured is within the statute unless "the goods are to be specially manufactured for the buyer and are not suitable for sale to others in the ordinary course of the seller's business and the seller, before notice of repudiation is received and under circumstances which reasonably indicate that the goods are for the buyer, has made either substantial beginning of their manufacture or commitments for their procurement." Under this provision, the seller need not be the manufacturer.

(2) A contract is enforceable "if the party against whom enforcement is sought admits in his pleading, testimony or otherwise in court that a contract for sale was made, but the contract is not enforceable under this provision beyond the quantity of goods admitted."

(3) The record requirement is dispensed with as to those items that have been received and accepted. Receipt means taking physical possession of the goods. Acceptance relates to an intention to keep the goods.

(4) The record requirement is also dispensed with as to goods "for which payment has been made and accepted." This seems to say that part payment should give rise only to partial enforcement. This should be true if a just apportionment can be made; if not, part payment should make the entire contract enforceable.

(5) A sufficient record (*see* V.C.4., *infra*).

(6) Promissory estoppel (*see* V.C.9.a., *infra*).

1) What Is Covered?

The section relates to "a contract to sell or sale of goods." This covers both a present sale of goods and a contract to sell goods at a future time. "Goods" are movable tangible things. The UCC provision does not, for example, apply to service contracts, real property contracts, or assignments of choses in action including securities. (*See infra.*)

2) Other UCC Provisions

Three other provisions in the UCC are, in effect, statutes of frauds. (1) While the original Article 8 provided that contracts for the sale (assignment) of securities must be evidenced by a signed writing, or that certain other tests be met, current Article 8 has no writing requirement and excludes the application of the one-year provision to such contracts. (2) UCC § 1–206 requires a writing signed by the party to be charged where there is an assignment of, or promise to assign, a general intangible, and the amount sought to be enforced exceeds $5,000. "General intangibles" include patents, royalties and certain rights under executory bilateral contracts. Revised Article 1 repeals this section, and it has been widely enacted. Most of the assignments that were governed by § 1–206 are now governed by Article 9. (3) UCC § 9–203 requires that a debtor sign a security agreement that contains a description of the collateral and the land, if any, involved.

3. Sufficiency of the Memorandum

a. Introduction

For the memorandum to be sufficient it must "amount to an acknowledgment by the party to be charged that he has assented to the contract that is asserted by the other party."

Comment: A record can satisfy the statute even though it is not formal or integrated. A note or memorandum will suffice. The memorandum may be in any form. It need not be made at the time the contract is entered into. It need not be prepared with the purpose of satisfying the statute and need not be delivered. It need not be in existence at the time of suit.

Example: The parties make an oral contract at a breakfast meeting. They memorialize their agreement on a paper napkin. This can be a sufficient memorandum.

b. Contents of the Record (Except for the UCC)

The record, including a memorandum of the contract, should (1) indicate that a contract has been made or that the signer has made an offer; (2) state with reasonable certainty (a) the identity of the contracting parties, (b) the subject matter and (c) the essential terms in contrast to details or particulars; and by whom and to whom the promises are made; and (3) be signed by the party to be charged.

Implied terms are deemed to be part of the memorandum.

c. What Is a Signature?

A signature is any mark, written, stamped or engraved that is placed by a party anywhere on the writing with intent to assent to and adopt (authenticate) the record as the party's own.

Discussion: For example, initials are sufficient. Also sufficient is a rubber stamp. A letterhead can be a signature. But if the statute says "subscribed," instead of "signed," some courts have held that the writing must be signed at the end.

d. Who Is the Party to Be Charged?

The party to be charged is the one against whom the claim or counterclaim is being made.

Discussion: If *A* sends a signed written offer to *B* and *B* orally accepts, the contract is enforceable against *A* but not *B*. But if *A* is to perform first, *A* may demand that *B* sign a sufficient record and if *B* does not, *A* need not perform. A memorandum is sufficient if signed by an authorized agent of the party to be charged. Further, the authority of the agent need not be expressed in a record, except under the real property provision, where the versions of many jurisdictions provide otherwise.

e. Parol Evidence and the Memorandum

1) Offered by Plaintiff

The interaction of the parol evidence rule and the statute of frauds produces complicated problems. If a plaintiff seeks to introduce evidence of essential terms not contained in the memorandum, for the purpose of enforcing them, the evidence will be barred by the statute of frauds whether or not there is an integration. But consistent additional non-essential oral terms may be shown unless there is a total integration and the parol evidence rule bars them.

2) Offered by Defendant

The defendant may show that the memorandum does not reflect the true agreement and, thus, defeat the claim, proving that the statute of frauds is not satisfied. However, if the parol evidence rule excludes such evidence, the record will be enforced as written. If it is a total integration, it cannot be contradicted or supplemented in order to defeat the claim. If it is a partial integration, the writing may not be contradicted, but it may be supplemented and, if the supplemental term is an essential term, the claim will be defeated because the term is not contained in the record.

3) Interpretation

Oral evidence is admissible in aid of interpretation unless it is excluded under the rules of interpretation.

f. Consideration

If the consideration is a promise that has yet to be performed, it must be stated in the record. In some states the consideration must be stated in the record even though it has been performed.

g. More than One Record

Where the terms necessary to satisfy the statute are in two or more documents, and only one is signed by the party to be charged, is the statute satisfied? The issues presented involve the connection among the documents and assent to the unsigned documents. If the unsigned document is physically attached to the signed document at the time it is signed, or if one of the documents by its terms expressly refers to the other, there is no problem; the statute is satisfied.

Even when this is not true, the unsigned document is part of the memorandum if the documents by internal evidence refer to the same subject matter or transaction. Extrinsic evidence is admissible to help show the connection between the documents and the assent to their contents by the party to be charged.

4. The Memorandum Under the UCC

a. Contents of the Record

Under the UCC, there are only three requirements governing the memorandum. It must:

(1) evidence a contract for the sale of goods;

(2) be signed by the party to be charged; and

(3) specify a quantity.

Thus, the memorandum is sufficient even though it omits other essential terms agreed upon. However, the contract is enforceable only as to the quantity of goods specified in the record.

b. Confirmation Between Merchants

If a merchant sends a signed memorandum to another merchant in confirmation of an agreement, and the memorandum is sufficient against the sender, it is also sufficient against the receiver, provided it is received and the party receiving has reason to know its contents, and fails to give written notice of objection to its contents within ten days after receipt.

Caveat: Such a written confirmation satisfies the UCC statute of frauds, but does not necessarily prove the existence of or the terms of the contract. Those questions are answered by the parol evidence rule.

5. Auction Sales

If goods having a price of $500 or more, or real property are sold at auction, the applicable statute of frauds must be satisfied. The auctioneer is authorized to sign a memorandum on behalf of both parties for a limited period of time after the sale.

6. Agent's Authority

A memorandum is sufficient if signed by an authorized agent of the party to be charged. By the great weight of authority, the agent's authority to sign need not be set forth in writing, but some statutes provide the opposite. Often, however, this requirement of a signed authorization is limited to the real property statute of frauds.

7. Effect of Non-Compliance with a Statute of Frauds

Under the view of the overwhelming majority of jurisdictions, failure to comply with the applicable statute renders the contract unenforceable rather than void. The oral contract is valid, but it may not be sued upon. Some consequences of this approach are:

(1) the statute must be raised as an affirmative defense or it is waived;

(2) the issue can be raised only by the parties to the contract and those in privity;

(3) the unsigned promise constitutes consideration for an unsigned counter-promise;

(4) if one party has signed and the other has not, the contract can be enforced against the party who signed by the party who has not signed.

Under the minority view, the contract is void; no contract is formed. If there is performance and the statute prevents enforcement, a quasi-contractual recovery will be allowed.

8. Part or Full Performance

Complete performance on both sides eliminates any statute of frauds problem. The effect of part performance varies under each version of the statute of frauds. This has already been discussed under the individual subdivisions, except that it has not been mentioned that full or part performance by the promisee has no effect under the suretyship statute of frauds.

9. Estoppel

a. Promissory Estoppel

Despite statutes of frauds, case law now allows recovery where there is substantial reliance upon an unenforceable oral promise. The phrase that is often used is "unconscionable injury." According to the Restatement (Second), the application of this doctrine of estoppel depends upon a number of factors, including the adequacy of other remedies, whether the reliance was substantial, reasonable, and foreseeable. Another factor is the extent to which the act of reliance corroborates the existence of the contract.

b. Estoppel in Pais

If a *representation* produces detrimental reliance an estoppel will be raised. For example, a party who represents to the other that a written memorandum of the contract has been signed will be estopped from raising the statute of frauds as a defense.

10. Effect of Some Promises Being Within and Others Outside a Statute of Frauds

Where one or more of the promises in a contract are within the statute and the others are not, no part of the contract is enforceable.

Exceptions: (1) Where all of the promises that are within the statute have been performed;

(2) Where the party who is to receive the performance under the only promise or promises within the statute agrees to abandon that part of the performance;

(3) Where a promisor makes a promise of alternative performances, one of which is within the statute and the other without, the promisee may enforce the promise that is outside the statute, except in the case of the one-year statute where either promise may be enforced. (*See* V.C.2.c.1.b., *supra.*)

11. Oral Rescission or Modification of a Contract Within a Statute of Frauds

a. Rescission

A written or otherwise recorded executory contract that is within the statute of frauds may be rescinded orally, except in the case of a contract to rescind a transfer of property within the Real Property or UCC statutes of frauds.

b. Modification

(1) If the new agreement is not within the statute of frauds, it is not only enforceable without a writing, but also serves to discharge the previous agreement, whether it was in a record or oral.

(2) If the new agreement is within the statute and is unenforceable because it is oral (or in an insufficient record), the former contract remains enforceable unless the new agreement is enforced under a theory of estoppel.

12. Relationship Among the Various Provisions

If a contract is within more than one statute of frauds provision, it must satisfy the most rigorous of the provisions.

Exceptions: (1) If a contract falls within the one-year section and the UCC statutes, it need only satisfy the less rigorous provision—the UCC statute of frauds.

(2) If a land contract is specifically enforceable under the doctrine of part performance, the other statute of frauds provisions do not prevent enforcement.

Review Questions *(Answers are in Appendix A)*

We suggest you first review HOW TO STUDY and EXAMINATION in the *Perspective* section, *supra.*

1. T or F *P,* seller, and *D,* buyer, entered into a detailed written agreement for the purchase and sale of 150,000 yards of fill. The writing concluded with a merger clause. At the trial, evidence was offered to the effect that *D's* obligation would be effective only if *D* obtained a contract with the City of Brockton. This evidence is inadmissible.

2. T or F *P* was the lessor of equipment. *P* entered into an integrated written agreement with *D* that provided in part that "discount and payment periods will start from the date of receipt of equipment by the Lessee." *D* offered evidence that, prior to signing the writing, the parties had agreed that payments were to be deferred until *D* started to show a profit as a result of the use of the equipment. This evidence is not admissible.

3. T or F Jobber (*J*) entered into a written agreement with supplier (*S*) by which *S* agreed to sell *J* its requirements of raw material for a stated consideration for an extended period. The agreement contained a merger clause. At trial, *J* sought to introduce evidence that *S* violated a contemporaneous oral agreement that *S* would sell 50 shares of its stock to *J* for an agreed price. *J's* evidence is inadmissible.

4. T or F *P* and *D* entered into an oral agreement for services for one year to be rendered by *P*. The service was to commence as soon as *P* could sever *P's* employment with *P's* present employer. The contract is within the statute of frauds.

5. T or F Twenty years ago, the defendant railroad orally agreed with plaintiff that if plaintiff contributed to the installation of a switch and siding, the defendant would maintain the switch and siding for the plaintiff's benefit for as long as the plaintiff needed it. Plaintiff made the agreed contribution and also built a sawmill adjacent to the siding. Although plaintiff still needs the switch and siding, defendant has torn it up. Plaintiff's action for breach will be defeated by the defense of statute of frauds.

6. T or F *D*, a grocer, sold his stock of groceries and his goodwill to *P*. It was orally agreed that *D* would not re-enter the grocery business in a limited area for two years. *P* sues for breach of this oral promise. Since the promise runs for a fixed term of two years, the promise is certainly within the statute of frauds.

7. T or F *P* lived in California, and *D* operated a dealership in Hawaii. In early April, they agreed that *P* would act as general manager for *D* starting on May 1. The hiring was for one year. *P* then left his job in California and moved to Hawaii and leased an apartment there. *P* worked for two months for *D* when he was terminated without just cause. *P* is not entitled to any recovery because the contract is within the one-year statute of frauds.

8. T or F Five years ago, *D* promised *P* that *D* would leave *D*'s entire estate consisting of tangible personal property and securities to *P* if *P* would take care of *D* for the rest of *D*'s life. *D* died five years later having made no provision for *P*. *P*, who duly performed, sues *D*'s representative. *D*'s representative has a defense under the statute of frauds.

9. T or F *P* and *D* railroad reached an oral agreement whereby for five years *P* would have the exclusive concession for advertising on *D*'s right of way, stations and cars. A written memorandum of agreement containing all of the terms was drawn by *D*'s staff and approved and signed by *D*'s president. The president later struck off the signature and placed the memorandum in the company's files. In an action by *P*, *D* may successfully plead the defense of statute of frauds.

10. T or F *D* wrote to *P* offering a brokerage franchise for two years on given terms. *P* accepted orally. In an action by *P* for breach, *D* may successfully plead the defense of statute of frauds.

11. T or F *P* entered into a written contract for two years employment as a physician with defendant clinic. After six weeks the parties orally agreed that the agreement would be rescinded immediately. *P* soon thereafter, and before any change of position by *D*, changed her mind, tendered her services that were refused, and brought suit to enforce the written contract. *P* may succeed since the second agreement was oral.

12. T or F Assume the same facts as in **11**, except that the oral conversation resulted in an agreement that the employment would expire in two months. The oral modification is enforceable.

13. T or F Assume the same facts as in **11**, except that the oral conversation resulted in an agreement that the employment term would be extended an additional six months. The oral modification is enforceable.

14. T or F The parties orally entered into a two-year employment agreement. *D*, the employer, prepared two memoranda. One was signed and contained all of the terms except the duration. The other was unsigned and contained the duration term and referred by internal evidence to the same subject matter. Since all of terms necessary to the statute of frauds were not contained in signed writings, the memoranda were not sufficient to satisfy the statute of frauds.

15. T or F *E,* the executor of *A*'s estate, in compromising a claim against the estate, orally promised to personally guarantee its payment. *E*'s promise is not enforceable under the statute of frauds.

16. T or F *X,* a salesperson for *S,* visited *B,* a physician, at his office and attempted to sell him a sailboat for $28,000. *B* said he would think about it for a week or two before deciding. *X* falsely reported to *S* that an oral agreement was reached, and *S* sent a written confirmation of the alleged sale. *B,* in annoyance, ripped up the paper and threw it in the wastebasket. A month later, *S* tendered the boat. *B* refused to take delivery and *S* sues. *B* would have the defense of statute of frauds.

17. T or F *S* and *B* entered into an oral contract for the purchase and sale of specified quantities of oats to be delivered over a 16-month period. *S* sent *B* a written confirmation of an oral contract bearing number 6077. After several months *B* wrote *S,* stating: "We have no further need for oats, consequently we will accept no further deliveries under contract number 6077." *S* brought suit, and *B* pleads the UCC and the one-year statutes of frauds. *B* would not have the defense of statute of frauds.

18. T or F *A* and *B,* an engaged couple, orally agree that after the marriage they will live in *A*'s house. In exchange *B* agrees to pay $20,000 to *A.* This agreement is within the statute of frauds.

19. T or F *A* and *B* are engaged to be married. *F,* who is *A*'s father, orally promised *A* and *B* a new Jaguar automobile as a wedding gift. *F* subsequently repudiated his promise. *F*'s promise is not enforceable. (In answering do not take into account the doctrine of promissory estoppel.)

20. T or F In an oral agreement *S* retained *X,* a licensed real estate broker, to procure a buyer who would pay $100,000 cash for Stoneacre. *S* orally promised *X* a commission of 6%. *X* produced *B,* who purchased Stoneacre for $100,000. In an action by *X* against *S* for a commission, *S* pleads the real property statute of frauds. *S* has not set forth a meritorious defense.

21. T or F *S,* the owner of a unique 16th century painting, orally authorized an agent, *A,* to sell it for $750,000. *A,* acting on behalf of *S,* reached an agreement with *B* to sell the painting to *B* at that price in a writing signed by *A* and *B,* but not by *S.* The statute of frauds is not satisfied because *A* was not authorized in writing to sell the painting.

22. T or F *S* orally agreed to transfer Stoneacre to *B,* and *B* orally agreed to pay the purchase price in six months. Pursuant to further terms of the agreement, *S* conveyed the property. At the end of six months, *B* has not paid. The statute of frauds is a defense to *S*'s action for the price.

23. Essay Engineering Company (*E*) agreed to do the inspection and testing needed during construction by Constructor Corp. (C) of a complex belt conveyor for an industrial plant. *C* estimated completion in fifteen months. *E* memorialized the agreement in writing and sent it to *C. C* received it and placed it in its files. *C* did not sign it.

During negotiations, the parties had agreed that if overtime (over 40 hours a week) became necessary, it should be added on a time-and-a-half basis. *E*'s written memorial, however, merely called for *C* to pay *E* $90,000 in fifteen monthly installments. It recited that "this contract may be amended only in a signed writing."

After three months, *C* having paid *E* $18,000 in three monthly installments, it became obvious that the conveyor would not be completed on time.

E told *C* that it would be necessary to hire workers for more months than anticipated and for more than 40 hours a week. *E* asked that the contract be amended accordingly. *C* orally agreed to pay *E* $6,000 per month until the job was completed, plus time-and-a-half for all employee hours worked over forty hours per week.

E submitted bills, when the job was completed, on this basis for an additional 6 months beyond the 15 months originally contemplated. *C* had not paid the bills on receipt, explaining it was short of cash. Upon completion *C* paid *E* $2,000, refusing to pay any additional amounts. *E* sues *C* for $6,000 for the additional 6 months work plus $15,000 for sums disbursed for overtime wages.

What are the rights of the parties?

24. Short Essay (consider issues from earlier chapters also).

George had been the personal manager of Connie Francis, the popular singer. Their contract had expired. Negotiations proceeded toward a new contract. Finally, an acceptable agreement for a three-year term seems to have been reached. Ms. Francis's lawyer sent the following letter to George.

> "Dear George:
>
> Enclosed in quadruplicate are the employment agreements between you and Connie Francis. . . . Please sign all copies, have Connie sign all copies and distribute the copies as follows:
>
> 1. One set for you;
> 2. One set for the office;
> 3. One set for me;
> 4. One set for your lawyer.
>
> Sincerely yours,
>
> /s Marv"

Connie Francis signed none of the four copies and decided to hire someone else for the position. George sues for breach of contract. Raise and resolve the contract issues in this case.

Chapter VI

Conditions, Performance and Breach

■ ANALYSIS

A. Nature and Classification of Conditions

1. Definition

A condition is an act or event, other than the lapse of time, that, unless excused, (1) must occur before a duty to perform a promise becomes due (condition precedent) or (2) that discharges a duty of performance that has already arisen (condition subsequent). A promise may be conditional, or it may be unconditional (independent, absolute).

Note: The distinction between condition precedent and condition subsequent can create considerable ambiguity in the analysis of a contract. In an effort to avoid confusion over what kind of "condition" the parties might be facing, Restatement (Second) tries to eliminate this set of conceptual choices by redefining the framework of conditions. Restatement (Second) § 224 defines the term "condition" more narrowly than the traditional common law as "an event, not certain to occur, which must occur, unless its non-occurrence is excused, before performance under a contract becomes due." Note that under this definition, only those events the occurrence of which give rise to a duty (traditionally "conditions precedent") are labeled conditions. (*See* Restatement § 224, comment e.) An event that terminates a duty (traditionally, a "condition subsequent") is treated separately in Restatement (Second) § 230 simply as an "event" that terminates and discharges a duty. The authors of the Restatement believed that this difference in meaning "is one of substance and not merely of the form in which the provision is stated." (Restatement § 230, comment a.) However, courts—even those that generally have endorsed Restatement (Second)—still often use the traditional condition precedent/condition subsequent terminology. For the sake of clarity and consistency, this Chapter will generally follow the traditional terminology.

Examples: (1) *A* promises to pay *B* $10,000 if *B* finds a buyer for Xanadu Acres on *A*'s terms. *A*'s promise is conditional. *A*'s duty to perform the promise becomes unconditional only if the event occurs. Here, *A* has made an offer to a unilateral contract. *B*'s performance creates the contract *and* operates as a condition to *A*'s duty to pay.

(2) *A* promises to pay *B* $10,000 if *B* finds a buyer for Xanadu Acres on *A*'s terms. *A* bargains for and receives *B*'s promise to use best efforts to find a buyer. The contract is bilateral, but *A*'s promise is again conditional. The contract is formed by the mutual agreement of the parties, but *A*'s duty to pay is conditioned on *B*'s performance.

(3) For a consideration, *A* promises to pay *B* $10,000 on July 5. *A*'s duty to perform arises after a lapse of time. Because a lapse of time is the only event that must occur before *A* must pay, *A*'s promise is, by definition, unconditional.

2. Classifications of Conditions

Conditions are classified in two ways. One classification is based on when the conditioning event is to occur in relation to the promise. In this classification, conditions are labeled as precedent, concurrent, and subsequent.

(1) A condition precedent must be performed or occur before a duty to perform a promise is due.

(2) Performance of a concurrent condition must be tendered before the promise of the other party must be performed. In essence, each party's performance is subject to the condition precedent that the other party tender performance.

(3) Conditions subsequent are relatively rare. Such a condition discharges a duty of performance after it has already become absolute.

The second classification is based on whether the condition has been agreed upon and placed in the contract by the parties (express or implied-in-fact condition) or has been imposed by the court to meet the ends of justice (constructive condition). The various classes of conditions are illustrated after VI.A.4., *infra.*

3. Effect of Failure of Condition

Liability for breach of contract attaches to breaches of promises, not for failures of condition.

Comment: Failure of condition may result in the inability to enforce a promise made by the other party, but it imposes no liability, unless the party protected by the condition has promised that the condition will occur.

4. Distinguishing Promises from Conditions

There is no conclusive or exclusive test to determine whether particular contractual language creates a condition or a promise. Certain introductory words almost always create conditions. Among these are: "on condition that" the ship sails, "provided that" the ship sails, "if" the ship sails, "subject to" the ship's sailing. Certain words are almost always promissory: "I will" sail the ship, I "promise" to sail the ship, I "warrant" that the ship will sail.

Express language of condition may also be the basis for finding an implied promise. Similarly, express language of promise may be construed to create an implied-in-fact or constructive condition.

Some contract terms are ambiguous as to their intended legal effect. "The ship is to sail on or before February 4," may be interpreted as creating either a condition or a promise (or both). the normal processes of interpretation are used to determine the intent of the parties.

If this intent cannot be determined, the court will treat the words as creating a promise rather than a condition.

Examples: (1) *S* agrees to sell and *B* agrees to buy a named book. *S* sues for the price without first tendering the book. In the absence of an agreement to the contrary, payment by *B* and delivery by *S* are constructive *concurrent* conditions. In order for *S* to put *B* in default, *S* must make conditional tender of performance or show that tender is excused. Similarly, if *B* were to sue, *B* would have to show tender of the price or the excuse of tender. Concurrent conditions occur primarily in contracts for the sale of goods and contracts for the conveyance of land.

(2) *I* insures *B* against loss by fire. *B*'s house is destroyed by fire and *B* has a claim against *I*. A provision in the insurance policy states: "No action shall be brought after the expiration of 12 months from the occurrence of any loss." *B* sues in the thirteenth month. *B*'s failure to

bring suit within twelve months discharges *I*'s duty of performance that had already arisen. This is a rare instance of a true condition subsequent.

Though true conditions subsequent are rare, at times conditions precedent are treated as subsequent because the language used is subsequent in form. (*See* the next illustration.) The distinction is often crucial to the issue of burden of proof. The claimant has the burden on conditions precedent, the other party on conditions subsequent. At times, a condition precedent is treated procedurally as a condition subsequent so that the burden of proof is placed upon the party with knowledge of the facts.

(3) *D* promised to pay *P* 60 cents per gallon for oil. *D* also promised to pay an additional 25 cents per gallon with the proviso that this second promise would be void if more oil should arrive in whaling vessels this year than last year's quantity. This is clearly an express condition precedent because payment for the oil was to be made at the end of the whaling season. Nonetheless, this court held the parties to the *form* of the language, thrusting the burden on the defendant to prove that more oil had arrived this year. Some other cases reach the opposite conclusion, holding that substance should prevail over form.

(4) *A* offers to pay $100 if *B* walks (unilateral) across Brooklyn Bridge. *B*'s walking the bridge is an express condition precedent to *A*'s duty to pay. If *B* does not walk, *B* is not entitled to the $100. However, *B* is not liable to *A* because *B* has not promised anything.

(5) *B* promises to paint *A*'s house by February 1. *A* promises to pay the agreed price. Painting the house is a constructive condition to *A*'s promise to pay *B*. The condition is constructive because there is no language of condition in the contract, only language of promise. Thus, on the general notion that one must do the agreed work before getting paid for it, unless otherwise agreed, the court constructs a condition that *B* must perform before *B* is entitled to be paid. Although express conditions must be strictly performed, constructive conditions require only substantial compliance.

(6) *Sub*, a subcontractor, promises to do certain painting work for *Jen*, a general contractor. *Jen* promises to pay *Sub* "when *Jen* is paid by the owner." *Sub* has completed the painting work. *Jen* refuses to pay *Sub* because *Jen* has not been paid by the owner. A few cases have held that *Sub* is entitled to be paid only after the owner pays *Jen*, because the owner's payment is an express condition precedent to *Jen*'s duty to pay. However, most cases have held that the "when" clause does not create a condition; therefore. *Sub* is entitled to payment within a reasonable time after performance even if *Jen* has not been paid. Courts reason that a general contractor is in a better position to gauge the ability of the property owner's ability to pay and should bear the burden of protecting against the risk of non-payment. Because a "when" clause is inherently ambiguous, extrinsic evidence is admissible to determine its intended legal effect. If no other persuasive evidence of intent exists, the court will generally follow trade usage; e.g., construction

subcontractors rarely work for contingent fees, but real estate brokers usually work for contingent fees.

(7) If the parties agree that *Sub* will be paid "on condition that Owner pays *Jen*," courts agree that a condition precedent has been agreed to. Traditionally, the condition has been effective. However, a strong recent trend holds that the condition is against public policy because it interferes with legislative policy to protect subcontractors by providing for mechanics' liens. If payment is not due, a mechanics' lien cannot be filed.

(8) *S* agrees to sell a paper mill to *B*, who promises to pay the purchase price in paper. *S* promises to instruct *B* how to manufacture paper. *S* fails to instruct. *S*'s promise to instruct *B* in the art of making paper is not a constructive condition but an implied-in-fact condition. An implied-in-fact condition is a true condition and must be strictly performed. Strict performance also applies to express conditions. The implied-in-fact condition must occur before *B* is required to pay. Implied-in-fact conditions are rare and ordinarily limited to situations involving cooperation.

(9) *S* and *B* enter into a contract for the sale and purchase of real property. The contract contains a clause that performance is "contingent upon *B* obtaining" a described mortgage loan. The phrase quoted clearly creates an express condition precedent, but, in addition, *B* has impliedly promised to use reasonable efforts to obtain the described loan. This means *B* could not back out of the sale by saying he can't obtain a mortgage if he hasn't tried in good faith to obtain one.

(10) A contract states, "in the event of any breach by the seller, the buyer shall give seller written notice of such breach within 30 days." Buyer commences an action for breach without complying with this provision. The question is whether the quoted language creates a promise or an express condition. If compliance with the notice provision is an express condition, the buyer's claim will be dismissed. If it is a promise, the breach would not be material and, under the rules stated in VI.B., *infra*, *B*'s action can proceed. When faced with the issue of whether particular words are language of express condition or language of promise, typically the court will presume that the words create a promise. If language is held to be a promise, the result is usually fairer.

B. Conditions and Promises as Related to Substantial Performance and Material Breach

Express conditions and implied-in-fact conditions must be fully performed but constructive conditions need only be substantially performed.

1. Failure of Condition and Breach of Promise

Discussion: The relationship of rules concerning failure of condition and the related question of breach of promise can be put into focus by the following illustration. *A*, in England, agrees to charter a vessel to *B*, in the United States, and *B* agrees to pay for the vessel when it arrives. The critical clause in the agreement states "the vessel to sail from England on or before February 4." The vessel in fact sails from England on February 5. There are three possible constructions of the quoted language.

(1) The quoted language creates only an express condition. If so, *B* is free to cancel the deal because the express condition has not been literally performed. However, *B* may not sue *A,* because, if the language only creates a condition, *A* did not make a promise.

(2) If the quoted language creates only a promise so that, although *B* has promised to cause the vessel to sail on or before February 4, there is no express condition, the case can be approached in two possible ways.

(a) If *A* sues *B* for refusing to accept the ship, the doctrine of constructive conditions is involved. Therefore, the issue is whether *A* has substantially performed the constructive condition.

(b) If *B* sues *A* because the ship sailed late, the issue is materiality of the breach. If *A's* breach is material, *B* would be (i) free to cancel because of the failure of constructive condition and (ii) also sue for a total breach; but if the breach is immaterial, *B* must perform and can only sue for a partial breach.

(3) If the quoted language created an express condition as in (1) but also gave rise to an implied promise, *B* would not only be free not to proceed whether or not the delay materially affected *B*'s interests, but *B* could also sue for total breach of contract.

Comment: Students must remember that substantial performance and material breach are usually opposite sides of the same coin. If a party has substantially performed, any breach by this party can only be immaterial. Conversely if a party has committed a material breach, this party's performance cannot be substantial. Thus, the way in which the issue is stated is ordinarily not of great importance. However, there are instances where the two ways of framing the issue are not interchangeable—when the two are not opposite sides of the same coin. For example, if one party has not yet performed *at all,* substantial performance has not been rendered, but a material breach has not necessarily occurred.

Examples: (1) *A* promises to restore *B*'s antique automobile and to fix a flat spare tire. *B,* in exchange, promises to pay $28,500. *A* delivers the restored automobile but fails to fix the tire. When the car was delivered, *A* had substantially performed and therefore there was no material breach. *A* is entitled to $28,500, minus *B*'s damages for *A*'s failure to fix the tire.

(2) Vendor agreed to deliver title to a certain lot and to pave the streets in the subdivision in which the lot is located. Vendor tenders a conveyance of title but has not paved the streets. Vendee rejects the tender and refuses to pay. Vendor has not substantially performed. Paving the streets is more important than fixing the flat tire was in the previous illustration. Although Vendor has not substantially performed, it may be that Vendor is not yet guilty of material breach. Consequently, on the bare facts stated we cannot determine if the

developer is guilty of a material breach that would justify an action by the vendee for total breach.

2. Factors Used to Determine Materiality of Breach (May the Aggrieved Party Cancel?)

In determining whether a breach is material, the court considers the following factors:

(a) to what extent, if any, has the contract been performed at the time of breach;

(b) the earlier the breach the more likely it will be regarded as material;

(c) a willful breach is more likely to be regarded as material;

(d) a quantitatively serious breach is more likely to be considered material;

(e) the degree of hardship on the breaching party;

(f) the extent to which the aggrieved party has or will receive a substantial benefit from the promised performance;

(g) the adequacy with which the aggrieved party may be compensated by damages for partial breach;

(h) the type of contract involved. For example, in a contract for the sale of goods, the "perfect tender" rule applies except in the case of installment delivery contracts. In construction contracts, and most other contracts, the doctrine of substantial performance is applied.

Example: Harrison, a dry-cleaner, leased a sign for a three-year term at $150 per month. During the term of the lease, Walker was obligated to maintain the sign. At the expiration of the lease, Harrison was to receive title to the sign. After the first month, someone splattered the sign with a tomato. Walker ignored many telephone demands by Harrison that it send someone to clean the sign. Angrily, Harrison telegraphed Walker that he was canceling the contract. Walker sues for the rent. Judgment for Walker. The damage was easily curable. If Harrison had hired someone to clean the sign, he could have recovered this sum from Walker. Harrison had the substantial benefit of the sign, and cancellation of the contract would result in a harsh forfeiture of Walker's performance.

3. Factors Used to Determine Substantial Performance (May the Defaulting Party Recover?)

(a) To what extent has the injured party obtained the benefits sought by contracting?

(b) To what extent may the injured party be adequately compensated in damages?

(c) To what extent has there been performance or preparation for performance?

(d) How great is the hardship if the breaching party is not permitted to recover?

(e) Was the breach willful?

(f) How certain can the court be that the party in breach would have completed performance?

Example: A agrees to build a house for *B*. One of the promises made in the contract is that Reading brand pipe will be installed. *A*'s plumbing subcontractor installs mostly Cohoes brand pipe. Although the piping is just as good as Reading, this is a breach by *A*. This breach was not discovered until after most of the plumbing was already encased in plaster walls. *B* refuses to pay *A* the final payment. The court found for *A*. *B* has obtained the desired result: a house that generally conforms to his contract. *A*'s deviation was not willful. *A* may recover the agreed price minus *B*'s damages, if any. A contrary result would impose a harsh forfeiture.

4. Effect of Delay

If the contract makes "time of the essence," ordinarily any lateness will be considered a material breach. Otherwise, a reasonable delay will not be considered a material breach. In the case of contracts for the sale of goods, however, the UCC makes time of the essence except in the case of installment contracts.

Examples: (1) *S* contracts to deliver a lathe to *B*'s plant on November 15. *S* tenders delivery on November 16. Under the "perfect tender" rule of the UCC (*see* VI.F.1., *infra*), *B* may reject the goods and hold *S* liable for total breach. Note, however, that sellers rarely contract for delivery on a date certain.

(2) *Builder* agrees to build a warehouse for *Wholesaler* to be completed by June 30. On June 30, the work is incomplete, and it appears that it will take two more weeks to finish. *Wholesaler* purports to cancel the contract. Absent extraordinary circumstances known to *Builder* at the time of contracting that makes completion by June 30 essential, such as the warehouse was needed on July 1 for Wholesaler to win a contract from a third-party supplier, *Builder's* delay is not a material breach. *Wholesaler*'s purported cancellation is a wrongful repudiation. Note carefully that although *Builder*'s delay is not material, the delay is a breach and *Builder* is liable for delay damages.

(3) *A* agrees to convey Xanadu Acres to *B* for $20,000 on June 30. The contract states that "time is of the essence." On June 30, *A* is unable to convey marketable title because of an ancient mortgage that is still of record. *A*'s lawyer informs *B* that a proceeding to clear the records had been started and a decree quieting title will likely issue in a day or two. *B* cancels. *B*'s cancellation is proper. The phrase "time is of the essence" indicates an intent that tender of performance by the date stated is an express condition precedent. Consequently, as in the case of other express conditions, the general rule is that strict compliance is required. However, there is a growing school of thought that indicates that "such stock phrases" do not necessarily have this effect. They are to be considered along with other circumstances in determining the effect of delay. Nonetheless, most courts employ the traditional rule and treat this stock phrase as creating an express condition.

5. The Satisfaction Cases

If a *party* to a contract promises to pay for a performance "on the condition that I am personally satisfied," payment will not be required if the party in *good faith* is dissatisfied. However, if the performance is one that is a matter of mechanical fitness, utility, or marketability, the courts rewrite the contract to mean that if the performance is objectively satisfactory, it must be paid for. This clearly violates the general rule that an express condition requires strict performance. However, in most jurisdictions where the personal satisfaction of a *third party* (e.g., an architect) is involved, the courts do not rewrite the contract. The only criterion is the third party's good faith.

Examples: (1) *A* agrees to rebuild a boiler in *B*'s factory and is to be paid "if the work is to the entire satisfaction of *B*." *A* does an excellent job but *B*, an honest but super-finicky eccentric, is not satisfied. If the jury finds that *B* is unreasonable, which it probably would, *B* must pay. Underlying reasons are (a) one ought not be a judge in one's own cause and (b) that an unconscionable forfeiture would otherwise occur. The result would be different if the person to be satisfied were an independent professional engineer rather than a contracting party.

(2) *A* agrees to paint a portrait of *B*'s daughter for $3,000, for which *B* only needs to pay if *B* is entirely satisfied. *A* paints a portrait that is critically acclaimed as a masterpiece. *B*, however, is not satisfied and rejects the portrait. *B* is not liable for the price. *B*'s judgment of the performance is a matter of taste and therefore the judgment is personal and subjective. Note that there is no element of unjust enrichment or forfeiture because if *B* rejects the portrait, *A* keeps it. Contrast the boiler in example (1) which, as a fixture, becomes the property of *B*, the factory owner. This is an important element in determining whether to apply a subjective test of good faith or an objective test of reasonableness. Note also that, although the standard is personal, the dissatisfaction must be genuine. If *B* manifests dissatisfaction with the *bargain*, for example, by stating that the price is too high, or by refusing to examine the portrait, *B* is liable. *B* is not dissatisfied with the performance but with the bargain.

6. Demand

If a promise is made to render a performance upon demand, demand is an express condition precedent. But it is generally held, as an exception, that a debtor's promise to pay upon demand is enforceable without demand.

C. Recovery Despite Material Breach or Failure to Perform Substantially

A party who does not substantially perform is not entitled to a recovery, unless performance is excused or the case comes under one of the following exceptions.

(1) Divisibility;

(2) Independent Promise;

(3) Quasi Contract; or

(4) Statutory Relief.

1. Divisibility

A contract is divisible if the performances of each party are divided into two or more parts and the performance of each part by one party is the agreed exchange for a corresponding part by the other party. If a divisible portion is substantially performed, recovery may be had for that portion despite a material breach of the overall contract.

Examples: (1) *A* and *B* agree that *A* will be *B*'s secretary for one year at a salary of $700 per week. *A* works for a week and quits for no good reason. *A* is entitled to $700 because *A* has performed one part of a divisible contract. *B*, however, is entitled to counter-claim for damages for the rest of the year. (Note also, that while most hirings are "at will," this illustration involves an employment contract for a specific term.)

(2) *T* agrees to transport five truckloads of widgets for *X* at $30 a mile. Four truckloads are duly delivered to their destination, but the fifth is totally demolished half-way to the destination. *T* sues for payment. *T* is entitled to payment for the four completed deliveries. Each has an apportioned calculable price and *independent value* to *X*. As to the fifth, *T* has no claim. The transport of the goods half-way to destination has no value to *X*. Indeed, *X* has an action against *T* for breach.

(3) A contractor agrees to make alterations for $3,075, payable as follows: $150 on signing the contract, $1,000 on delivery of materials to the site, $1,500 on completion of rough carpentry and $425 on completion of the job. The first two payments are duly made. The contractor wrongfully repudiates upon completion of the rough carpentry and sues for $1,500 on a theory of divisibility. The contractor does not recover as the contract is not divisible. It can hardly be said that $150 was the agreed equivalent for signing the contract or that delivery of plaintiff's materials was worth $1,000 to defendant. Construction contracts are rarely divisible.

2. Independent Promises

A promise is independent (unconditional) if it is unqualified or if nothing but a lapse of time is necessary to make the performance of the promise presently enforceable. The promisee may enforce an independent promise without rendering substantial performance of the promisee's part of the bargain.

Example: A promises to paint *B*'s house and *B* promises to pay *A* $5,000 upon completion of the work. *A*, without justification, fails to start the job within a reasonable time. *A*'s promise is unconditional because *A* must paint before *B* must pay, and there are no other express or implied conditions to *A*'s duty of performance. Consequently, *B* may cancel and sue for total breach despite *B*'s own nonperformance. *B* need only prove that he or she would have been ready, willing and able to pay had *A* performed.

Caveat: Relativity of the Definition. In special circumstances, such as destruction of the house before *A* has an opportunity to start performance (*see* VI.D.4., *infra*), or *B*'s repudiation, conditions may be constructed to protect *A* in the light of the facts. Although, in the above example, *A*'s promise to paint is said to be unconditional by definition, the definition is relative to the facts given.

a. Independent Promises in Leases

Under the traditional common law, the doctrine of constructive conditions did not apply to leases. Consequently, a tenant's duty to pay rent was treated as independent of the landlord's covenants to repair and to provide services. Even if the landlord did not fix a flight of stairs, for example, the tenant still had to pay rent. This rule has been abolished or eroded in most jurisdictions as to residential tenancies.

b. Independent Promises in Insurance

Absent a provision in an insurance policy that makes payment of the premium an express condition, the insurer's duty is not conditioned on payment of the premium. Consequently, if a casualty loss ensues, the insurer must pay although the premiums are in arrears. This rule does not prevent the insurer from inserting a clause permitting it to cancel a policy for non-payment. Until the cancellation is effectuated, however, the insurer's promise remains independent of the payment of premiums.

3. Quasi-Contractual Recovery

Although all jurisdictions recognize the availability of quasi-contractual relief where services are rendered under a contract that is defective for reasons such as indefiniteness, or non-compliance with writing requirements, or that fails because of impossibility of performance, there is disagreement with respect to giving relief to a party who has breached the contract. The orthodox and still prevailing view is that a party in default may not recover from the other party even though the breaching party has conferred benefits on the other party in excess of the damages caused by the breach. The modern trend, however, permits such recovery.

4. Statutory Relief

a. Introduction

A number of statutes permit a defaulting party to recover. For example, legislation in most states requires that workers be paid at periodic intervals, and that accrued wages be paid when the employment relation ends, regardless of any contract condition to the contrary.

b. The UCC

Article 2 of the UCC allows a defaulting buyer to obtain restitution to the extent the buyer's payments exceed the smaller of (a) $500 or (b) 20% of the purchase price. The buyer's claim for restitution is subject to an offset in the amount of the seller's actual damages and the value of benefits received by the buyer.

Example: *B* contracts to purchase living room furniture from *S* for $2,100, paying $700 of the purchase price. *B* repudiates and sues for restitution of the down payment. *B* obtains restitution of $700 minus the lesser of $500 or 20% of the price ($420). Since $420 is less than $500, *B* obtains judgment for $700–420, that is, $280.

D. Excuse of Conditions

1. Prevention

A condition is excused by wrongful prevention, substantial hindrance or the failure to cooperate. Moreover, in every contract there is a constructive condition that one will not wrongfully prevent or substantially hinder the other party's performance.

Examples: (1) A nephew agreed to care for his granduncle for the rest of the granduncle's life. The granduncle promised his nephew that he would be paid by his estate. Later, the granduncle pointed a gun at his nephew and unjustifiably ordered him to leave. The nephew sues for damages and recovers. Although the nephew's performance under the contract was a constructive condition precedent to the granduncle's duty to pay, this condition was excused because the granduncle prevented its occurrence.

(2) Assume all the facts in example (1), except that the granduncle sues the nephew for breach of the nephew's promise to take care of him for life. Case dismissed. There is a constructive condition to the granduncle's rights that he not prevent his nephew from performing. Because this condition failed, he has no cause of action.

(3) *B* lists a house for sale with *A*, a real estate broker, agreeing to pay a commission conditioned "upon closing of title." *A* procures a purchaser who signs a contract of purchase. Later at the purchaser's request, *B* agrees to a mutual rescission of the contract. *A* sues *B* for the agreed commission. *A* recovers. *B*'s conduct actively prevents the condition that title close. Consequently, the condition is excused.

(4) Assume the same facts as in the previous example, except that no mutual rescission occurs. Instead, the purchaser repudiates the contract. *B* retains the down payment but takes no action against the purchaser. *A* sues *B*, contending that *B* should have sued the purchaser for specific performance thereby bringing about the condition to *B*'s own duty to pay a commission to *A*. Action dismissed. Although there are times when one must cooperate affirmatively to bring about a condition to one's own duty, heroics are not required. An action for specific performance involves expense, annoyance and risks.

(5) *S* agrees to sell Xanadu Acres to *B* for $100,000 and *B* agrees to purchase, subject to *B*'s obtaining a mortgage loan of $75,000 at specified terms. *B* makes no effort to get financing. *S* sues *B* for breach. *S* recovers. Although a condition to *B*'s duty to purchase has not occurred, the condition is excused (meaning that the condition need not occur) because *B* failed to cooperate by using reasonable efforts to obtain a mortgage loan. An affirmative duty of cooperation is implied, because the condition cannot occur without *B*'s cooperation. A duty of affirmative cooperation is implied when it accords with "justice, common sense and the probable intention of the parties."

(6) *S* agreed to sell to *B* 2,600 tons of widgets for $41 a ton. *S* failed to deliver and set up as a defense that widgets were in short supply because *B* bought up the widgets from the suppliers from whom *S* planned to buy, driving up the market price. Judgment for *B*. Although

there was substantial hindrance by *B,* there was no wrongful conduct by *B*. Sellers who agree to sell goods they do not possess ("selling short") assume the risk of market forces, including the possibility that the buyer may be actively purchasing in the market.

(7) Assume the same facts as in the prior example, except that *B* has bought up all the widgets available on the world market ("cornered the market"). *S* will be excused, because *B* has made it impossible for *S* to perform.

2. Estoppel, Waiver and Election

a. Equitable Estoppel (Estoppel in Pais)

Equitable estoppel has traditionally been held to exist where one party has misrepresented a fact, and the other party has injuriously relied upon that misrepresentation. Today, an estoppel may be based upon even an innocent misrepresentation of fact or upon a promise.

b. Waiver

A waiver is generally defined as an intentional relinquishment of a known right. This definition is absurd. One important thing to remember is that even though there is a waiver under this definition, it may be without effect. Another thing to remember is that, generally speaking, waivers of rights are totally ineffective, and this discussion concerns waiver of *conditions* and *not* the renunciation of a *right* to damages or the discharge of a contract, both of which are discussed in the section on discharge, VII.D., *infra*. Another thing to remember is that many waivers are unintentional. One more thing—many waivers occur where the waiving party does not know his or her legal options.

1) Waiver Before Failure of Condition

A waiver of a condition that constitutes a material part of an agreed exchange is ineffective in the absence of consideration, its equivalent, or an estoppel.

A waiver of a condition that is not a material part of the agreed exchange is effective, but it may be reinstated by notice prior to any material change of position by the other party.

An effective waiver disables the party from canceling but does not discharge the aggrieved party's right to damages.

Examples: (1) *A* agrees to paint *B*'s house, and *B* promises to pay $5,000. Immediately after the agreement, *B* promises to pay the $5,000 even if *A* does not paint. The waiver of condition is ineffective; any other rule would completely subvert the doctrine of consideration. Thus, what has occurred is an attempted modification without consideration, its equivalent, or an estoppel. *B*'s second promise is unenforceable.

(2) *A* agrees to build a garage for *B* before January 1. They make time of the essence. Before January 1, *B* tells *A* that the performance will be accepted even if it is not complete until February 1. On January 30, *A* completes the performance and

B refuses to pay. *A* sues. Judgment for *A*. Although the condition that time is of the essence is material, it is not a material part of the agreed exchange. The waiver is effective even without an estoppel. The practical result is that the waiver is effective even if it can be shown that *A* could not have finished the building by January 1.

(3) Assume the facts given in example (2), except that the day after *B* had made the waiver and before any change of position by *A, B* communicated a retraction of the waiver. The condition that time is of the essence is reinstated.

2) Who Can Waive

Only the party for whose benefit the condition has been imposed can waive it.

Example: S and *B* agree to the sale by *S* to *B* of Xanadu Acres, "subject to *B*'s obtaining financing" on specified terms. *B* fails to obtain the financing but decides to dip into savings to make the purchase. As the condition is clearly for *B*'s protection, *B* may waive it. *S* cannot.

Perspective—Waiver Before Contracting: At times one party will present a pre-printed form contract to the other for signature. After discussion, the party who is proposing the form may assure the other that a given term of the printed form will not be applied in this case. Many courts have treated the situation as involving waiver although the *real* issue is the parol evidence rule. Generally, if the words of assurance have induced the adhering party to sign, the court will rule that the propounding party is estopped from enforcing the term in question.

3) Waiver After Failure of Condition

A waiver after a failure of an express or constructive condition is an election. An election may take place by conduct or by promise. No consideration is needed for an election and, according to the majority rule, an election once made cannot be withdrawn.

Examples: (1) *A* promises to charter a vessel from *B* on the condition that the vessel arrive on or before February 4. The vessel arrives on February 5. The express condition clearly has failed, and *A* can elect to cancel the deal because *A* is entitled to literal performance. However, if *A* elects to continue, both parties are bound.

(2) *A* promises to build a house in exchange for *B*'s promise to pay. *A* falls so behind schedule that there is a material breach. There is a failure of a constructive condition that gives *B* the right to elect to continue the contract and sue for a partial breach or to terminate *B*'s obligations under the

contract and sue for a total breach. The election may be by conduct, as where *B* makes a payment to *A* after *B*'s right to elect has arisen.

4) Repeated Waivers

If a party repeatedly waives a condition, the other party can reasonably expect that future waivers will be made unless the first party reinstates the condition by reasonable notice.

Example: A mortgagee had consistently waived the condition of timely payment by accepting late payments. Then without giving any prior notice, the mortgagee refused to accept a late payment and began a foreclosure action. Case dismissed. The mortgagor had reason to believe that late payments would be accepted. The mortgagee is estopped from insisting on its right to timely payment until it has given the mortgagor reasonable notice that the condition is reinstated.

3. Excuse of Conditions Involving Forfeitures

A condition may be excused if (1) it involves an extreme forfeiture, (2) its occurrence is not a material part of the agreed exchange and (3) if one of the foundations for equitable jurisdiction exists.

Discussion: If a case is an equity case, in the sense that earlier in our history the case would have been brought in a separate court of equity, certain special rules and maxims apply, including the maxim that "equity abhors a forfeiture." Whenever a party seeks, and plausibly is entitled to, specific performance, specific restitution (except replevin), or an injunction, the case is an equity case even though in nearly every jurisdiction law and equity are administered in the same court.

Example: Holiday Inns obtained a 4½ year option to purchase certain vacant land from Knight for $200,000. The consideration for the option was $10,000 paid on acquiring the option and four additional $10,000 payments payable on July 1 of each of the next four years. The option agreement provided that the dates of payments were of the essence. Two of the annual installments were duly made. The third, tendered on July 2, was rejected. Equity jurisdiction exists because each parcel of land is deemed unique. The court rules that the option is in effect. The failure of condition is slight, and the forfeiture is extreme—$30,000 already paid for the option. The plaintiff is not attempting to extend the option period, but only to obtain relief from forfeiture that would be caused by a late installment payment.

4. Excuse of Conditions Because of Impossibility

Impossibility excuses a condition if it becomes impossible for it to occur, it is not the fault of the party, the condition is not a material part of the agreed exchange, and a forfeiture would otherwise occur.

Example: A agrees to erect a building for *B*. *B* promises to pay on the condition *A* produce the certificate of satisfactory completion signed by a named architect. After *A* substantially performs the work, the named architect dies. *A* is entitled to enforce *B's* promise to pay, because the condition is excused. The result would be otherwise if the architect died prior to the contractor's commencement of performance.

E. Prospective Unwillingness and Inability to Perform: Repudiation

1. Repudiation as a Breach Creating a Cause of Action

A repudiation is a promisor's unjustified statement positively indicating that he or she will not or cannot substantially perform, or the promisor's voluntary act that renders the promisor's substantial performance impossible or apparently impossible. A repudiation is a total breach whether or not performance is due now or in the future.

Discussion: The only exception is the case of a unilateral obligation not yet due (*see* VI.E.9., *infra*). To establish a cause of action, the aggrieved party must prove (1) the contract, (2) the breach by repudiation, and (3) that he or she would have been ready, willing and able to perform but for the repudiation. Note that this last requirement, for whatever reason, often tends to be overlooked by students.

The Restatement (Second) softens the requisites of a repudiation. While much case law requires a "positive" or "unequivocal" statement of unwillingness or inability to perform, Restatement (Second) § 250, cmt. C, states: "a party's language must be sufficiently positive to be reasonably interpreted to mean that the party will not or cannot perform."

2. Prospective Unwillingness and Inability as a Prospective Failure of Condition Creating a Defense

If a party repudiates the obligations of the contract or appears unwilling or unable to perform, under the doctrine of prospective failure of condition, the other party may, depending on the circumstances, (1) continue performance; (2) suspend or withhold performance; (3) change position or declare that the contract is canceled.

Discussion: If the prospective unwillingness is a repudiation, the other party has no power to elect to waive the breach but must cease performance except in the rare case where continuation of performance will minimize damages. In cases not involving a repudiation, which of the responses is permissible depends on the facts of the case. "The question must resolve itself into one of degree and probability." The Restatement (Second) suggests that if the insecure party fails to take the interim step of demanding assurances, the insecure party acts at its peril if it cancels the contract or takes other action that proves to have been improper because the other party is able to prove that it would have been ready, willing and able to perform pursuant to the contract but for the insecure party's conduct.

Examples: (1) *S* agrees to sell and *B* agrees to buy a specific car, delivery to be made on June 1. On April 25, *S* tells *B* that *S* will not perform. Result: *S* has repudiated. Therefore, *B* may, first, sue now for anticipatory breach or sue after June 1 for actual breach, and, second, change position or otherwise indicate that the contract is at an end. Thus, *B* may elect any of the responses indicated above, except that *B* cannot continue performance or make plans based upon obtaining the car on June 1.

(2) *S*, instead of telling *B* that the car will not be delivered, sells the car to *X*. *B* has precisely the same rights as in the preceding illustration because *S*'s conduct amounts to a repudiation.

(3) *A* agrees with *B* to sing the lead part in an opera for two months. Prior to opening night, *A* becomes ill, and her physician expresses the opinion that she will not be able to sing for two weeks. Although her illness excuses the prospective non-performance, the prospective inability to perform is serious, and *B* may respond by hiring a substitute and declaring the contract at an end. *A* cannot recover in any suit for breach. The Restatement (Second) suggests that before changing position *B* should demand assurances from *A*. According to the Restatement (Second), if *A* does not first demand assurances and *B* shows up ready, willing and able to sing on opening night, *A* will be liable for breach of contract.

(4) A serious shortage of steel exists because of wartime conditions. A general contractor asks the steel subcontractor whether it will be able to get sufficient steel to perform. The subcontractor states that it is unable to give a positive promise that it will be able to perform. It has not repudiated, because it has not positively stated it will not perform but has indicated prospective inability.

Although the general contractor has no cause of action, it would be justified in changing position by contracting with a steel subcontractor who can assure it of performance. If the UCC were applicable, (it is not applicable because the construction contract is basically a service contract) the first subcontractor would be liable for breach because it failed to give adequate assurances (*see* UCC § 2–609). However, because wartime conditions were impeding the procurement of steel, the subcontractor conceivably may have had the defense of impossibility of performance.

(5) *S* contracted to sell certain real property to *B*. Closing was set for December 15. On November 30, *B* wrote to *S* that there were certain defects in title, and *B* was therefore canceling the contract and demanding the return of the down payment. *B* did not specify what defects had been discovered. There were defects, but they were curable within a reasonable time after December 15. *B* sues for restitution, and *S* counterclaims for damages to the extent these exceed the down payment. Judgment for *S*. Although *B*'s title search showed that *S* was prospectively unable to perform, it did not conclusively establish inability. Consequently, *B*'s cancellation was an overreaction and, therefore, a repudiation. While *B* would be justified in withholding any payments due before or at the closing date, *B* was not free to cancel absent a finding that title was incurable. Unless (a) title is incurable or (b) the seller repudiates, the buyer can place the seller in default only by (c) tendering the buyer's own performance coupled with a demand for a conveyance of marketable title within a reasonable time followed by failure of the seller to tender such a conveyance. *In short, tender, demand and breach.*

The seller also recovers on the counterclaim. To place a buyer in breach, the seller must normally show the buyer's breach as well as seller's own tender and demand. Here, however, tender is excused by the buyer's repudiation. The seller need only show the buyer's repudiation and that the seller would have been ready, willing and able to perform within a reasonable time but for the repudiation.

3. Role of Good Faith

A promisor's good faith, but unjustified, cancellation of the contract is a repudiation.

Example: *See* example involving the tomato-streaked dry-cleaning sign, VI.B.2., *supra*.

4. Retraction of a Repudiation or Prospective Failure of Condition

A repudiation may be retracted, and a prospective unwillingness or inability to perform can be cured unless the aggrieved party has canceled or materially changed position or otherwise indicated that the contract is at an end.

Example: S contracts to deliver steel to *B* in ten monthly installments, commencing June 1. On May 1, *S* repudiates the contract. On May 5, threatened by a lawsuit and advised by counsel of the probability of an adverse judgment, *S* notifies *B* that the steel deliveries will be made as scheduled. The withdrawal of the repudiation effectively reinstates the duties of the contract. The result would be different if *B* had already contracted with another steel supplier: in that case, *B* could hold *S* liable for total breach of contract.

5. Urging Retraction

The aggrieved party may urge the repudiator to retract without prejudice to the aggrieved party's rights.

Example: S contracts to deliver steel to *B,* deliveries to commence on June 1. *S* repudiates on May 1. *B* immediately begins to negotiate with *C* for steel to replace the steel expected under *B*'s contract with *S*. Simultaneously, *B* urges *S* to retract. On May 6, *B* enters into a replacement contract with *C*. Later that day, *B* receives a retraction from *S*. The retraction is ineffective. By urging *S* to retract, *B* was not being underhanded and did not lose the right to change position.

6. Effect of Impossibility on a Prior Repudiation

Subsequent impossibility will discharge an anticipatory breach and partial impossibility will limit damages for the breach.

Examples: (1) Writer *(W)* hires a translator (*T*) for a one-year term commencing June 1. On May 11, *W* repudiates. On May 25, *T* dies from a snake bite. *T*'s estate sues *W* for breach. *T*'s estate fails to establish a cause of action. Although *W* was guilty of committing an anticipatory breach, *T*'s estate cannot establish that *T* would have been ready, willing and able to perform but for the repudiation.

(2) Assume the same facts as in example (1), except that *T*'s death occurs on June 30, after the one-year term began. *T*'s estate establishes

a cause of action, but under the prevailing view, recovery is limited to damages for a thirty-day period. This view is the better view because it fully takes into account all facts known at the time of trial. The other view is that *T*'s rights vest at the time of the repudiation.

7. Constructive Repudiation Under the UCC and Restatement (Second)

Under § 2–609 of the UCC, if a party has reasonable grounds for insecurity, that is, reasonably fears that the other party is unable to or unwilling to perform, that party may demand adequate assurance of performance and also has the right to suspend performance until such assurance is received. Failure to give adequate assurance within a reasonable time, not exceeding 30 days, operates as a repudiation.

a. Is the Common Law Displaced?

Whether the right to demand adequate assurance displaces other rights (e.g., to change position) or is simply an additional right is not yet clear. The Restatement (Second) takes the position that other rights are displaced.

b. What Are Adequate Assurances?

The adequacy of an assurance varies greatly with the commercial context. Words of assurance from a reputable party may suffice, but where the prospective inability is grave even a reputable buyer may be required to offer more than sweet talk, such as furnishing a financial statement or producing a bank letter of credit.

c. The Restatement (Second)

The Restatement (Second) follows the lead of the UCC and permits the insecure party to demand adequate assurances and suspend performance until such assurances are received. If assurances are not furnished within a reasonable time, the demanding party may treat the failure to provide them as a repudiation. Under the Restatement (Second), the right to demand assurances replaces other permissible reactions to prospective inability or unwillingness, except the permissible responses to a repudiation or insolvency. Thus, except in the case of a repudiation or insolvency (*see* VI.E.8., *infra*), the insecure party can cancel or change position *only at its peril*. If the other party tenders or demands timely performance, the insecure party will itself be in breach if it is no longer able or willing to perform. (Recall Example 3 in VI.E.2., *supra*.) The courts have not yet accepted the Restatement position.

8. Insolvency

a. Insolvency Defined

A particular form of prospective inability is insolvency—at least in cases where a party's solvency is relevant. (The insolvency of an employee, for example, may be irrelevant to performance of the employment contract.) UCC § 1–201(23) [revised 1–201(24)] enumerates three kinds of situations that constitute insolvency:

(1) cessation of payment of debts in the regular course of business;

(2) inability to pay one's debts as they mature;

(3) insolvency within the meaning of the Federal Bankruptcy Act. Subject to complex qualifications beyond the scope of a *Contracts* course (11 U.S.C. § 100(26)), this occurs when one's debts are greater than one's assets.

b. The Effect of a Buyer's Insolvency

When a seller discovers that a buyer is insolvent, the seller may take the following steps:

(1) Refuse delivery except for cash, including payment for all goods previously delivered under the same contract;

(2) Stop delivery of goods in transit;

(3) Reclaim goods delivered on credit to a party while insolvent, provided that demand for their reclamation is made within ten days of receipt by the buyer.

(4) Reclaim goods delivered on credit to a party while insolvent, irrespective of the ten-day period, if the buyer has made a misrepresentation of solvency to the particular seller in writing within three months before delivery.

c. Effect of a Seller's Insolvency

The buyer who has paid in whole or in part for goods identified to the contract but who has yet to receive them may rightfully recover the goods if the seller became insolvent within ten days after receipt of the first installment of their price. The buyer's rights may be subordinate, however, to the rights of secured creditors and of the trustee in bankruptcy.

9. Repudiation of a Debt

The doctrine of anticipatory breach was greeted with skepticism in this country. It was early held that the doctrine of anticipatory repudiation cannot be used to accelerate a debt. This early exception remains entrenched in our law. The exception is usually stated to be that no action lies for repudiation of a unilateral obligation to pay a sum of money at a fixed time or times.

Examples: (1) Plaintiff purchases a disability insurance policy that promises to pay $500 a week for life in the event of permanent total disability. Plaintiff, after duly paying premiums, becomes permanently and totally disabled. The insurer refuses to pay. Plaintiff sues for total breach, claiming the present value of all payments due. The action for total breach fails. Plaintiff is entitled only to the payments due at the time of judgment. Now, you might be inclined to scream, "That's unfair! Does he have to sue after every week?" Note, however, that the plaintiff may also be able to obtain a mandatory injunction ordering the insurer to make future payments.

(2) Defendant promises to pay $500 a month for ten years to plaintiff in exchange for a parcel of land to be conveyed at the end of that period. After making six payments, defendant repudiates. Plaintiff may sue immediately for total breach. The case falls outside the exceptional category of repudiation of a debt. There are interdependent obligations—defendant's duty to pay and plaintiff's duty to convey.

10. Repudiation and Right to Elect

As a general rule, the aggrieved party may elect to continue the obligations of the contract despite a material breach. However, if the other party has repudiated, the aggrieved party cannot elect to continue the contract. There is no right to recover damages that could have been avoided by ceasing performance or preparation for performance. Under the UCC, this principle is relaxed to a slight extent. The aggrieved party may urge retraction and "may for a commercially reasonable time await performance by the repudiating party."

Example: A Corp. contracts with *B*, a municipality, to construct a bridge. Prior to performance, *B* repudiates. *A* angrily insists that it has a contractual right to build the bridge, builds it, and sues for the price. Although *A* recovers under the doctrine of anticipatory breach, *A* failed to mitigate damages. *A* does not recover the price but only the profit that would have been made under the contract; that is, the contract price minus cost of performance.

F. Performance of the Sales Contract

1. Obligations of the Seller

The seller must tender goods conforming in every respect to the contract. If tender is not perfect, unless otherwise agreed, the buyer may reject the whole, accept the whole or accept any commercial unit or units and reject the rest.

a. Perspective

The perfect tender rule is so undermined by exceptions and qualifications that it may be misleading. Nevertheless, if none of the qualifications or exceptions applies, a buyer can tell a seller's delivery agent to "take them away, there is a defect" or, after delivery (but before acceptance), tell the seller, "pick them up, there is one short-weighted box out of a hundred."

b. Qualification and Exceptions

1) "Unless Otherwise Agreed"

The express terms of the contract may restrict the perfect tender rule, for example, it may provide that the buyer can't reject the whole but has to allow seller to replace the defective item. A trade usage that constitutes an implicit term of the contract may be inconsistent with the perfect tender rule. For example, a trade usage may limit the buyer's remedy to a price adjustment for certain kinds of defects.

2) Cure (UCC § 2–508(1))

a) Within the Contract Time

If a non-conforming tender is made and the time for performance has not yet expired, the seller may seasonably notify the buyer of the seller's intention to cure and may then within the contract time make a conforming delivery.

Example: B contracts to purchase a new Aston-Martin automobile from *S*. On tender of delivery, *B* notices some small dents and scratches that were made in the course of shipment from the factory to *S*. *S* offers to cure by delivering a conforming undamaged replacement, and the time for delivery has not expired. *S* has the right to cure.

b) A Further Reasonable Time (UCC § 2–508(2))

Where the buyer rejects a non-conforming tender which the seller had reasonable grounds to believe would be acceptable with or without a money allowance the seller may, if it seasonably notifies the buyer, have a further reasonable time to substitute a conforming tender.

Discussion: There are two kinds of situations where the seller may have reasonable grounds to believe that the buyer will accept a non-conforming tender.

(1) The Seller Knows of Non-Conformity

A seller may know of the non-conformity and still be reasonable in tendering the goods.

Example: The contract between a buyer and a dealer calls for hearing aid model A-660. The manufacturer delivers to the dealer model A-665 which it describes as an improved version of model A-660. The dealer is reasonable in tendering A-665 to the buyer. Again, a seller can reasonably believe the buyer will accept, say, Cohoes pipe instead of Reading pipe, or will accept short-weight shipments (with a price allowance). In each of these instances, if the buyer rejects, the seller has additional time to make a conforming tender.

(2) The Seller Does Not Know of the Non-Conformity

Discussion: Goods are often shipped in sealed containers. Distributors buy and resell to retailers without opening the containers. Retailers also deliver factory-sealed containers to consumers. Absent a history of non-conforming goods in the same kind of containers from the same source or other special information, it is reasonable for the seller to believe that the goods are acceptable. If, upon inspection, the goods are properly rejected, the seller has a reasonable additional time to cure.

Example: S contracted to sell to *B* a tankerload of oil, testing out at .5% sulfur or less. *S* then purchased a tankerload that was on the high seas from *T* who gave *S* a certificate from a refiner that the cargo of oil had a .5% sulfur content. When it was tendered on February 14, *B*'s inspection revealed that the sulfur content was .9%, too high to meet the contract terms. *S* offered to cure by delivering the cargo of another ship arriving on February 28. *B* refused. (Among *B*'s reasons was a 25% drop in the market price of crude oil between the time of contracting and February 14). It was held that *B*'s refusal was a wrongful repudiation. *S*, relying in good faith on the certificate, had reason to believe that the tender would be acceptable and therefore had a further reasonable time to cure.

3) Acceptance (UCC § 2–606)

Once goods have been accepted, rejection is no longer possible, although revocation of acceptance may be an available alternative.

a) Express Acceptance

If, after a reasonable opportunity to inspect the goods, the buyer signifies to the seller that the goods are conforming or that they will be kept despite their non-conformity, the buyer has accepted. A buyer who signs a seller's form stating the goods have been inspected and are conforming has not accepted under this rule unless there genuinely was a reasonable opportunity to make more than a cursory inspection.

b) Failure to Make an Effective Rejection

Failure to reject does not operate as an acceptance until the buyer has had a reasonable time to inspect the goods. To make an effective rejection, the buyer must seasonably notify the seller of the rejection. After a rejection is properly communicated, it is to be remembered that the seller often has the right to cure. Consequently, the UCC provides in § 2–605 that when goods are rejected the buyer must state all defects that are discoverable by reasonable inspection. To justify a rejection or a claim of breach, the buyer cannot rely on any discoverable unstated defect that the seller could have cured.

Between merchants, a more drastic rule prevails. When a seller requests in writing a full and final statement of all defects on which the buyer proposes to rely as grounds for rejection, the buyer cannot rely upon unstated defects (even if the defects could not be cured) that reasonably could have been discovered.

c) "Acts Inconsistent with the Seller's Ownership"

According to UCC § 2–606(1)(b), acceptance takes place if the buyer does "any act inconsistent with the seller's ownership." This provision is not to be read literally, because the right to inspect often includes the right to use. For example, a vehicle inspection requires a test drive. However, the use of the vehicle after the defects are known may be inconsistent with the seller's ownership. Use after a rejection is certainly wrongful. (UCC § 2–602(2)(a)). When the acceptance is by wrongful conduct, there is an acceptance only if the seller opts to treat it as an acceptance.

4) Revocation of Acceptance (UCC § 2–608)

The buyer may revoke acceptance of a lot or commercial unit whose non-conformity substantially impairs its value to the buyer provided (a) the goods were accepted on the reasonable assumption that the seller would cure and the non-conformity has not been seasonably cured or (b) acceptance was reasonably induced by the difficulty of discovery or by the seller's assurances.

a) "Substantially Impairs the Value to the Buyer"

Revocation of acceptance is grounded on material breach rather than on perfect tender. (*See* VI.B.2., *supra*, on the question of what breaches are material). Materiality of the breach under the UCC is based on a personal standard ("value to the buyer") of the effect of the non-conformity upon the particular buyer.

b) Time Limitation

Revocation must take place "within a reasonable time after the buyer discovers or should have discovered the ground for it and before any substantial change in the condition of the goods which is not caused by their own defects." Notification is required.

Example: B purchases a new station wagon and accepts delivery. During the next 12 months it was returned to the dealer for repair on 30 occasions. New piston rings, a new carburetor, and a new fuel pump were installed. The vehicle continued to break down and consumed oil heavily. Revocation of acceptance is permitted. The value of the vehicle was seriously impaired. The seller's repair attempts were continued assurances of cure, justifying retention and use of the vehicle for 11 months.

c) Effect

After a valid revocation, the buyer has the same rights and duties with respect to the goods in question as if the goods had been rejected.

5) Installment Contracts (UCC § 2–612)

a) Presumption Against (UCC § 2–307)

Unless otherwise agreed, all goods called for by the contract are to be tendered in one lot. An agreement to the contrary can be inferred from circumstances, as where it is known that the buyer cannot store the full quantity. Despite the presumption against installment deliveries, if the contract either explicitly or implicitly requires or authorizes delivery in separate lots, it is subject to the rules of installment contracts despite a contractual agreement to convert each delivery into a separate contract. Such a term of the contract is void.

b) Effect

The perfect tender rule does not apply to installment contracts. Where a non-conformity with respect to one or more installments *substantially impairs* the value of the whole contract, the buyer is justified in rejecting the delivery in question and canceling the whole contract. However, if the non-conformity of an installment substantially impairs the value *only* of that installment, the buyer must accept the installment if it can be cured and the seller gives adequate assurance of its cure. If the seller cannot or does not assure its cure, the buyer may reject the installment.

Example: B contracted to buy 20 carloads of plywood from *S*. Nine percent of the first carload consisted of non-conforming sheets of plywood. *B* canceled the contract. *S* sued. *B* is liable for breach. As Professor Quinn points out: "It is tough to reject any single installment under an installment contract, and even tougher to get rid of the rest of the whole contract." A substantial impairment of the value of the installment of the contract does not substantially impair the value of the entire contract. Moreover, it is doubtful whether *B* could have rejected the first carload since it was only 9% afflicted. Even if its value is substantially impaired, *S* is entitled to attempt a cure. One method of cure would have been a price allowance for the non-conforming plywood.

6) Improper Shipment (UCC § 2–504)

In a shipment contract, the seller is obligated to make a reasonable contract with a carrier for transportation and give prompt notice of shipment to the buyer. These obligations are not subject to a perfect tender rule. A buyer may reject because of breach of these obligations only "if material delay or loss ensues."

2. Obligations of the Buyer

Absent an agreement to the contrary, receipt of the goods and tender of payment are concurrent conditions. UCC § 2–511(1). Thus, even in a shipment contract where the seller delivers the goods by placing them on board a carrier, payment is not due until the goods are received at their destination. UCC § 2–310(a).

a. How Much Must Be Tendered?

Unless credit has been extended the buyer must tender the entire amount.

b. Form of Tender

Under Federal legislation a seller may insist on "legal tender" (i.e., currency) instead of a check. Under the UCC, however, if a seller insists on legal tender, the buyer is given more time to gather the cash. "Tender of payment is sufficient when made by any means or in any manner current in the ordinary course of business unless the seller demands payment in legal tender and gives any extension of time reasonably necessary to procure it." (UCC § 2–511(2)).

c. Buyer's Duty to Accept Goods

Failure to accept conforming goods or wrongful revocation of acceptance constitutes a breach.

1) Perspective

"Accept" is here used in its technical sense. Remember, the mere fact that a buyer pays for and takes possession of goods does not mean that the goods have been accepted.

2) Right of Inspection (UCC §§ 2–512, 2–513)

Unless otherwise agreed, the buyer's duty to accept and pay for a tender of goods is subject to the buyer's right to inspect them at any reasonable time and in any reasonable manner. When the seller is required or authorized to send the goods to the buyer, the inspection may occur after arrival and for a reasonable time after receipt of possession.

a) Exception

Unless otherwise agreed, the buyer has no right to inspect prior to payment if the contract provides that delivery is C.O.D. or payment is to be against documents of title. (Documents of title include bills of lading and warehouse receipts that evidence possession of goods.) Even in these cases, however, the buyer has the right to inspect before acceptance.

b) Place and Method of Inspection

If the parties agree upon a place or method of inspection, it is presumed to be exclusive. If inspection as stipulated becomes impossible, or if there has been no agreement on these matters, then the buyer may inspect at any reasonable time and place and in any reasonable manner. However, if the parties clearly meant for the inspection to be carried out as agreed, and it cannot be done, the rights and obligations of the parties would be discharged.

d. Buyer's Duties with Respect to the Rejected Goods (UCC §§ 2–602—2–604)

If the buyer properly rejects (or revokes acceptance of) goods, the buyer must refrain from any acts of ownership over the goods, and must hold them with reasonable care at the seller's disposition for a time sufficient to permit a seller to remove them.

1) Extra Duties of Merchant Buyer

After rejection, the merchant buyer is under a further duty to follow any reasonable instruction of the seller with respect to the goods. This is contingent on the seller providing indemnity for expenses upon demand by the merchant buyer, and on the seller having no agent. If no instructions are given and if there is no local agent of the seller, the merchant buyer must make reasonable efforts to sell perishables or other goods that are likely to decline in value quickly. For example, if the buyer receives non-conforming leather jackets, it cannot store them outside where rain could ruin them.

2) The Seller Is Silent

Aside from the rule with respect to perishables and the like, the buyer who receives no instructions within a reasonable time after rejection has no duty to sell or return the goods, but merchant and non-merchant buyers alike have the option to sell, return or store rejected goods without thereby tortiously "accepting" the goods.

G. Warranties in the Sales Contract

1. Express Warranties (UCC § 2–313)

An express warranty is a description, affirmation of fact, or promise with respect to the quality or future performance of goods that becomes part of the basis of the bargain. The affirmation may be in words or by sample or model. An affirmation merely of the value of the goods or merely of the seller's opinion of the goods is not a warranty.

a. "Merely" an Opinion

If a seller of a used car describes it as being in "A-1 condition," is this merely the expression of an opinion or is it an affirmation of fact? This kind of case has divided the courts for over a century. Is the seller honestly expressing an opinion? If not, whether or not there is a warranty, the description may be a fraudulent misrepresentation, for which identical remedies are available. (UCC § 2–721). If the speaker is an expert speaking to a non-expert, the expression is not "merely" opinion. There is a large grey borderland between fact and opinion.

b. Basis of the Bargain

The affirmation or promise must be part of the basis of the bargain. It need not be the inducing cause of the buyer's purchase. If the buyer did in fact rely, a warranty is created. Additionally, if the statement is one that would naturally induce a purchase, a warranty exists. This second standard is objective: a buyer can enforce a document entitled "limited warranty" that accompanied goods even if the buyer neither read it nor was aware of its existence. A statement of fact or promise made after a contract of sale may also be an express warranty, effective as a modification without consideration under UCC § 2–209. How can a subsequent statement be part of the basis of a bargain? It seems to qualify as such if it in part induced the buyer to use the goods in a particular way, or if it soothingly induced the buyer not to request a rescission of the contract.

2. Implied Warranties

a. Merchantability (UCC § 2–314)

If the seller is a merchant with respect to the kind of goods in question, unless effectively disclaimed, there is an implied warranty that the goods be such as "pass in the trade under the contract description" and "are fit for the ordinary purposes for which such goods are used."

Discussion: Perfection is not required. If goods of a certain description are acceptable in the trade despite 3% or less of the lot being rotten, the warranty is not breached by rotten goods within this range. In many cases where the warranty of merchantability is raised, personal injury or physical injury to property has occurred, and the tort perspective about strict product liability dominates. The following examples are limited to purely economic losses.

Examples: (1) *B* purchased a used car from *S*, a dealer in used cars. While *B* was driving the car home, the transmission fell out. This was repaired, and soon thereafter the brakes failed. *B* returned the car and properly revoked acceptance of it. A car with a defective transmission and brakes is not fit for the *ordinary* purpose—driving—for which a car is used. *S*, a merchant, should not have sold it in the regular course of business.

(2) *B* purchased floor tiles from *S*, a merchant. Shortly after installation, the tiles began to yellow. *B* sues for damages. *B* recovers. The tiles are unmerchantable, not fit to be sold. A tile that discolors shortly after installation is not of fair average quality.

b. Fitness for Particular Purpose (UCC § 2–315)

If the seller has reason to know that the buyer wants the goods for a particular purpose and knows that the buyer is relying on the seller's skill and judgment, unless effectively disclaimed, there is an implied warranty that the goods shall be fit for that purpose.

Example: B, a sawmill operator, went to *S*, a Mobil dealer, and asked for oil that would be suitable for use in the sawmill's hydraulic system. When asked by *S* to describe the system, *B* accurately described it. *S* checked with Mobil and suggested Ambex 810, which *B* used for two and one half years, at which time *B* discovered not only that Ambex 810 was unsuitable for the hydraulic system, but was also the cause of frequent breakdowns and production losses. *S* is liable for general and consequential damages for breach of warranty of fitness for a particular purpose. *B* relied on the Mobil organization in selecting the appropriate oil. Mobil was aware that inappropriate oil would lead to the breakdown of a sawmill.

Comment: In the illustration above the buyer expressly discussed the particular purpose with the seller, but all that is required is that the seller have reason to know the buyer's purpose and reason to believe that the buyer is relying on the seller's judgment and skill. Note that even a non-merchant may make this warranty.

c. Free and Clear Title

Unless effectively disclaimed, a seller impliedly warrants that the title conveyed is good, that its transfer is rightful, and that the goods are free from any security interest or lien of which the buyer was unaware at the time of contracting.

Comment: This warranty applies whether or not the seller is a merchant.

d. Infringement (UCC § 2–313(3))

A merchant who regularly deals in the kind of goods in question warrants, unless effectively disclaimed, that no patent or trademark is being infringed, but if the buyer furnishes the specifications, the buyer must hold the seller harmless against any third-party claim of infringement arising out of the use of the specifications.

3. Disclaimer of Warranties

a. Disclaimer of Express Warranties

It is lawful for a contract to provide that no express warranties are given. Problems arise primarily in two situations. In the first, suppose that a written contract provided that there are no express warranties, but elsewhere in the writing affirmations of fact or promises are made that constitute express warranties as defined in UCC § 2–313. A rule of construction is provided in UCC § 2–316(1) that mandates that whenever possible the two contractual provisions be construed as consistent with each other. If consistency cannot be attained, the disclaimer is inoperative and an express warranty exists. (If both the express warranty and the disclaimer are oral the same rule prevails.)

In the second situation, the written contract disclaims express warranties, but an express warranty has been made elsewhere by statements in an advertisement or orally by an authorized agent of the seller. The substantive rule is again the same, but the practical question is whether the parol evidence rule will bar evidence extrinsic to the contract. This, of course, depends on whether a court deems the writing to be the final and complete expression of the parties' intent. Even if it so finds, remember that some warranties may constitute misrepresentations and be admitted on that theory in a tort or restitution action.

b. Disclaimer of Implied Warranties

All implied warranties (except free and clear title) can be disclaimed if the buyer is warned by language such as "as is," "with all its faults," or similar phrases. Implied warranties are also eradicated as to discoverable defects if the buyer had an opportunity fully to examine the goods. Implied warranties can also be excluded or modified by course of dealing or course of performance or trade usage. If the disclaimer is by contractual language other than phrases such as "as is," certain distinctions are made.

1) Merchantability

The warranty of merchantability is difficult to exclude. If the exclusion is in writing, the language of exclusion *must use the word "merchantability"* and must be conspicuous. Conspicuousness is often achieved by highlighting the exclusions by larger or bolder type or contrasting color. The conspicuousness requirement is to avoid surprise. Consequently, even if an inconspicuous clause is used, it is effective if the buyer is aware of it.

2) Fitness

The implied warranty of fitness for a particular purpose can be excluded *only in writing* and only if the exclusion is conspicuous. The word "fitness" need not be used. (Do not lose sight of the fact that there is no implied warranty of fitness in most sales.)

Example: A contract conspicuously states: **"THERE ARE NO WARRANTIES THAT EXTEND BEYOND THE DESCRIPTION ON THE FACE HEREOF."** The implied warranty of fitness is effectively disclaimed. Evidence of *extrinsic* express warranties are likely barred by the parol evidence rule but the implied warranty of merchantability is not disclaimed because the word "merchantability" is not used.

3) Free and Clear Title

The implied warranty of free and clear title can be excluded or modified only by specific language or circumstances that give the buyer reason to know that the seller does not claim title or is only purporting to sell such right as the seller has. Thus, in addition to unusual cases where the seller reveals special circumstances casting doubt on the seller's own title, there is no implied warranty of title at a sheriff's or other forced sale, or at a sale by an executor.

c. Proposed Revision

The 2003 proposed revision of UCC § 2–316 (withdrawn in 2011) would have made it more difficult to disclaim warranties in consumer contracts. The disclaimer of merchantability must be in a record, be conspicuous, and include the following language: "the seller undertakes no responsibility for the quality of the goods except as otherwise provided in this contract." To disclaim the warranty of fitness in consumer contracts the following language needs to be used: "the seller assumes no responsibility that the goods will be fit for any particular purpose for which you may be buying these goods, except as otherwise provided in this contract."

d. Limitations on Remedies

Even if there is no disclaimer, remedies for breach of warranty may be limited pursuant to the provisions of UCC §§ 2–718 and 2–719.

Review Questions *(Answers in Appendix A)*

We suggest you first review HOW TO STUDY and EXAMINATION in the *Perspective* section, *supra.*

U called *N,* his nephew, and stated, "If you promise to take care of me for the rest of my life, and if you carry out the promise, you shall have free room and board in my house and $25,000 on my death." *N* made the promise and commenced performance. Shortly thereafter, *U* evicted *N* without cause.

1. T or F Since an express condition to *U*'s promise was not fulfilled, taking care of the Uncle for his life, *N* may not recover damages against *U* but is entitled to the reasonable value of his services.

2. T or F If before *N* started to perform, *U* had told *N* that he was withdrawing from the deal, *U* would be under no liability because, in effect, he would merely be revoking an offer.

Brush, a portrait painter, agreed to paint a picture of Handsome, promising to complete it before June 20, Handsome's birthday. In exchange, Handsome promised to pay $5,000 on completion "on condition Handsome was satisfied it captured Handsome's essence."

3. T or F The satisfaction clause is so subjective that Handsome's promise is illusory.

4. T or F Assume that on June 1 the painting had not been started and Handsome heard accurate information from a reliable source that Brush had left for Europe to teach summer courses. Handsome, under the doctrine of indirect revocation, would be free to retain a substitute painter without liability.

X Corp. entered into a contract to construct a 10-mile length of *Z* Railroad's line. One mile of it was to be tunneled through a mountain. The price was to be $10,000,000. At the completion of each mile *Z* was to pay *X* $1,000,000.

5. T or F If *X* repudiates after completing three miles, *X* is entitled to a contractual recovery of $3,000,000 minus any damages suffered by *Z*.

6. T or F If the contract had not called for installment payments and if there is no custom for such payments, *X* would not be entitled to any payment until it had completed the work.

Insured had a disability policy that provided for payment of $500 per week in any period during which insured was totally disabled.

7. T or F If insured sustained a total permanent disability which the insurer refused to recognize, refusing to make any payments, the insured could not sue for total breach.

8. T or F The policy is a divisible contract.

A, an architect, contracted on February 1 with *Z* to prepare plans for the construction of a building. *A* agreed to start work on the plans by June 1. On May 1, *A* suffered a stroke. When *Z* inquired, *A* referred *Z* to *A*'s doctors who predicted that *A* would be disabled from working for at least 10 months. Thereafter, on May 15, *Z* contracted with *B* for preparation of the plans. *A*'s doctors were, however, wrong in their prognosis and on June 1, *A* was ready, willing and able to perform.

9. T or F In an action by *A* against *Z, Z* has the defense of prospective inability to perform.

10. T or F In an action by *B* against *Z* (assuming *Z* refused to honor the contract with *B*), *Z* has the defense of impossibility of performance by virtue of *Z*'s prior contract with *A*.

B contracted in a subscribed writing to purchase a house and lot from *S*. Title was to be conveyed free of any encumbrance on June 1. A title search made on March 1 revealed that a mortgage existed as a lien upon the property.

11. T or F *B* may cancel on grounds of prospective inability to perform.

12. T or F *B* may sue *S* for anticipatory breach.

13. T or F *B* writes *S* on March 1 saying, "I will take title despite the mortgage." On March 3, *B* writes *S* saying, "I have reconsidered. I will not take title unless the mortgage lien is removed." *B* is not obligated to take title encumbered by the mortgage.

B contracted in a subscribed writing on February 1 to purchase a house and lot from *S*. Title was to be conveyed on June 1 of the same year. The contract recited: "Time is of the essence." It further recited valid and sufficient reasons why time should be of the essence.

14. T or F Tender of marketable title by *S* on June 1 is an express condition to *B*'s duty to pay the price.

15. T or F Tender of marketable title by *S* on June 1 is a constructive condition to *B*'s duty to pay the price.

16. T or F Failure by *S* to tender marketable title on June 1 is a failure of condition but not a breach of contract.

17. T or F Failure by *S* to tender marketable title on June 1 is a breach of contract but not a failure of condition.

18. **Essay** Constructor, Inc. entered into a contract with Housing Authority to be the general contractor for a housing project. The contract provided that the facility would be completed "no later than July 16" of the following year. Constructor then entered into a contract with *X* whereby *X* would do the masonry work. Constructor's contract with *X* also provided for a completion date of July 16. *X's* work was delayed partly because of weather conditions. When it seemed clear that *X* could not complete on time, Constructor brought in another contractor, *Y*, to do part of the masonry work. *Y* began paying its masons above the union scale with the result that many of *X's* employees went to work for *Y*. In early July, Constructor fired the carpentry sub-contractor, and to some extent this slowed *X's* progress. Similar delays had occurred earlier. As of August 2, *X* had completed only 65% of the work that still was allocated to *X*. On that day, Constructor notified *X* that *X's* contract was canceled.

The contract provided that delays caused by delays of other sub-contractors should be credited to *X*, but only if a written claim was made within 48 hours from the beginning of such a delay. No such written claim was ever made. *X*, however, offers evidence that a representative of Constructor had stated on a number of occasions that *X* would be credited with delays caused by other subcontractors.

What are the rights of the parties? Explain.

19. **Essay** Don's life was insured by Magna Insurance Company for $50,000, with double indemnity ($100,000) for accidental death. The policy provided that "Notice of death for which a claim may be made shall be given in writing to the Secretary within ten days from the date of such death, and failure to give notice within said ten days shall invalidate any claim for loss by death." It also provided that "coverage is voided if the death is causally related to intoxication." Don disappeared on January 1, 1995. His wife, the named beneficiary, reported him missing to the police. On March 1, 1995, after diligent efforts, Don's body was located in his car at the bottom of the river. Experts examining the car concluded that brake failure resulted in an accidental death. However, there is some evidence that Don was depressed and had talked about suicide. (If the cause of death were suicide, coverage would exist, but not for double indemnity.) There was an empty bottle of bourbon in the car, but the body had deteriorated to the extent that it could not be determined whether Don had been drinking. Don's widow immediately reported the discovery of the body, and all the circumstances of his disappearance and the recovery of the corpse to Magna. The company sent her forms for filing a claim and sent an expression of sympathy. She promptly returned the completed forms. Company representatives met with her to discuss pay-out options, but later refused to pay anything. Raise and resolve the legal issues presented by these facts.

20. **Short Essay** The City of Albany contracted with Chris Constructor, Inc., whereby Chris would dredge at two locations on the Hudson River, which for convenience will be called point X and point Y. The contract provided that point X would be dredged first and at the completion of this dredging the sum of $125,000 would be paid. Chris would next proceed to point Y. When this dredging was complete, the sum of $85,000 would be paid. Chris commenced to dredge at point X. When the job was almost complete, Chris stopped performance because it was unable to meet its payroll. The dredging was completed by another contractor. Chris asks the City to compensate it for the work done. Is Chris entitled to payment?

Chapter VII

Defenses

■ ANALYSIS

- 2) Exceptions
- b. Illegal Bargains Executed in Whole or in Part
  - 1) Reprise
  - 2) Divisibility
  - 3) Not in Pari Delicto
  - 4) Locus Poenitentiae (Room for Repentance)
- c. Change of Law
  - 1) Legalization of the Activity
  - 2) Supervening Illegality
  - 3) Supervening Illegality of an Offer
- d. Change of Facts

D. Discharge of Contractual Duties
- 1. Mutual Rescission
  - a. Rescission Requires a Mutual Agreement
  - b. Implied Rescission
  - c. Cancellation Versus Rescission
- 2. Executory Accord, Accord and Satisfaction, Substituted Agreement, and Unilateral Accord
  - a. Executory Bilateral Accord
  - b. Unilateral Accord
  - c. Accord and Satisfaction
  - d. Substituted Contract
- 3. Novation
- 4. Account Stated
- 5. Release and Covenant Not to Sue
  - a. Release
    - 1) Generally
    - 2) UCC
  - b. Covenant Not to Sue
- 6. Acquisition by the Debtor of the Correlative Right
- 7. Alteration
  - 1) Waiver of the Alteration
  - 2) Negotiable Instruments
- 8. Performance—to Which Debt Should Payment Be Applied?

A. Impracticability

1. Introduction: Impossibility and Impracticability

Contract liability is strict liability. An obligor is therefore liable in damages for breach of contract even if the breach occurs without fault on the part of the obligor, and even if circumstances have made the contract more burdensome or less desirable than had been anticipated. However, contract duties may be excused by the occurrence of an event if the contract was made on the basic assumption that this event would not occur. Events that excuse performance include those that make performance of the contract literally impossible and events that make performance commercially "impracticable," what is often referred to as "practically impossible." Indeed, in modern practice, the two concepts seem to have merged, and "impossibility" in the traditional sense may seem simply to be an extreme example of "impracticability."

The Restatement (Second) implicitly recognizes this conceptual merger. Restatement (Second) § 261, cmt. d, explains:

> *Although the rule . . . is sometimes phrased in terms of "impossibility," it has long been recognized that it may operate to discharge a party's duty even though the event has not made performance absolutely impossible. This Section, therefore, uses "impracticable," the term employed by Uniform Commercial Code § 2–615(a), to describe the required extent of the impediment to performance.*

Accordingly, in the discussion that follows in this section, we focus on "impracticability" as the basic point of reference.

2. Impracticability Is Not Necessarily a Defense

The general rule is that when a contractual promise is made, the promisor must perform or pay damages for the failure to perform no matter how burdensome performance has become as a result of unforeseen changes. The doctrine of impracticability is an exception to this rule of no-fault liability.

3. When Impracticability Is a Defense

When a performance becomes impracticable because of an event that the parties assumed would not occur when making the contract, the duty is discharged, unless the language or situation points to a contrary result.

a. Three-Part Test

In determining whether the defense of impracticability applies, three questions are considered. (1) Was there, *contrary to a basic assumption of both parties,* an unexpected contingency? (2) Did this event make performance impossible, or under the modern and UCC view, impracticable? (3) Upon whom should the risk of the unexpected contingency be placed?

1) The Basic Assumption

Certain assumptions are more basic than others. Both parties may assume a stable market, reliable sources of supply, and the continued financial ability of a purchaser of goods and services. Yet sudden market instabilities (unless caused by war or other catastrophe) and loss of financial ability are not deemed to violate basic assumptions. Therefore, contracting parties assume certain understood risks, including market shifts, interruption of sources of supply, and financial capability.

Traditional categories in which basic assumptions have been found to have been violated involve: (1) destruction of the subject matter or of the means of performance; (2) death or illness of a person essential for performance; (3) supervening illegality or prevention by law; (4) reasonable apprehension of danger to life, health or property; and (5) failure of the contemplated mode of delivery or payment.

2) Upon Whom Is the Burden of the Event Placed?

Assuming that a basic assumption has failed because of one of these events and that performance has been made impracticable, is non-performance excused? It is not, if the party claiming the excuse (a) is contributorily at fault for the occurrence of the event or (b) if there is a contractual term allocating the risk to this party. If the contract does not allocate the risk, the court will generally allocate it to the party claiming the excuse if (c) the event was reasonably foreseeable, if (d) normal business understanding allocated the risk to this party or (e) such an allocation seems fair.

Examples: (1) *D* promised to license to *P* the use of a Music Hall on certain dates. Prior to the performance, the Music Hall was destroyed by fire without any fault on *D*'s part. *D* has the defense of impossibility of performance. If the Music Hall had been closed because of a mortgage foreclosure, the result would have been different, because the impossibility would be "subjective." This is another way of saying that *D* would have assumed the risk of financial ability to perform.

(2) *S* promised to deliver 2,000 tons of Regent potatoes to be grown upon *S*'s farm. Through no fault of *S,* a pestilence struck the farm and destroyed the potato crop. *S* has the defense of impossibility of performance. The result would be the same even if the particular farm was not mentioned in the agreement, provided both parties assumed that the crop was to be grown on this land. The mere fact that *S* is a potato farmer does *not* prove, without more, that such a basic assumption existed.

(3) *C* (contractor) agrees to construct a building on land owned by *O,* "the building to be completed and delivered by May 5." On April 30, the nearly completed building is destroyed by fire without either party being at fault. Although impossibility or at least impracticability certainly exists, *C* does not have the defense. Some believe this result is proper because it is the contractor who has control of the job site and is best able to guard against accidental fires, negotiate for excuses, and arrange for insurance. Others believe the result is rooted primarily in *stare decisis,* because American cases in the early nineteenth century refused to excuse contractors in this kind of situation on the ground that it is possible for the contractor to start over again.

(4) *C* agrees to repair *O*'s roof. After the repair work is underway, a gas explosion destroys the building without fault on the part of either party. *C* is excused. Performance *is* impossible. *O* is liable in quasi contract for *C*'s part performance. The same analysis is made as to the rights of sub-contractors against general contractors.

(5) *S* agrees to transport wheat from Texas to India. The parties contemplate that the vessel will use the Suez route, and freight charges are calculated on that basis. After the vessel was underway, the canal is closed as a result of war between Israel and Egypt. *S* does not have the defense of impracticability because substitute routing around Africa is available, albeit at extra cost. Moreover, the event was foreseeable, and its possibility was discussed in the press. Foreseeability is an important factor in deciding whether a risk is assumed. The reasoning is that if an event is foreseeable the party should negotiate protective clauses.

(6) *S*, the owner of a glove factory, agrees to sell its output to *B*. After the agreement, the government requisitions the factory to produce gloves for the military. Therefore, *S* is unable to produce the kind of goods that were promised *B*. Prevention by *supervening* domestic law, regulation, court order, or the like is grounds for the successful assertion of the defense of impracticability, unless the court order or requisition is based on the fault of the party. Under UCC § 2–615(a) it is irrelevant whether the requisition was valid or not.

(7) *A* agrees to work for *B* for one year under *B*'s personal supervision. *A* dies. *A*'s estate has the defense of impossibility. (Note the relativity of the criteria. Death of any human is, of course, foreseeable. Foreseeability is down-played in death and illness cases.) If *B* had died, *B*'s estate would have the same defense. The rationales are that *A*'s duties as employee are non-delegable and *B*'s duties of *personal* supervision are also non-delegable. Note, however, that in most cases death of the employer would not discharge the contract.

(8) *A*, a general contractor, agrees to construct a building for *B*. During the course of construction both *A* and *B* die. *A*'s estate is obligated to complete the building and *B*'s estate is obligated to pay. The duties of a general contractor, as well as the duties of payment, are delegable.

(9) *A* agrees to work for *B* for one year in Venezuela. When *A* arrives at the job site from the United States, *A* learns that an epidemic of a serious contagious disease is in progress. No vaccine exists for this disease, and how long the epidemic will last is impossible to predict. *A* returns home. *A* has the defense of impracticability based on reasonable apprehension of danger to health.

(10) *S* agrees to sell certain goods to *B* for $100,000. As a result of inflation *S*'s production costs have tripled. Performance of the contract would cause *S* to lose a substantial sum on the transaction. *S* reveals these facts to *B*, stating that delivery will not be made unless *B* agrees to pay an increased price. *B* refuses, and *S* does not deliver. *S* does not have the defense of impracticability. Increased costs are within the scope of the risks assumed by a fixed price contract. If the increased costs were the result of a severe shortage of raw materials or supplies caused by an event such as war, embargo, etc., the defense of impracticability could be sustained if it is not undercut by contributory fault, assumption of the risk or similar arguments. (*See* UCC § 2–615, Comment 4.)

4. Temporary and Partial Impracticability

When the impracticability of a performance is temporary or partial, the promisor is obligated to perform to the extent practicable unless the burden of performance would be substantially increased. However, the promisee may reject any delayed or partial performance if the tendered performance is less than substantial.

Example: A movie star, under a multi-year contract with a studio, is drafted into the army during World War II. The army discharges him while his contract still has several years to run. Clearly, his inability to perform during military service excuses his performance. Whether he must fulfill the balance of the contract depends on whether the burden of performance will have been substantially increased by the interruption of the contractual relationship.

5. Temporary and Partial Impracticability Under the UCC

The UCC includes rules with respect to temporary and partial impracticability that agree with the common law rule stated in the preceding paragraph. The Code is, however, somewhat more specific.

a. Temporary Impracticability Under the UCC

If the seller expects to be late in tendering delivery and *if the lateness is excusable because of impracticability,* the seller must seasonably notify the buyer of any expected delay. The buyer may then cancel any non-installment contract. The buyer may cancel any installment delivery or an installment contract under the criteria for their cancellation discussed in connection with exceptions to the perfect tender rule. On the other hand, the buyer may within a reasonable time, not exceeding 30 days, agree to accept the delayed delivery or deliveries.

b. Partial Impracticability Under the UCC

Allocation is the key concept when the seller, *on grounds of impracticability,* can deliver only part of the promised goods. As in the case of excusable delay, the seller must seasonably notify the buyer of the shortfall and communicate the estimated quota allocated to the buyer. The quota must be fixed in a fair and reasonable manner. In fixing quotas, the seller may include allocations for regular customers who are not under contract, and also an allocation for its own needs. The buyer has a reasonable time, not exceeding 30 days, to accept the allocation. Otherwise, the seller's duties are discharged. If the contract is an installment contract, the buyer's rights to cancel are subject to the criteria for canceling installment contracts discussed in connection with exceptions to the perfect tender rule.

6. Impracticability of Means of Delivery or Payment

a. Delivery

If an agreed type of carrier, docking facilities, or manner of delivery becomes unavailable, the UCC requires that a commercially reasonable substitute be employed and accepted. (UCC § 2–614(1).)

Comment: "*Substituted performance*" is the apt caption for the UCC provision that deals with unavailability of agreed upon transportation. Although the method of delivery may be of serious concern, it is not usually at the core of the bargain. Note that substituted performance is *not* the UCC solution for the problem of goods that are not available.

b. Payment Before Delivery

If the agreed means or manner of payment becomes unavailable because of domestic or foreign government regulation, the seller's obligation to deliver is discharged.

However, if a substitute means or manner of payment that is commercially reasonable *is available, the buyer has the option to use the substitute, which reinstates the seller's duty to deliver.*

c. Payment After Delivery

If the agreed means or manner of payment becomes unavailable because of governmental regulations after the goods are delivered, the buyer may pay in the means or manner provided in the regulation. The buyer is discharged from paying via the agreed means even when the regulatory means or manner is not a commercially reasonable equivalent as long as it is not "discriminatory, oppressive or predatory."

Comment: This provision is directed mainly toward foreign government regulations controlling the movement of currency.

7. Impracticability and Conditions

Perspective: The present topic deals with impracticability as a defense to non-performance of a *promise*. Earlier we considered how impracticability relates to excuse of conditions.

8. Existing Impracticability

If performance is impracticable at the time the contract is made, and the party against whom enforcement is sought was unaware of the impracticability and did not otherwise assume the risk, the agreement is void.

B. Frustration

1. What Constitutes Frustration

Where the objective of one of the parties is the basis upon which both parties contract, the duties of performance are constructively conditioned upon the attainment of the object.

a. Impracticability Compared

In impracticability cases, one party cannot perform or can perform only in a more burdensome way than had originally been contemplated. In frustration cases, performance is practicable, but the purpose of at least one of the parties is frustrated to the extent that the performance contracted-for has become valueless (or nearly so).

b. Elements

The defense of frustration has rarely been allowed. It requires:

(1) An event that frustrates the purpose of one of the parties and the occurrence of this event must be the basis on which *both parties* entered into the contract;

(2) The frustration must be total or nearly total;

(3) The party who asserts the defense must not, expressly or impliedly, have assumed the risk of this occurrence or be guilty of contributory fault.

In addition, the defense will be disallowed if the court determines that community standards would allocate the risk of the event to the party whose purpose has been frustrated.

c. Perspective

Frustration cases closely resemble mistake cases. Frustration arises when the parties are mistaken as to a future event. As in mistake cases, the presence of unjust enrichment is often the chief underlying factor that points towards relief.

Examples: (1) Krell advertised his apartment as available for use for viewing the coronation procession of King Edward VII. Henry responded, and a contract was agreed upon whereby Henry was to have the use of the apartment for two days in exchange (in today's equivalent) for several thousand dollars. The coronation was canceled because of the illness of the King. Henry has the defense of frustration. Note that there is no impossibility of performance. Henry can pay, and Krell can let Henry have the rooms. Krell has not breached. He has not promised that the coronation would take place. Yet it is clear that the coronation was the basis on which both parties entered into the contract. The contract was senseless but for the expected coronation and Krell's enrichment was unearned.

(2) *B* was about to be married and ordered a wedding gown from *C*, who made the gown. Before the wedding, *B* died. *B*'s estate does not have the defense of frustration because the occurrence of the wedding was not the basis upon which both parties entered into

the contract. That there was no unjust enrichment bolsters this conclusion—*C*'s enrichment is earned by labor and material expended in the ordinary course of business.

(3) *T* operated a saloon under a lease which provided that: "It is expressly agreed that the only business to be carried on in said premises is the saloon business." A National Prohibition Law was enacted. *T* has the defense of frustration against the landlord's claim for rent. The quoted clause shows the basis on which the parties entered into the contract, and it is totally frustrated.

(4) Lloyd leased to Murphy certain premises for a five-year term under a lease signed four months before U.S. entry into World War II. The lease stated that it was "for the sole purpose of conducting thereon the business of displaying and selling new automobiles (including servicing and repairing thereof and of selling the petroleum products of a major oil company) and for no other purpose . . . except to make an occasional sale of a used automobile." After the U.S. entered World War II, sales of new automobiles were severely restricted by government regulation. Lloyd told Murphy that he waived the restrictive clause and would allow a sublease. But Murphy vacated, claiming frustration. Lloyd sued. Judgment for Lloyd. The frustration defense fails on two grounds. First, the frustration is not total; other uses, such as selling gas, were permissible. Second, entry into the war and the consequent curtailment of civilian auto sales was foreseeable at the time the lease was entered into. Since the event was foreseeable, failure to guard against it indicates an assumption of the risk.

d. Restitution After Discharge for Impracticability or Frustration

When a contract is discharged for impracticability or frustration, the executory duties are at an end. Yet, one or both parties may have partly performed. Compensation for part performance is available in the restitutionary action of quasi-contract.

C. Illegality

1. What Is an Illegal Bargain?

a. Generally

A bargain is illegal, if either its formation or its performance is criminal, tortious or contrary to public policy. Subject to exceptions, an illegal bargain is not enforceable. The court generally leaves the parties where it finds them.

Examples: (1) *A* delivers heroin to *B* in exchange for a cash payment of $50,000 and *B*'s promise to pay $50,000 in one week. Neither party is licensed to possess heroin. The bargain is illegal because the Criminal Code prohibits such transactions. Neither party can recover from the other.

(2) *A* promises to kill *X* in exchange for *B*'s promise to pay him $10,000. The agreement is illegal because its performance is criminal. If *A* performs, the court will not enter judgment for *A*.

(3) *B*, a newspaper reporter, promises *A* $500 if *A* procures certain confidential files from *A*'s employer. *A* performs. The agreement is illegal because it involves commission of the tort of conversion.

(4) *B*, a service company, promises *A*, an actual or potential competitor, $10,000 a year if *A* refrains from opening an office in *B*'s city. Even in the absence of anti-trust legislation, the agreement is illegal as a restraint of trade. Buying off competitors is against public policy.

Comment: The above examples involve obvious kinds of illegality. Under the general rule stated below (VII.C.2.a.), it is clear that *A* can recover in none of these cases. The difficult cases are those where the illegality is somewhat remote from the agreement. Remoteness will be illustrated by four kinds of situations:

(1) bribery,

(2) license violations,

(3) depositary cases, and

(4) instances where one party has knowledge of the illegal purpose of the other.

b. Bribery Cases

An agreement is illegal if it calls for the payment of a bribe, is procured by a bribe, or is performed by bribery.

Examples: (1) *B* promises *A*, who is purchasing agent of *X* Inc., the sum of $1,000 if *A* purchases certain of *B*'s products for *X*. *A* makes the purchase for *X*. The agreement between *B* and *A* is illegal because commercial bribery is criminal.

(2) *B* pays *A*, who is purchasing agent for *X*, Inc., the sum of $1,000 in exchange for *A*'s agreement to purchase certain goods for *X*. The ensuing agreement between *B* and *X* is illegal because it was *procured* by an illegal act.

(3) *B* hires *A* as *B*'s agent to purchase certain movie rights from *Y*. *A* obtains the rights by bribing an agent of *Y*. *A*'s conduct in *performing* the contract was illegal; therefore, the contract between *B* and *A* has become illegal according to some strong modern authorities. Traditionally, the illegal conduct was regarded as too tangential, collateral or remote to infect the contract itself with the taint of illegality.

c. Licensing Cases

If a license is required to control the skill or moral quality of persons engaged in a trade or profession, an agreement to practice that trade or profession by an unlicensed person is illegal. If the license is solely a revenue raising measure, the agreement is not illegal. If the license is required for other purposes, the courts will decide on a case-by-case basis.

Examples: (1) *A,* an unlicensed plumber, installs plumbing pursuant to an agreement with *B.* Plumbing licenses are issued only after a difficult examination of plumbing skills. The agreement is illegal.

(2) *A,* an unlicensed plumber, installs plumbing pursuant to an agreement with *B.* In this locality, plumbing licenses are issued to everyone who applies and pays an occupation tax of $500. The agreement is a binding contract.

(3) *A,* an unlicensed milk dealer, sells milk on credit to *B.* Licenses to act as a milk dealer are obtained by a showing of financial ability to pay one's debts. The court will attempt to ascertain the legislative intent of the licensing statute. In all likelihood, a court will find that the agreement is legal despite the unlicensed status of *B,* unless the court finds that the legislative intent was to invalidate agreements made by unlicensed milk dealers.

(4) *A,* an unlicensed liquor dealer, sells liquor to *B* on credit. Liquor licenses are required primarily to screen out organized crime elements from the liquor industry. The court will find that the agreement is illegal. B doesn't have to pay his tab.

d. Depositaries

A depositary of the fruits of a crime may not refuse to return the money or goods deposited unless the depositary is a party to the illegal transaction.

Examples: (1) *A,* a swindler, illegally obtains money from *B. A* deposits the money with *C. C* cannot refuse to repay the money to *A.* The deposit is viewed as remote from the crime.

(2) *B* gives a sum of money to *A* for the purpose of bribing purchasing agents. *A* pockets the money, and *B* seeks restitution. The defense of illegality will be sustained. *A* is not a mere depositary but a participant in an illegal scheme.

e. Knowledge of Illegal Purpose

Knowledge by the seller of goods or services of the illegal purpose of the buyer taints the contract with illegality only if the intended purpose involves "serious moral turpitude" or if the seller does something to further the illegal purpose of the other.

Examples: (1) *S* sells cigarettes to *B* on credit knowing that *B* intends to smuggle them into a neighboring state where cigarettes are taxed at a much higher rate. The contract is not illegal and may be enforced.

Caveat: Some states make "criminal facilitation" a crime. Under such a statute, knowledge of the illegal purpose would make the contract criminally illegal. The next two examples are decided under the traditional rule which does not outlaw criminal facilitation.

(2) *S* sells a rifle to *B* on credit knowing that *B* intends to kill *X*. The contract is illegal because the intended purpose involves serious moral turpitude.

(3) *S* contracts to sell ammunition to *B*, knowing that *B* intends to export the purchase and also knowing that *B* does not have an export license for ammunition. *S*, at *B*'s request, packs the ammunition in boxes marked "plumbing fixtures." The contract is illegal because *S*'s assistance had passed the point of mere knowledge of the scheme.

2. Effect of Illegal Bargain

a. Illegal Executory Agreements

An illegal executory bargain is void, so that neither party to the agreement can enforce it.

1) Comment

In each of the examples in the first part of this chapter ("What is an Illegal Bargain") where there was a finding of illegality, the agreement would not be enforced.

2) Exceptions

(a) If a party is justifiably *ignorant of the facts* creating the illegality and the other is not.

Example: A enters into a contract of employment with *B*, an insurance company, for a five-year term. Unbeknownst to *A*, *B* has not obtained a license necessary to enable it to lawfully do business. *A* can recover compensation for any services rendered before discovery of the illegality and, on establishing that he or she would have been ready and willing to continue had the performance been legal, also for breach of the executory portion of the bargain.

(b) If the illegality is minor and the party who is *ignorant of the law* justifiably relies upon an assumed special knowledge by the other party of the requirements of law, the contract may be enforced by the innocent party.

Example: O, an owner, and *B*, a building contractor, make an agreement for the construction of a building. The contract provides that the building code be followed. *B* misrepresents to *O* minute regulations of the building code, and builds based on those misrepresentations. *O* can recover against *B* for breach. This is an exception to the general proposition that a person is responsible for knowing the law. Here *B* has special knowledge that *O* does not have and cannot be expected to have.

(c) Certain statutes, enacted to protect a certain class, mark only one party as the wrongdoer. Contracts in violation of such statutes are enforceable by the protected party.

Example: L and *T* enter into a lease under which *T* agrees to pay rent that is illegally high under rent-control legislation. The legislation is designed to protect tenants and penalizes landlords who violate its terms. *L* breaches the lease by failing to maintain and repair the premises as covenanted in the lease. *T* may enforce the provisions in the lease concerning maintenance and repair.

(d) If an illegal provision does not involve serious moral turpitude and if the parties would have entered into the contract irrespective of the offending provision, the illegal portion of the agreement is severed, and the balance of the agreement is enforceable. The illegal provision must not be central to the party's agreement.

Examples: (1) Over-broad covenants not to compete (VIII.C.6.c., *infra*).

(2) Illegal penalties (VIII.A.6.a., *infra*).

(e) If an agreement can be interpreted so that either a legal or illegal meaning can be attributed to it, the interpretation giving the agreement a legal meaning will be preferred. An illegal contract can also be *reformed* to make it legal.

Example: A and *B* agree on a mortgage loan. The documents are drawn up by a title insurance company. The title company uses a pre-printed form which provides for usurious interest in the event of a default. The agreement can be reformed by excision of the illegal clause, provided the parties did not knowingly agree to the usurious interest provision.

b. Illegal Bargains Executed in Whole or in Part

Where there has been performance under an illegal bargain the court will not aid either party and will leave the parties where it finds them.

Examples: (1) *S* pays *A,* who is purchasing agent for *B,* the sum of $1,000 in exchange for *A*'s promise to place certain orders with *S*. *A* breaches the agreement, and *S* seeks restitution. Restitution is denied. Also, as discussed above, *S* cannot successfully sue for breach.

(2) Suppose that the facts in the above example are modified so that *A* places the orders as agreed. *B,* upon discovery of the bribe, refuses to pay for the goods delivered. *S* sues for the price. Recovery denied.

Exceptions:

1) Reprise

The exceptions under "Illegal Executory Agreements" also apply here. In addition, where performance has been rendered, there are several additional exceptions discussed immediately below.

2) Divisibility

If a performance is illegal, but other performances under the agreement are legal, recovery may be had for the legal performance if the illegal performance does not involve serious moral turpitude.

Discussion: "Divisibility" is not used in this context in the same sense as it is used in the chapter on performance. Divisibility is not determined according to fixed rules but by the judicial instinct for justice.

Example: A, a licensed plumber, agrees to remodel a bathroom for $8,000. *A* has no electrician's license, but does the entire job, including electrical work. Although there is no apportioned price for the electrical work, the court will treat the contract as divisible, allowing recovery for the reasonable value of the non-electrical work, but not exceeding the contract rate.

3) Not *in Pari Delicto*

A person who has performed under an illegal bargain is entitled to a quasi-contractual recovery if this party is not guilty of serious moral turpitude and, although blameworthy, is not equally as guilty as the other party to the illegal bargain.

Comment: There are two classes of cases in which the notion of not *in pari delicto* is generally available. In the first kind, the party enters into the illegal bargain under duress or circumstances close to duress. In the second kind, the rule that makes the bargain illegal is designed to protect one class of persons against another.

Examples: (1) *A,* a refugee, gave *B* jewels to be used to bribe border guards so that *A* could escape Hitler's army. *B* absconded with the jewels. Years later, *A* discovers *B* and sues for the value of the jewels. *A* can recover from *B* as *A* was not *in pari delicto*. A person who makes an agreement in dire necessity and motivated by self-preservation has not committed an act of serious moral turpitude.

(2) *A* borrows money from *B* at a usurious interest rate. *A,* a member of the class that usury laws aim to protect, may recover the excess interest *A* has paid.

4) *Locus Poenitentiae* (Room for Repentance)

Even if a plaintiff is *in pari delicto* and therefore as blameworthy or more blameworthy than the defendant, plaintiff is entitled to avoid the bargain and obtain restitution if plaintiff acted in time to prevent the attainment of the illegal purpose for which the bargain was made, unless the mere making of the bargain involves serious moral turpitude. The plaintiff is generally not permitted to recover if the withdrawal comes after any part of the illegal performance is consummated. Repentance also comes too late if it comes after attainment of the unlawful purpose is seen to be impossible.

Example: A gives $1,000 to *B* to bribe a public official. Before *B* makes any attempt to carry out the illegal purpose, *A* demands that *B* return the money. *A* may recover. The result would be different if the public official had rejected the bribe.

c. Change of Law

1) Legalization of the Activity

If an agreement is illegal when made and subsequently becomes legal because the law is changed, the change does not validate the agreement, except where the repealing statute expressly or impliedly so provides. One might assume that the repealing statute always impliedly validates such an agreement, but that is not so. Statutes generally look ahead, not back.

Example: A borrows money from *B,* promising to pay a usurious rate of interest. Before the time for performing the bargain, a statute is enacted allowing such a rate of interest. The bargain is still illegal unless the statute manifests an intention to validate such bargains.

2) Supervening Illegality

If a contract is lawful when made, but the performance is outlawed prior to full performance, the case is governed by the doctrine of impracticability of performance. (Or, depending on what part of the performance is made illegal, by the doctrine of frustration of purpose. Remember the saloon and Prohibition example in VII.B.1.c., *supra*.)

3) Supervening Illegality of an Offer

If a lawful offer is made, but performance of the proposed contract is subsequently outlawed, the power of acceptance is terminated.

d. Change of Facts

Where the bargain is illegal and a change of facts removes the cause of the illegality, the contract remains illegal. However, the parties with full knowledge of the facts may subsequently ratify the agreement.

Example: A, who is not a member of the bar, is retained by *B* to file a tort claim against *X* on *B*'s behalf. *A* is subsequently admitted to the bar and successfully obtains a recovery against *X* for *B*. *B* need not pay *A*'s fee. The result would be different if, before complete performance, *B,* with full knowledge of the facts, had ratified the contract.

D. Discharge of Contractual Duties

Perspective: Many methods of discharging a contractual duty are discussed elsewhere; for example, non-fulfillment of a condition, anticipatory repudiation, impracticability of performance, disaffirmance for lack of capacity, etc. In this chapter several consensual kinds of discharge will be discussed.

1. Mutual Rescission

a. Rescission Requires a Mutual Agreement

If A and B enter into a bilateral executory contract, they can rescind it by mutual agreement. The surrender of rights under the original agreement by each party is the consideration for the mutual agreement of rescission.

Discussion: Within limits, parties to a contract are free to end the obligations of the contract by agreement. The limits are imposed by the doctrine of consideration. Three situations must be distinguished:

(1) rescission occurring before any performance;

(2) rescission occurring after part performance by one or both parties;

(3) rescission occurring after full performance by one party.

In the first two situations, the surrender of rights under the original agreement by each party constitutes the consideration. In the third situation, the rescission is void for want of consideration.

Examples: (1) *A* and *B* enter into a contract in which *A* agrees to work for *B* for a period of one year, and *B* agrees to pay $500 every week. Before performance begins, the parties mutually rescind their duties under the contract. The rescission is effective, because each party is suffering a bargained-for detriment—the surrender of the performance to be rendered by the other party.

(2) In example (1), if *A* works for a week and then the parties mutually rescind, there is no consideration problem for the same reason as example (1). The only question is whether *A* should be paid for the work *A* performed. This is a question of interpretation and logically depends upon whether the parties intended to rescind only the executory part of the contract, or to discharge all duties under the contract including the duty to pay.

(3) In example (1), if *A* had completely performed and the parties then agreed to mutually rescind, the agreement would be ineffective because *B* would not be suffering any detriment. The result may be different by statute or if a gift has been completed.

b. Implied Rescission

While rescissions are ordinarily expressed in words they can be implicit in conduct. Some courts call an implied rescission an "abandonment."

Example: S and *B* enter into a contract by the terms of which *S* agrees to manufacture and sell to *B* a given machine and *B* agrees to pay $50,000. Neither party has any experience in the design or manufacture of such a machine. The contract provides that first *B* is obligated to provide more precise specifications, and *S* is to provide preliminary design sketches. Neither party acts. After a reasonable time, there is an implied rescission. Both parties' failure to cooperate in its performance is regarded as an abandonment of the contract. From another perspective, if either party sued the other, the plaintiff could not establish due compliance with all conditions precedent.

c. Cancellation Versus Rescission

In the face of a material breach, the injured party may properly cancel the contract. In canceling, the aggrieved party may incorrectly use expressions such as "I rescind." According to UCC § 2–720, which restates the sounder common law cases, "unless the contrary intention clearly appears, expressions of cancellation or 'rescission' of the contract or the like shall not be construed as a renunciation or discharge of any claim for damages for an antecedent breach."

Examples: (1) *A* promises *B* that a structure will be completed before January 1, and it is agreed that time is of the essence. Because of delays by *A*, it is obvious the structure will not be completed on time. Despite this delay, *B* permits *A* to complete the structure. Because *B* has effectively waived the express condition that *A* perform on time, *B* is required to pay. The question remains whether *B* can successfully sue for the breach based upon late performance or whether *B* has renounced the right to damages. The question is one of interpretation. Did *B* manifest an intent to renounce the right to damages? If *B* did, the renunciation is effective without consideration.

(2) *S* and *B* enter into a contract for the development of software. *S* commits a material breach. *B* writes to *S* stating, "I rescind the contract." *B*'s expression effectively cancels the contract but does not amount to a renunciation of the right to damages. It should be noted that, if *B*'s notice manifested an intent to surrender the right to damages, it could have this effect without consideration.

2. Executory Accord, Accord and Satisfaction, Substituted Agreement, and Unilateral Accord

a. Executory Bilateral Accord

A bilateral executory accord is an agreement that an existing claim shall be discharged in the future *by the rendition of a substitute performance.*

Discussion: Prior to performance or breach of the executory accord, the existing claim is suspended. Upon performance, there is an accord and satisfaction that discharges the claim. If, however, the debtor breaches, the prior obligation revives and the creditor has the option of enforcing the original claim or the executory accord. If the creditor breaches, the debtor may ordinarily obtain specific performance of the accord.

Comment: The common law did not regard executory accords as binding contracts. Today most states enforce them. New York, by statute, only enforces them if they are in writing and signed by the party against whom enforcement is sought.

b. Unilateral Accord

An offer by a creditor or claimant to accept a performance in satisfaction of a credit or claim is known as a unilateral accord.

Comment: At early common law the offeror could, with impunity, refuse the tender of performance even if the performance was tendered prior to any revocation. Under modern law, if tender is refused, the debtor may sue for damages for breach of the accord, or, in a proper case, for specific performance. New York requires that the offer be in writing and signed by the offeror.

c. Accord and Satisfaction

An accord and satisfaction is formed in one of three ways:

(1) Performance of an executory bilateral accord; or

(2) Acceptance of an offer to a unilateral accord; or

(3) Creation of a substituted contract.

d. Substituted Contract

A substituted contract resembles an executory bilateral accord, but in this transaction the claimant or creditor agrees that the claim or credit is immediately *discharged in exchange for the promise of a future performance.*

Discussion: The prior claim or credit is merged into the substituted contract. Consequently, in the event of its breach, it alone determines the rights of the parties. There would be no right to enforce the prior claim, unless the new agreement is void, voidable, or unenforceable.

Examples: (1) *C* (creditor) writes to *D* (debtor), "I promise to discharge the debt you owe me upon delivery of your black Mercedes if you promise to deliver it within a reasonable time." *D* promises. This is an executory bilateral contract of accord; it is a bilateral agreement that relates to the satisfaction or discharge of a claim at some *future time*—here upon the delivery of the automobile. If the Mercedes is delivered and accepted, an accord and satisfaction is formed. If it is not tendered within a reasonable time, *C* may pursue the original debt. *C* may instead sue for damages for breach of contract to deliver the car.

If *D* tenders the automobile within a reasonable time and *C* refuses the tender, *D* can resist any action by *C* to collect the debt by counter-claiming for specific performance.

(2) *C* writes to *D,* "If you will promise to deliver your black Mercedes within 30 days, I will immediately treat the debt you owe me as satisfied and discharged." *D* accepts the offer. There is a substituted agreement. The factual difference between this case and case (1) is that here *C* agrees to discharge the claim when *D*

makes the promise rather than when the promise is performed. *C* may enforce only the substituted contract.

(3) *C* writes to *D,* "If you *deliver* your black Mercedes within a reasonable time, I promise to discharge your debt." If *D* delivers the automobile, and *C* accepts, there is a binding accord and satisfaction. If *D* tenders the Mercedes and *C* refuses to take it, *D* may sue for damages for breach of a unilateral contract of accord or, in a proper case, sue for specific performance.

3. Novation

A contract is a novation if it does three things: (a) discharges immediately a previous contractual duty or a duty to make compensation, (b) creates a new contractual duty, and (c) includes as a party one who neither owed the previous duty nor was entitled to its performance.

Example: A owes *B* $100. *B* and *C* agree that *C* here and now assumes *A*'s duty, and that *B* here and now releases *A* from the obligation to pay $100. There is a novation, even though *A* has not suffered any detriment and *A* has not assented to the arrangement. *A* is a third party beneficiary and *A*'s assent is presumed, but *A* is empowered to disclaim the discharge if *A* so desires.

Perspective: It is necessary to distinguish an executory accord from a novation. A novation is a substituted contract that operates immediately to discharge an obligation. If the discharge is to take place upon performance, the tripartite agreement is merely an executory accord.

4. Account Stated

An account stated arises where there have been transactions between debtor and creditor resulting in the creation of matured debts and (a) the parties by agreement compute a balance which the debtor promises to pay and which (b) the creditor promises to accept in full payment for the items of the account.

Discussion: An account stated often results from an implied agreement—the sending and retention of the account without objection for more than a reasonable time. But the inference of assent is generally held to be rebuttable. Consideration is *not* necessary to support the account, but the promises are enforceable only to the extent of the previous obligation. Thus, the main effect of an account stated is to shift the burden of going forward with the evidence to the party who claims the account is incorrect.

Example: S made various shipments of seed to *B. S* sent *B* monthly statements showing the shipments and the price of each of them. A February shipment was billed together with other shipments for three successive months. *B* fails to pay. *S* sues, alleging an account stated. *B* alleges that the February shipment was never received. *S* succeeds in the action. It is irrelevant whether *B* received the seed. *B*'s failure to object to the item of account for three successive months results in an objective manifestation of assent.

5. Release and Covenant Not to Sue

a. Release

1) Generally

A release is a writing manifesting an intention to discharge another from an existing or asserted duty. A release supported by consideration discharges the duty. At common law, consideration was not necessary if the release was under seal. This is still the law in some jurisdictions. Today, the effectiveness of a release of a duty without consideration is largely dependent upon local statutes.

2) UCC

UCC § 1–107 provides that: "Any claim or right arising out of an alleged breach can be discharged in whole or part without consideration by written waiver or renunciation signed and delivered by the aggrieved party." Section 1–306 of the revision is substantively in accord, but delivery is not required.

b. Covenant Not to Sue

A covenant not to sue is a promise by a creditor not to sue either permanently or for a limited period of time. This promise must be supported by consideration.

Comment: A release is an executed transaction while a covenant not to sue is executory. A covenant not to sue is sometimes used to circumvent the common law rule that the release of one joint obligor releases all of them.

6. Acquisition by the Debtor of the Correlative Right

Acquisition by the debtor of the correlative right in the same capacity in which the duty is owed discharges it.

Example: A owes *B* $100. *A* is *B*'s next of kin. *B* dies without a will, so that *A* inherits all of *B*'s personal property. The duty to *B* is discharged by the acquisition by *A* of the correlative right.

7. Alteration

A fraudulent alteration of a written contract by one who asserts a right under it extinguishes the right and discharges the obligor's obligation.

a. Waiver of the Alteration

The aggrieved party may forgive the alteration, thus reinstating the contract according to its original tenor.

b. Negotiable Instruments

A holder in due course of an instrument altered by a prior holder may enforce it according to its original tenor. UCC § 3–407.

8. Performance—to Which Debt Should Payment Be Applied?

A duty is discharged by performance. However, a common problem involves a debtor who owes several debts to the same creditor. When the debtor sends a sum of money to the creditor which debt should be credited?

Where a person owes several debts to a creditor, payments are to be applied in the following sequence:

(a) *in the manner manifested by the debtor unless the manifestation violates a duty to a third person such as a surety;*

(b) *if the debtor manifests no intention, the payment may be applied at the discretion of the creditor, provided it is not applied to a disputed, unmatured or illegal claim, and also provided it is not applied so as to violate a duty of the debtor to a third person of which the creditor is aware, and is not applied as to cause a forfeiture;*

(c) *if the creditor manifests no intent on receipt of payment, the law will allocate payment in the manner deemed most equitable.*

Review Questions *(Answers in Appendix A)*

We suggest you first review HOW TO STUDY and EXAMINATION in the *Perspective* section, *supra.*

A, a producer, hired *B,* an inexperienced actor, to play a minor part. A license was required for *A* to put on the performance. The license was to protect the public from overcrowding, fire hazards and the like. At the time of contracting and performing, *B* was unaware that *A* was unlicensed or even that a license was required. *B* performed the agreed upon services, but *A* has not paid.

1. T or F *B* can recover on the contract, because *B* was unaware that *A* did not have a license.

2. T or F In an action by *B* on the contract it is not relevant that *B* was unaware of the licensing requirement because ignorance of the law would not excuse *B.*

S entered into an agreement with *B,* an agent for an unfriendly foreign power, promising to procure certain governmental documents classified as "Top Secret" and to paint *B*'s house. Each of these performances had a separately apportioned price.

3. T or F The executory bilateral agreement is void.

4. T or F If *B* performed his promises (turning over top secret documents and painting), *B* could recover the price for painting under the doctrine of *locus poenitentiae.*

Brush, a portrait painter, agreed to paint a portrait of Beauty, promising to commence on May 4 and to complete it by June 20, Beauty's birthday. A down payment was paid, and the balance was due on completion. The painting was started and destroyed by fire when half completed.

5. T or F Brush would have the defense of impossibility.

6. T or F If Brush died before starting the painting, Beauty could recover back the down payment.

A agreed to work for *B* for 6 months, and *B* promised to engage *A*'s services for 6 months. After two months of performance, *B* asked *A* if *A* would be willing to rescind their agreement and work for *C* for the remaining 4 months. *A* agreed as did *C*.

7. T or F *B* continued to be liable to *A*.

8. **Essay** Landlord (*L*) and tenant (*T*) entered into a 25-year written and subscribed lease commencing January 1, 2009, whereby *T* agreed to build facilities at *T*'s own expense on the premises for the sole purpose of operating a drive-in movie theater and the sale of popcorn, soda pop, and snacks. No rent was payable until June 1, 2009. From and after this date *T* was to pay rent in the amount of $3,000 a month.

On March 1, 2009, after *T* had diligently commenced and continued construction of the facilities in accordance with the contract, the County Board of Supervisors voted to authorize the condemnation of the parcel for use as a park. *T* immediately stopped construction. The County condemned the land on August 1, 2009.

(a) *L* has commenced an action against *T* for rent for the months of June and July. May *L* recover?

(b) Assume that prior to commencement of the suit, *L* and *T* negotiated as to whether *T* should pay rent, and *L* agreed to take $3,000 in full satisfaction of T's demand for $6,000. However, *L* refused to accept *T*'s tender of $3,000 in cash. May *T* raise these facts as a defense?

(c) Assume that *C*, the construction contractor retained by *T*, was not licensed by the township in which the drive-in theater was being built. A township ordinance required such a license, which is granted upon a showing of financial stability, the payment of a $1,000 application fee, and the identification of corporate officers if the applicant is a corporation. In an action by *C* against *T* what is the consequence of *C*'s lack of a license?

Chapter VIII

Contract Remedies

■ ANALYSIS

5. Relationship Between Specific Performance and Damages
    a. Specific Performance Plus Damages
    b. Specific Performance and Liquidated Damages
    c. Effect of Denial of Specific Performance
6. Restraining Orders
    a. Employment Contracts with Affirmative and Negative Duties
    b. Trade Secrets
    c. Covenants Not to Compete
        1) Ancillary to Sale of Business
        2) Ancillary to Employment

A. Damages

1. Goal of Damages

The aggrieved party receives "gains prevented" (expectancy interest) plus "losses sustained" (reliance and restitutionary interests), subject to the limitations imposed by the doctrines of foreseeability, certainty and mitigation.

Discussion: The basic goal of contract damages is to place aggrieved parties in the same economic position they would have achieved had their contracts been fully performed. The aggrieved party is entitled to the "benefit of the bargain."

Example: Purchaser contracts with manufacturer for the production of a custom-made oil drill and repudiates the contract after production has been started. The manufacturer recovers lost profits (contract price minus what the full cost of production would have been) plus losses sustained (cost of labor and supplies actually expended to the extent such costs are not salvageable). To break down this hypothetical further, say the contract price for this custom-made oil drill was $400,000, and the full cost of production would have been $360,000. The manufacturer's losses sustained are $4,000 for labor (repudiation happened soon after production started) and $17,000 for non-salvageable supplies. Total supplies had cost $100,000 but the manufacturer was able to sell $83,000 worth to a third party. (Note the manufacturer is under a duty to minimize damages.) Here, the manufacturer would recover $61,000: $40,000 for lost profits (contract price minus production costs) and $21,000 for losses sustained ($4,000 for labor and $17,000 for supplies).

2. Foreseeability—General and Consequential Damages

Contract damages cannot be recovered unless they are foreseeable to the parties at the time of contracting.

a. Application

"General damages" are those foreseeable to a reasonable person similarly situated. "General damages" are calculated by the standardized rules discussed below. "Special" or "consequential" damages are those which are foreseeable because at the time of contracting the party in breach knows that in the event of breach no substitute performance will be available. If UCC Article 2 applies, the seller will be held responsible for the buyer's damages that were foreseeable at the time of contracting *or* at the time of breach.

Examples: (1) *S* contracts to make deliveries of flour to *B,* knowing that *B* operates a large bakery and also knowing that because of a severe shortage, flour is almost unavailable on the spot market. *S* fails to make a scheduled delivery. Because of *B*'s inability to acquire flour in a timely fashion, *B* is forced to shut down the bakery for a week. In addition to "general damages," *B* may recover for loss of a week's profits.

(2) *S* contracts to deliver large quantities of sugar to *B,* knowing *B* is a wholesaler who sells sugar to large users. The first scheduled delivery is April 1. Unbeknownst to *S, B* contracts to

deliver to *T* on April 1 the sugar that *S* promised to deliver. Also unknown to *S*, *B* contracted to deliver "*S* brand" sugar to *T* and not just "sugar." *S* fails to deliver on April 1. *B* cannot cover because "*S* brand" sugar is unavailable. *T* sues *B* for damages and recovers. *B* now sues *S*, claiming lost profits on the resale and reimbursement for the damages paid to *T*. *B* does not recover for these damages. Although *S* knew *B* bought for resale it had no reason to know that this contract of resale allowed so little time between *S*'s delivery date and the date for redelivery. Moreover, it had no reason to know *B* contracted to deliver sugar by brand name and thus had disabled itself from being able to cover.

b. Particular Situations

1) Sale of Goods

a) Seller's Non-Delivery

Purchaser recovers as general damages the difference between market price and contract price, or between cover price (price reasonably paid for substitute goods even if in excess of the "market") and contract price.

Examples: (1) *B* contracts to purchase sugar from *S* at 17 cents a pound for delivery on April 1. *S* fails to deliver. On April 1, the market price is 22 cents. *B*'s general measure of damages is 5 cents per pound.

(2) *B* contracts to purchase sugar from *S* at 17 cents per pound for delivery on April 1. On April 1, the market price could be found by a jury to be 22 cents. However, some spot sales were for as much as 29 cents. Supplies were thin and spot prices erratic. *S* failed to deliver, and *B* called a reputable broker who found a spot seller who delivered covering sugar to *B* at 26 cents. *B*, who has acted in a commercially reasonable way, may recover the difference between the cover price and the unpaid contract price. In addition, *B* may recover any broker's fee as "incidental" damages.

b) Seller's Breach of Warranty

Purchaser can recover as general damages the difference between the value the goods would have had if they had been as warranted and their actual value. Value is determined as of the time and place of acceptance.

Comment: Notice that this rule is a rule of "difference in *value*." Price is *not* a factor.

Example: S, a merchant advertises a sale to close out a line of machinery. *B* purchases from *S* a new grinding machine for $1,000. Comparable new merchantable machines are valued at $2,000. The machine has a hidden defect which makes it unmerchantable and worthless. Absent an effective limitation of liability or disclaimer, *B* is entitled to $2,000 in damages. If the defect had reduced the market value of the machine to $500, instead of $0, *B* would be entitled to $1,500.

c) Buyer's Breach

For total breach by the buyer as to goods the buyer has not accepted, the seller may recover the difference between the contract price and the market or resale price. If the seller has an unlimited supply of the goods involved, however, the seller has lost the profits on the sale, so the seller may instead recover "the profit (including reasonable overhead) which the seller would have made from full performance by the buyer." UCC § 2–708(2).

Discussion: The rule gives three optional measures of recovery. (In addition, a seller may have an action for the price [*see* d), *infra*].) The last of the three measures applies to a merchant who contracts to sell stock in trade; for example, the automobile dealer. The economic injury done to the seller by the buyer's total breach is that the seller has lost the profit on a sale. Unless the car is unique, its resale to another buyer does not make the seller whole, because the dealer could have procured a similar car for the second buyer; the dealer would have made that second sale even if the first buyer hadn't breached. If it can be shown that the dealer has a limited supply of cars and could not have procured a similar car for a second buyer, this measure of damages is not applicable.

In the case where the dealer could have made a second sale, the contract price-market price formula will not make the dealer whole as presumably the sale was at or near the market price.

The contract price-resale price formula is most appropriate for contracts for the sale of unique goods and goods that are not part of the seller's stock in trade.

The contract price-market price measure is most appropriate for contracts for the sale of commodities and other fungible goods for which there is an active market.

d) Seller's Price Action

If the buyer has accepted the goods, or if the goods are destroyed after risk of loss has passed to the buyer, the seller can recover the price. A price action is also available if the goods are identified to the contract and the seller cannot reasonably resell them.

e) Consequential and Incidental Damages in Sales Cases

Consequential damages are available to a buyer if the foreseeability test is met. *See* VIII.A.2., *supra*. Sellers *cannot* claim consequential damages (UCC § 1–106. revision § 1–305), but frequently can get incidental damages. Buyers can claim incidental damages, too. These include, but are not limited to, brokerage commissions, storage charges, advertising costs, and auctioneer's fees made necessary by the other's breach.

2) Employment Contracts

a) Employer's Breach

Employees who have been discharged in breach of contract may recover the wages or salary that would have been payable during the contract term minus the income that they have earned, will earn, or could with reasonable diligence earn during the contract term. In the case of a long-term contract the "present worth" doctrine (see VIII.A.5., infra) will be applied.

Discussion: Notice that a contract price minus market price formula is not used in this context. *Prima facie* the employee is entitled to the contract price. This is reduced only if the employer meets the burden of proving that the discharged employee obtained another job or could reasonably have obtained one during the contract term.

b) Employee's Breach

If an employee quits in breach of contract, the employer recovers the difference between the market value of the employee's service minus the contract price.

Discussion: In other words, the employer recovers more than nominal damages only if the employee was underpaid. Although, in theory, consequential damages are available, only a handful of cases have granted consequential damages against a breaching employee. These mostly involve performing artists whose breach destroys the production of a film.

3) Construction Contracts

a) Contractor's Delay

Damages for delay are measured by the rental value of the completed premises for the period of delay.

b) Contractor's Failure to Complete

Failure to complete is compensated by the additional cost of completion plus delay damages.

c) Defect in Construction

If the breach consists of a defect in construction, the damages are the cost of correcting the defect, unless this would constitute unreasonable economic waste.

Examples: (1) *C* (Contractor) promised to comply with each of *O*'s (Owner's) specifications. One of these was the use of Reading pipe. *C* breached by installing Cohoes pipe, a brand of comparable quality. The breach was not discovered until most of the pipe was walled in by plaster. Correcting the breach would involve economic waste—the cost of tearing down the plaster, installing the correct pipes, and re-plastering. *O*'s damages are limited to the difference in value between the structure as it should have been built and the value it has as it was built—a zero sum here. This is the same rule as for breach of warranty in sales cases.

(2) *C* contracted to build a suburban house for *O* with a garage and driveway. Rather than excavate a rock formation, *D* built the driveway with a 22½% grade, which is so steep the driveway cannot be used safely and conveniently. A 12½% grade is considered the permissible maximum. The cost of redoing the driveway and lowering the garage would be $20,000. The full purchase price was $68,000. The defendant offered evidence to show that the property's value, even with the defect, exceeded the contract price. Despite this evidence, *O* recovers the cost of curing the defect. The difference in value rule will not be applied where the defect affects the usability and safety of the premises. Normally, it will not be applied where the defect is willful, which also appears to be the case here.

d) Owner's Breach

If no work has been done, the contractor recovers the anticipated profit, that is, the contract price minus the projected cost of performance. If the work has been started, the contractor recovers the anticipated profit plus the cost of labor and supplies actually expended.

Perspective: If the contract was an unprofitable one, the contractor will normally prefer to sue for restitution rather than damages. (*See* VIII.B., *infra.*)

e) Consequential Damages in Construction Cases

If foreseeability is shown, consequential damages are available against a breaching contractor, but if an owner breaches by failure to pay or by repudiating, consequential damages are *never* available to the contractor.

Example: C promised to complete a one family residence for *O* by September 30. Before contracting, *O* informed *C* that *O* had contracted to convey *O*'s present residence to *T* by October 1 and would be liable to *T* for liquidated damages of $200 a day for any delay in conveying. Consequently, it was urgent that *C* complete the new residence on time. *C* did not substantially perform until

October 15, when *O* was able to occupy the new house. As a result of the delay, *O* was liable to *T* for $3,000. *C* is liable to *O* for at least the sum of $3,000 as consequential damages.

4) Contracts to Sell Realty

a) Vendee's Total Breach

If a contract vendee totally breaches the contract, the vendor may recover the difference between the contract price and the value of the realty.

Perspective: This is the same rule as is applied to breach by a purchaser of goods. Contrast the rule as to vendor's breach, stated below.

b) Vendor's Total Breach

(i) *English Rule. For total breach, the vendee may recover only the down payment plus reasonable expenses of a survey and examination of title.*

Comment: The vendee, under this orthodox view, is not entitled to the expectancy interest. The rule originated because land titles in England were often insecure and registry systems were poor. Consequently, many good faith vendors were unable to convey marketable title. Close to half the states follow this English rule.

Exception: If the vendor (a) refuses to convey or (b) is aware of the title defect at the time of contracting, the vendor is liable for the difference between contract price and market value. Because the rationale for the English rule is not applicable, the vendee's expectations are protected.

(ii) *American Rule. Under the "American Rule," followed in a bare majority of jurisdictions, no matter what the reason for the breach, the vendor is liable for the difference between contract price and market value.*

Perspective: This is the same as the primary rule of damages applicable where a seller of goods totally breaches.

c) Consequential Damages

Consequential damages against a vendor in default is a strong possibility under both the American rule and the exceptions to the English rule.

Example: V advertised real property for sale. *P,* who told *V* that the purchase was for speculation and that he anticipated a rising market and probable quick resale, entered into a contract with *V* on January 15 to purchase the property for $100,000, conveyance to be on February 28. On February 1, *P* entered into a contract with *T* for the resale of the property for \$120,000. *V* repudiated. Because *V*, at the time of contracting, was aware of *P*'s purpose and knew that this purpose could not be accomplished if *V* breached, *V* is liable to *P* for the \$20,000 loss of profit.

d) Vendor's Delay

If the breach consists of a delay in conveying, the vendee may recover for the rental value of the premises during the period of delay.

3. Certainty

a. General Rule

The fact of loss and its amount must be proved with reasonable certainty.

Discussion: The standard of certainty requires a higher quality of proof on the issue of damages than for other issues in a lawsuit. It is applied with special stringency to lost profits, particularly lost profits as consequential damages.

Examples: (1) *S* agrees to sell sugar to *B*, who, as *S* well knows, operates a bakery. *S* is also aware of a sugar shortage. *S* breaches. *B* is unable to cover and is forced to close the bakery for a week, losing profits. This is the kind of consequential damages claim that is most closely scrutinized. If *B* were operating a new business, almost certainly *B* would be unable to prove these damages. (For an alternative measure of damage, *see* "Alternatives Where Expectancy Is Uncertain," *infra.*) If *B* had an established business with a relatively stable record of profitability and adequate records, proof could be made with sufficient certainty. Exactness of damages need not be shown, but a reasonable basis for computation must be proved.

(2) *A*, a publisher, totally breaks a contract to publish a novel by *B*, a previously unpublished author. *B* was to be compensated strictly on a royalty basis. *B* cannot establish the loss of royalties with sufficient certainty.

b. Alternatives Where Expectancy Is Uncertain

1) Protection of Reliance Interest

Where the aggrieved party cannot establish the lost expectancy interest with sufficient certainty, the aggrieved party can recover expenses for preparation and part performance as well as other foreseeable expenses incurred in reliance on the contract.

Caveat: If the defendant can show that the contract would have been a losing proposition for the plaintiff, an appropriate deduction will be made for the loss that was not incurred.

Example: Defendant promised to use diligence in marketing, at \$1 a box, 90,000 boxes of Christmas cards produced by plaintiff. The cards were of unique designs that related to the events of the year. Defendant totally breached, and plaintiff had no alternative way of marketing them in time for the Christmas season. Because of the "novelty" nature of the designs, plaintiff cannot prove that the 90,000 boxes would have been sold. The salvage value in the following year is trivial. Nonetheless, plaintiff may recover expenditures for labor and material ($17,000) minus the net salvage value of the cards ($2,000). Defendant has the burden of proving that full performance of the contract would have resulted in a loss to plaintiff and what the amount of that loss would have been. If defendant can show what that loss would have been, the loss would have been subtracted from plaintiff's $15,000 recovery.

Split of Authority: Can expenditures incurred prior to contracting be compensated? In the example immediately above, plaintiff could not recover the cost incurred prior to contracting of the plates from which the cards were printed. Other courts disagree, and allow such costs on the theory that these are opportunity costs that would have been incurred even if the plaintiff had contracted with another distributor.

2) Rental Value of Profit-Making Property

If the breach disables the aggrieved party from using profit-making property, the aggrieved party may recover the rental value of the property.

Example: S delivers and installs a defective furnace in *B*'s new glass factory. As *S* could have foreseen at the time of contracting, the defect prevents the opening of the factory for a prolonged period. Because *B*'s factory is new, it is unlikely that *B* can prove lost profits with sufficient certainty. Nonetheless, *B* may recover the rental value of the factory for the period it was closed because of the breach. If rental value is unclear, it can be inferred by calculating the going rate of interest upon the cost of the factory.

3) Value of an Opportunity

If a duty is conditioned upon a fortuitous event, and the breach makes it uncertain whether the event would have occurred, the aggrieved party may recover the value of the chance that the event would have occurred.

Example: Plaintiff was one of fifty semi-finalists in a beauty contest in which twelve finalists would receive cash prizes, the lowest of which was $4,000. The defendant neglected to notify plaintiff of the time and place of the final competition. A jury verdict for $1,000 is upheld. The plaintiff had roughly a 1 in 4 chance of being selected as a finalist.

Discussion: The rule only applies to aleatory contracts, such as contests and insurance policies.

4. Mitigation

Damages that could have been avoided by reasonable efforts cannot be recovered. Conversely, the aggrieved party may recover reasonable costs incurred in an effort to minimize damages.

Discussion: The aggrieved party need take only reasonable action to avoid damages. Heroics are not required. The notion of mitigation is built into many rules of damages. For example, an aggrieved purchaser cannot recover consequential damages if "cover" is possible; *i.e.*, comparable goods could have been bought in the market at the time of learning of the breach. An employee who has been wrongfully fired should take a comparable job if one is available. In addition, it is a doctrine to be applied to any case where damages could reasonably have been minimized.

Example: Shirley MacLaine contracted with *D* to play the female lead in "Bloomer Girl," a musical to be filmed in California for a minimum agreed compensation of $750,000. *D* decided not to produce "Bloomer Girl." In substitution *D* offered Ms. MacLaine the lead in "Big Country," a Western to be filmed in Australia. She declined to play in "Big Country" and sues for $750,000. Because the offer of the substituted role was comparable neither in the kind of role played nor in the location of the filming, she has not acted unreasonably in refusing the role. Note, however, that had she taken the substitute role or accepted any other employment for the contract period, earnings from such employment would have been subtracted from her recovery.

a. Exception

One is not required to enter into another contract with the breaching party even if the offered contract would have minimized damages. This is an alternate ground for the prior illustration.

b. Non-Exclusive Contracts

The principle of mitigation is not necessarily applicable in cases where the relationship between the parties is not exclusive. If the aggrieved party is free to enter into other similar contracts, entry into such a contract after breach does not reduce damages.

Examples: (1) *A*, the owner of a car rental fleet, contracts to rent a car for one year to *B*, who repudiates. *A* then rents the car that had been earmarked for *B* to *C*. *C*'s rental payments do not reduce the damages recoverable against *B*, provided that it can be shown that *A* had a sufficient supply of cars to accommodate both *B* and *C*. The basic idea is the same as in the case of an action by an automobile dealer against a repudiating buyer discussed in VIII.A.2.b.1.c., *supra*.

(2) Mr. Plumber, a plumbing subcontractor who employs about 20 workers at different job sites, is hired by Mr. Jeecy, a general contractor, to install plumbing at a new condominium complex. In addition to Plumber's regular workers, he has access to additional plumbers from the union hiring hall. Jeecy breaches. Mr. Plumber

sends the four plumbers he would have sent to Jeecy's job to another job at a trout hatchery. Mr. Plumber is still entitled to receive full damages, as he would have had the hatchery job regardless of Jeecy's breach.

5. Present Worth Doctrine

Where damages include payments that were required to be made in the future, the value of the payments must be calculated at their present worth.

Example: *D* repudiates a contract that requires payment to *P* of $20,000 per year for 20 years. The contract is not exclusively a unilateral obligation to pay a sum of money. (*See* VI.E.9., *supra*). Consequently, an action for anticipatory breach is available. *P* sues to recover $400,000—20 years times $20,000: *P* does *not* recover $400,000. That sum invested at 5% would return $20,000 per year and at the end of 20 years would be intact. Instead, *P* is entitled to judgment for a sum of money which could purchase an annuity that would yield $20,000 per year for 20 years. The cost of such an annuity depends upon the interest rates in effect at the time of purchase.

6. Liquidated Damages

a. Penalties Distinguished

Liquidated damages clauses are valid. Penalty clauses are void. A clause will be deemed a valid liquidated damages clause if it is a reasonable and good faith attempt to pre-estimate the economic harm that would flow from breach. In contrast, penalty clauses are designed to deter breaches by the prospect of punishment. Distinguishing the two is important—penalty clauses are often disguised as liquidated damage clauses. Traditionally, the test is whether the pre-estimate was reasonable as of the time of contracting. The modern view is to validate the clause if it is reasonable in the light of foresight or in the light of the actual harm done.

Comments: (1) Note that the key element in distinguishing a liquidated damages clause from a penalty clause is its *purpose*.

(2) Note also that courts are more prone to uphold a provision as a liquidated damages clause if the injury caused by the breach is difficult or impossible to estimate accurately.

Example: *P*, an oral surgeon, hired *D*, also an oral surgeon, to work as an assistant in *P*'s Gloversville office. A clause provided that *D* would not practice oral surgery in Gloversville, except in association with *P*. It further provided that if *D* violated this promise, *D* would pay the sum of $60,000 to *P*. Courts will uphold the clause if it seems that the sum realistically deals with the probable financial injury that a breach would cause. The clause in this case is particularly likely to be upheld because actual damages are very difficult to prove with a reasonable degree of certainty.

b. Formulas Are Acceptable

Valid liquidated damages clauses are often expressed in formulas rather than in exact dollar amounts. Such an expression does not affect the validity of the clause.

Example: *V* contracts to sell a residence to *P*. A deed of conveyance and possession are to be delivered on October 1. *P*, who is married and has four children, intends to move into the house on October 1 and explains this to *V* prior to contracting. At *P*'s insistence, the contract provides that for each day's delay in delivery of possession *V* will pay liquidated damages of $500. The sum is reasonable in the light of alternative lodging costs in the area, increased cost of food, storage of furniture, etc. The clause will be upheld.

c. Shotgun Clauses Are Dangerous

A clause providing that "$50,000 will be paid for breach of this contract" may be deemed a penalty because it does not proportion the damages to any particular kind of breach. Instead, there is just one amount for any breach. Notice that in each of the illustrations of valid liquidated damages clauses given above, the clause targets the kind of breach that triggers the liability for liquidated damages. The question is one of interpretation. If it is possible to interpret the clause as targeted solely at a total breach (or other specific kind of breach), then it is *not* a "shotgun clause" and is *not* invalid under the rule applicable to such clauses.

d. Can't Have It Both Ways

The courts will strike down a clause that attempts to fix damages in the event of breach while giving the aggrieved party the right to obtain judgment for additional actual damages that may be established. Such a clause does not involve a reasonable attempt to definitively pre-estimate the loss.

e. Specific Performance Not Excluded

A valid liquidated damages clause does not give a breaching party an option to pay liquidated damages or perform. Therefore, the presence of such a clause does not preclude a decree for specific performance. However, the aggrieved party cannot normally have both remedies. If the aggrieved party obtains a decree for specific performance, the decree may also quantify such actual damages as may have been sustained between the time of the breach and the time of the decree.

f. Additional Agreed Damages—Attorneys' Fees

The award of damages does not ordinarily include reimbursement of the successful party's attorney's fees. However, a contract can provide that, in the event of breach, the aggrieved party may recover reasonable attorneys' fees incurred. In this situation, the victorious party recovers an agreed amount in excess of the damages that would accrue by operation of law.

7. Limitations on Damages

The UCC and the common law permit the parties to limit damages "as by limiting the buyer's remedies to return of the goods and repayment of the price or to repair and replacement of non-conforming goods or parts." UCC § 2–719(1)(a). The UCC further provides that: "Consequential damages may be limited or excluded unless the limitation or exclusion is unconscionable. Limitation of consequential damages for injury to the person in the case of consumer goods is prima facie unconscionable but limitation of damages where the loss is commercial is not." UCC § 2–719(3).

Discussion: The general approach of the UCC, which is similar to that of the common law, is to uphold agreed upon limitations of liability. The primary restriction on parties' contractual freedom to limit liability is unconscionability. Limitations on commercial losses are routinely upheld.

Example: *A* operates a business that heavily depends on the "Yellow Pages" phone book as a source of customers. The telephone company, in breach of contract, placed *A*'s name and number in the wrong category of listings. This caused a drastic diminution in the amount of *A*'s business during the year. *A*'s contract with the telephone company provides that *A*'s remedy for breach is limited to restitution of the amount paid for advertising in the directory. The limitation is valid.

a. Failure of Essential Purpose

"Where circumstances cause an exclusive or limited remedy to fail of its essential purpose, remedy may be had as provided in this act." UCC § 2–719(2).

1) Discussion

This rule is statutory and does not exist at common law. It is far less broad than an initial reading might convey. The issue is not conscionability of a limitation clause. Rather, the issue is the *purpose of the limitation clause.*

Example: A contract for the sale of a new car limits the purchaser's warranties to repair and replacement of defective parts. The car has numerous defects. Despite many trips to the dealer's service department for replacement of defective parts, the car does not operate properly. The purpose of the clause limiting the buyer's remedies has failed. It was designed to limit the dealer's liability but *also to* provide the buyer with a serviceable car for the warranty term. Consequently, the buyer may return the car and obtain restitution of the purchase price and recover general and consequential damages for breach of warranty. Compare the previous example concerning the "Yellow Pages." There the purpose is solely to limit liability. Assuming the UCC were applicable to the Yellow Pages case (it, of course, is not), the clause does not fail of its purpose.

8. Punitive Damages

Punitive damages are not available in a contract action unless the breach involves an independent tort.

Examples: (1) *S* contracts to deliver sugar to *B* on February 1. *S,* out of malice, withholds delivery. *B* may recover general damages and consequential damages (if the test of foreseeability is met). *B* may not recover punitive damages.

(2) *S* contracts to provide services to *B* commencing February 1. *B* no longer desires the services contracted for and prevents *S*'s performance by hiring *S*'s key employees in breach of their contracts with *S*. *B* is liable for punitive damages. Why? Because in addition to *B*'s breach by prevention, *B* has committed the tort of wrongful interference with the contractual relation between *S* and *S*'s employees.

Comments: (1) Some jurisdictions grant punitive damages where elements of fraud, malice, gross negligence or oppression "mingle" with the breach as in example (1) above. Although the UCC specifically bars punitive damages except where specifically provided (§ 1–106(1), revision § 1–305), courts sometimes overlook the UCC provision in these cases.

(2) Many jurisdictions grant punitive damages against insurance companies in cases where in bad faith the company refuses to settle a claim. For example, the insured has automobile liability insurance for a maximum coverage of $50,000, and an injured passenger offers to settle for that amount. The insurer rejects the offer and takes the case to trial and the court enters judgment for the passenger against the insured on a verdict of $1,000,000. This sets the stage for an action by the insured against the insurer in which punitive damages are available if the insured proves bad faith—the insurer's reckless disregard of the insured's interests.

(3) California will also grant punitive damages where there is a bad faith refusal to recognize the existence of a contract.

9. Mental Distress

The law does not compensate for mental distress caused by a contractual breach in most contractual contexts. In a few atypical cases (*e.g.*, breach of contract for funeral arrangements) such compensation has been allowed.

10. Nominal Damages

Every breach of contract creates a cause of action. If the aggrieved party suffers no economic harm or cannot prove such harm with sufficient certainty, nominal damages can be recovered, *e.g.*, six cents.

11. Efficient Breach Theory

Discussion: This theory holds that if a party breaches, and is still better off paying damages to compensate the victim of a breach than going ahead with performance, the result is preferable because it is economically efficient. That is, considered as a unit, the parties are better off, and the breach makes no party worse off. Consequently, the party who will benefit from the breach should breach, and the courts should not deem such a breach to be blameworthy.

Critique: (1) The theory fails to account for transaction costs—the costs of litigation or settlement negotiations.

(2) The theory fails to account for damages that are real but noncompensable because of the rules of foreseeability and certainty.

(3) The theory does not reflect the law except to some extent in the 7th Circuit. The tort of interference with a contract reflects the legal system's reality; the breach and the incitement to breach are treated as legal wrongs.

B. Restitution

1. Goal of Restitution

The basic goal of actions at law or in equity for restitution is to place the aggrieved party in the same economic position this party had enjoyed prior to entering into the contract. This is accomplished by requiring the defendant to restore to the plaintiff what defendant has received from the plaintiff. Such restoration will not fully recapture the *status quo ante* if the plaintiff has incurred expenses in reliance upon the contract, but which have not benefitted the defendant. A modern but unorthodox trend permits recovery of such expenditures in a restitution action.

2. When Is Restitution Available?

Restitution is available in six principal kinds of contractual situations:

a. Total Breach of Contract.

b. Avoidance of a Contract for Incapacity, Duress, Misrepresentation, Mistake, etc.

c. The Agreement is not a Contract Because of Indefiniteness, Misunderstanding, Agent's Lack of Authority, etc.

d. The Agreement is Unenforceable Because of a Statute of Frauds and Certain Kinds of Illegality.

e. The Agreement is Discharged Because of Impracticability or Frustration.

f. The Defaulting Party Seeks to Recover for Part Performance.

Restitution under all of these categories, except Total Breach of Contract, is quasi-contractual. Discussion here is limited to restitution's role as a remedy for a total breach of contract.

3. The Party Avoiding Must Offer to Return Property

As a precondition to an action for restitution, a party who seeks to avoid a contract must offer to return any property received. The offer may be conditional on the other party's restitution of what that party received.

Exceptions:

a. Equitable Action

Specific restitution may be decreed in an equitable action despite the plaintiff's failure to offer to make restitution. This is because a decree in equity can be conditioned upon the plaintiff's restoration. In many states, judgments at law do not have this flexibility. It must be remembered that there must be grounds for equitable intervention before specific restitution will be granted.

b. Worthlessness

If the property received was worthless or became worthless because of its defects, failure to offer its return will not defeat the plaintiff's action.

c. Consumption or Loss of Possession

If services have been received, they, of course, cannot be returned. If the goods received have been consumed or disposed of, return is not possible. Consequently, the requirement of an offer to return is dispensed with. Instead, the value of the services or goods will be subtracted from the plaintiff's recovery.

d. Divisibility

If the contract is divisible into several agreed exchanges and the grievance does not relate to all of them, the plaintiff does not need to offer to return those things received pursuant to an uncontested divisible portion.

4. Defendant's Refusal to Accept an Offered Return

If a defendant improperly refuses an offer of return of goods, the plaintiff may assert a lien on the goods and can sell them. The price will be credited to the restitution claim.

5. Measure of Recovery

The plaintiff receives the reasonable value of services rendered, goods delivered, or property conveyed less the reasonable value of any counter-performance received, irrespective of any enrichment.

Comment: "Unjust Enrichment," the principal philosophical underpinning of the restitution remedy, does not provide the measure of recovery.

Examples: (1) An attorney contracted to try a divorce case for $7,500. After nearly completing the trial, the client wrongfully fired the attorney. The reasonable value of the services was $10,000. The attorney recovers $10,000.

(2) *C* contracts to add a porch of rather ugly design on *O*'s house for $15,000. Before the work is completed, *O* wrongfully orders *C* to cease performance. *C* recovers the reasonable value of services rendered even though the ugly and incomplete porch diminishes the value of *O*'s realty.

6. No Restitution After Complete Performance

Restitution is not available if a debt has been created.

Example: An attorney contracts to try a divorce case for $7,500. After completing the trial, the client wrongfully repudiates. The attorney has no restitution action and is limited to an action for $7,500 even though the reasonable value of services was $20,000.

7. Election of Remedies

In the absence of a statute, a plaintiff cannot recover both restitution and damages. Under the UCC, recovery may be had under both headings.

Examples: (1) A seller tenders a defective machine for which the purchaser has paid. The purchaser may reject it, or revoke acceptance of it. The purchaser may then recover the purchase price (if paid) and, under the UCC, recover damages as well. Damages are usually measured by the increased cost of replacing the machine with a substitute.

(2) *A* assigns a patent to *B* who promises to pay a royalty and to use best efforts to promote the patented invention. *B* totally breaches. Because the UCC is not applicable, *A* may elect to sue for damages or to seek restitution at law for the value of the patent, but cannot have restitution plus damages. A third possibility is a decree in equity for specific restitution of the patent.

8. Specific Restitution

Specific restitution will be ordered where the legal remedy is inadequate.

Discussion: The typical restitution action at law for the reasonable value of one's performance is a "quasi-contractual" action and in which the judgment is for a sum of money. In equity, through various devices, such as a decree canceling a deed, or the imposition of a constructive trust, specific restitution of property transferred or wrongfully acquired may be compelled. The remedy at law is deemed inadequate where property is transferred in exchange for the promise of something other than money, and the exchange will not be forthcoming (Example 1), and also where the contract breacher has acquired money or property in violation of a relationship of trust and confidence (Example 2).

Examples: (1) *A* conveys his or her house and land to *B* in exchange for *B*'s promise to support and take care of *A* for *A*'s life. *B* repudiates. *A* may have specific restitution. *A*'s remedies at law are inadequate. Damages are speculative. Restitution at law for the value of the property is not an adequate remedy as *A* has evinced no intent to convey at market value.

(2) *A* contracts with the CIA to be an intelligence agent and agrees not to publish any material about CIA operations without the CIA's clearance. In violation of the contract, *A* writes and causes to be published a book about CIA activities. A constructive trust is imposed upon *A*'s royalties from the book. Note that normally a plaintiff *cannot* recover the profits that a defendant has made from a breach of contract. Here, however, there are grounds for such relief in equity because of the confidential relationship between the CIA and its agent.

C. Equitable Enforcement

1. Inadequacy of the Legal Remedy

Equity will enforce a contract by decreeing specific performance or by a restraining order only if the legal remedy of damages or restitution is inadequate.

a. Uniqueness

Equity will order specific performance to a contract purchaser if the subject matter of a contract of sale is unique. The legal remedy is inadequate because the disappointed purchaser cannot replace the subject matter on the market.

Examples: (1) Real property is always deemed unique—each parcel is deemed to have its individual character;

(2) Heirlooms, works of art, and other one-of-a-kind objects; and

(3) Patents, copyrights, closely held stock, and other intangibles not readily available on the market.

b. Affirmative Rule of Mutuality

If a purchaser could have obtained a decree of specific performance in the event of the seller's breach because the purchaser's legal remedy would have been inadequate, the converse is true—the seller can obtain a decree of specific performance in the event of the purchaser's breach.

Example: *V* contracts to sell a house to *P* for $200,000, payable in cash. *P* repudiates. *V* may obtain a decree of specific performance although there is nothing unique about *P*'s performance—the payment of money.

c. Conjectural Damages

The legal remedy is inadequate if damages are conjectural, although the contract is sufficiently definite, and restitution does not carry out the ends of the contract.

Examples: (1) *S* contracts to supply *B*'s requirement of natural gas for a ten-year term. In the third year, *S* repudiates. *B* sues for specific performance. *B* can obtain equitable enforcement because damages for failure to supply gas for the next seven years are highly conjectural.

(2) Contracts of insurance, annuity contracts based on life expectancy, and contracts to give security are other illustrations in which damages for breach are highly conjectural. Consequently, specific performance is typically available in those instances as a remedy for breach; *e.g.*, a repudiation by the insurer prior to the happening of the insured event.

2. Defenses to Specific Performance

a. Validity of the Contract and Value

Equity will not enforce a contract that is invalid. Moreover, it requires that the contract be for value. Nominal consideration will not suffice, and a contract under seal without consideration will not suffice. Value consists of any consideration in fact bargained for or the existence of an antecedent debt. For example, a right is exchanged for value if it is given as security for, or in total or partial satisfaction of, a pre-existing debt.

Exception: An option contract for a nominal consideration or under seal (in those jurisdictions where the seal is still viable) will be specifically enforced, provided that it looks to further performances for a fair exchange.

Example: *V* offers to sell Bleak House to *P* for $250,000, a fair price. *V* also agrees to make the offer irrevocable for 30 days in consideration of $1. The following day, *V* purports to revoke the offer, and *P* thereafter gives *V* a notice of acceptance and brings an action for specific performance. Despite the fact that the consideration for the option is nominal, equity will decree specific performance.

b. Certainty of the Contract

Equity requires that the parties' performances be described in the contract with greater precision than is the case in an action at law. Because the penalty for non-compliance with a decree is punishment for contempt, the parties and the court must know what to do with reasonable certainty.

c. Impossibility

Equity will not order a defendant to render a performance that is impossible even where impossibility will not excuse a breaching party in an action for damages.

Example: *V* contracts to sell Bleak House to *P*. Subsequently, *V* breaches the contract by conveying to *T*, a bona fide purchaser for value. Because the impossibility is self-induced, *V* does not have the defense of impossibility of performance in an action at law. Nevertheless, the court will not order specific performance, because *V* no longer has the capability of performing.

3. Judicial Discretion as to Equitable Remedies

Specific performance is never a matter of pure entitlement. The court has wide power of discretion in determining whether or not to grant the remedy. The factors considered by the court in deciding against enforcement are reducible to certain doctrines, such as "difficulty of supervision," discussed below.

a. Difficulty of Supervision

Equity, in its discretion, will refuse to order specific performance of contracts where supervision of performance by the court will be unduly burdensome.

Only rarely will a court specifically enforce a contract to build or repair a structure. Yet, the court will do so where the "injustice from refusal to enforce outweighs the probable burden of supervision." For example, a court has ordered specific performance of a railroad's contractual promise to a city to elevate its tracks. Specific enforcement of a contract to build has also been ordered in circumstances where the performance is to be on the *defendant's* land, e.g., where defendant agrees to build a structure in its shopping center and lease it to the plaintiff. In such a case, the plaintiff cannot hire a contractor to do the job and sue for damages (the contractor would be trespassing).

b. Personal Service Contracts

Employment contracts are not specifically enforced against the *employee*. Such decrees would reek of involuntary servitude and possibly would run afoul of the Constitution. At times, however, an employee may be *enjoined* against working for another, resulting in indirect enforcement. Enforcement against an *employer* is normally denied because of the difficulty of supervision, or because of the adequacy of the legal remedy of monetary damages. But arbitration awards of reinstatement have been enforced.

c. Undue Risk

If performance of the contract would impose an undue risk that the counter-performance will not be received, specific performance will be denied.

Discussion: It used to be the general rule that if for any reason specific performance could not be decreed against one party (e.g., difficulty of supervision), it could not be decreed against the other. This negative rule of "mutuality of remedy" has been abandoned and the undue risk doctrine is what remains of it.

Example: *V* contracts to sell Bleak House to *P*. *V* is to convey title on *P*'s making of a down payment, and *P* is to make further payments in installments over a ten-year period. *V* repudiates, and *P* seeks a decree of specific performance. The court may condition a decree for specific performance on *P*'s executing a mortgage to secure *V*'s right to payment.

d. Unconscionability

Under the doctrine of unconscionability, equity has refused to enforce contracts that are valid at law. Inadequacy of consideration coupled with any wrongful non-disclosure, overreaching, abuse of confidential relationship, etc., can result in a refusal of specific performance even where the inequitable conduct would not enable the party to avoid the contract.

e. Unclean Hands

Specific performance will be denied if the plaintiff is guilty of any inequitable conduct with respect to the transaction, even if the questionable conduct was done in concert with the defendant so that no unconscionability exists.

Example: *D*, a professional athlete of extraordinary skill, entered into a voidable contract to play baseball for *Philadelphia* while under the age of majority. *Chicago* induced him to play for it at a higher salary. *D* disaffirmed his contract with *Philadelphia,* and after attaining the age of majority, entered into a binding contract with *Chicago*. *Philadelphia* then induced *D* to breach the contract with *Chicago* to play for it. *Chicago* sues *D* to enjoin him from playing with *Philadelphia*. *D* sets up the defense of unclean hands. Injunction denied. *Chicago,* which inequitably interfered with *D*'s contract with *Philadelphia,* cannot equitably complain of *D*'s similar behavior at a later time in concert with *Chicago*.

Perspective: "Unclean hands" is related to illegality, but conduct short of illegality may give rise to the doctrine.

f. Laches

Even if the statute of limitations has not run, specific performance will be denied if the plaintiff's failure promptly to commence a lawsuit prejudices the defendant, as by causing the defendant to change position or where the plaintiff has remained inactive until the subject matter has risen in value.

g. Balancing Hardships

Specific performance will be denied where the hardship to the defendant or to the public will be greatly in excess of any benefit to the plaintiff.

Examples: (1) A railroad breached its contract to erect a private railroad crossing that had little or no value to the plaintiff and would involve considerable cost to the defendant. Specific performance was denied.

(2) A defendant railroad breached its contract to share trackage. The defendant's employees threatened to strike if the contract were to be performed. Hardship to the defendant and to the public were cited as grounds for denial of equitable relief. The railroad didn't have to share trackage and the strike was averted. Remember, however, the plaintiff can still claim damages or restitution at law.

4. Specific Performance with an Abatement

When a vendor's title to real property is encumbered so that the vendor is unable to convey the interest specified in the contract, the vendee may obtain a decree of specific performance with an abatement in price. Specific performance with an abatement has also been decreed where specific property has been damaged, as by fire, after contracting and before conveyance.

Comment: In essence, this decree involves specific performance with an offset for damages for a partial breach. In rare cases, specific performance will be refused if only a radically different kind of estate can be conveyed from that contracted for.

Examples: (1) *V* contracts to sell a farm to *P*. A title search reveals the land is encumbered by easements that had not been disclosed by *V*. These easements diminish the value of the land by 15%. The court may order specific performance with a 15% reduction in price.

(2) *V* contracts to sell a farm to *P* for $500,000. A title search reveals that *V* only has a life estate. Because *V*'s life expectancy is limited, the value of *V*'s interest is $100,000. *P*'s action for specific performance with an abatement will be denied.

5. Relationship Between Specific Performance and Damages

a. Specific Performance Plus Damages

A decree for specific performance is often accompanied by an award of damages. Often this will be an award of damages for delay in performing, say, a contract to convey real property. In other cases, it may be an award of damages for partial breach of, say, an output contract.

b. Specific Performance and Liquidated Damages

The presence of a liquidated damages clause does not preclude an award of specific performance.

c. Effect of Denial of Specific Performance

If the court denies specific performance because of the adequacy of the legal remedy or because of the exercise of equitable discretion, the plaintiff may thereafter commence an action for damages or restitution at law. The denial of specific performance on equitable grounds does not deprive the plaintiff of the legal remedy. Under modern practice, in many jurisdictions, plaintiff may join the equitable action with the law action in one lawsuit. In such a suit, if the equitable remedy is denied, the legal remedy may be granted.

6. Restraining Orders

Specific relief, of a sort, is often obtained by a restraining order. While these are most often sought in personal service contracts, they are not limited to such contracts.

Example: *S* contracts to sell *S*'s entire output to *B*. For breach of this contract a court can enjoin *S* from selling to others. Such a negative order frees the court from the need to supervise sales to *B*.

a. Employment Contracts with Affirmative and Negative Duties

Where an employee promises to work exclusively for an employer for a given period, although equity will not compel the employee to work, it will enjoin the employee from working for another if the employer can show irreparable harm from breach of the express or implied negative covenant not to work for another.

Example: An opera singer breaches a contract to sing with plaintiff's company and signs on with a competing company in the same city, which draws on the same clientele. An injunction restraining the singer from performing for the competitor may be granted. A contrary result will be reached if the singer signs up with a company from a distant city because there would be no injury from breach of the negative covenant.

b. Trade Secrets

A covenant not to divulge trade secrets will be enforced by injunction. Even in the absence of such a covenant, a duty not to divulge will be implied and enforced by injunction.

c. Covenants Not to Compete

An agreement not to compete is void if it is unconnected with another transaction. An ancillary covenant connected with the sale of a business, an employment contract, a lease, and certain other transactions may be valid, if reasonable.

Comment: If the covenant is unreasonable, the orthodox view was that the entire covenant fell. The modern cases in some jurisdictions allow partial enforcement, limiting the injunction to a reasonable time and area.

1) Ancillary to Sale of Business

Reasonableness is judged by whether the duration and territorial area of the restraint is in excess of the area in which the seller enjoyed goodwill or of the period of time the goodwill can reasonably be expected to continue.

Example: A local dry cleaner sells his store in Brooklyn, N.Y., promising not to compete "within New York State." This covenant, specifically its geographical reach, would be ruled unreasonable if the store's new owner tries to stop the dry cleaner from setting up a new shop with new clientele in Buffalo, N.Y., hundreds of miles away.

2) Ancillary to Employment

Covenants of this kind are tested by stricter criteria. Equity will enforce such a covenant (1) to the extent necessary to prevent an employee's use of trade secrets and confidential customer lists or (2) where the employee's services are "special, unique and extraordinary." An injunction will be limited to the area and time necessary to protect the employer's interests.

Example: *P*, a nationwide firm specializing in advising businesses on how to minimize unemployment insurance costs, hired *D* eleven years ago. *D*'s employment contract provided that if *D* left *P*'s employ, *D* would refrain for three years from competing in seven named counties, one of which was the place of employment. *D* became vice-president in charge of operations and was thoroughly conversant with all aspects of the operation but had little involvement with sales. *P*'s services were sold to major companies listed in industrial directories. After eleven years, *D* resigned and set up a competing business in the same community. *P* seeks an injunction: (1) prohibiting *D* from operating a competing business, and (2) permanently enjoining *D* from soliciting *P*'s customers.

All relief is denied. *D* may solicit *P*'s customers as there is no secret customer list. In addition, under the orthodox view, still widely followed, the covenant is over-broad in its geographical range and therefore is void in its entirety. While the modern view permits limited enforcement of an over-broad covenant, there must be a substantive basis for enforcement. Here, there are no trade secrets, nor are *D*'s services "unique and extraordinary," despite the fact *D* is a talented and skilled professional.

Review Questions *(Answers in Appendix A)*

We suggest you first review HOW TO STUDY and EXAMINATION in the *Perspective* section, *supra*.

On April 15, Vendor contracted to sell to Vendee, a wholesaler, 10,000 yards of satin, delivery to be made on September 15 of the same year at a price of $5.00 a yard, which amount was paid in full on signing the contract. Payment before delivery enabled Vendee to purchase at a price lower than the market.

On April 16, Vendee contracted to sell 5,000 yards of the satin to Shrunk, Inc., at the price of $9.00 per yard and 5,000 yards to Shriek, Inc. at $7.00 a yard. Vendee promptly notified Vendor of the resale contracts and instructed Vendor to deliver the satin directly to Shrunk and Shriek who were retailers in the trade.

Because of a series of business misfortunes, Vendee's liquid assets became dangerously short, and Vendor became aware of this. Vendor, whose son was jilted by Vendee's daughter, maliciously and with intent to injure Vendee, failed to deliver the satin.

On the evening of September 15, Vendee demanded that if the satin were not delivered, Vendor should immediately make restitution of the $50,000 paid and begin negotiations on the issue of additional damages. Vendor replied that he would consider it "when I have time, maybe when I get back from Acapulco in February."

On September 15, the market price of satin was $8.00 a yard. Shrunk agreed with Vendee to rescind their contract and they exchanged releases. Shriek demanded immediate delivery of the satin or payment of damages. With the proceeds of a loan, Vendee was able to satisfy Shriek and other creditors. Vendee went out of business and has ulcers and hypertension proximately caused by Vendor's breach.

1. T or F Because Vendor's breach was malicious, Vendee may recover punitive damages.

2. T or F Because Vendor's breach was malicious, Vendee could have successfully brought an action for specific performance.

3. T or F Vendee is not entitled to restitution of the payment because Vendee's damages remedy is adequate.

4. T or F Vendee's general damages against Vendor are measured by the difference between contract price and the market price on September 15.

5. T or F Vendee is not entitled to damages for the medical problems caused by the breach.

6. T or F Because Vendor was unaware of the resale price, Vendee cannot recover for loss of profits on the resale to Shrunk.

7. T or F Because the resale price to Shrunk was above the market price, Vendee cannot recover from Vendor his full loss of profits on the resale contract to Shrunk.

8. T or F Assuming Shriek had sued Vendee instead of settling, Shriek would have been entitled to the difference between the contract price and the market price even if Shriek had not covered.

9. T or F Because Vendee and Shrunk voluntarily exchanged releases, Vendee is not entitled to damages from Vendor for lost profits on the resale contract with Shrunk.

10. **Essay** Edwards secured a patent on a converter for transforming landline telephones (traditional wired phones) so that they had all the capabilities of the latest cellphones. The invention had worked in laboratory tests and was believed to be capable of mass production at moderate cost.

Lacking funds for development, Edwards entered into an agreement with Uncas. The latter provided a substantial capital investment and received 100% of the stock and the position of President in a newly formed corporation called Telefonica.

Edwards assigned the patent to Telefonica and received a contract to serve as general manager of the corporation for twenty-five years at a salary of $150,000 per year plus 5% of the net profits of the corporation during the life of the patent. All these arrangements were made in October 2008. It was anticipated that a plant would be built and production under way in one year. Contracts were let for construction of the plant and for the purchase of raw materials.

In particular, Telefonica contracted on October 30, 2008, with International Metals for the purchase of 10,000 linear yards of standard wire such as is generally used in electronic circuitry. International Metals was told of the use to which the wire would be put and of the fact that Telefonica had contracted with Titanic, Inc., for delivery of 500,000 converters provided that in Titanic's sole discretion the converters would satisfactorily perform their function.

In early 2008, a shortage of wire of this type developed because of explosive growth of microcomputer production, coupled with strikes in the world's largest copper mines. Realizing that it would be unable to meet its commitment to Telefonica from its own plants, International Metals contracted with Japan Metals, Inc., which agreed to manufacture the wire and deliver it directly to Telefonica.

Japan Metals failed to perform its agreement. As a result, Telefonica, which had acquired a plant and all necessary personnel and materials, was forced to delay production for one year. Uncas, who wrongfully suspected that Telefonica's failure to obtain the wire was due to Edwards' incompetence, fired him. Edwards decided, instead of seeking other employment, to build a home laboratory and to develop a practical water desalinization process.

(a) What remedies are available to Edwards?

(b) What is the extent of the liability of International Metals to Telefonica?

(c) What is the extent of the liability of Japan Metals to International Metals?

11. Multiple Choice:

A. Walsh Construction has entered into a contract with Jones to build her a house for $300,000. Jones repudiated the contract after she has paid Walsh Construction $60,000. At this point, the house was one-third constructed. Walsh Construction sued for breach and proved that it would have cost it a total of $255,000 to perform the contract, of which it has already spent a total of $90,000 in materials and labor in performing the contract. It was able to salvage $10,000 by sales of some of these materials to other contractors after Jones repudiated the contract.

1. Walsh Construction's damages recovery measured by its expectation interest is:

   a) $45,000

   b) $65,000

   c) $90,000

   d) $100,000

   e) $115,000

   f) $125,000

g) $135,000

h) $255,000

2. Walsh Construction's damages recovery measured by its reliance interest is:

a) $20,000

b) $30,000

c) $60,000

d) $80,000

e) $90,000

f) $125,000

B. Construction Co. had entered into a contract with Resort to construct an 18-hole golf course for $200,000. Because of mistakes in judgment, it had underpriced the job; the cost to construct the entire 18 holes would be $250,000. After Construction Co. had finished half the work, at a cost of $125,000, and Resort had paid $50,000 in progress payments, Resort cancelled the contract without justification and Construction Co. immediately stopped the work. Assume that $300,000 is the market value of the services under the contract (building 18 holes), and that "half the work" equals half the market value.

1. Which measure of recovery will give Construction Co. the highest recovery?

a) Expectation

b) Reliance

c) Restitution

d) (a), (b) and (c) result in the same recovery.

2. If Construction Co. sues Resort for restitution, it would be entitled to:

a) $25,000

b) $75,000

c) $100,000

d) $150,000

Chapter IX

Avoidance or Reformation for Misconduct or Mistake

■ ANALYSIS

A. Duress
   1. What Constitutes Wrongful Conduct
      a. Violence or Threats of Violence
      b. Imprisonment or Threat of Imprisonment
      c. Wrongful Seizing or Withholding of Property, Including the Abuse of Liens or Attachments
      d. The Abuse of Legal Rights or the Threat Thereof
      e. Breach or Threat to Breach a Contract
   2. Coercion by a Third Person
   3. Voidable or Void?
      a. Does It Make a Difference?
      b. When Does Duress Make a Transaction Void?

B. Undue Influence

C. Misrepresentation
   1. Requirements
      a. Scienter Is Not a Requirement
      b. Deception
      c. Reliance
      d. Justification
      e. Injury Not Usually a Requisite
      f. The Misrepresentation Must Be of Fact and Not Opinion or Law
         1) The Representer Is or Claims to Be an Expert
         2) The Representer Has Superior Access to the Facts upon Which the Opinion Is Based
         3) There Is a Relationship of Trust and Confidence Between the Parties

A. Duress

Any wrongful act or threat that is the inducing cause of a contract constitutes duress and is grounds for avoiding the contract. However, where the coercion involves economic pressure rather than a threat of personal injury or the like, duress is usually not present unless the party coerced can show that there was no reasonable alternative but to assent.

1. What Constitutes Wrongful Conduct

a. Violence or Threats of Violence

Example: *A* threatens *B* with physical injury unless *B* signs an acceptance of *A*'s offer. *A*'s threat would not coerce a person of ordinary firmness, but does induce *B*, who is easily susceptible to threats. The contract is voidable. A subjective test is used to determine whether *B*'s acceptance was induced by the threat.

b. Imprisonment or Threat of Imprisonment

Examples: (1) An employer discovers that an employee has been embezzling money. The employer threatens the employee with criminal prosecution unless the employee makes restitution. The employee is induced to sign a promissory note in the amount of $5,000 payable to the employer. According to the Restatement (Second) the note is voidable. The cases, however, are in disarray and, if part of the consideration is the employer's promise not to prosecute, courts often deny contractual relief on grounds of illegality. Even if the note is voidable, the employer's claim for restitution of the amount embezzled is not barred.

(2) *A* is arrested as a result of mistaken identity. After the mistake has been ascertained, the prosecutor tells *A* that charges will be dismissed if *A* signs a release of claims for false arrest and false imprisonment. *A* signs. Subsequently, *A* sues for false arrest and false imprisonment. The release is voidable because of the implicit threat of continued wrongful imprisonment.

c. Wrongful Seizing or Withholding of Property, Including the Abuse of Liens or Attachments

A wrongful threat to detain, or the wrongful detention of property of another, amounts to duress if it coerces the assent of the other to an unfair transaction and the coerced party had no reasonable alternative but to assent.

Examples: (1) An attorney who has been fired by his or her client exercises a retaining lien on documents for a corporate merger and agrees to release them only on payment of an outrageous fee. Because of the urgency of the situation, and because there is insufficient time to obtain judicial relief, the fee is paid. The fee may be recovered to the extent it is excessive.

(2) A foreign traveler's baggage is attached in order to coerce a settlement in excess of what is owed. This is done despite the fact that the traveler has other attachable assets in the jurisdiction. The excess may be recovered if the court is convinced that the

traveler had no reasonable alternative but to assent to the settlement. This illustration is based upon an old case that found duress. In today's world of international credit cards and electronic funds transfers, a factual finding that there was no reasonable alternative is more doubtful.

d. The Abuse of Legal Rights or the Threat Thereof

Discussion: Rights exist to protect certain interests. At times rights are exercised or threatened to be exercised to attain ends other than for which they exist. If used for illegitimate ends, the rights are abused, and a transaction coerced by such an abuse may be set aside if the coerced party was induced to consent because of such coercion. The Restatement (Second) takes the position that duress does not exist if the coerced party had any reasonable alternative; but the cases in this category seem to consider that factor as just one circumstance to determine whether coercion was the inducing cause of the consent.

Examples: (1) An employer threatens to fire an employee whose hiring is at will unless the employee sells certain shares of stock to the employer. The shares are recoverable, subject to the plaintiff's repayment.

(2) A husband threatens a custody battle on grounds of the wife's adultery unless the wife surrenders shares of stock owned by her. She surrenders them. The shares or their value are recoverable.

e. Breach or Threat to Breach a Contract

A threatened breach of contract constitutes duress if the breach would result in irreparable injury because of an absence of an adequate legal or equitable remedy or other reasonable alternative such as a substitute supplier. In addition, however, the breach or threatened breach must be a violation of the duty of good faith and fair dealing.

Example: *S*, a supplier of component parts to *B*, a radar manufacturer acting under a Navy contract, threatens not to deliver components promised under a contract except at a greatly increased price and only if it is awarded a second contract to supply similar components to *B* under a second government contract that has been awarded to *B*. No other supplier of similar components can make delivery for eight months. Failure to agree would expose *B* to damages for breach of its contract with the Navy and would prejudice its ability to get future government contracts. Duress exists. The excess payments can be recovered, and the second contract avoided. Note that the threat to breach unless the second contract is signed is clearly a breach of the duty of good faith and fair dealing.

The threat to breach unless the price is raised is not necessarily such a breach. According to the Restatement (Second) a party may insist upon a price rise if there is economic justification for it. However, if, as in this example, the purchaser is known to be committed to a third party, under a fixed-price contract, it would seem that the threat to breach unless more money is paid is a violation of the duty of fair dealing, even if there were some economic justification for the price rise.

At any rate, everyone would agree that the threat not to deliver unless the second contract was awarded is an outrageous violation of the duty of good faith and fair dealing.

Perspective: Courts will first look to see if the renegotiated contract lacks consideration, but the UCC has abolished the requirement of consideration for contract modifications in cases involving the sale of goods.

Example: *D* owes *C* a debt of $5,000 that is overdue and uncontested. *C* desperately needs cash. *D*, who knows of *C*'s needs, offers *C* $4,000 in full satisfaction of the debt, threatening not to pay until a judgment is entered. *C* agrees and signs a release. *C* can sue for the balance under the rule of *Foakes v. Beer* as there is no consideration for the release. In a jurisdiction where a signed release is effective without consideration, *C* can avoid the release on grounds of duress if *C* can show there was no reasonable alternative but to sign the release.

2. Coercion by a Third Person

If the wrongful pressure is applied by a third person, the transaction can be avoided if the other contracting party knows of the coercion, or the other party does not give value. If the other party gives value without notice of the wrongful conduct, the coerced party cannot avoid the contract.

Perspective: This is a variation upon the *bona fide* purchaser for value rule of property law.

Examples: (1) *A* threatens *B* with physical harm unless *B* pays *A* $10,000 by the end of the month. To raise the money, *B* puts Blackacre on the market asking its reasonable value—$50,000. *C*, knowing of the threat, offers *B* $15,000 for Blackacre. Because *B* has no other offers, and is in terror of *A*'s threat, *B* agrees to the sale provided the price is paid before the end of the month. *B* may avoid the sale.

(2) The facts are the same as stated in (1), except that *C* has no knowledge of the threat. Although *B* lowered the asking price because of the threat, *B* cannot avoid the sale.

3. Voidable or Void?

a. Does It Make a Difference?

Discussion: Throughout the discussion of duress we have been presupposing a valid transaction and its possible avoidance. The general run of duress cases involve voidable transactions. Just below, we will point out one situation where duress renders a transaction void. There are several consequential differences between voidable and void transactions. (1) Good title to property that is acquired in a voidable transaction can be transferred to a bona fide purchaser for value. (2) A voidable transaction can be ratified. Neither of these two propositions apply to a void transaction.

b. When Does Duress Make a Transaction Void?

A transaction is void because of duress if it is in no sense the consensual act of the party. A contract signed because a shotgun is pointed at one's head is consented to if one has a general idea of what one is signing. The contract is voidable. If one does not have any idea of the contents of the writing, one is in no sense consenting. The document is void. These cases are rare.

Perspective: Compare the rule concerning fraud-in-the-factum (IX.C.6, *infra*).

B. Undue Influence

Discussion: The gist of undue influence is unfair *persuasion* rather than coercion. Persuasion is unfair in two classes of cases. First, where a person uses a position of *trust and confidence* to convince the other to enter into a transaction that is not in the best interests of the party. Second, persuasion is also unfair where a person uses a *position of dominance* to influence a transaction against the best interests of the subservient party.

Comment: The foremost indicator of undue influence is an unnatural transaction resulting in the enrichment of one of the parties at the expense of the other.

Examples: (1) Plaintiff, an elderly and financially inexperienced housekeeper, inherited a good deal of money and property. Harold and Faye, an elderly couple experienced in business, promised her a home with them for life if she would advance them money for the construction of a motel to be repaid without interest. She relied totally on Harold, advancing him money without keeping records or even recollecting the amounts. She was forced to leave because of conflicts with Faye. Thereafter she entered into a settlement agreement relying on Harold's figures as to the amount he had received. These figures considerably understated the amounts. The settlement was set aside. Plaintiff's trust and confidence in Harold was total. He exerted his influence in a manner inconsistent with her interests and enriched himself. She is entitled to an accounting and an equitable lien on the premises.

(2) Confidential relations include cases such as example (1), but typically involve husband-wife, parent-child, trustee-beneficiary, guardian-ward, attorney-client, administrator-legatee, physician-patient, clergyman-parishioner, and fiancé-fiancée.

(3) *A* is old, infirm, and bedridden and lives in the home of *B,* one of his children. *B* threatens to cease supporting and caring for *A* unless *A* deeds his real property to *B*. *A* does so and soon thereafter dies. *A*'s estate may successfully sue to set aside the deed unless it can be shown that the value of the property is not greatly in excess of the value of the services. Note that, in addition to the confidential relationship of parent-child, *B* was in a position of dominance.

C. Misrepresentation

If a misrepresentation constitutes an actionable tort, avoidance is allowed, but all of the elements of tortious misrepresentation are not required for avoidance.

1. Requirements

a. Scienter Is Not a Requirement

Discussion: A misrepresentation is an assertion that is not in accord with existing facts. Avoidance may be based on a negligent or even an innocent misrepresentation. However, an *intentional* misrepresentation *need not be material,* while an *unintentional* misrepresentation *must be material*. A representation is material if (a) it would influence the conduct of a reasonable person or (b) the person using the words knows that it would likely influence the conduct of the other party even if it might not influence a reasonable person.

Rationale: If the misrepresentation is intentional, the wrongdoer has accomplished his or her intended purpose even if the statement was immaterial, whereas one who innocently or carelessly misstates a seemingly unimportant fact has no reason to know that the statement will cause action.

Example: *V*, a seller of farmland, tells *P*, a prospective purchaser, that the land was once the site of the principal lodge of the Delaware Indians. *V* had been told this story in his youth and believed it to be true, but it is false. The representation is not material to the ordinary reasonable purchaser and will not give grounds for avoidance unless *V* is aware of any special influence this story might have upon *P*'s decision to contract to purchase at the price *P* did. If *V* was aware of the inaccuracy of the statement or knew that the story was of dubious veracity, *P* could avoid the contract of purchase provided the other elements of avoidance (deception, reliance and justification) are made out.

b. Deception

The party must have been deceived. If the party did not believe the representation, it cannot later be used as a basis for avoidance.

c. Reliance

The party must have relied upon the representation in the sense that the party regarded the representation as an important fact and that it influenced the decision to enter into the contract.

d. Justification

Discussion: The old idea that a party could not avoid a contract for fraud unless there was a "right to rely" has largely been superseded by the idea that avoidance will be allowed even "to the simple and credulous." The law is in flux on the question, but if the representation is purely factual (as opposed to a representation of fact and opinion or fact and intention) the modern law regards reliance as justified in almost every case. A party is justified in relying even if the party is negligent in investigating the facts or in not investigating the facts. Some states, such as New York, reject the modern law and will not allow avoidance if the party had an opportunity to check the veracity of the representation.

Example: *V* advertised certain real property for sale. *V* described it as having 580 feet of road frontage and that an engineering report showed that the land had a gravel content of 80,000 cubic yards. *V* believed these representations, both of which were based on representations made to *V* by the prior owner. *P*, relying on the advertised facts, purchased and subsequently sought to avoid the purchase after discovering that the gravel bed was exhausted after 6,000 cubic yards were removed and that the road frontage was only 415 feet. *V* was successful in this action to avoid the purchase, despite the fact that, prior to purchasing, *V* did not have the land surveyed and did not check out the engineering report. The court points out that the misrepresentations, although innocent, were material. As in sale of goods cases, the rule of caveat emptor is dead. Even a negligent purchaser need not offer justification for relying on the seller's statements of fact.

Courts in a good number of states would disagree and would hold that since *P* had an opportunity to verify the truth of the representations, *P*'s reliance was unjustified.

e. Injury Not Usually a Requisite

Even if a party gets something as valuable as, or more valuable than, the performance promised, a party may avoid the contract. The rationale is that when a party has been given false information that prevents the exercise of the party's own best judgment, the party's autonomy has been tinkered with.

Example: *B*, negotiating a purchase of a fur coat for his friend *T*, told the seller, *S*, that he would pay no more than $4,000 for a particular coat. *T* secretly told *S* that she would pay the balance of *S*'s $5,000 asking price. *S* then told *B* that he could have the coat for $4,000, and an agreement was reached with *B* for the sale at that price. *T* made the secret payment of the balance. *B* was permitted to avoid the sale despite the fact that *B* received a $5,000 coat for only $4,000 out of his pocket.

Exception: Most cases hold that where a purchaser of land misrepresents the purpose for which the purchase is being made, avoidance is not permitted unless the seller owned adjacent land which will decrease in value because of the intended use.

Example: Purchaser buys a farm at fair market value, representing the intention to farm it. Instead, the purchaser is acting on behalf of a power company that is assembling a site for a power plant. Seller is upset because, had the seller known the facts, Seller could have held out for a much higher price. Avoidance will not be permitted.

f. The Misrepresentation Must Be of Fact and Not Opinion or Law

Discussion: A party is not justified in relying on a statement merely of opinion such as "buy an umbrella today; tomorrow it's likely to rain." Nonetheless, many statements of opinion also imply a factual assertion. "It's uncomfortably hot and muggy today," expresses an opinion but does imply certain facts about the temperature and humidity. An assertion of law is sometimes a statement of fact; (e.g., "Iowa has adopted the UCC"), but more often is a statement of opinion, as when the person making an assertion prognosticates how the Iowa courts will solve a "battle of the forms" case. Although one may not rely on what is merely an opinion, one may rely on the implied facts contained in an opinion if it is reasonable to do so. The following are categories of cases in which such reasonableness is likely to exist. In each case it is assumed that the other elements of avoidance (deception, reliance and justification) exist.

1) The Representer Is or Claims to Be an Expert

Example: "This car is in excellent condition," spoken by an auto dealer is a representation of fact. When spoken by a non-expert owner, it is not, unless it falls into category (4) below.

2) The Representer Has Superior Access to the Facts upon Which the Opinion Is Based

Examples: (1) "This is an original engraving by Paul Revere and has been in our family since 1770." Normally a statement of authorship of an antique work of art is treated as a statement of opinion. In this case, however, the opinion is ostensibly based upon family tradition and is a factual representation.

(2) A franchisor of a chicken-raising system advertises that the franchise would "return to the careful broiler raiser an income roughly equal to half as much as is obtained on an average size farm in the Midwest—and it will do so for about 6 hours of one person's attention daily." The statement is treated as a representation of fact because the franchisor quite clearly has unique access to facts upon which it is based. Note also that this case fits under the expertise category as well.

3) There Is a Relationship of Trust and Confidence Between the Parties

Example: *A*, who has been *B*'s trusted adviser in financial matters, offers to buy Blackacre from *B* for $100,000, stating, "in my opinion that is a fair price." *B* accepts the offer without making any inquiry as to Blackacre's value. *A* soon thereafter resells Blackacre for $150,000. Statements of value are at the very core of the opinion rule and are generally *not* treated as representations, but in this instance, because of the relationship of the parties, *B* is justified in relying upon *A*'s statement of value. Alternatively, this could be viewed as a case of undue influence.

4) The Opinion Intentionally Varies Radically from Reality

Examples: (1) *S*, the owner of a car, has recently had major unrepaired difficulties with his transmission and clutch. *S* tells *B*, a prospective purchaser, that the car is in A-1 condition. *B*, who is deceived, makes the purchase. *S*'s statement clearly varies radically from reality. It is intentional. It is treated as a factual misrepresentation. Consequently, *B* can avoid the sale.

(2) Plaintiff, a widow seeking new interests in life, enrolled in defendant's school for ballroom dancing lessons. Although she had no dance aptitude and little sense of rhythm, she was repeatedly the target of "a constant and continuous barrage of flattery, false praise, excessive compliments, and panegyric encomiums" inducing her to enter into a number of contracts for an aggregate of 2,302 hours for lessons for a cash outlay of $31,000 (in 1961 dollars). The court indicates she is entitled to avoid the contracts. Note that this case also smacks of undue influence.

5) The Representation Is of the Law of Another Jurisdiction

Discussion: If the person making an assertion of law is a lawyer, that assertion can be treated as a factual representation under the expertise category. If the representer is not an attorney, the assertion is treated as merely an opinion unless the case falls under a different exceptional category.

If, however, the assertion, whether or not made by a lawyer, relates to a law of another jurisdiction, it is treated as a representation of fact.

g. Promissory Fraud and Statements of Intention

The making of a promise without an intention to carry it out is a misrepresentation of fact, as is a statement of intention when one has no intention to carry it out.

Discussion: "The state of a man's mind is as much a fact as the state of his digestion." Consequently, if the promisor does not intend to carry out the promise, the promisor is lying. Similarly, a non-promissory statement of intention is a representation.

Example: A developer of tract housing tells a prospective purchaser of a house in the tract that the development company intends to install tennis courts and a golf course nearby. The company has no such intention. The developer has made an intentional misrepresentation. If the other elements (deception, reliance, and justification) are present, the purchaser may avoid the contract of sale. The same result is reached if the contract expressly promised that such sports facilities would be installed, and it can be proved that there was no intent to carry it out.

Where Promise Is Unenforceable: There is no consensus whether the promissory fraud rule can be applied to a promise that is void or unenforceable on grounds of lack of consideration, the parol evidence rule, a statute of frauds, etc. Some courts have refused to apply the rule to such promises on the belief that such application would subvert the rules with respect to the validity and enforceability of promises. Many courts and the Restatement (Second) take the view that the promissory fraud doctrine does apply to such cases. In other words, if a contracting party makes a promise that cannot be enforced because it is barred by the parol evidence rule and does not intend to keep the promise, the contract can be avoided for misrepresentation.

Caveat: *Mere Non-Performance Does Not Prove Misrepresentation.* It is important to note that mere non-performance of a promise does not prove that the promisor never intended to perform. It must be proved that there was a lack of intent to perform at the time of promising.

h. Non-Disclosure

General Rule: *There is no duty to disclose facts that would tend to discourage the other party from entering into a proposed deal.*

Comment: This general rule is being eroded by exceptions.

Exceptions:

(1) *Statutory disclosure rules, such as securities disclosure rules, Truth-in-Lending Act, etc.*

(2) *Concealment (Positive Action to Hide) Is the Equivalent of a Misrepresentation.*

Example: Prior to offering a machine for sale, the owner paints over a crack on the engine block. This is a misrepresentation of fact, and if the other elements (deception and reliance) are present, the purchaser can avoid the contract.

(3) *Where Partial Disclosure Is Misleading.* In the law, silence is better than a half-truth. A truthful statement that omits important qualifying facts is a misrepresentation.

Examples: (1) *A*, a hospital, offers *B*, who is in the Philippines, a position in Oregon. *B* is aware that the hiring is at will, but is unaware that the Board of Trustees has before it a proposal to abolish the position. Upon arrival in Oregon, *B* is told that the position has been abolished. *B* has a tort action for deceit because of the non-disclosure of the full facts. Whenever there is a right of action for deceit, there is alternatively a right to avoid the contract.

(2) *A* reads to *B* a proposed contract, omitting from the reading certain material clauses. *B* assents and signs the document. *B* can avoid the contract even though *B* was negligent in not reading it. Note that if *A* had read none of the contract to *B, B* would be bound under the "duty to read" concept and would have no power of avoidance.

(4) *Changing Circumstances and New Information. If S* makes a true assertion, but changing circumstances cause the assertion to no longer be true, *S* has a duty to inform the other of the change. Similarly, if *S* honestly but incorrectly makes an assertion and discovers the error, what had been an innocent misrepresentation has now become intentional.

(5) *Where a Party Becomes Aware That the Other Is Operating Under a Mistake as to a Vital Fact.* This rule is similar to and, to a large extent, coextensive with the doctrine of unilateral palpable mistake. (*See* IX.D.7., *infra.*) The duty to disclose does not run to all kinds of vital facts. Certainly, there is a duty to disclose latent defects such as termite infestation where the seller knows that the buyer is unaware of such infestation. On the other hand, a party need not disclose superior information about market trends. The ethics of the community are the ultimate resource to determine where to draw the line. The rule requiring disclosure is but an emanation of the obligation of good faith and fair dealing. The Restatement (Second) points this out in the two illustrations given below.

Examples: (1) *P* learns from published government surveys that *V*'s land contains valuable minerals and knows that *V* does not know this. *P* offers to purchase the land without disclosing this information. *V* accepts. The contract is not voidable because *P*'s conduct is not a breach of the obligation to act in good faith. The discretionary remedy of specific performance may, however, be denied.

(2) *P* learns of the valuable mineral deposits on *V*'s land by trespassing. *P*'s failure to disclose is the equivalent of a representation that the land contains no valuable mineral deposits. The contract is voidable if the other elements (deception, reliance, justification) for avoidance are present.

(6) *Where There Is a Confidential Relationship.* Where there is a confidential relationship (e.g., husband and wife, parent and child, priest and penitent, etc.) that falls short of a fiduciary relationship in the strict sense, there is nevertheless a duty to disclose all *material facts* that bear on the transaction. This duty is not limited to vital facts and includes the disclosure of publicly available information as well as privately obtained information about market trends and land values that bear on the transaction. Compare this rule with the last two examples above and with the doctrine of undue influence (*See* IX.B., *supra*).

(7) *Where There Is a Fiduciary Relationship.* If the relationship is a fiduciary one in the strict sense (trustee-beneficiary, attorney-client, executor-beneficiary), the duty of disclosure is more stringent than in a confidential relationship. Fiduciaries must reveal all relevant facts that they know or *should know*. Beneficiaries must be aware of their legal rights. Even if these requirements are met, the transaction can be avoided if it is not on fair terms.

(8) *Suretyship, Marine Insurance, Partnership and Joint Ventures*. In each of these kinds of contracts, broad disclosure rules have been laid down by the courts. These rules are generally akin to those governing *confidential relationships*.

(9) *Where Specific Performance Is Sought.* Where the remedy sought is specific performance, relief will be denied because of non-disclosure of material facts even if there is no special relationship between the parties.

Non-Disclosure in Perspective: In sale of goods cases, non-disclosure by a seller is often irrelevant because, unless warranties have been excluded, relief can be had on an implied warranty.

i. Misrepresentation by a Third Person

If a misrepresentation is made by an agent of a party acting within the scope of the agency, the party is chargeable as if the party had made the statement.

Comment: If a party, prior to contracting, has received false or otherwise incorrect information from a third person who is *not* an agent of the other party, that party cannot avoid a contract induced by this information, unless the other party learned of the misrepresentation prior to contracting. These rules are variants of the *bona fide* purchaser for value principle.

2. Cure of a Misrepresentation

If after a misrepresentation is made but before the deceived party has avoided the contract, the facts are brought into line with the representation, the contract is no longer voidable.

Example: *V*, seeking to induce *P* to purchase *V*'s land, falsely informs *P* that the land is zoned for light industrial use. *V* knows that this is incorrect, but a proposed change is pending. *P* contracts to purchase the land. Before *P* learns of the deception, the zoning ordinance is changed so that the land is now zoned for light industrial use. The contract is no longer voidable by *P*.

3. Merger Clauses

Despite a "merger" clause, or a "there are no representations" clause, parol evidence is admissible to show that a misrepresentation was made. An "as is" clause excludes warranties, but does not exclude evidence of representations.

Comment: The New York rule agrees but holds that if the alleged misrepresentation contradicts a specific recital of fact made in the contract, evidence of it is inadmissible.

Rationale for the General Rule: Remember that the parol evidence rule does not exclude evidence tending to show that a contract is void or voidable.

4. Election of Remedies

If the misrepresentation and ensuing deception, reliance and injury constitute a tort, the deceived party must elect between either a tort action or the exercise of the power of avoidance followed by a restitutionary action.

Exception: Under the UCC, both remedies are available, but items of recovery cannot be duplicated.

Example: *S* sold a horse to *P*, representing it to be a stallion although *S* knew it to be a gelding. Before discovering the deception, *P* incurred costs for caring for and feeding the horse. Upon discovering the deception and in the absence of a statute, *P* may offer to *return the gelding,* avoid the contract and sue for return of the purchase price, thereby forgoing the ability to recover other expenses. Alternatively, *P* could sue for breach of warranty but must *keep the gelding* and recover the difference between the value of the horse as warranted and its actual value plus consequential damages. A third possibility is an action for deceit. This requires *P* to *keep the gelding* and obtain tort damages. Under the UCC, *P* need not choose among these three options but may pursue all three. *P* may return the horse (revoke acceptance of the horse), get restitution of the purchase price, and collect damages as well. Thus, *P* should end up with the purchase price, the costs of care and feeding, and the additional cost of obtaining a stallion of the kind represented minus the value (if any) of the use of the horse. Remember, however, that the common law still governs if the contract is not for the sale of goods.

5. Restoration of *Status Quo Ante*

Where restitution is sought at law (in a non-UCC case), the plaintiff must, before suing, offer to restore any tangible benefits received under the contract. Plaintiff need not have done so if what has been received has perished because of its defects, is worthless, or consists of money that may be offset. However, in an equitable action no prior offer to restore is required, but the equitable decree can be conditioned upon such restoration. An equity action is available if something other than, or in addition to, a money judgment is sought; e.g., cancellation of a deed.

6. Fraud-in-the-Factum: A Rarity

Where a party signs a document that is radically different from that which the party was led to believe was being signed and the circumstances are such that a reasonable person similarly situated would have signed it, the document is void.

Discussion: In almost all cases of legally cognizable misrepresentation, the contract, at most, is voidable. The kind of misrepresentation discussed up to this point has been called "fraud in the inducement." In rare cases, fraud renders a transaction void. This is quaintly known as "fraud-in-the-factum" (or fraud in the execution). The chief consequence of this kind of fraud is that a bona fide purchaser for value from the defrauding party does not take good title. In the usual case of fraud, (fraud in the inducement), a bona fide purchaser for value from a defrauding party acquires good title.

Example: A husband asks his wife to sign a document and represents to her that the document is a property division solely for the purpose of saving on income taxes. She has habitually trusted him in all financial affairs. She signs, without reading, a separation agreement. The agreement is void.

Perspective: Compare the case where duress makes a contract void rather than voidable (*See* IX.A.3.b., *supra*).

D. Mistake

1. Perspective

Certain kinds of mistakes may prevent the formation of contracts. These include misunderstandings (*See* VIII.B.2.c., *supra*) and mistakes in transmission. Here, however, the discussion centers on mistake as a ground for avoiding a transaction.

2. Mistake of Fact Versus Mistake in Judgment

For avoidance, the mistake must relate to a basic assumption as to vital existing facts. Risks of mistake in judgment are characteristic contractual risks from which the court will not relieve a party.

Comment: Risks as to *changing facts* are governed by the rules of *impracticability* and *frustration*.

Examples of Mistakes in Judgment: These include, for example, wrong judgments regarding the profitability of stock purchases, the number of labor hours required to complete a task, and the amount of rock in an area to be excavated.

3. Mutual Mistake

Where both parties are mistaken about a basic assumption upon which they base their bargain, the transaction can be avoided. However, it can only be avoided if a substantially different exchange of values occurs because of the mistake, and the risk of the mistake is not otherwise allocated by agreement of the parties or by the court because such other allocation is reasonable.

Examples: (1) A pregnant cow of excellent breeding stock is mistakenly believed by both parties to be sterile and is sold at a price far below what she otherwise would bring. The sale can be avoided because "A barren cow is substantially a different creature than a breeding cow. There is as much difference between them as there is between an ox and a cow." This case treated the facts as a mistake of subject matter.

(2) A charity and a landowner work out a transaction whereby it is believed that the landowner will be able to receive a large charitable deduction. But for the deduction, the transaction would be of no interest to the landowner, and both parties know this. Existing regulations barred charitable deductions of this kind. The transaction may be avoided. Notice that the vital fact about which they had a mistaken assumption does *not* relate to the identity or quality of the

subject matter. Older cases insisted that the mistake had to relate to the subject matter, as in example (1).

(3) *A*, a 55 year old man, purchases an annuity contract from *B*, an insurance company, whereby *B* is to pay a fixed sum monthly to *A* for life. At the time of contracting, unknown to *A* and undetected by a medical examination required by *B*, *A* has a terminal illness that causes death six months later. Before dying, *A* purports to avoid the contract. The transaction cannot be avoided. Despite the existence of a mutual mistake as to a vital fact, the court will determine that it is reasonable that *A* assume the risk of mistake. Both parties to an annuity contract should understand that it is an aleatory contract; that is, a contract of hazard.

4. Mistake Versus Uncertainty

Where the parties are uncertain or consciously ignorant of a vital fact there is no right of avoidance.

Example: A woman found a stone that appeared to be a gem. She took it to a jeweler who honestly stated his ignorance of its nature and offered her $1 for the stone. She agreed and made the sale. The stone was an uncut diamond worth $700. Avoidance was not permitted because the parties were uncertain rather than mistaken.

5. Mutual Mistake as to Injuries

The orthodox view is that a release of a personal injury claim can be avoided if there are unknown injuries but not if there are unforeseen consequences of known injuries.

Discussion: Diagnosis is distinguished from prognosis. However, some jurisdictions allow avoidance also if there is a vital mistake as to the nature and effect of known injuries.

Example: Plaintiff suffers a blow to the head in an automobile collision. The injury appears slight. Plaintiff releases the claim against the negligent driver for $200. Subsequently, it appears that serious permanent injuries were caused by a blood clot on the brain that resulted from the blow. Even under the stricter view, plaintiff may set aside the release. Knowledge of a blow to the head is not knowledge of injury to the brain.

6. Mutual Mistake as to Acreage

a. Avoidance

If the number of acres contracted to be conveyed or actually conveyed are discovered to be materially different from what the parties believed, the aggrieved party may avoid the contract or conveyance. Avoidance is permitted whether the sale is on a per acre basis or in gross.

b. Restitution

If the contract or conveyance is on a per acre basis, the purchaser may have pro rata restitution of the purchase price for any shortage of acres. The seller has a restitution action for payment for additional acres. If the purchaser has not paid, the remedy is an abatement in price rather than restitution.

Discussion: If a sale is in gross, the only available remedy is avoidance. If the sale is on a per acre basis, the aggrieved party may have restitution (or an abatement) as an alternative to avoidance. However, in a per acre sale, the discrepancy is not always material. In such a case only restitution (or an abatement) is available.

Examples: (1) *V* contracts to sell a farm to *P*. The price is calculated on the basis of $3,000 an acre. The acreage is assumed to be 220 acres because a property description prepared for *V*'s ancestor so states. After paying the price, receiving a deed of conveyance, and taking possession, *P* orders the land surveyed. The survey reveals that the land contains 190 acres. Because there was a mutual mistake as to quantity, and the price was set on a per acre basis, *P* can obtain restitution of $3,000 for each "missing" acre. Because the discrepancy is large enough to be deemed material, *P*, alternatively, can avoid the deed and obtain restitution of the entire purchase price.

(2) *V* advertised the XYZ ranch for sale for $750,000, describing it as containing 900 acres, a grazing permit on federal land, and some described horses and equipment. Some of the land was nearly worthless. *P* contracted to purchase the ranch for $750,000 after *V* agreed to throw in additional equipment. *P* had the land surveyed. The survey showed a deficiency of 70 acres. *P* demanded an abatement for the deficiency. When *V* refused, *P* purported to avoid the contract. *P* sues for restitution of the down payment, and *V* sues for damages. *V* receives judgment for damages. The sale is *not* on a per acre basis since it includes goods and a grazing permit on other land. In addition, the land was of uneven quality, some acres being worth much less than the rest. Consequently, *P* is not entitled to a reduction in price. The deficiency of less than 10% in area is not deemed material enough to justify avoiding the contract. *P*'s unjustified attempt to avoid the contract is a repudiation.

Perspective: These cases are treated under mistake despite the fact that the vendor has made a misrepresentation of fact. The reasons are historical.

7. Unilateral Palpable Mistake

A mistake by one party of which the other is, or ought to be, aware is grounds for avoidance. Cases of this kind are sometimes treated, with the same result, as cases of fraudulent non-disclosure. (See IX.C.1.h., *supra.)*

8. Unilateral Impalpable Mistake

Avoidance is allowed for unilateral impalpable mistake if (a) the mistake if computational, clerical or something of that sort rather than a mistake in judgment, (b) enforcement of the contract would be oppressive, resulting in an unconscionably unequal exchange of values, and (c) avoidance would impose no substantial hardship on the other party.

Example: A construction company enters its bid for constructing a building, making a computational error that would result in doing the job at a substantial loss. It discovers its mistake the day its bid is accepted. It may avoid the contract, but the result would be different if the mistake were not vital or if the discovery of the mistake came significantly later so as to prejudice the other party. Note that the other party's loss of the expectancy engendered by a favorably low bid is not deemed prejudicial for purposes of this rule.

9. Mistake of Law

Discussion: The orthodox view is that a mistake of law (except for mistake of the law of another jurisdiction) is not grounds for avoidance, but the modern trend and the Restatements take the position that relief will not be denied merely because the mistake is one of law. However, mistake of law is not, in all respects, treated as a mistake of fact. If the mistake relates to something other than the legal consequences of words or conduct, the mistake, if vital, may be grounds for avoidance. Generally, a person is bound by the legal consequences of his or her acts such as making an offer, an acceptance, a waiver etc., whether or not the person knew the legal consequences of the act.

Examples: (1) *V* contracts to sell a parcel of land to *P*, who intends to construct a health club on the premises, and *V* knows this. Both parties think this is a lawful use of the land. However, several days before contracting, the zoning ordinance was amended to prohibit such use. Because of the revision of the ordinance, the market value of the land is substantially diminished. The contract is voidable by *P* for mutual mistake.

(2) *S* contracts to sell goods to be delivered to *B* on January 2. *S* tenders delivery on January 3 when the market price has fallen well below the contract price. *B*, in total ignorance of the perfect tender rule, accepts delivery. This act of acceptance cannot be avoided.

10. Mistake in Performance

Recovery may be had for payments, overpayments, deliveries of returnable goods, and conveyances of excessive land made in the mistaken belief that the performance was owed under a contract with another, even if the mistake is negligent and unilateral, but there must be a mistake rather than uncertainty.

Examples: (1) An insured under a life insurance policy disappears under circumstances that make it probable but not certain that the insured perished. The policy amount is paid to the beneficiary. The insured is later found alive suffering from amnesia. The payment cannot be recovered because there was conscious uncertainty rather than mistake. The result would be different if a corpse had mistakenly been identified as the insured; the parties would have been certain but mistaken.

(2) Because of its own computer programming error, a commercial tenant pays rent twice a month rather than monthly and does so for two years. The excess payments may be recovered.

Exception: If the party who mistakenly pays has a moral obligation to do so, restitution is not allowed.

Example: *X* pays money to *Y* although, unknown to *X*, *Y*'s claim is unenforceable or barred by the statute of limitations. The payment may not be recovered.

Perspective: The rule stated for mistake in performance refers to money, returnable goods and land, but makes no reference to services. Services rendered by mistake cannot be returned. Consequently, there is no duty to pay for such services.

11. Defenses to Avoidance or Recovery for Mistake

a. Change of Position

A contract cannot be avoided, or the value of a performance recovered for mistake, if the other party has detrimentally changed position in reliance upon the contract or performance.

Example: Defendant asks plaintiff broker to sell defendant's shares of XYZ Company. The broker mistakenly assumes the shares to be of XYZ Co. of America, a valuable listed security. Instead, the shares are of XYZ of Colorado, an unlisted security of little value. Because of the mistake, the defendant is paid $30,000 in excess of the value of the shares and uses the sum to pay off a mortgage loan. The plaintiff can recover the money. Paying off the mortgage or keeping the money in a bank equally enriches the defendant unjustly. Consequently, the change of position is not detrimental.

b. Voluntary Payment

Where a party with full knowledge of the facts pays money to the other restitution is not available.

Example: Take the example, above, of the commercial tenant who overpays the rent through its own carelessness. Change the facts so that the landlord wrongfully overbills the tenant who pays without contesting the overcharge. Restitution will be denied.

c. Affirmance of the Transaction After Discovery of the Mistake

(*See* IX.H., *infra.*)

d. Failure to Avoid the Contract with Reasonable Promptness After Discovery of the Mistake

(*See* IX.H.2.b., *infra.*)

E. Reformation for Mistake, Misrepresentation or Duress

1. Reformation for Mistake

Reformation of a writing for mistake is available if three requisites are met.

(1) There must have been a prior agreement.

(2) There must have been an agreement to put the agreement in writing.

(3) *Because of a mistake, there is a variance between the prior agreement and the writing.*

a. The Prior Agreement

The prior agreement may have been oral or written. An indefinite or tentative agreement suffices. If by error, rather than by modification, clauses earlier agreed upon are misstated or omitted, the writing may be reformed based on mistake.

If one party, without the consent of the other, intentionally omits a term that has been agreed upon, reformation is available on grounds of misrepresentation.

Example: *C*, a construction company, bargains for the right to deposit demolition waste on *O*'s land. They reach agreement whereby permission is granted in exchange for a sum of money. In addition, *C* promises *O* that before depositing the waste, the topsoil will be removed and then replaced onto the waste. *C* prepares a writing, representing to *O* that it contains their entire agreement. The promise with respect to the topsoil removal and replacement is not contained in the writing. *O* signs the writing without reading it. The writing may be reformed. Alternatively, as the misrepresentation goes to a vital existing fact—the contents of the writing as to a material term—*O* may avoid the contract.

b. The Agreement to Reduce to Writing

Reformation is not available if the parties intentionally omit or misstate a term.

c. The Variance

Frequently the variance is an arithmetical error. Sometimes it is a misdescription of the subject matter, as a typist's error in a metes and bounds description of real property. At times, the parties mistake the legal effect of their writing. Reformation is available in each of these circumstances.

Examples: (1) *V* agrees to sell Blackacre to *P*. They agree that *V* can remove a mill, but *V* fails to tell *V*'s lawyer about the mill agreement. *V*'s lawyer prepares a deed conveying Blackacre and "all improvements" thereon. *V* signs without reading the document or, alternatively, reads but does not comprehend that the legal effect is to transfer the mill. Under either alternative, *V* can obtain reformation.

(2) *A* contacts an insurance company (*I*) and asks about "term" life insurance and is quoted accurate rates for "term" insurance and agrees to purchase a "term" policy. *I*'s secretary mistakenly takes a form for a "whole life" policy, types *A*'s name and beneficiaries thereon as well as the term insurance premium. A whole life policy is far more expensive than term insurance and builds up a cash value while a "term" policy does not. *I*'s agent delivers the policy to *A*. Some years later *A* asks *I* for the cash value of the policy. Only then does *I* realize that a mistake has been made. *I* can obtain reformation of the policy.

(3) *V* contracts to convey Blackacre to *P*. Blackacre is agricultural land consisting of 100 acres and the going rate for

farm acreage in this vicinity is $3,000 per acre. The contract price is $300,000. Neither party is aware that the land is zoned for industrial use making it worth $900,000. Reformation is *not* permitted because the mistake does not go to the transcription of their agreement. The mistake may be grounds for avoidance unless the court allocates the risk to *V*.

2. Reformation for Misrepresentation

If one party misrepresents the content or legal effect of a writing to the other, the other may elect to avoid the contract or to have it reformed to express what was represented.

Example: *C*, a construction company, bargains for the right to deposit demolition waste on *O*'s land. They reach agreement whereby permission is granted in exchange for a sum of money. In addition, *C* promises *O* that before depositing the waste, the topsoil will be removed and then replaced onto the waste. *C* prepares a writing, representing to *O* that it contains their entire agreement. The promise with respect to the topsoil removal and replacement is not contained in the writing. *O* signs the writing without reading it. The writing may be reformed. Alternatively, as the misrepresentation goes to a vital existing fact—the contents of the writing as to a material term—*O* may avoid the contract.

3. Reformation for Duress

Reformation for duress requires that (1) the parties have made a binding contract preliminary to entering into a more formal contract; (2) one party is coerced into agreeing to a more formal contract that is at variance with the original agreement.

Example: *B*, a bank, makes a binding commitment to *A* to provide specified financing at 7% interest to be secured by a mortgage on premises *A* has contracted to purchase. On the day prior to the date set for closing, the bank informs *A* that the loan will not be made unless *A* signs a bond and mortgage calling for 9% interest. Because of the surrounding circumstances, *A* has no reasonable alternative but to yield. *A*'s suit for reformation will be successful.

4. Reformation and the Parol Evidence Rule

The parol evidence rule is inapplicable in an action for reformation.

Comment: Although the parol evidence rule is inapplicable, a decree for reformation must be based on "clear and convincing" evidence, a higher standard than is normally required in a civil suit.

5. Defenses to Reformation

a. Bona Fide Purchaser for Value

Reformation will not be granted if the effect of the decree would infringe on the rights of a bona fide purchaser for value or other third persons who have justifiably relied upon the document as written.

b. Equitable Defenses

Reformation is an equitable action. Consequently, it is subject to equitable defenses such as unclean hands and laches. (See VIII.C.3.e., f., supra.) A decree for reformation may be withheld in the sound discretion of the court.

c. The Effect of Negligence

Negligence is no bar to reformation. Refer back to the previous examples. In a number of them, the plaintiff committed multiple acts of carelessness.

It is important to note, however, that reformation is not available if one party carelessly believes that a writing will contain a particular provision. Unless this belief was shared or induced by the other, no proper case of reformation is made out. This is not because of negligence. Rather, it is because the writing is not at variance with the agreement.

F. Unconscionability

1. Unconscionability in Equity

For centuries, equity has refused to grant specific performance of contracts that were unconscionably obtained or unconscionable in content. Such decisions do not necessarily invalidate contracts but leave the parties to their legal remedies.

Example: *V* had an oil lease on federal land with one poorly producing well on it. *P*, by checking public records ascertained that oil in large amounts had recently been found in the vicinity of *V*'s leasehold. *V* was unaware of these recent discoveries. *P* telephoned *V* and asked him if he would sell the lease. *V* said yes, stating that his price was $5,000. The parties executed a document giving *P*, in exchange for $100, a 90-day option to purchase an assignment of the leasehold for $5,000. In light of the recent discoveries, this was considerably less than the value of the leasehold. *P* exercised the option, but *V* repudiated. Specific performance is denied. Equity *does* consider the adequacy of the consideration. Note that the price was set by *V*. The information possessed by *P* was publicly available. Nonetheless, the imbalance between price and value is deemed unconscionable especially in view of *P*'s non-disclosure.

2. Unconscionability at Law

Since enactment of the UCC § 2–302, courts in sales cases and in non-sales cases have exercised the power to strike down or limit contracts or contract clauses on grounds of unconscionability. Prior to enactment of the UCC, courts sometimes reached similar results by indirection, particularly by spurious interpretation.

3. What Constitutes Unconscionability

The UCC comments to § 2–302 indicate that there are two kinds of unconscionability. First, "unfair surprise," termed by some as "procedural" unconscionability. Second, "oppression," termed by some as "substantive" unconscionability.

a. Unfair Surprise (Procedural Unconscionability)

A burdensome clause that does not come to the attention of a party adhering to a contract will be struck down if a reasonable person would not expect to find it in the contract and the reason it was not noticed was its burial in small print, or the inability of the adhering party to comprehend the language.

Examples: (1) *A* checks a coat in a hotel checkroom and is given a plastic token that bears an identification number. On the reverse is language purporting to limit the hotel's liability to $25. The limitation of liability is ineffective unless it can be shown that *A* was aware of the language on the token. Traditionally, this result has been based on lack of mutual assent. This result is correct, because normally *A* would have no reason to know that contractual terms had been proposed. Today, similar analysis is applied to specific clauses in what a party understands to be a contract. Although a party may have given blanket assent to a contract by signing it, the party can be relieved from the burden of one-sided clauses that one would not reasonably expect to be in the contract.

(2) A franchise agreement between a petroleum company and a filling station operator contains a clause whereby the latter agrees to indemnify the petroleum company against liability for the negligence of the petroleum company's employees on the premises. An employee of the company negligently loses control of a tank-truck hose while filling the franchisee's tank, spraying the operator and others. The indemnity provision is unexpected and constitutes "unfair surprise" because of the shift of the normal risks. The court rules that, unless the operator is made aware of the provision and actually assents to it, it is invalid. The provision, although perhaps one-sided, is not necessarily oppressive. If the operator was aware of the clause, perhaps the risk could have been insured against.

b. Oppression (Substantive Unconscionability)

Provisions of a contract that are assented to but are grossly one-sided may be voided or modified by the court. A contract that suffers from total overall imbalance; that is, one that is grossly one-sided, may be voided.

Examples: (1) An impoverished, non-English speaking consumer promises to pay $1,145 for an appliance worth $348. The court limits recovery to a reasonable price.

(2) A homeowner agrees to pay $2,500 for home improvements worth $1,000. Little work is done before the homeowner repudiates. The court permits no recovery by the contractor.

c. The Hybrid—Surprise and Oppression

Analytically, the surprise and oppression cases can be distinguished. However, where unconscionability has been found, the facts generally contain a mixture of lack of knowledgeable assent and a clause or contract that unduly benefits the party who has drafted the contract.

Example: *B*, an impoverished person of limited education, purchased furniture on the installment plan from *S*. While still indebted to *S*, she purchases a stereo set from *S* on credit. The purchase agreement provides: "all payments now and hereafter made by *B* shall be credited pro rata on all outstanding leases, bills and accounts due *S* at the time each such payment is made." The effect of this "cross-collateral clause" is to give *S* a security interest in all the goods sold by *S* to *B* until her debt is reduced to zero. *B* defaulted, and *S* moves to replevy all the goods ever sold to *B* by *S*. Replevin denied. The clause is "procedurally" suspect because it is not readily comprehensible, even to a college graduate. Moreover, it is substantively suspect because the cross-collateral clause is, or may be, unreasonably favorable to *S*. This combination has led at least one court to rule that unconscionability exists.

4. Judge Versus Jury

Unconscionability is a question of law for the court, not for the trier of fact.

Comment: The court must allow evidence of the commercial setting and purpose of a provision prior to ruling on the question. Consequently, it is almost always impossible to read a contract and decide that it, or any part of it, is unconscionable. Extrinsic evidence is necessary prior to deciding.

5. The Irrelevance of Hindsight

Unconscionability must be judged by looking at the circumstances existing at the time of contracting, without reference to future events.

Comment: Supervening oppressiveness is governed by the doctrine of impracticability.

6. Consumer Protection

In the great majority of cases in which unconscionability has been found, the party protected by the finding has been a consumer. Generally, business organizations are expected to have a greater ability to protect themselves. There have been a few cases protecting a small business against a corporate giant. *See* example (2) under Unfair Surprise, above, and *see* the next paragraph, below.

7. Termination Clauses and Sales of Goods

Under UCC § 2–309(1), a contract for the sale of goods that is indefinite in duration is not terminable except on reasonable notice. The focus here is on retail franchises and wholesale distributorships which envisage a continuing, often exclusive, relationship. But other relational contracts are also included; *e.g.*, requirements contracts of indefinite duration. UCC § 2–309(3) provides that an agreement dispensing with reasonable notice is invalid "if its operation would be unconscionable."

Example: *B* was the exclusive dealer in Northern New Jersey for aluminum siding produced by *S* and had so acted for 8 years. After *S* had decided to terminate the agreement, but before notifying *B* of its intention, *B*, with the knowledge and encouragement of *S,* leased additional land and expanded its warehouse. The court finds that 20 months notice of termination is appropriate under the circumstances. A contract provision dispensing with a reasonable period of notification would have been unconscionable.

8. Limitation on Consequential Damages—Personal Injuries

Another provision of the UCC (§ 2–719) makes specific reference to unconscionability. Section 2–719 deals with limitations on consequential damages. Although the UCC permits limitations on damages and permits the exclusion of consequential damages, it indicates that the exclusion is subject to the rule of unconscionability. "Limitation of consequential damages for injury to the person in the case of consumer goods is prima facie unconscionable but limitation of damages where the loss is commercial is not." UCC § 2–719(3). Of course, it is possible to have a finding of unconscionability in the case of the exclusion of commercial losses based on the general criteria for unconscionability. However, this would be most unusual.

G. "Duty" to Read

1. Rule

Assent to a document that purports to be a contract or other consensual transaction implies assent to the terms contained therein.

Perspective: The material discussed here repeats rules stated elsewhere, but this general discussion may help crystallize the effect of not reading a document to which one assents.

Example: *B* negotiates with *S* for the purchase of a new car, for its financing, and for its insurance. After shaking hands on the dickered price, payment terms, insurance coverage, and fees, *S* presents *B* with a mass of documents for signature. These documents faithfully contain all of the terms discussed. But they also contain considerably more terms. The additional terms protect the interests of *S,* as dealer, as well as the interests of the manufacturer, the finance company, and the insurer. *B* signs at the places indicated by *S.* Other unsigned documents, labeled "limited warranty" and "Automobile Insurance Policy" are handed to *B. B* is bound by the terms of the documents unless one of the exceptions mentioned below applies.

2. Exceptions

1) If the document or particular provision is not legible;

2) If the provision is placed in such a way that it is not likely to come to the attention of the other party;

Example: A limitation of liability is printed on a box containing goods sold. The limitation is not binding on the purchaser unless it can be shown the buyer was aware of the limitation.

3) Fraud

(i) *Fraudulent Inducement.* Where one party materially misrepresents the contents of a writing, the modern cases permit a defrauded party, despite a failure to read, to avoid such a contract, if they were deceived and relied upon the representations. Alternatively, the contracts may be reformed to conform to the representations.

(ii) *Fraud-in-the-Factum.* A contract is void where the misrepresentation (1) goes not only to the content of the document but also to the nature of the document, and (2) the document is radically different from the kind represented and (3) it was not unreasonable for the party to sign it.

4) Mistake

(i) *Unilateral Mistake.* If only one party assents to a document under the mistaken belief that it contains, or does not contain, certain provisions, this party is generally bound by the document. In two situations, however, relief may be available.

(a) *Palpable Mistake.* If the other party is or ought to be aware of the mistaken belief, the mistaken party may avoid the contract or have it reformed to conform to what the mistaken party thought the document contained.

(b) *Impalpable Mistake.* If the other party has no reason to know of the mistake, the mistaken party cannot have reformation but may avoid the contract, provided that enforcement of the contract would result in an unconscionably unequal exchange of values, and avoidance would impose no substantial hardships on the other.

(ii) *Mutual Mistake.* If both parties share the same mistake as to the contents of a writing, it can be reformed to conform to their belief.

5) Unconscionability.

Discussion: As indicated earlier, for analytical purposes, two kinds of unconscionability are distinguished: unfair surprise and oppression. The second category is unrelated to "duty" to read, because even if an oppressive clause is read and comprehended it can be invalidated by a court. The first category goes to the heart of this topic. Modern cases scrutinize, and sometimes hold void, burdensome, unexpected clauses that have not been read by, or explained to, a party adhering to a form contract.

H. Affirmance or Ratification

1. Discussion

Affirmance and ratification are equivalent terms. Upon discovering a misrepresentation or mistake, and on escaping duress or undue influence, a party has choices. One of these choices is to continue to accept the obligations of the contract. A manifestation of intent to continue with the transaction is an affirmance. No consideration is required for an affirmance. After affirmance, the power of avoidance and the right to seek reformation are lost.

2. Affirmance by Conduct

a. Exercise of Dominion

After a party's power to choose between affirmance and avoidance ripens, the continued exercise of dominion over property received under the contract or continued acceptance of benefits under the contract affirms the contract.

Examples: (1) Plaintiff, a salesperson under contract for one year's service, agreed to a new contract at considerably diminished pay. He agreed to this new contract as a result of threats made by his employer of being fired and deported. These threats constituted duress. He continued in this job for nine months. At no time during this period did he protest the new terms and conditions. His many communications with his employer (who usually was in a distant city) were friendly. By accepting the benefits of the coerced contract, after the coercion has been removed, he ratified the contract.

(2) *B* purchases land from *A*. The deed is voidable for mutual mistake. "On discovery of the mistake, *B* tenders a deed back to *A*, who refuses to accept it. *B* continues to occupy and use the land. *B*'s conduct amounts to affirmance and he is precluded from avoiding the contract." Restatement (Second) Contracts § 380, ill. 4.

b. Delay

An affirmance occurs if a party fails within a reasonable time to avoid the contract after the power to do so has ripened.

Discussion: What is a reasonable time is normally a question of fact. If the party seeking to avoid has received no benefits under the contract, and the other has not taken any action in reliance on the first party's silence, a reasonable period of time can be long indeed.

If the aggrieved party has received speculative securities, anything more than slight delay would constitute affirmance. It would be inequitable to allow even a defrauded party to speculate at the other's risk.

Fault is also a factor. The more odious the duress or misrepresentation, the longer a period of reasonable time the party has to avoid. On the other hand, the negligence in discovering the grounds for avoidance by the party who seeks to avoid is grounds for abbreviating the period.

In short, three factors dominate the determination of reasonableness of time to avoid: (1) reliance by the other; (2) speculative benefit gained by stalling; and (3) fault.

3. The Party Avoiding Must Offer to Return Property Received

This requisite and its exceptions are discussed in connection with the remedy of restitution.

Review Question *(Answers in Appendix A)*

We suggest you first review HOW TO STUDY and EXAMINATION in the *Perspective* section, *supra.*

B, a lawyer, asked a clerk in *S,* Inc.'s lumber yard for a price quote for 5,000 linear feet of pressurized 2″ × 4″ lumber. *S* quoted a price of $625, whereupon *B* placed the order for 5,000 linear feet. The lumber was delivered with a bill for $625 which *B* paid. At *S*'s regular selling price the bill should have been $1,250. The error in the price quote and bill resulted from a mistake in calculation by *S*'s clerk. *B* used the lumber to construct a deck. Upon discovery of the mistake, *S* demanded payment of an additional $625.

1. T or F *S* can recover because the mistake should have been obvious to *B*.

2. T or F *S* cannot recover because the mistake was unilateral.

3. T or F *S* cannot recover because the mistake was caused by negligence.

4. T or F *S* cannot recover because *B* changed position.

5. Essay Mrs. Klaus, a property owner and a Lutheran, was greatly interested in furthering her church and particularly in healing conflicts among the several organizational groups, known as synods, of the church. A group of leaders of various Lutheran synods came up with a proposal to erect an intersynodical Lutheran high school and to further this purpose organized the Lutheran High School Association of Jefferson County. In 2001, Mrs. Klaus signed an agreement turning over possession of a 20-acre wooded tract of land to the Association. In return the Association agreed to pay a total of $40,000, in 40 equal annual installments, without interest. ($40,000 was the fair market value for a cash sale.) Concurrent with the last payment Mrs. Klaus was to execute a conveyance of the tract to the Association.

The Agreement provides that "no part of said land shall be developed and used by said purchaser, its successor or assigns, for any other than religious and educational purposes for a period of 40 years from the date of this agreement."

The Association made all payments called for by the agreement, but was unable to raise sufficient funds for a high school until 2009 when a large cash grant made it feasible to start construction. The Association, however, determined to build the school on a more centrally located tract of land. In 2009, the Association announced its plan to assign the contract with Mrs. Klaus to the Alliance, a non-Lutheran Protestant group, which has immediate plans for constructing a seminary on the still undeveloped Klaus tract. We do not know the price paid by the Alliance, but the fair market value of the tract is now $200,000. Mrs. Klaus died in 2008 and her heirs have varying mixtures of religious piety and economic hunger. They feel that the Association has taken advantage of their ancestor who, they assert, was not interested in furthering the religious work of non-Lutheran religious groups. They offer evidence in this regard.

They have asked you what are the remedial possibilities and the prospects of success as to each of them. What will you tell them? Explain.

Chapter X

Third Party Beneficiaries

■ ANALYSIS

A. Types of Beneficiaries

Except for intended beneficiaries, persons not in privity may not recover on a contract.

1. Operative Concepts and Categories

a. Privity

Only promisors and promisees in a contract are in privity with each other.

b. Intended Beneficiary

A person for whom a promisee extracted the benefits of a promisor's promise is an intended beneficiary.

Discussion: Several tests have been used to determine who is an intended beneficiary. The most commonly used tests are:

1) to whom is the performance to run (if it is to run directly to the third person, this person is an intended beneficiary); and

2) whether the promisor reasonably understood that the promisee intended to benefit the third person; that is, whether the third person was an ultimate intended beneficiary of the promisor's performance.

Comment: The parties' intentions are but one factor used to determine if a beneficiary is intended or not. The courts have also openly and covertly employed policy considerations.

c. Who Is the Promisor?

Throughout this chapter there are references to the "promisor" and the "promisee." In a bilateral contract there are at least two promisors. Under the tests for intended beneficiaries, "promisor" refers to the party who is to render the performance that most directly inures to the beneficiary. Normally, it is the "promisee" who is bargaining for the other party's promise to benefit the third party.

Example: *B* owes $300 to *T*. *B* promises to lend $300 to *A* in exchange for *A*'s promise to pay $300 to *T*. Although *A* and *B* have both made promises, for purposes of third party beneficiary analysis, *A* is the promisor, because *A*'s promised performance is to deliver money to *T*, a person not in privity.

d. Incidental Beneficiary

A party who receives benefits from a promisor's performance, but who was not intended to be a beneficiary is an incidental beneficiary and therefore has no rights in the contract. (See, *e.g.*, examples (4) and (9) *infra*.)

e. Creditor Beneficiary

If a promisee extracts from the promisor a promise to render a performance to a third person because the promisee is indebted to the third person, then the third person is a creditor beneficiary.

Comment: Motive should not be confused with intent. For instance, in example (3) below, *B* wants *A* to pay *T*. *B*'s motive is not likely to be affection or benevolence. *B* wants the creditor to be paid so as to be free of the debt. *B* seeks to accomplish this by having *A* pay *T*. While the motive is not benevolence, it is accomplished by a payment to *T*, which is a benefit to *T*.

f. Donee Beneficiary

If the promisee's purpose in extracting the promise is to confer a gift upon the third person, the third person is a donee beneficiary. (See examples (2), (5), (10) and (12) infra.)

Comment: The distinction between donee and creditor beneficiaries is not ordinarily important on the issue of intent to benefit but may be important on other issues, such as when rights vest (*see infra*).

g. Promises of Indemnity

The promise of an indemnitor against loss does not ordinarily give rise to a third party beneficiary situation because the intent to benefit is deemed to run to the promisee. However, the promise of an indemnitor against liability sometimes is held to create third party beneficiaries, especially in public contracts. (*See* examples (6), (7) and (8) *infra*.)

h. The Municipality Cases

Municipal contracts that create enforceable rights in third persons are of three types. These are:

(1) where a contractor agrees to perform a duty that the municipality owes to individual members of the public and the breach of which would create tort liability against the municipality;

(2) where the contractor promises the governmental body to compensate members of the public for injuries done them despite the absence of a governmental duty; and

(3) where the governmental body enters into a contract to gain advantages for individual members of the public.

i. The Surety Bond Cases

The typical performance bond involves a guaranty by a surety company to the owner that the contractor will perform. Workers, suppliers, and subcontractors are not third party beneficiaries of a performance bond because the purpose of the bond is to assure payment of damages to an owner in the event of a contractor's non-performance.

A payment bond is a guaranty by a surety that the contractor will pay its debts incurred on a specific project. Laborers, suppliers, and subcontractors are generally held to be third party beneficiaries of a payment bond. While the motive of an owner-promisee in procuring a payment bond is to protect itself from mechanics' liens, the intent is also to benefit the laborers, suppliers, and subcontractors by seeing to it that they are paid.

It is presumed that these third parties are not intended beneficiaries of a joint performance-payment bond. If a joint bond were not deemed to solely benefit the promisee-owner, the bond might be dissipated in paying third parties without paying the promisee.

Examples: (1) *B* owes *T* $300. *B* sells a quantity of hay to *A* who promises *B* and *T* to pay $300 for the hay to *T*. All three parties are present at the time *A*'s promise is made. *T* is a promisee, in privity with the promisor, *A*. Consequently, the concepts peculiar to third party beneficiary contracts, such as the concept of vesting, are inapplicable to these facts.

(2) A son promised his father to pay $1,000 to his sister if the father would forbear from selling certain property. The father forbore. The sister, a person not in privity, is an intended donee beneficiary. Intended, because the performance of the promise (payment) runs directly to her; donee, because the promisee-father intended to confer a gift upon her.

(3) *B* owes $300 to *T*. *B* then lends $300 to *A* in exchange for *A*'s promise to pay $300 to *T*. *T* is an intended creditor beneficiary. Intended, because the performance (payment) is to run directly to *T*; creditor, because *B*'s purpose in entering into the contract is to discharge of a debt that *B* owed to *T*.

(4) *A*, a bank, promises *B* a loan with which to pay *B*'s creditors. The creditors are incidental beneficiaries because the performance (disbursing the loan) by *A* runs to *B* and not to *B*'s creditors. As incidental beneficiaries, *B*'s creditors have no rights against *A*.

(5) *A*, a lawyer, drafts a will for *B*. *T* is a beneficiary under the will. Because the will was improperly drawn, *T* received less under the will than the testator had intended. Although the promised performance (drawing a will) runs to *B*, the promisor understood that the promisee's ultimate intent was to benefit *T*, a beneficiary of the will. Therefore, under the second test given above for intended beneficiaries, *T* is an intended beneficiary of the contract between *A* and *B*. If the first test were employed, *C* would not be an intended beneficiary.

(6) *A* promises *B* to reimburse *B* in the event that *B* is compelled to pay *T*. *B* is compelled to pay *T*. *A* is an indemnitor against loss. *A*'s performance (payment) runs to *B*. Therefore, *T* is an incidental beneficiary.

(7) *A* promises *B* to discharge *B*'s legal liability in the event *B* becomes liable to *T*. *B* incurs a liability toward *T*. *A* is an indemnitor against liability. Although ordinarily *T* would be a third party beneficiary under the first of the two tests, frequently the contract will provide that no third party has an enforceable right under the contract. This is the case with most if not all liability insurance policies. If the contract has such a provision, *T* is not a third party beneficiary.

(8) *B*, a municipality, owes a duty to the public to keep its streets in repair. *A*, a street railway, contracts with *B* to maintain the

streets and to indemnify *B* if *B* is liable for damages because of *A*'s improper performance. *T* suffers damages as a result of *A*'s breach. *T* is a third party beneficiary. It should be noted that the duties owed by municipalities to the public are defined by tort law.

(9) *B,* a city, entered into a contract with *A,* a water company, whereby *A* agreed to furnish water at a specified pressure in *B*'s fire hydrants. *T*'s house, located in *B,* was destroyed by fire because *A* failed to provide water at the specified pressure. *T* is not an intended beneficiary because the performance of the promise—supplying water at specified pressure in *B*'s hydrants—runs to *B* and not to *T.* Policy considerations lead to the same result. If *A* were liable, it would be a crushing burden not factored into its water rates. Also, most property owners carry fire insurance. If *A* were liable, it would essentially be a reinsurer (an entity that insures insurance companies).

(10) *B,* a city, entered into a contract with a contractor whereby the latter agreed to lay certain sewer lines. The contractor promised *B* to be liable to members of the public for damage done to private property. *T*'s property was damaged as a result of the contractor's construction work. *T* is an intended donee beneficiary because the promised performance is a promise of compensation and runs directly to members of the public.

(11) *B,* a city, entered into a contract with *A,* a water company, which provides a maximum schedule of rates to be charged to users. *T,* a property owner, is billed for water at a rate in excess of the contract rate. *T* need not pay more than the contract rate. The water was furnished directly to the property owners. The rate limitation was intended to benefit individual members of the public.

(12) *X* owns real property and, in exchange for a loan, mortgages it to *T. X* sells the property to *B* who takes "subject to" the mortgage which means that, although the land is encumbered by the mortgage, *B* accepts no personal liability for the debt. *B* subsequently sells the property to *A* who "assumes" the mortgage, which means that *A* promises *B* to pay the debt. Although *A*'s promised performance runs directly to *T* and by the usual test *T* is an intended beneficiary, there is substantial authority to the effect that *T* has no rights in the contract. Because *B* had merely taken subject to the mortgage and was not *T*'s debtor, *T* cannot be classified as a creditor beneficiary because the promisee was not indebted. Because it is unlikely that *B* had any donative intent, many courts have refused to treat *T* as a donee beneficiary. Others have, however, recognized *T* as an intended donee beneficiary.

B. Promisor's Defenses

1. Defenses from the Third Party Beneficiary Contract

In the absence of agreement to the contrary, the promisor can assert against the beneficiary any defense the promisor has against the promisee.

Examples: (1) *B* promises not to cut down certain timber in exchange for *A*'s promise to pay *T* $1,000. *B* is not obligated to *T* and intends that the $1,000 be a gift. *B*, contrary to the agreement, cuts down the timber. Although *T* is an intended donee beneficiary who has standing to sue, *T* does not prevail in an action against *A* because *A* has the defense of non-performance against *B* which can be used against *T*.

(2) *B* promises to do certain carpentry for *A* in exchange for *A*'s promise to pay $1,000 to *T*, a creditor of *B*. *B* fails to substantially perform the carpentry. Although *T* is an intended creditor beneficiary of *A*'s promise to *B*, *T* cannot recover against *A*, because *A* has the defense of failure of constructive condition (non-performance) against *B*, which is also available against *T*.

Exceptions:

(1) *Where the parties agree that the beneficiary will have enforceable rights despite any defense that the promisor might be able to assert against the promisee.*

Example: Fire insurance policies purchased by homeowners often cover the interests of both the homeowner and the mortgagee. These frequently provide that the mortgagee (as third party beneficiary of the policy) may recover despite the failure of the owner to pay the premium. In the event a fire occurs after the owner's failure to make timely payment, and before any notice of cancellation is received by the mortgagee, the mortgagee may recover on the policy although the owner may have no right to recover for injury to the owner's interest in the property.

(2) *Where the rights of the beneficiary have vested, the rights may not be varied by subsequent agreement between the promisor and the promisee.*

Discussion: Re-examine examples (1) and (2) at the beginning of X.B.1. In each of them, the beneficiary's rights have been effectively destroyed by the promisee's material breach of the contract. This destruction of rights occurs whether or not the rights of the beneficiary have vested. If we vary the examples so that *A* and *B* *mutually agree* to curtail *T*'s rights, the agreement would be ineffective against *T*.

2. When Do Rights Vest?

a. Omnipotence of the Contract

The parties may provide as they wish with respect to vesting.

Example: The contract may validly provide that rights of third parties are always divestable or that they vest immediately, or that they vest in ten years, etc.

b. Creditor Beneficiaries

Unless the contract provides otherwise, the rights of a creditor beneficiary vest, at the latest, when the beneficiary brings an action to enforce a contract or otherwise materially changes position in reliance on the contract.

Comment: The tendency today is to hold that rights vest as soon as the beneficiary learns of the promise and assents to it. Silence is assent in this context because the beneficiary can only benefit from the contract.

c. Donee Beneficiaries

According to the original Restatement, the rights of a donee beneficiary vest immediately upon making the contract, but the Restatement (Second) and much case law have indicated that the same rule that applies to creditor beneficiaries should be applied to donees.

Example: *B* promises not to cut down certain timber in exchange for *A*'s promise to pay *T* $1,000. Before *T* learns of the agreement, *B* and *A* enter into a substituted contract, discharging *T*'s rights. *T*'s rights are effectively discharged if *T* is a creditor beneficiary. If *T* is a donee beneficiary, *T*'s rights are effectively destroyed under the modern view incorporated in the Restatement (Second).

d. Perspective

Vesting has a very limited role. It does not give the beneficiary the equivalent of a fee simple absolute in the promise. It only insulates the beneficiary from a curtailment of rights by mutual agreement of the promisor and promisee. It does not insulate the beneficiary from defenses such as failure of constructive condition.

3. Counterclaims

The promisor can effectively raise against the beneficiary a counterclaim that the promisor has against the promisee only if it is in the nature of a recoupment; that is, if it arises out of the same transaction upon which the promisor is being sued. The recoupment may be used only as a subtraction from the beneficiary's claim and not for affirmative relief.

4. Promisee's Defenses Against the Beneficiary

Suppose after *A* makes a promise to *B* for the benefit of *T*, a supposed creditor of *B*, *A* discovers that *T* is not a creditor because *B* has a valid defense against *T*. The availability of this defense to *A* depends upon the interpretation of the contract. If the promisor promises to pay irrespective of any such defense, it is not available. If *A* promises merely to perform to the extent *B* is obligated, the defense may be raised. If the promise is to pay a specific debt, it is generally held that the promise is to pay irrespective of such a defense.

Example: *T* sold an oil burner to *B* on credit. When *B* sold the house, *A*, the purchaser, agreed to assume the payments still due on the oil burner contract. These amounted to $800, and *A* received a credit of that amount against the purchase price. *A* failed to make the payments, alleging that *T* materially breached a warranty made to *B*. *T* is a third party beneficiary of *A*'s promise to assume the debt. *A* may not raise the defense of breach of warranty, because *A* has assumed a specific debt and the preferred interpretation is that *A* has promised to pay irrespective of *B*'s defense against *T*. This interpretation is preferred because (1) *A* has received a credit from the promisee for the assumption, and (2) *B* does not want to be involved in litigation with *T* over an oil burner in which *B* has no further interest. (As indicated below, *A*'s assumption of the debt does not discharge *B*'s liability.)

C. Cumulative Rights of the Beneficiary

1. Creditor Beneficiary

A creditor beneficiary has rights against both the promisor and the promisee and may obtain judgment against both. The beneficiary may only receive one satisfaction.

Novation Contrasted: If a creditor beneficiary releases the promisee in exchange for the promisor's assumption of the obligation, the substituted contract between promisor and beneficiary is called a novation. No novation occurs in a normal third party beneficiary contract, because the beneficiary does not impliedly release the debtor when the beneficiary assents to, or even attempts to enforce, the promisor's assumption. The beneficiary may obtain judgment against the promisee on the original debt and against the promisor on the third party beneficiary contract. Although entitled to judgment against both, the beneficiary is entitled only to one satisfaction.

Examples: (1) *B* is indebted to *T* in the amount of $10,000. *A*, for a consideration, agrees with *B* to assume *B*'s obligation to *T*. *A* fails to pay. *T* may obtain judgment against *B* on the original debt. *T* may also obtain judgment against *A* on the contract of assumption. However, *T* is entitled to collect only the sum of $10,000 plus interest and costs.

(2) *B* is indebted to *T* in the amount of $10,000. *A*, *B*, and *T* work out a three-party substituted contract whereby *T* agrees to *discharge B*, and *A* agrees to pay the $10,000 to *T*. This three-party arrangement is a novation. *T* has rights only against *A*.

2. Donee Beneficiary

Although a donee beneficiary has rights against the promisor, the donee has no rights against the promisee unless after the donee's rights have vested, the promisee has received a consideration to discharge the promisor. The donee's remedial rights are limited to the value of the consideration.

Example: *B* promises not to cut down certain timber in exchange for *A*'s promise to pay *T* $1,000. *T* is not a creditor of *B*, and *B*'s motive is to confer a gift on *T*. *T*'s rights subsequently vest. *A* and *B* subsequently agree that in consideration of $200 *A* will be discharged from the obligation to *T*. *T*, as a donee beneficiary, ordinarily would have no rights against *B*, but because *B* received $200 as consideration for discharging *A*, *T* is entitled to recover $200 from *B*.

D. Rights of the Promisee Against the Promisor

In addition to the promisor's liability to the beneficiary, the promisor is under an obligation to the promisee for performance of the contract.

Although this chapter has focused on the rights of the beneficiary, it should not be forgotten that the promisor's contract is with the promisee. In the case of a donee beneficiary contract, the promisee usually suffers no damages by a promisor's breach, and restitution may not be a satisfactory remedy. In such a case the legal remedy may be inadequate and, if so, an action for specific performance will be entertained.

In a creditor beneficiary contract, breach by the promisor can cause substantial harm to the promisee. If such damages occur, they are recoverable. The terminology is that the promisor is primarily liable and the promisee is secondarily liable. As far as the beneficiary is concerned, primary and secondary liability is totally irrelevant. Both are liable. However, between the promisor and promisee the status as primary or secondary obligor is very important. The party who is secondarily liable and is made to pay has an action over against the party who is primarily liable.

Examples: (1) *B* owes *T* \$10,000. For a consideration, *A* assumes the duty to pay. Because *A* breaches, *B* is forced to pay *T*. *B* has an action against *A* for \$10,000.

(2) In a separation agreement, the husband promised his wife that he would leave, by will, certain specified legacies to their children. He died without complying with the promise. The children, as intended third party donee beneficiaries, can enforce the promises made for their benefit against their father's estate. Alternatively, the wife has an action for specific performance against the estate of the husband. Note, because she suffered no economic injury, the wife's remedy at law is inadequate, and therefore she is entitled to specific performance.

Review Questions *(Answers in Appendix A)*

We suggest you first review HOW TO STUDY and EXAMINATION in the *Perspective* section, *supra*.

B purchased a tractor from *T*, financing the purchase by signing a note and giving a security interest in the tractor. Subsequently, *B* sold the tractor to *A* who in writing stated: "I hereby assume and promise to pay off the note you owe to *T* for the purchase of this tractor."

1. T or F In an action by *T*, *A* may properly raise as a defense facts tending to show that the tractor was defective when *T* sold it to *B*.

2. T or F If the agreement between *B* and *A* contained an additional clause stating, "*T* shall have no right to enforce this agreement," *T* would be barred from recovering judgment against *A*.

3. **Essay** Starr, Inc., a manufacturer, was losing money. It owed \$100,000 to State Bank. Starr sold its business to Enterprise, Inc., representing falsely that its annual gross sales had averaged \$15,000,000. In fact, they had averaged about \$8,000,000. Enterprise paid \$500,000 in cash for the assets of the business and agreed to pay \$100,000 to State Bank and also agreed to honor existing warranties on products Starr had sold. Neither Enterprise nor Starr notified State Bank or holders of warranted products of this contract. After six months of operation Enterprise learned of the falsity of Starr's representation.

About the same time, one of Starr's products failed to operate properly. It caused an explosion that resulted in personal injuries and property damage to a warranty holder.

The damage was evaluated at about $1,000,000. The failure that occurred involved a defect in manufacture that was expressly warranted against.

State Bank and holders of the warranty learned of the Starr-Enterprise deal only after they unsuccessfully tried to reach Starr's officers or directors. They managed to find a former employee of Starr who had a vague recollection of the contract. State Bank has brought an action against Enterprise for the $100,000 debt owed by Starr. The persons injured by the explosion have sued Enterprise for damages. A copy of the Starr-Enterprise contract was produced in pre-trial discovery proceedings. Decide the cases. Explain.

4. **Essay** Mr. *B* contracted with Mrs. *S* to purchase her house for $210,000, making a down payment of $21,000. The contract provided that closing would take place in 60 days and that title would be conveyed by Mrs. *S* to Ms. *T*, Mr. *B*'s sister. A week after the contract was signed, Mr. *B* was killed in an accident. Ms. *T* has asked Mr. *B*'s executor to pay the balance and complete the purchase. The executor refuses. Ms. *T* has asked Mrs. *S* to sue Mr. *B*'s executor for specific performance. Mrs. *S* refuses, stating that she is content to keep the down payment, cancel the contract, and forget the whole thing. The closing date has passed with no further action by the parties. What are the rights of Ms. *T*? Explain.

Chapter XI

Assignment and Delegation

■ ANALYSIS

- 10. Defenses and Counterclaims of the Obligor Against the Assignor
    - a. Defenses
    - b. Counterclaims
        - 1) Same Transaction (Recoupment)
        - 2) Different Transactions (Set-Off)
    - c. Circumventing Rule
        - 1) UCC Rule
        - 2) Exceptions for Consumer Paper
- 11. Rights of the Assignee Against the Assignor
    - a. Express Warranties or Disclaimers of Implied Warranties
    - b. Implied Warranties

B. Delegation of Duties

- 1. What Is a Delegation?
- 2. Liability of the Delegant
- 3. Liability of the Delegate
- 4. Non-Delegable Duties
    - a. What Duties Are Non-Delegable?
    - b. Delegation in Sales Contracts
    - c. Effect of Improper Delegation

A. Assignment of Rights

1. What Is an Assignment?

An assignment is a manifestation of intent by the owner of a right to effectuate a present transfer of the right. The manifestation of intent must be addressed to the assignee or someone on the assignee's behalf.

Perspective: An assignment's closest analogy is to a sale of goods or a conveyance of land. It is an executed transaction. It transfers the property in a contract right. Consequently, words of promise do not create an assignment. An order communicated to the debtor alone is not an assignment.

Examples: (1) *D*[ebtor] owes *C*[reditor] $1,000. *C* gives a writing to *A* that states that *C* transfers *C*'s credit against *D* to *A*. *C* has assigned the right to payment to *A*.

(2) *D* owes *C* $1,000. *C* promises *A* to assign this credit to *A*. No assignment is created. Assuming the promise is for a consideration and is otherwise enforceable, *A* has rights similar to those of an assignee of future rights discussed below. This is because *A* has a right to specific performance.

(3) *D* owes *C* $1,000. *C* writes to *D*, "Please pay the balance due me to *A*." This is an order to pay. No assignment is created.

(4) *D* owes *C* $1,000. *C* owes *A* $500. *C* writes *A*, "I will pay you out of money that *D* owes me." *A* is not an assignee of a portion of *C*'s right against *D*. This is merely a promise to pay out of a fund.

2. UCC Coverage

In its simplest form an assignment is an outright transfer, but an assignment is frequently made as a security device. The right is transferred as security only. It is similar to a mortgage of real property rather than the conveyance of a fee simple. Although UCC Article 9 focuses primarily upon security devices, it governs the assignment of an "account" whether the assignment is an outright transfer or the creation of a security interest.

Definition: An account is "a right to payment of a monetary obligation, whether or not earned by performance . . ." UCC § 9–102(2) (1999).

Non-Coverage: (1) The assignment of rights, other than rights to payment are not governed by Article 9. Because rights other than rights to payment are sometimes the subject of an assignment, a party who is entitled to performance is called an "obligee" and the party who is under an obligation to perform is called an "obligor." Article 9 calls a person who owes money an "account debtor."

(2) Ironically, for purposes of UCC Article 9, the term "account" does *not* include "deposit accounts." (These are governed by UCC Articles 3 and 4.)

3. UCC Exclusions

Although UCC Article 9 governs assignments of accounts regardless of the purpose of the assignment, specific exceptions are enumerated in the UCC. These include (there are others, § 9–109 enumerates them):

(a) Assignments of accounts in connection with the sale of a business from which they arose;

(b) An assignment of rights under a contract coupled with the delegation of the assignor's duties to the assignee; and

(c) The assignment of a single account to an assignee in whole or partial satisfaction of a preexisting indebtedness.

Where the transaction is not governed by UCC Article 9, the common law rules apply. In some instances, other legislation applies. For example, the FTC has outlawed wage assignments in consumer credit transactions. UCC Article 2 has several provisions that govern the assignment of rights in contracts for the sale of goods.

4. Deviations from the Norm

There are three types of assignments that deviate from the norm and create problems that ordinary assignments do not have.

a. Gratuitous Assignments

The fact that the assignor makes a gift of a right against the obligor is not a defense available to the obligor. An assignment, as an executed transaction, requires no consideration. But, as between the assignor and the assignee, the gift must be complete. If it is not complete, the assignee's rights can be terminated by the death of the assignor, by a subsequent assignment of the same right, or by a notice of revocation communicated to the assignee or to the obligor.

A gift is not complete unless the subject matter is delivered. Since a right cannot be physically delivered, the gift can be completed by substitute delivery methods such as: (1) by the receipt of payment by the assignee, (2) by the assignee's entering into a substitute contract with the obligor, (3) by delivery to the assignee of a symbolic writing that incorporates the debt, or (4) by application of the doctrine of promissory estoppel.

An assignment given for a pre-existing debt is for "value" and is not deemed to be gratuitous. The pre-existing debt constitutes "value."

b. Voidable Assignments

An assignment may be voidable by the assignor because of infancy, insanity, fraud, duress, etc. The same rules that apply for avoiding a contract also apply here.

c. Assignment of Future Rights

Definition: An assignment of a future right is the assignment of a right that will arise under a contract that has not yet been made.

Rule: *The common law rule is that an assignment for value of a future right is an equitable assignment.*

Discussion: At common law, the rights of an equitable assignee are superior to those of the assignor. But they are subordinate to those of a subsequent assignee for value of the same right without notice, and to the rights of a subsequent attaching creditor of the assignor who is without notice of the claim of the assignee, provided the attachment is made before the right comes into being.

UCC: The rule under UCC Article 9 is very different. Generally speaking, under the UCC, if the assignee of future rights complies with the perfection requirements of the UCC, the assignee will prevail.

Examples: (1) *C* enters into a contract with *D* whereby *C* is to construct a building for *D* and is to be paid as the work progresses. *C* borrows money from *A* bank and to secure repayment of the loan, assigns the rights to payment to *A*. *A* receives a legal assignment even at common law. The right to payment is a present conditional right, not a future right.

(2) *C*, a construction contractor has no pending work. *C* borrows money from *A*, and assigns to *A* its right to payment under *C's* next construction contract. *C* subsequently obtains a contract to build a garage for *D*. Pre-UCC, this assignment would be an equitable assignment. Under Article 9, it is a legal assignment.

(3) In consideration of a preexisting debt, *C* assigns to *A* the right to payment of a loan that *C* expects to make to *D*. This case falls under one of the UCC exclusions (the assignment of a single account in satisfaction of a preexisting debt) and no other statute governs. *A* has an equitable assignment that is subordinate to the rights of *C's* attaching creditors.

5. Formalities

In the absence of statute, an assignment may be oral. Under UCC Article 9, a writing is required unless the assignee is in possession of the collateral involved. Possession of an account is not possible; consequently, if the assignment of the account is governed by UCC Article 9, a writing is required. If there is no writing, the assignment is not enforceable against anyone.

An assignment or promise of assignment of rights that is not governed by UCC Article 8 or 9 is not enforceable unless it is in writing if the remedy sought is in the amount or value of $5,000 or more. (UCC § 1–206.) Revised Article 1, adopted by many states, would repeal this provision, but the assignment of most of the obligations covered by that provision are now governed by UCC Article 9 and its writing requirements.

6. Attachment and Perfection of Security Interests in Accounts

a. Attachment

"Attachment" relates to the relative rights of the assignor and assignee. Once the rights of an assignee attach, the assignee's rights are superior to those of the assignor.

Unless there is an agreement to the contrary, the rights of the assignee attach as soon as there is "agreement, value, and collateral," specifically that

(1) there is an agreement that it attach,

(2) value has been given, and

(3) the account in which the assignee has rights is identified.

It is important to remember that if UCC Article 9 governs, the assignment must be in writing for the assignee's rights to attach.

b. Perfection

"Perfection" relates to the rights of the assignee against third parties. Perfection cannot occur until the assignment attaches. The filing of a notice of assignment (financing statement) in a public record office is the normal method of perfecting the assignment. Filing is not required to perfect a security interest in an account where the assignment (either by itself or in conjunction with others) does not constitute a significant part of the accounts of the assignor. In this case, the rights of the assignee are perfected on attachment.

7. Priorities

Under the UCC, an assignee who has perfected the security interest in an account has priority over a party whose rights are subsequently perfected, including lien creditors and a trustee of the assignor's bankrupt estate.

a. Comment

The business purpose of taking assignments of accounts as security for loans is to give the lender priority over other creditors of the assignor, just as a mortgagee has priority in a mortgagor's real property. In the event that the assignor becomes unable or unwilling to pay debts as they mature, the assignee can insist that the obligor pay the assignee rather than the assignor or the unsecured creditors of the assignor. The UCC permits the realization of this business purpose provided the assignee's rights are perfected.

b. Unperfected Assignments

A subsequent secured creditor, a subsequent lien creditor, and a subsequent bona fide assignee for value will prevail over the rights of an assignee who has not perfected the assignment. A lien creditor is an unsecured creditor who has acquired a lien by attachment, levy or the like and includes a trustee of the assignor's estate in bankruptcy.

c. Non-UCC Cases

1) Assignee Versus Attaching Creditor

At common law, the priority between an assignee and a creditor who had attached the assigned right is governed by the rule: "prior in time, prior in right." Consequently, priority depends on the relative time of the attachment and of the assignment. However, the assignee may be estopped from asserting this priority. For example, it is often held that the assignee loses this priority if the *obligor* has not received notice of the assignment in sufficient time to call the assignment to the attention of the court in the attachment proceedings. The more modern view deprives the assignee of priority only if the assignee fails to give notice of the assignment prior to payment by the obligor to the attaching creditor.

2) Successive Assignees

At common law there are three competing rules to determine priority among successive assignees of the same obligation:

(a) ***New York Rule.*** Prior in time is prior in right.

(b) ***English View.*** The first assignee to notify the obligor prevails provided this assignee has taken the assignment for value and without notice of any prior assignment.

(c) ***Four Horsemen Rule.*** (Rule of the Restatements and the Prevailing Rule). Prior in time is prior in right unless a subsequent assignee who pays value in good faith (1) obtains payment from the obligor; or (2) recovers judgment from the obligor, or (3) enters into a substituted contract with the obligor; or (4) receives delivery of an instrument that incorporates the debt.

3) Latent Equities

An assignment to a bona fide assignee for value without notice destroys any latent equities third persons may have in the right.

Example: *D* owes *C* $1,000. *T* induces *C* to accept $100 for an assignment of this right to the payment by misrepresenting material facts. *T* subsequently assigns the right to *X* who takes in good faith, for value, and without notice of *C*'s right to avoid the assignment to *T*. *C* has no rights against *D* or *X*. Although *C* may have a tort claim against *T*, *C* has lost all rights in the account against *D*.

8. Floating Lien

UCC § 9–204 expressly validates a floating lien on a shifting stock of accounts.

a. Comment

This rule permits a debtor to grant to the creditor a security interest in the shifting stock in trade and a security interest in shifting accounts. This permits the debtor to dispose of the goods and collect the accounts without being required to account to the creditor for the proceeds. The agreement may provide that the creditor's lien or interest automatically attaches to newly required stock in trade and to newly created accounts.

b. Prior Law

Prior to the UCC, the law had difficulties with the floating lien. Under the rule of *Benedict v. Ratner,* the lien was regarded as void because the creditor's failure to police the debtor was considered to be a fraud on other creditors. The UCC, however, takes notice of the practice of lenders to allow free rein to debtors until such time as the debtor's financial status appears shaky. Another difficulty was that the floating lien purported to cover goods and accounts not yet in existence; the common law had difficulty accepting a lien on things not in being. Under the UCC, however, if the creditor files a financing statement that identifies the assigned rights, the assignment of future rights is treated as if it were the assignment of present rights.

9. Non-Assignable Rights

A right is assignable except where the assignment:

(1) would materially change the duty of the other party;

(2) would materially vary the burden or risk of the other party;

(3) would impair materially the other party's chance of obtaining return performance; or

(4) would be contrary to public policy.

Examples: (1) *D* owes *C* $1,000. *C* is in San Francisco. *C* assigns the right to payment to *A*, who is in Chicago. Although *D*'s duty is varied to a slight extent, the right is assignable. Sending a check to Chicago is not materially different from sending it to San Francisco.

(2) *D* agrees to paint *C*'s portrait for a fee. *C* purports to assign the rights to *A*, intending for *D* to paint *A*'s portrait. The purported assignment is ineffective. The assignment would materially change *D*'s duty.

(3) *D* insures a house owned by *C*. *C* sells the house to *A* and purports to assign its insurance coverage to *A*. The house is destroyed by fire. Neither *C* nor *A* can recover from *D*. *C* no longer has an insurable interest in this house and the assignment to *A* is ineffective. *D*'s risk would be materially changed if the assignment were valid. *D*'s risk is affected by the identity of the owner of the premises.

(4) *C* has a yearly retainer contract with *D*, an attorney. *D* assigns the rights and delegates the duties to *A*, another attorney. The assignment is ineffective. Although *D*'s *right* to receive payment is assignable, the *duty* to perform legal services is non-delegable (*see* XI.B.4., *infra*, for non-delegable duties). Because the duty is non-delegable, the purported delegation impairs *C*'s chance of obtaining return performance. Therefore, the assignment with which it is coupled is ineffective. To generalize, an assignment that is coupled with a delegation of non-delegable duties is ineffective.

(5) *A*, a public officer, purports to assign a portion of a yet unearned salary. The assignment is against public policy. The same rationale forbids assignments of government pension rights and alimony and support payments.

a. Standing to Complain

An assignor cannot effectively complain that the assigned right is non-assignable. Only the obligor may complain. If the obligor expressly or tacitly consents to the assignment there is an effective waiver.

b. Contractual Prohibition of an Assignment

1) Common Law Rule

At common law, a provision in a contract prohibiting an assignment of rights was generally sustained as valid under the general principle of freedom of contract, although several courts did strike down such provisions as illegal restraints on alienation. If, however, the court was able to find that the provision was not drafted with sufficient clarity to accomplish the purpose of voiding the assignment, the anti-assignment clause was treated as a promise not to assign. An assignment would breach the promise and give the obligor an action for breach, but the assignment was valid. Because damages for breach of the provision are ordinarily nominal, the anti-assignment clause was frequently of no practical value.

2) The UCC Rule

Under UCC Article 9, an anti-assignment clause is ineffective to prohibit the assignment of an "account." Also, UCC Article 2 permits the assignment of the right to damages for total breach or of a right arising out of the assignor's due performance of the assignor's entire obligation, despite a clause purporting to prevent assignment.

Comment: In the clash between freedom of contract and freedom of alienation, the UCC comes out strongly in favor of freedom of alienation. All accounts covered by Article 9 are freely alienable. In addition to accounts, in a sale of goods situation, the right to receive delivery of goods that have been paid for and the right to damages for total breach are also freely alienable despite an attempted restraint on alienation.

3) Interpretation Under Article 2

UCC Article 2 provides—and the Restatement (Second) agrees—that general language purporting to prohibit "assignment of the contract" should be construed as barring only the delegation of duties, unless the circumstances indicate the contrary.

Comment: Although assignment and delegation are two distinct legal concepts, the UCC recognizes that contracting parties do not always make the distinction. It also takes note of the probability that the primary concern of a party drafting an anti-assignment clause is that the performance of the other party not be delegated.

c. Contractual Authorization of an Assignment

A contract provision that authorizes an assignment will be honored (even if the rights are not otherwise assignable).

Comment: However, a merely routine clause to the effect that the contract "shall inure to the benefit of heirs and assigns" will not have that effect.

d. Option Contracts

The offeree's rights in an option contract are assignable, provided the rights are otherwise assignable and the duties otherwise delegable and any promise expected to be made by the offeree has been made.

Comment: Option contracts are offers but are also contracts. While offers are not assignable, option contracts generally are.

Examples: (1) *D,* for a consideration, offers to sell Whiteacre to *C* for $50,000 cash, the offer to be irrevocable for 60 days. *C* assigns the right to purchase to *A* who tenders $50,000 to *D* within the 60-day period. *D* refuses the tender. *A* can successfully pursue a claim for specific performance or damages.

(2) *D,* for a consideration, offers to sell Whiteacre to *C* for $50,000, payable $20,000 in cash and $30,000 by a purchase money bond and mortgage executed by *C,* the offer to be irrevocable for 60 days. *C* assigns the right to purchase to *A* who tenders $20,000 in cash and a bond and mortgage executed by *A.* *D* refuses the tender. *D* properly refused the tender. The offer looked to the credit of *C,* not *A.* If *A* had tendered $20,000 cash and a bond and mortgage executed by *C,* then *D* would be obligated to convey.

10. Defenses and Counterclaims of the Obligor Against the Assignor

a. Defenses

The obligor may assert against the assignee any defense which the obligor could have asserted against the assignor. The same general rule applies to a sub-assignee. The maxim is that the assignee stands in the shoes of the assignor.

Example: *D* contracts to pay $5,000 to *C* in exchange for carpentry work which *C* promises to perform. *C* assigns the right to payment to *A.* *C* does not perform the work. *D* may successfully resist *A*'s claim to payment because there is a failure of the constructive condition that work be performed before payment is due.

Comment: Defenses that can be raised may run the entire gamut of the defenses to a contract, including formation problems such as lack of consideration or fraud, and supervening defenses such as impracticability.

Exception: *When the rights of the assignee have vested, they may not be discharged or curtailed by a subsequent agreement or other voluntary transaction between the obligor and assignor. Vesting occurs when the assignee notifies the obligor of the assignment.*

Example: *D* promises to pay *C* $5,000 for certain carpentry work. *C* assigns the right to payment to *A,* who notifies *D* of the assignment. *C* performs the carpentry and subsequently purports to release *D* from the duty to pay. The release is ineffective because it is a voluntary transaction between *D* and *C* purporting to discharge *A*'s rights. If, however, *C* had failed to perform the work, *A* could not compel *D* to pay even though *A*'s rights had vested (*see* prior example).

Qualification of the Exception: Under UCC Article 9, even after notice to the obligor, the assignor and obligor have a limited right to curtail the rights of the assignee. If the assigned right to payment has not yet been earned by performance, the assignor and obligor may, in good faith and in accordance with reasonable commercial standards, modify or substitute for the contract. When this occurs, the assignee has rights under the new agreement.

Example: Raintree County contracts with *C* for the construction of a new county courthouse for $25,000,000. *C* assigns the rights to payment to *A*, a bank, which extends *C* a line of credit to be drawn upon as *C* purchases supplies and meets the payroll. Many citizens denounce the project as extravagant. In response to these criticisms, county officials have the architects redesign parts of the building so as to cut the cost. The county renegotiates the contract with *C* resulting in a smaller courthouse at a reduced contract price of $18,000,000. *A*'s rights are effectively curtailed. Note that *A* is not injured by the change except as it may have to locate other creditworthy borrowers.

b. Counterclaims

To what extent may an obligor raise as a counterclaim against an assignee a claim that the obligor has against the assignor? Under UCC Article 9, this depends, in part, on whether or not the counterclaim stems from the same transaction.

1) Same Transaction (Recoupment)

If the obligor's counterclaim arises out of the same contract from which the assignee's rights stem, the obligor may raise the counterclaim by way of defense. This defense, known as recoupment, cannot be used for affirmative relief against the assignee but only by way of subtraction.

Example: *D* purchases a printing press from *C* for $100,000, paying $20,000 down. The balance is to be paid in 60 days. *C* assigns the right to payment of the $80,000 balance to *A*. Because the press contained a defect that breached the implied warranty of merchantability, *D* suffered consequential damages of $250,000. *A*'s action for $80,000 will be defeated. *D* may recoup $80,000 from *A* but cannot get a judgment for money damages against *A*.

2) Different Transactions (Set-Off)

If the obligor's counterclaim arose from a different transaction with the assignor, this counterclaim may be raised against the assignor only if it accrues before the obligor receives notice of the assignment. This defense, known as set-off, cannot be used for affirmative relief against the assignee but only by way of subtraction.

Comment: The rule focuses on when the obligor receives notice of the assignment. The obligor does *not* receive notice when the assignee files a financing statement. Filing gives constructive notice to subsequent creditors, but it does not give constructive notice to the obligor.

c. Circumventing Rule

To circumvent the rule that an assignee stands in the shoes of the assignor, a waiver of defense clause is frequently employed. Sellers who sell on credit often use credit instruments drafted by the bank or finance company to whom they will assign the credit instrument. These instruments frequently provide that the assignee shall not be bound by any defense or claim that the obligor has against the assignor. Such a clause lends to the instrument some of the traits of a negotiable instrument.

1) UCC Rule

Under UCC Article 9, waiver of defense clauses is valid, provided the assignee takes the assignment in good faith, for value, and without notice of the claim or defense, except that such a clause cannot effectively prohibit the raising of a real defense. (§ 9–403). Real defenses are: voidability for infancy, voidness for total incapacity, illegality or fraud in the factum, and discharge in insolvency proceedings.

2) Exceptions for Consumer Paper

The UCC provision validating waiver of defense clauses subordinates the rule to "any statute or decision which establishes a different rule for buyers or lessees of consumer goods . . ." Many states have invalidated such clauses in consumer protection legislation, as has the Federal Trade Commission. The rule validating waiver of defense clauses continues to be viable in non-consumer transactions.

11. Rights of the Assignee Against the Assignor

a. Express Warranties or Disclaimers of Implied Warranties

Within broad limits, the assignee and assignor may agree as they wish as to warranties. Thus, the assignor will be held to any express warranty that is made. A warranty disclaimer is similarly upheld where the parties agree to the disclaimer.

b. Implied Warranties

In the absence of an express agreement to the contrary, an assignor warrants that:

(1) *the assignor will do nothing to defeat or impair the value of the assignment;*

(2) *the right exists and is subject to no defenses or limitations not stated or apparent; and*

(3) *any document delivered is genuine and what it purports to be.*

The implied warranties do not run to a sub-assignee (an assignee of an assignee).

Comment: The assignor does not impliedly warrant that the obligor is solvent or that the obligor will perform; that is, the assignor is not a guarantor.

B. Delegation of Duties

1. What Is a Delegation?

A delegation occurs when an obligor (delegant) appoints another person (delegate) to render a performance that is owed to a third person. There are many kinds of delegations and delegates. At the simplest level, an employee who is told to deliver a package of goods owed to a third person is a delegate. Somewhat more complex is the status of a construction subcontractor to whom a portion of the work is delegated. More complex yet is the status of a person to whom the entire performance of the obligations of a contract is delegated.

2. Liability of the Delegant

Obligors cannot free themselves from liability by delegating duties.

Comment: This is perhaps the only immutable rule in the law of contracts. There is no way an obligor can be freed from liability other than by consent of the obligee, the decree of a bankruptcy court, or by operation of law such as the passage of time under a statute of limitations. One type of consensual transaction whereby the obligor-delegant can be discharged from liability is a novation. A novation is a three-party agreement whereby the delegate assumes the duties of the obligor and the assumption is *accepted by the obligee in substitution for the original obligor's liability*. A novation is not an exception to the rule. The discharge occurs only by consent of the obligee.

3. Liability of the Delegate

The delegate becomes liable to the third party only if the delegate makes a promise that is for the benefit of the third person.

Examples: (1) *D* agrees to build a house for *C*. *D* subcontracts the plumbing work to *A*. *A* fails to complete the work within the time agreed upon in the original contract. *C* seeks to hold *A* liable for delay damages. *C* has no cause of action. The promise of the subcontractor is not deemed to be for the benefit of the owner but solely for the benefit of the delegant. Based on *stare decisis* it is generally held that the owner is only an incidental beneficiary of a construction subcontract. Of course, there are also contrary cases.

(2) *D* owes *C* $10,000 secured by a mortgage on Greenacre. *A* purchases Greenacre from *D* who delegates to *A* the duty to pay *C*. *A* promises *D* to pay $10,000 to *C*. *C* is a third party beneficiary of *A*'s promise. *A*, who is a delegate of *D*, has also "assumed" an obligation to *C*. There is no novation because *C* has not agreed to discharge *D*. *C* may obtain judgment against both *D* and *A*, but is entitled to only one satisfaction. In other words, when *A* "assumed" the mortgage, *C* became a third party intended creditor beneficiary of *A*'s promise to pay.

(3) In the prior illustration assume that, in exchange for *A*'s assumption of *D*'s obligation, *C* discharged *D*. The result is a novation. Only *A* is liable to *C*.

(4) *C* and *D* enter into a bilateral contract. *D* delegates the duty to *A* who agrees to assume the duty. *D* informs *C* of the delegation and assumption and states that because of the assumption *C* no longer should look to *D* for performance or liability in the event of nonperformance. Thereafter *C* accepts *A*'s performance. There is substantial authority to the effect that when *C* deals with *A* in the face of *D*'s repudiation an implied novation occurs. The Restatement (Second), however, follows the lead of Article 2 of the UCC and rules that the obligee can prevent an implied novation by notifying the delegant or delegate that performance will be accepted under protest.

(5) *D* and *C* enter into a bilateral contract. *D*'s duty is non-delegable but *D* delegates it to *A* who agrees for a consideration to assume the obligation. *C* deals with *A* knowing of the delegation. Because *C* has dealt with *A*, the non-delegability has been waived, and *C* may no longer complain that the duty was non-delegable. Of course, *D* remains secondarily liable to *C*.

Perspective: The above illustrations duplicate in part those given in the section of this outline on third party beneficiaries. We are now adding a new dimension to our study of these illustrations by considering the delegation of duties that appear in these cases.

4. Non-Delegable Duties

a. What Duties Are Non-Delegable?

Certain duties are delegable; others are not. The test is whether performance by the original obligor or under the obligor's personal supervision is required by the contract. Such a requirement may be expressed in the contract. If it is not, such a requirement will be implied in two kinds of cases:

(a) Where the contract is predicated on the unique skills of the obligor, and

(b) Where the contract is predicated on the trust and confidence that the obligee has placed in the obligor.

Examples: (1) *D* agrees to paint *C*'s portrait. Subsequently, *D* delegates the duty to paint to *A*, an able and better-known portrait painter. The delegation is ineffective. *C*'s selection of an artist is presumptively based on *C*'s judgment of the artist's style. *C*'s exercise of taste, even if idiosyncratic, is given effect.

(2) *C* retains *D*, a lawyer in a distant city, to defend a lawsuit. *D* delegated the retainer and assigned the right to payment to *A*, who was successful in causing the case to be dismissed. *C* need pay neither *A* nor *D*. The duties were improperly delegated to *A*. The relationship of attorney and client is based on the trust and confidence of the client. Although the attorney may delegate a substantial part of the duties of preparing a defense to law clerks, associates, partners and even outside counsel, the attorney cannot delegate the duty of overall management and supervision of the case without the consent of the client.

(3) *C* contracts with *D* to have an addition built onto a house. *D* delegates the plumbing work to *A*. The delegation is proper. The

skills are mechanical. *D* could have performed the contract by hiring a crew of plumbers, each of whom could have been changed on a day-to-day basis. When this can happen, the contract duties are delegable.

(4) *C* contracts with *XYZ,* Inc., a small, specialized company that does applied scientific research, and which has a reputation for excellence. The contract looked to the development of a prototype of a battery-operated furnace. *XYZ,* Inc., assigned its rights and delegated its duties to *A,* Inc. The delegation is proper. The delegant is a corporation and its scientists could be changed at any time. Nothing in the contract required the personal performance of any given person.

b. Delegation in Sales Contracts

Article 2 Rules: In general, the delegation rules of the UCC are the same as the common law. It will be recalled that, under UCC Article 2, a general clause prohibiting assignment of the contract has the effect of prohibiting the delegation of duties.

Also, under UCC Article 2, unless the language or circumstances point to a contrary intention, an assignment in general terms is treated as doing three things: (1) assigning the rights, (2) delegating the duties, (3) and creating an assumption of duties.

UCC Article 2 also authorizes the obligee to demand assurances from the delegate whenever the other party assigns rights and delegates duties to a delegate.

c. Effect of Improper Delegation

An attempted delegation of a non-delegable duty is ineffective. It is also a breach. If persisted in, the breach is material.

Review Question *(Answers in Appendix A)*

We suggest you first review HOW TO STUDY and EXAMINATION in the *Perspective* section, *supra.*

S, a distributor of footballs, and *B,* a sporting goods retailer, entered into a contract whereby *S* agreed to sell and *B* agreed to buy 1,000 Brand X footballs of an agreed model at $25 per football, payment to be made 90 days after delivery. The contract provided that any assignment of rights in the contract would be void. Before delivery of the footballs, *S* purported to assign *S*'s rights to *C.*

1. T or F The purported assignment to *C* was ineffective.

2. T or F My answer to the previous question would be different if the purported assignment was made after delivery of the footballs.

Assume that there is no anti-assignment clause, and that *S* made a second assignment to *D* who paid value and took without notice of the first assignment, and that *D* gave notice of the assignment to *B,* who paid *D* before learning of the assignment to *C.*

3. T or F Under none of the competing common law rules can *C* recover from *D*.

4. T or F If the UCC applies, the result in question 3 today may depend on a factor or factors not mentioned in the facts.

Assume hereafter that the assignments previously mentioned had not been made by *S*. Instead, before delivering the footballs, *S* had, for a valuable consideration, signed and delivered a writing to *X* that read "I hereby assign my contract with *B* to *X*."

5. T or F This would be interpreted as only a delegation of duties.

Assume hereafter that there was only an attempted delegation of duties from *S* to *X* with an agreement by *X*, for a consideration, to assume the duties of *S*.

6. T or F *B* may treat the delegation as creating reasonable grounds for insecurity.

7. T or F The duties attempted to be delegated were non-delegable.

8. T or F Assume the duty was delegable and that upon delegating the duty *S* stated to *B* that *S* no longer considered itself obligated by the contract and that *B* should look solely to *X* for performance. If *B* deals with *X* thereafter, there would be a novation.

9. Essay On January 2, 1999, Abel contracted in writing subscribed by both parties to sell to Baker 1,000 bales of cotton on or before May 1, 2009, at the price of $50,000, payable $20,000 cash on delivery. On delivery of the cotton, Baker was to execute a promissory note in the amount of $30,000 payable in one year. The contract also stated that "this contract is non-assignable." On March 1, 2009, Caleb bought Baker's business. At the bottom of the contract with Abel, Baker wrote, "I hereby assign this contract to Caleb." This document was delivered to Caleb. Abel was notified by letter of this transaction. Abel in reply, on March 6th, wrote to Baker and Caleb saying, "Since you have wrongfully assigned, I regard the contract as terminated and am selling the cotton elsewhere."

(a) Assume that Caleb sued Abel on March 7, 2009, without tendering anything. What are the rights of the parties?

(b) Assume that no action has been commenced and on April 15, 2009, Abel wrote Caleb and Baker, "I retract my letter of March 6th. I will make delivery on May 1st." What are the liabilities of Caleb and Baker if Caleb refuses to accept delivery?

Appendix A

Answers to Review Questions

CHAPTER II. MUTUAL ASSENT—OFFER AND ACCEPTANCE

1. ***True.*** The answer is supplied by the statement that a reasonable person in P's position would conclude that *A* was not serious. Under the objective theory of contracts and the reasonable person approach, there is no contract.

2. ***True.*** The parties here clearly agreed that this was a sham arrangement and therefore intended that no legal consequences would attach to the writing.

3. ***False.*** If a doctor promises to follow a certain procedure, the doctor has made an enforceable commitment. On the facts, the doctor appears to have made such a promise. If so, she has a cause of action. The most that can be argued on the other side is that this is a question of fact.

4. ***False.*** This is similar to the cases involving ads for the sale of goods. First, it is doubtful if there is language of commitment. The fact that the Tribune will refuse certain types of advertisements does not mean that it will accept all others. In any event, there is no statement of quantity. Thus, an offer was not made.

5. ***True.*** As a common law proposition an announcement that an auction will be held is deemed to be a statement of intention. Under the Uniform Commercial Code, even after the goods have been put up for sale, the auctioneer may withdraw the goods from sale except where the auction is "without reserve" and a bid is received within a reasonable time.

6. ***False.*** *P*'s first communication was only an inquiry. *D* then asked for an offer. When *P* named a sum *P* made an offer. But this was rejected by *D*. *P* then made an additional inquiry. *D*'s statement is not language of promise or commitment. Rather *D* is saying that an offer for less than $56,000 would not be considered. Thus, the only offer that is made is *P*'s offer to pay $56,000 which was made when *P* said "I accept." This offer was not accepted.

7. ***False.*** Although *B* may have been legally bound to return the watch so that there is no consideration, there is an additional reason why B may not recover. B did not know of the offer or intend to accept.

8. ***False.*** *B* clearly knew of the offer. The issue is intent to accept. Under one view, the offeree may testify to his or her state of mind. If *B* testifies to having a subjective intent to accept and is believed, *B* will prevail. Under a second view, there is a presumption that *B* intended to accept, and *B* is not permitted to testify as to subjective intention. The presumption is rebuttable. On the facts, whether the presumption is rebutted is probably a question of fact.

9. ***False.*** Although a reasonable person could conclude that this was an offer looking to a series of unilateral contracts, it could also be concluded that the act called for was the discontinuance of publication and that there was one unilateral contract with a series of performances. In either event, abstaining from publication for a week is a condition precedent to *A*'s obligation to pay $10 each week. The main difference is that if *A*'s words amounted to an offer looking to a series of unilateral contracts, *A* would be free to revoke prospectively. This is not true under the second analysis.

10. ***False.*** *A* is not contractually bound under the rules of acceptance by silence because A did not have a reasonable opportunity to reject the services. In addition, under the rules of property law *A* would not be guilty of an act of wrongful dominion by occupying the house because the structure is *A*'s.

11. ***False.*** Since *A* was unconscious, *A* did not expressly or impliedly agree to anything. B is entitled to a quasi-contractual recovery measured by the reasonable value of B's services.

12. ***False.*** It depends upon whether a reasonable person in the position of *A* would conclude that *B* expected to be paid for the work to be done prior to the contract or that *B* was doing the preliminary work in hopes of obtaining the contract. The custom of the trade supplies the answer. Brokers normally work for contingent fees.

13. ***False.*** Although there seems to be an offer and an acceptance by an act of dominion, the Restatement, Second, states that the offeree is not bound by the offered terms where, as here, they are manifestly unreasonable. If there is no contract there is a conversion and *A* should have the option of suing in contract, tort, or quasi-contract, but nevertheless the Restatement based on case law takes the position that *A* should be limited to a reasonable value recovery in this contractual action.

14. ***True.*** Because the counter-offer is effective when it is received, and was lost, it does not act as a rejection. The letter of acceptance is authorized (reasonable) and is effective when sent (2 P.M.) even though it was lost. Under the majority view, a revocation is effective when it is received. Therefore, there is a contract. Under the minority view that a revocation is effective when sent, the result would be different.

15. ***True.*** Despite the quoted language, the offer is revocable. There is no consideration to support the promise of irrevocability. UCC § 2–205 does not apply, because the case involves real property. The rejection terminated the revocable offer as did the revocation.

16. ***False.*** Because no time period is stated, the offer is open for a reasonable time. Because the offer is to sell at a fixed price in a fluctuating market, it is clear that the offer should be open for a relatively short period—long enough to give the offeree a reasonable opportunity to consider the offer. This time had long since elapsed when the attempted acceptance occurred.

17. ***False.*** The manifest purpose of the offeror is the conviction of the criminal. This can happen until the statute of limitations expires. When this happens depends upon the law of a particular jurisdiction, but under the facts it is clear that it had not.

18. ***False.*** The offeror may stipulate in the offer that the power of acceptance shall terminate upon the happening of a certain event. If the event happens before the acceptance, the power of acceptance lapses even though the offeree is not informed that the event has occurred.

19. ***True.*** When an offer is made in a face to face or telephone conversation or in any situation where there are direct negotiations, the offer is deemed, in the absence of a manifestation of a contrary intention, to be open only while the parties are conversing.

20. ***False.*** A revocable offer looking to a series of contracts may be terminated prospectively. Under the majority view, an adjudication of incompetency followed by the appointment of a guardian terminated the offer even though B was unaware of what transpired. Under this view, A is liable only for the first delivery.

21. ***False.*** The "equal publicity" doctrine does not apply because *A* knew of *B*'s existence and address. *A* was bound to personally notify *B*.

22. ***True.*** The payment of $100 makes the offer irrevocable. Under the modern view, the counter-offer does not terminate the original offer. Therefore, it can still be accepted by *B*.

23. ***True.*** Whether the 7 days are measured from Jan. 2 or Jan. 3, an acceptance sent on Jan. 9 is timely if sent in an authorized (reasonable) manner, which is the case here. In computing 7 days, the day from which the computation is made is not ordinarily considered.

24. ***False.*** Under the provisions of UCC § 2–311 there is a contract.

25. ***False.*** The traditional common law rule is that an agreement to agree as to a material term renders the agreement too vague and indefinite to be enforced (void). But here the quoted words indicate that the parties have agreed to make a good faith effort to reach agreement. A breach of that promise will amount to a breach of contract.

26. ***False.*** Although there are two views on the intention to accept an offer to a unilateral contract such as a reward offer, under either view *B* cannot recover. Under the older view it is clear that *B* did not subjectively intend to accept. Under the newer view of the Restatement (Second), if *B* manifests an intent not to accept prior to *A's* performance, *B* is not entitled to recover.

27.(a) (1) Thompson's question was an inquiry and created no legal consequences.

(2) Case's reply amounted to an offer. The reply contained language of commitment ("I will sell the tractor to you"). The offer was sufficiently definite. It contained subject matter, price and delivery terms. It was made to one person. The phrase "or to anybody else for that matter," is best understood as a comment to Thompson indicating an intent to sell to someone else if Thompson did not accept. (*See* 6 *infra*).

(3) Did the offer lapse? (a) Because the parties were face to face, the offer presumably lapsed after the conversation. But the words "upon an agreement" could indicate the contrary. (b) Was the acceptance within a reasonable time? Probably not, but essentially this is a question of fact.

(4)(a) Proper mode of acceptance. As a common law proposition, the words "upon an agreement" indicate an offer looking to a bilateral contract and, even if the offer is considered ambiguous, it would still be deemed to look to a bilateral contract. (b) Under the UCC if the offer "unambiguously" looks to a bilateral contract, it must be accepted by promise. If the offer is ambiguous or indifferent, it may be accepted by any reasonable means including promise, performance or the commencement of performance. Thompson, however, has not performed because Thompson has not paid. At most, picking up the tractor is the beginning of performance in which case the offeror may treat the offer as having lapsed if the offeror does not receive notification within a reasonable time. Is notification after two weeks reasonable? Probably not, but this is a question of fact. (*See* 3b *supra*). But the offeror may overlook the lapse of time and treat the offeree's conduct as creating a good acceptance.

(5) Alternatively, Thompson may be viewed as having accepted by an act of wrongful dominion. The act of dominion would be wrongful if Thompson could accept only by promise and failed to make one, or if the offer had lapsed. In the event that there is a wrongful act of dominion, Case would have the option given by UCC § 2–606; i.e., he could hold Thompson to an acceptance of the offer or, at Case's option, as a tortfeasor.

(6) Was an offer made to Petersen? (i) The offer to Case is not transferable to Petersen. (ii) There was no general offer to the public. The offer was communicated to Thompson alone. (*See* 2 *supra*). The only way in which it can be said that there was an offer to Petersen would be if Case had made Thompson Case's agent for this purpose. This seems unlikely on the facts presented.

(b) If (a) is answered thoroughly, there is little to say here. If you eliminated the quoted language, then the offer is indifferent (ambiguous) as to the manner of acceptance.

(c) At common law, the sentence relating to the arbitration clause would appear to make the communication a counter-offer. (Could it be a mere comment on the terms?) Under the UCC, the first question is whether there is a definite and seasonable expression of acceptance. This seems to be the case and the acceptance is clearly not conditional. Thus, there is a contract. The additional term does not become part of the contract whether or not the parties are merchants. The offeror did not assent to the term and the additional term is a material alteration under most of the cases decided on this issue. Therefore, there is a contract, but it does not include the arbitration clause.

28. (1) The first paragraph merely provides factual background and raises no legal issues.

(2) In the next paragraph, plaintiff made an offer requesting by way of acceptance a 60-day option on the plaintiff's terms. A signature line suggested a means of acceptance, but did not prescribe such a means. The point becomes irrelevant by ensuing facts and the presence or absence of consideration also becomes irrelevant.

(3) The reply by defendant does not accept the plaintiff's offer. Does it make an offer? Although it contains detailed terms, it lacks language of commitment and contains language that demonstrates a lack of present commitment.

"We would be willing to sell . . . *if such an offer were made today,*" either indicates a lack of commitment or, at best, is an offer open for a day. The phrase "letter of intent" also normally shows a lack of commitment. More conclusively, there is a further reference to an offer to be made by plaintiff that will be a "firm and binding one." Perhaps contradictory is language that: "you are assured . . . we will enter into a contract . . ." Such language appears promissory. Nonetheless, taken as a whole, the communication is at best ambiguous as to its legal effect. Offers are not construed from weak language. They must be clear expressions of commitment.

(4) Even if the letter were construed to be an offer, the letter contains terms that are indefinite. "Suitable assurances," unless fleshed out by usage, appears vague as to what such assurances might be and what personnel are involved. "Mutually satisfactory arrangements" is also quite indefinite. Even if this language is construed as requiring bargaining in good faith by plaintiff, Conroy is not a contracting party and Conroy would be under no such obligation.

(5) Even if the letter were construed as an offer and it was sufficiently definite, did plaintiff accept? Its expression of assent indicated that plaintiff was intending to make an offer, not to accept one. Nonetheless, it is a manifestation of willingness to

enter into a contract on defendant's terms. However, plaintiff labels its communication as an offer. One would suspect that a court would hold an apparently sophisticated business to its own conclusion as to the nature of its communications.

(6) Moreover, its reference to the preparation of a formal agreement by the parties' general counsels would indicate that important details still needed to be worked out and that it did not intend to be bound until the general counsels had done their work of preparing a formal agreement. We are dealing with an apparently sizable corporate acquisition, and it is unlikely that there was an intent to be bound until the details were worked out.

(7) The large sums of money spent by plaintiff was doubtless in reliance upon defendant's manifestation of intention to enter into the contract. Recently, courts have protected the reliance interest of a party who in good faith expends money in reliance upon continued good faith negotiations. The cases involve an extension of the doctrine of promissory estoppel. The facts do not indicate whether defendant broke off negotiations in bad faith.

29. Short Essay

The communication appearing in the window of the envelope had all the earmarks of an offer to a unilateral contract. It contains a clear expression of promise to a given individual, promising a specific quantity, and requests a specific act of acceptance (opening the envelope). This analysis is perhaps too literal. The skeptical reasonable adult may well understand that the hidden internal wording is likely to contain a catch. Yet should not *Time* be held to the false impression it tried to create? Isn't this one of the foundations of the objective theory? Anyway, it is not unprecedented for an advertiser to offer an incentive to read its message. Life insurance companies frequently offer "free gifts," if, in exchange, the offeree will listen to a sales pitch. Land developers in resort areas do this all the time.

Assuming the circular creates an offer, can Joshua's mother accept? Normally, only the offeree can accept. It is arguable however that Joshua's mother acted as his agent.

As for the members of the class who had not demanded a watch, there is a common law view that the offeror of an offer to a unilateral contract must be notified of acceptance if the offeree knows that the offeror is unlikely to know that the act of acceptance has taken place. This is adopted by UCC Section 2–206. This provision is applicable here as a watch is a good. Consequently, those who had not notified *Time* of their acceptance by demanding a watch cannot recover.

CHAPTER III. CONSIDERATION AND ITS EQUIVALENTS

1. ***True.*** Both elements of consideration are present. The mother suffered detriment in naming the child as desired by the putative father. This was clearly bargained for by the father. The mother in turn knew of the offer and intended to accept.

2. ***False.*** *P* suffered detriment in delivering the goods. This was bargained for by *D*. *P* knew of the offer and intended to accept. The fact that *D* promised to pay for past deliveries is not important because of the rule that one consideration will support many promises.

3. ***False.*** *D*'s promise is not enforceable because under the law of Guardian and Ward *P* in returning etc., was only doing what *P* is legally obligated to do and did not suffer detriment. Thus, there is no consideration to support *D*'s promise. The duty discussed here is not imposed by the law of contracts.

4. ***True.*** When *D* promised to guaranty payment, *D* made an additional promise and there was no consideration because *P* never did anything other than what *P* was legally obligated to do. Thus, there was no consideration for this promise.

5. ***True.*** Under the majority view, plaintiffs were only doing what they were legally obligated to do. There was no consideration to support the promise of *D* to pay an additional sum.

6. ***True.*** Under the First Restatement, *D*'s promise to pay more would not be enforceable because there was no impossibility of performance. Under the Restatement, Second, the promise is binding even though not supported by consideration "if the modification is fair and equitable in view of circumstances not anticipated when the contract was made." Before this rule can be applied, additional facts must be known. In any event, the applicable rule is UCC § 2–209(1) which provides that a modification is binding without consideration even though it is oral. Under the UCC, *D* would be required to pay the additional sum provided *P* is acting in good faith and has a legitimate commercial reason for seeking a modification.

7. ***False.*** The common law rule is that the agreement may be modified despite the contrary provision in the initial agreement. UCC § 2–209(2) could not change the result because it relates only to a contract for the sale of goods.

8. ***True.*** *B*'s promise to pay *A* a fair share of the profits is too vague and indefinite to be enforced and the result is a void bilateral contract under the doctrine of mutuality of consideration. Although *A* complies with the two minimum rules for forging a good unilateral contract out of a bad bilateral contract, *A* is still not able to enforce the contract, because despite *A*'s performance *B*'s promise is too vague and indefinite to be enforced. Thus, *A* is not entitled to a contractual recovery but may recover in quasi contract.

9. ***False.*** *D* has promised alternative performances. The rule is that for detriment to exist each alternative must be detrimental. On the facts, *D* must either sell or give 5 days notice. Each alternative is detrimental. Under UCC § 2–309, there may be a question of unconscionability, but the facts given in the question do not raise the issue.

10. ***False.*** Here *B* has made only one promise (to buy 12 carloads) and *S* has made two promises (to sell 12 carloads and give *B* the option of buying 13 more carloads). The rule is that one consideration (*B*'s buying) will support many promises. Thus, *B*'s promise is consideration for *S*'s promise to sell an additional 13 carloads. As to these 13 carloads, *S* has made an irrevocable offer (option contract). *S* is not free to revoke this offer. *B* is entitled to receive the additional 13 carloads.

11. ***False.*** Because the work is requested, it is clear, under modern law, that in the absence of a promise to pay a specific sum, *B* would be entitled to the reasonable value of the services. The issue is whether, under the law relating to moral obligation, *B* is entitled to $7,200 or $8,000. According to most, *B* may recover $8,000. While Corbin would limit the enforcement to an amount not disproportionate to the value of the services, the disparity between the reasonable value and the amount promised is within the same ballpark and could not be deemed disproportionate. The Restatement, Second, is unclear.

12. ***True.*** It is clear that there was substantial injurious reliance on the part of *D* on the gift promise made by *F*. Thus, the doctrine of Promissory Estoppel applies. Under the First Restatement, where a court could choose either a contractual recovery or nothing, it is possible that $17,000 would be awarded. Under the notion of flexibility of remedy espoused by the Restatement Second, *D* would probably be limited to reliance damages—$2,000. (The actual case gave her a judgment for $17,000.)

13. ***True.*** This is a case of gratuitous agency under the doctrine of promissory estoppel. Despite the fact that all of the elements for a promissory estoppel exist, under the traditional approach in a gratuitous agency situation, the promise will be enforced only where there is misfeasance—negligent performance. Here, there is only non-feasance—failure to perform. Thus, *P* will not recover under the traditional rule.

14. (1) It is clear on the facts that there was no consideration in the classical sense for *A*'s promise. *B*'s "kindnesses" amounted to past consideration. *A* apparently was not bargaining for *B* to come to the United States or for *B* to work in the business.

(2) The next question is moral obligation. Receipt of unrequested benefits does not ordinarily create a legal obligation. If a subsequent promise is made to pay for these benefits, the majority of cases hold that the promise is unenforceable. A strong minority current would permit enforcement of the promise. The Restatement, Second, would take the same position with respect to benefits received in an emergency. Recovery would also be permitted under the California statute mentioned in the text.

(3) "Permanent employment," standing alone, amounts to a hiring at will in the absence of a consideration over and above the employment. Here under the conclusions reached in (1) above there was no such consideration. However, in a jurisdiction that accepts the moral obligation concept embraced by the Restatement, Second, such consideration would be held to exist.

(4) Moreover, *B* took substantial action in reliance upon *A*'s promise. It would appear that *B* may recover under a theory of promissory estoppel if it can be established that the action involved injury to *B*. The question is, how his damages should be computed? Should he be limited to reliance damages, or should he obtain a full contractual recovery? The law is very much in flux on this question.

Full contractual recovery would entitle *B* to the value of *A*'s promise. Assuming the promise means *B* will have a job for his working life, *B* would be entitled to wages for that period of time, minus what *B* earns or reasonably could earn at substitute employment. (Wages as a truck-driver appears to be a proper standard because the parties defined "employment" by practical construction, i.e., course of performance.) Reliance damages would likely be more appropriate here. *A* generously extricated *B* from his difficulties abroad, paid *B*'s travel expenses and gave *B* a start in a trade. Justice might dictate some small, if any, recovery for what *B* gave up when he left Poland, to the extent that these exceeded the benefits *B* received under the contract.

15. Plaintiff's response to Defendant was a counter-offer. It differed from the offer in several respects. It makes reference to a performance and payment bond. This is not a term of the offer. It ignores the third exclusion in the offer. It provides for rough-in work in the kitchen and kitchen equipment not required to be furnished by others—which may or may not be implied in the offer. Consequently, there is no contract formed by the process of offer and acceptance.

When Plaintiff promised Defendant that it would use Defendant's bid in its calculations, no contract was formed. Plaintiff's offer (bid) was not accepted even conditionally. Moreover, there was no consideration for Plaintiff's promise. The promise to use Defendant's bid in calculating its own bid was not bargained for by Defendant.

Is Defendant estopped from revoking its offer? Plaintiff's reliance on Defendant's figure was reasonable, foreseeable and foreseen. Nonetheless, Defendant's attempt in its acceptance to impose different terms in the contract indicates it did not rely totally on the bid and therefore an estoppel is inappropriate.

16.

I. The option is valid.

A. Consideration

An irrevocable offer (option) requires consideration or its equivalent. The same consideration—payment of rent—that supports the other promises of Lessor supports the irrevocability of the offer. One consideration supports many promises. [Moreover, in N.Y., and some other jurisdictions, an irrevocable offer can be created by a signed writing containing language of irrevocability.]

B. Indefiniteness

The option is somewhat indefinite. Outside the UCC, only a few frontier cases recognize the validity of agreements to agree, holding that such agreements impose a duty to bargain in good faith. We need not go to the frontier in this case as the agreement provides a precise mechanism for determining the rent if the parties fail to agree. Consequently, the option does not fail for indefiniteness.

II. The Acceptance

A. Counter-offer.—Repudiation

Lessee's proposal may have amounted to counter-offers which act as rejections to terminate the power of acceptance of revocable offers. However, an irrevocable offer is not terminated by a rejection. Lessee's demand that the Lessor finance him may have amounted to a repudiation of the option. However, Lessee's subsequent conduct implicitly retracted any repudiation.

Lessee made it clear that it intended to accept the offer. A clear manifestation of intent to accept is an acceptance. Consequently, once the option is accepted and the parties are unable to agree on the rent they are under a duty to arbitrate. By agreeing to appoint arbitrators they clear up any indefiniteness with respect to *when* the appropriate time was to select arbitrators. Moreover, if Lessee had not accepted earlier, the agreement to select arbitrators was a clear manifestation of acceptance.

III. The breach by Lessor.

When Lessor failed to name an arbitrator within a reasonable time and refused to return Lessee's phone calls he was guilty of a material breach of the option contract.

IV. The check is not an offer.

Lessee's check and accompanying letter was not clearly an offer to an accord and satisfaction nor to an agreement fixing the rent. The statement reeks of tentativeness. Nothing indicates that Lessor must accept it, if at all, as full payment for January rent or that Lessor recognizes the renewal of the lease.

V. The effect of protest.

Assuming the check and accompanying lease were an offer to an accord and satisfaction for the January rent, at common law the protest would be futile. Cashing the check in defiance of the conditions attached by the debtor is an acceptance by exercise of dominion irrespective of assent or dissent. Some cases ruled that the common law rule was changed by a provision of Article 1 of the UCC. (According to some of the cases, the UCC is applicable because Article 3 governs check law, and Article 1 governs all provisions of the UCC.) In the 1990's Article 1 was changed to overturn those cases. Forty-eight states have adopted the change, thereby restoring the common law rule.

VI. Estoppel

The mention of "other arrangements" raises the question of promissory estoppel. If there were any defect in the option or in the acceptance, Lessee did not have ordinary contractual rights. Lessee may invoke promissory estoppel either showing Lessor's bad faith in negotiating or a promise (e.g., the promise to name arbitrators) and justifiable conduct in reliance on the promise. On the analysis of this question given above, promissory estoppel is not needed to aid Lessee's case as he can successfully enforce the contract on more traditional grounds.

Note how the above answer was strengthened by dividing it by captioned headings. This format helps the examiner see the structure and logic of the answer. [Material in square brackets should be a part of your answer only if the examiner asks that local statutes be considered.]

CHAPTER IV. LEGAL CAPACITY

1. ***True.*** The infant may disaffirm an executed transaction for a reasonable time after reaching majority. Here *A* disaffirms immediately after reaching maturity. The action is timely. Since *A* seeks restitution *A* must account for the consideration received. *A* should tender return of the money.

2. ***True.*** Here the contract is executory at least as far as the adult is concerned. The youth has obtained no benefit under the contract, and there is no injustice to the adult in allowing the youth to disaffirm. The only other question is whether *A* ratified the contract after majority by telling the seller that another payment would be made. A statement that payment will be made is not generally a ratification.

3. ***False.*** Normally, if the incompetent's executed contract is on fair terms and the other party has no reason to know of the incompetence, the transaction cannot be disaffirmed unless the status quo ante can be restored.

4. **Essay** Despite a misrepresentation of age the majority view allows the infant to disaffirm. On disaffirmance the infant must return any consideration received which the infant still has or anything traceable to the consideration. An interesting question is whether the grandfather's reimbursement falls into this category. If so, it would appear that the airline would be entitled to only $150, the value of the flight, rather than $200 or $300.

Another question is whether the flight is a necessary. It is questionable whether a college education at a distant location is a necessary. If the education is a necessary, however, it would seem to follow that the flight is also. If it is, Janice is liable for the reasonable value of the flight.

CHAPTER V. INTERPRETATION AND PROPER FORM (WRITING REQUIREMENT)

1. ***False.*** The writing is a total integration that may not be contradicted or supplemented. But this rule does not apply where there is an express condition precedent to the formation of a contract. This is the situation here.

2. ***True.*** If there is a total integration, the writing may not be contradicted or supplemented. If there is a partial integration, the writing may not be contradicted but it may be supplemented by a consistent additional term. The offered term is contradictory and therefore it makes no difference whether the integration is total or partial. In either event, the term is inadmissible. *D* does not allege a condition precedent to the formation of the contract, but a condition precedent to performance.

3. ***False.*** Whether or not the written requirements contract is a total integration, the evidence is admissible because the stock agreement has its own separate consideration on each side. The only issue is whether this agreement contradicts the written agreement. Since it is clear that there is no contradiction, the evidence is admissible.

4. ***False.*** The issue involves the one-year statute of frauds. Logically, the contract is not within the statute, as the severance could legally occur the same day. Since the day of contracting is disregarded as a fraction of a day, the contract is performable within one year.

5. ***False.*** The one-year statute of frauds is not violated if the promise by its terms may be performed within one year, however unlikely or improbable that may be. Here, it is possible that the plaintiff may not need the switch, for example, after six months. Therefore, the defendant's promise is not within the one-year statute of frauds.

6. ***False.*** Under one view the promise not to compete for two years is within the statute of frauds. But under another view, since the essential purpose of the promise would be attained by the death of the promisor, the promise is not within the statute of frauds. Note the wording of the question: "the promise is *certainly* within the statute of frauds."

7. ***False.*** It is clear that the agreement cannot be performed within one year from the *making* thereof. However, the court permitted a contractual recovery on the theory of promissory estoppel because "unconscionable injury" should not be permitted.

8. ***False.*** *D*'s promise is not within the one-year statute of frauds because *P* could have died within one year from the making of the promise. In a few jurisdictions, the statute is supplemented by a lifetime or a testamentary disposition provision. Under these statutes, restitution would be available.

Article 8 of the UCC (securities) no longer has a statute of frauds provision. Article 2's statute of frauds (sale of goods) is satisfied because *P* has fully paid for the goods.

9. ***False.*** As soon as the memorandum was signed, the statute was satisfied. Delivery is not needed.

10. ***False.*** An oral acceptance of a written offer to a contract that is within the statute of frauds results in a contract enforceable against the offeror.

11. ***False.*** The oral rescission is effective, despite the fact that the original agreement was within the statute of frauds and in writing.

12. ***True.*** The oral modification is enforceable, because the new agreement is not within the statute of frauds.

13. ***False.*** The oral modification is unenforceable, because the agreement, as modified, is within the statute. As a result, the written contract stands unmodified.

14. ***False.*** Even though one of the writings containing an essential term is not signed, under the majority rule, if the documents by internal evidence refer to the same subject matter or transaction, and the writing that establishes the contract is signed, the memoranda are sufficient to satisfy the statute of frauds.

15. ***True.*** The executor is orally promising to be personally liable for a debt of the estate. The executor is therefore promising to answer for the debt, default, or miscarriage of another, and has a defense under the suretyship statute of frauds.

16. ***True.*** The amount involved is in excess of $500. *B* is not a merchant, and the written memorandum is not effective against *B*. The result would be different if *B* were a merchant. *See* UCC § 2–201(2).

17. ***True.*** Here, both parties are merchants, and the confirmatory memorandum is sufficient to satisfy the UCC statute of frauds. But, in addition, there is a problem with the one-year section of the statute of frauds. According to some authorities, the more stringent requirements of that statute's rule with respect to a memorandum must be met. *B*'s letter incorporates the confirmatory memorandum and satisfies the one-year statute of frauds.

18. ***False.*** Although marriage is a contemplated condition of the contract it is not the consideration. The agreement is, therefore, not within the section of the statute of frauds that relates to an "agreement made upon consideration of marriage."

19. ***True.*** If *F* is bargaining for them to marry, marriage is the consideration, and a writing is needed. If marriage is not the consideration, the statute is not involved and there would be no consideration to support the promise.

20. ***True.*** The real property statute of frauds is not applicable to a brokerage contract which is a service contract. The real property aspect is only incidental. In a number of jurisdictions, a separate statute requires a broker's retainer to be in writing.

21. ***False.*** The statute of frauds does not require a writing to evidence the agent's authority. Some local variations on the statutes of frauds do require a writing but usually only for the real property statute.

22. ***False.*** If the vendor of the property conveys the property to the vendee, the promise of the vendee will be enforced even though it is oral.

23. Because *C* was obligated to pay *E* $90,000 in fifteen monthly installments, the agreement, by its terms, may not be performed within one year from the making thereof. Thus, the one-year statute of frauds requires a writing.

In addition to the statute of frauds problem, there is a parol evidence rule problem. We are told that during negotiations (presumably prior to the writing) the parties had agreed "that if overtime became necessary it should be added on a time-and-a-half basis." Whether this evidence is admissible depends upon whether the writing was an integration and if so whether it was a total integration. If it is a total integration, it may not be contradicted or supplemented. If it is partial, it may not be contradicted but it may be supplemented by consistent additional terms. Here, it is debatable whether the term offered is consistent or contradictory. In addition, under the various views discussed in this outline, different conclusions as to whether the integration was partial or total could be reached. For example, under Williston's view, it would appear that it would be natural to have included this term in the writing and so the integration would be total with the result that this term would be excluded. The writing is likely to be characterized as a total integration of the contract. Although we are not informed whether the writing contained a merger clause, the clause about amendments only by a signed writing points to an intent to have a complete writing. The UCC parol evidence rule would not apply because the agreement does not involve the sale of goods.

A later oral agreement of the parties provided, in part, that *C* would pay *E* "a time-and-a-half for all worker hours worked over forty hours per week." Here, the parol evidence rule is inapplicable, because this agreement was subsequent to the writing and the parol evidence rule does not apply to subsequent agreements.

The issue is, was there consideration for *C*'s promise to pay *E* $6,000 per month until the job was completed, plus time-and-a-half for overtime? If the time-and-a-half provision was in the original agreement this would not be a problem, but the problem would still exist as to the promise to pay $6,000 per month. At first blush, it would appear that *E* is not suffering any detriment. UCC § 2–209(1) does not affect the problem because it relates only to sale of goods.

However, under the view of the Restatement (Second), if the need for overtime and additional months of work was a result of unanticipated circumstances as represented by *E*, and the modification is fair and equitable, the modification is binding without consideration.

The validity of the modification is not affected by the clause in the original agreement that recited "this contract may be amended only in a signed writing." Under the common law rule, the agreement may be modified by a subsequent agreement despite the existence of such a clause. There is a contrary UCC provision (UCC § 2–209(2)) which does not apply because the agreement is not for the sale of goods.

The subsequent agreement does not contravene the statute of frauds because *by its terms* it may be performed within one year, however unlikely or improbable that may be. Because the new agreement is not within the statute of frauds, it is enforceable, as far as the statute of frauds is concerned. Under the majority rule, the new agreement is not only enforceable without a writing but also serves to discharge the prior written agreement.

Thus, the subsequent agreement would appear to be binding if the viewpoint of the Restatement (Second) on consideration for contract modifications is followed.

24. Short Essay

There are two issues here, mutual assent and the statute of frauds. Was the written employment agreement intended to be merely a written memorial of a contract that has already been made or was it intended to be binding only upon the signing of the document in quadruplicate? This issue of intent is really a question of fact. [Stating that it is a question of fact is an acceptable answer, but the N.Y. Ct. of App. said that there was no contract as a matter of law. Among other factors, the court pointed out that the fact that one copy would go to George's lawyer showed that the latter would have an opportunity to review the proposal before George signed it. *See* 26 NY2d 466].

Assuming that there was an intent to contract, the statute of frauds must also be satisfied as the contract is for a three-year term. The document has not been signed. Can we piece together the signed letter and the document and regard Marv's signature as the subscription of the contract? Assuming Marv is authorized to act as Ms. Francis's agent [lawyers are rarely authorized by their clients to contract on their behalf], the signature does not purport to authenticate the contract; it clearly refrains from doing so by asking that George get Ms. Francis's signature on the four copies. Consequently, the statute of frauds would bar enforcement of the contract, if there were one.

CHAPTER VI. CONDITIONS, PERFORMANCE AND BREACH

1. ***False.*** The condition is excused by *U*'s prevention. An action for damages is available to *N*.

2. ***False.*** The offer ripened into a bilateral contract by *N*'s promise. While an offer can be revoked, a contract is not revocable.

3. ***False.*** Handsome must make the determination in good faith. This requirement is a sufficient restraint on his freedom so that his commitment is genuine.

4. ***False.*** The appropriate doctrines are prospective failure of condition and anticipatory repudiation.

5. ***False.*** The contract is not divisible. Although the payout is on a per mile basis, it is apparent that a major part of the price is allocated to the tunnel.

6. ***True.*** In a service contract, absent agreement to the contrary, the rendition of services is a constructive condition precedent to payment.

7. ***True.*** The doctrine of anticipatory breach does not apply to a case where the repudiating party is under an obligation solely to pay money at a fixed time or fixed times.

8. ***False.*** The insurer's installment obligations are not apportioned exchanges for agreed installment obligations by the insured.

9. ***True.*** *A* appeared totally unable to perform and *A* was unable to provide assurances. *Z*'s conduct in hiring a substitute was permissible.

10. ***False.*** In view of the response to the prior question, *B*'s contract with *Z* is clearly binding upon *B* and *Z*. It is important to note that even if *Z* was not justified in hiring a substitute, he did enter into a contract with *B*, and the fact that *Z* would then be liable to *A* would not make it impossible to honor the contract with *B*.

11. ***False.*** Under any view of the matter, cancellation is too precipitous. Under the Restatement (Second), *B* may suspend any performance and demand assurances. Under the old Restatement, the inquiry would include the question of whether *S* had a right to prepay the mortgage or a justifiable expectation that the mortgagee will accept prepayment.

12. ***False.*** Even if *B* had the right to cancel, there would be no right to sue for anticipatory breach. *S* has not taken any action, after contracting, that is inconsistent with the obligations of the contract.

13. ***True.*** The waiver made on March 1 may be retracted until such time as there has been a change of position in reliance upon it. No such change of position is stated.

14. ***True.*** A clause that makes time of the essence creates an express condition that performance be rendered at the stated time.

15. ***False.*** Because it is an express condition, it cannot be a constructive condition.

16. ***False.*** It is both. *S* has a duty to tender title on June 1 and *S*'s rights are conditioned on such tender.

17. ***False.*** *See* the discussion of the answer to the preceding question.

18. As a general rule a date specified in a contract for completion of performance is not of the essence; that is to say, failure to complete on time is not, standing alone, a material breach. Consequently, the aggrieved party cannot treat such delay as a failure of condition. Cancellation is not a permissible response.

The cancellation took place almost three weeks after the scheduled completion date. About two-thirds of the work remained to be done. It would appear from this that on July 16, *X* was in material breach. Although failure to complete on that date was not *per se* a material breach, substantial lack of completion would be a material breach. If so, Constructor waived the constructive condition of substantial performance by the due date, resulting in an obligation by *X* to complete within a reasonable time. Whether August 2 is the end of a reasonable period of time is basically a question of fact.

It would have been better for Constructor to have fixed a new reasonable completion date on July 16, stating that this new date was of the essence. If Constructor justifiably canceled, it has an action against *X* for total breach. If, however, the cancellation is unjustified, *X* has an action for total breach against Constructor.

X's breach may be excused. Delays caused by weather are, however, seldom excused. Barring extreme and unforeseeable conditions, a construction contractor assumes the risk of weather. [*See* Chapter VI on Defenses]. Delays caused by delays of other subcontractors were specifically made excuses by the contract, but conditioned on filing a timely notice of claim. *X*'s evidence that a representative of Constructor waived the condition of timely written notice is relevant and admissible. As it is subsequent to the making of the contract it is not barred by the parol evidence rule. Waiver of a condition that is not a material part of the agreed exchange is effective without consideration. The condition of timely notice is not part of the agreed exchange which essentially is a trade of money for masonry. If a substantial part of *X*'s delay was excusable on this ground, *X* would be absolved of any charge of material breach.

The bringing in of *Y* raises a number of problems. If *X* was not materially in breach when *Y* commenced work, Constructor repudiated the contract by bringing in *Y*, unless the bringing in of *Y* was justified because of the prospective inability of *X* to substantially perform. In all likelihood, however, when *X* acquiesced in the bringing in of *Y* there was a modification of the contract by conduct. There is no indication that *X* protested. At any rate, the existence of this modification is a question of fact.

Y's conduct in offering a higher rate of pay gives *X* no rights against *Y*. There is no privity between subcontractors. [Chapter IX on Third Party Beneficiaries]. It is doubtful whether Constructor is responsible for *Y*'s actions. *X* will argue that the paying of higher wages to masons hindered *X*'s performance, excusing the resulting delay. Yet Constructor is not responsible for such hindrance unless, as discussed in the previous paragraph, the bringing in of *Y* was wrongful and the hindrance is a proximate result of that wrong. This seems doubtful because there would appear to have been an implied modification of the contract.

19. Compliance with the ten-day notice of death provision was impossible and is excused. When a *condition* is impossible to perform it is excused if failure to excuse it would result in forfeiture and the condition is not a material part of the agreed exchange. This rule precisely covers the facts of this case.

The burden of proof on the cause of death (was it accidental or not) is on the widow because accidental death is a condition precedent to the Magna's duty to pay double indemnity.

The burden of proof on whether the death was causally related to intoxication is on Magna. Logically, one can argue that it is a condition precedent to Magna's liability that Don not be intoxicated. However, the company chose language of condition subsequent: "coverage is voided." Courts frequently give effect to the language rather than the logic of a condition. When you add to that tendency the rule that insurance policies are construed against the drafter, the inevitable construction is that the language will be treated as creating a condition subsequent.

The discussions with the widow by Magna representatives constitute a waiver of the conditions of notice and cause of death. According to most authorities, conduct recognizing the existence of liability after a condition has failed is treated as an irrevocable election.

Short Essay

Construction contracts are rarely divisible. Payments made on the attainment of particular landmarks are generally regarded as progress payments. This contract, however, appears to be divisible. We cannot know for sure if the two dredging projects are independent or interdependent, but from the facts as stated it appears that they are independent, and each appears to have independent value. If this is so, and if "almost complete" meets the standards of substantial performance, that is to say, is in the high 90's of percentage of completion of a severable part of the contract, it has met the standard as the breach was not willful and the City can be compensated in damages for the increased cost of completion.

In many jurisdictions, Chris could recover, even in the absence of substantial performance, on a theory of quasi contract, receiving the reasonable value of the services rendered minus the City's damages.

CHAPTER VII. DEFENSES

1. ***True.*** Ignorance of facts making a contract illegal insulates a party from the charge of illegality.

2. ***False.*** In the law of contracts ignorance of the law insulates one from the charge of illegality when one relies on the presumed expertise of the other party. The inexperienced actor can rely on the presumed expertise of the producer.

3. ***True.*** The illegal provision is central to the agreement.

4. ***False.*** The doctrine of *locus poenitentiae* is engaged when one party withdraws from an illegal agreement.

5. ***False.*** It was not impossible to complete the portrait prior to the fire and it is not impossible to start again.

6. ***True.*** The death of the artist discharges the contract because the performance is personal. Generally, the law attempts to restore the status quo ante when such discharges occur.

7. ***False.*** A novation has been formed. Note that *B* consented to a discharge of the agreement *B* had with *A*.

8. (a) The question boils down to the issue of whether *T* may successfully raise the defense of frustration of purpose. *T*'s performance (paying money) is surely not impossible to perform. Nonetheless, once condemnation became imminent it would have been senseless for *T* to continue with the construction of the theater facilities. *T*'s basic purpose in entering into the lease appears to have been frustrated. This is the starting point for the defense to be considered, but it is not sufficient in itself.

Was the ability to operate a theater a basic assumption shared by both parties? The lease was for a long term and for a restricted use. It would appear that *L* shared with *T* the assumption that a theater could be operated on the site as a long-term proposition. Nonetheless, we must ask whether the risk was assumed by *T*. This in part turns on whether the condemnation was foreseeable as a possibility. If it was foreseeable, then *T* will be held to have assumed the risk. A foreseeable risk is assumed when a party fails to negotiate an exemption from it.

Was the frustration total? Frustration is not a defense unless the event totally or almost totally frustrates the purpose of the contract. It seems clear that the drive-in theater was frustrated in its totality, but we do not know if the land could have been used for any other purpose during June and July. The lease permits the selling of snack food. Absent further facts it is difficult to gauge whether this was a viable use or whether the selling of snacks (clearly intended as accessory to the use of the land as a drive-in theater) at the location would be so impracticable as to be equated with total frustration. Moreover, we do not know if other uses (e.g., a parking lot) could have been made of the land with the consent of *L*. The burden is on *T* to prove the defense. If the facts given are all *T* has proved, the defense should not be allowed.

Thus far this essay is written on the assumption that the lease does not allocate the risk of condemnation. To the extent that it does, the lease itself provides the answer to our question.

(b) *T*'s second defense is that of discharge by accord and satisfaction. *T* will argue that the settlement was a substituted contract resulting in the discharge of the rent claim and its substitution by the settlement agreement. The new agreement acts as an accord while at the same time it acts as a satisfaction of *L*'s claim. The consideration for *L*'s agreement is *T*'s surrender of *T*'s good faith and not unreasonable defense of frustration.

L may prefer to view the settlement agreement as an executory accord. This kind of an agreement is unenforceable at common law and is still unenforceable in some jurisdictions. For example, in New York an executory accord is enforceable only if it is in writing.

The distinction between an executory accord and a substituted contract is that the latter is intended to discharge immediately the pre-existing claim. In an executory accord the intention is to discharge the claim upon performance of the accord. Consequently, the classification of the agreement is a question of interpretation. If the parties have not made themselves clear, the greater the deliberateness and formalization of the agreement, the more likely we are dealing with a substituted contract. Of course, under the modern view it would make no difference on these facts into which class the agreement fell.

(c) *C*'s lack of a license is not necessarily fatal to its claim against *T*. When a licensing requirement is based upon a legislative determination to control the moral fitness or skills of a licensee, it is generally held that the lack of a license is a bar to recovery of fees allegedly earned by the practice of the unlicensed activity. Because the practice of the activity without a license is illegal, contracts made in direct connection with the activity are deemed illegal. This is based upon a presumed legislative intent to bar the collection of fees wrongfully earned.

When, however, the licensing requirement serves other ends, the law is less clear. In searching for legislative intent, the courts have generally held that if the purpose of the statute is to impose an occupation tax, a contract entered into by an unlicensed practitioner is not invalid. Where the purpose, as here, is less clear, each case must be decided on its own facts.

In the case at bar, revenue is being raised but there is some control exercised over the licensee by requiring financial stability and requiring disclosure of the corporate officers. Because of the last two requisites, it is obvious that the police power is being engaged. Consequently, the case is closer to the cases where the licensing requirement is designed to control the fitness of the licensee. *C* may not recover from *T*.

[Alternative conclusion: Because no effort is made to weed out applicants who lack professional skills or who are morally unfit, the licensing requirement is far removed from the class of cases that hold that unlicensed professionals, such as lawyers, doctors and plumbers cannot recover from their clients. *C* may recover from *T*.]

CHAPTER VIII. CONTRACT REMEDIES

1. ***False.*** The weight of authority disallows punitive damages for contractual breaches.

2. ***False.*** The precondition for specific performance is the inadequacy of the legal remedy. Malice is not usually relevant on this question.

3. ***False.*** Restitution at law is one of the options a party aggrieved by a breach has, whether or not the damages remedy is adequate.

4. ***True.*** The buyer's general damages are measured by the difference between market price and contract price on the day the buyer learns of the breach.

5. ***True.*** Damages for breach of contract do not include mental distress, etc.

6. ***False.*** The seller is liable for consequential damages if the seller knows the buyer's needs and that the buyer is unable to cover. The seller knew that Vendee had contracted to resell to Shrunk. It is not relevant that Vendor did not know the resale price.

7. ***False.*** Vendee's expectation of making a profit that is somewhat greater than is made by other sellers is entitled to protection.

8. ***True.*** There is no requirement that an aggrieved buyer cover.

9. ***False.*** Once again, Vendee's expectation of making resale profits is protected. The fact that Shrunk released Vendee should not inure to the benefit of Vendor.

10. (a) The firing of Edwards was wrongful. Consequently, Edwards has an action for breach of contract. Specific performance is not an available remedy as courts will not order an employer to reinstate an employee for breach of contract. The rationale is that due performance is too difficult for a court to supervise and that a court is unwilling to force continuation of a personal relationship.

Edwards must opt for either restitution or damages. Because Edwards has transferred a unique thing—rights to a patent—to Telefonica in exchange (in part) for a percentage of the profits from its exploitation, the remedy at law is less than adequate. Consequently, an action in equity for specific restitution is available. In such an action the court can decree the revestment of the patent. In addition, the court can order the payment of damages for breach of the employment aspects of the relation. The identical measure of damages as is applied in a court of law (*see infra*) would be applied.

Another restitutionary remedy would be a quasi-contractual action. In this action Edwards can receive judgment for the reasonable value of the patent. This is likely to be an undesirable choice. Although Edwards receives the value of the patent—assuming it can be established by expert witnesses—Edwards cannot receive damages for breach of the expectations engendered by the employment aspects of the contract. One cannot get contractual and quasi-contractual relief for the same breach, except as modified by statute.

The third option is an action for damages. Normally, this is measured by the value of expectations—the benefit of the bargain. As for loss of salary, Edwards is entitled to the promised salary less what is earned or reasonably should be earned by exercising reasonable diligence during the term of the contract. Whether the choice of activities was reasonable raises essentially questions of fact. The value of the research services to himself or herself may be deducted from the salary. The recovery will also be reduced by application of the present worth doctrine.

In the action for damages Edwards would also be entitled to the expected 5% of profits. The difficulty, however, is whether this amount can be proved with reasonable certainty. The converter is new and has never been mass produced, much less marketed. Whether it would be a success, and whether it would be profitable, is unknown. Also unknown is whether Titanic will regard the products as satisfactory. To assess 5% of unknown profits would be speculative. Should Telefonica before trial develop a history of profitability, however, this fact may remove the uncertainty.

(b) Generally, a seller in default is made to pay the difference between the market price (or cover price) and the contract price. In a seller's market, the market price generally exceeds the contract price and Telefonica is entitled to damages on this basis. But here, Telefonica's economic loss doubtless exceeds this by far. Because it was unable to cover, (assuming it proves there was no reasonable way to cover), it suffered serious consequential injury. Damages for such injury are available if the seller had reason to know of the needs of the buyer and the buyer cannot minimize the loss by cover. International knew Telefonica's needs and Telefonica apparently could not cover. Consequently, International is liable for Telefonica's lost profits.

As discussed in (a) these may be too speculative. Alternatively, Telefonica's reliance damages can be redressed. These would include the rental value of the plant, wasted salaries, unsalvageable materials and the like. It would also include damages Telefonica may have to pay to Titanic, but not damages payable to Edwards, because the breach with Edwards was not proximately caused by International's breach.

(c) Although International may recover for breach against Japan Metals and may recover market price minus contract price damages, it may not recover consequential damages. There are no facts indicating that Japan Metals knew the particular needs of Telefonica.

Multiple Choice Answers

A. b. Walsh's expectation of a profit is $45,000 ($300,000 price minus $255,000 cost of performance). In addition, Walsh is entitled to its sunk costs which it cannot salvage—$80,000 ($90,000 minus $10,000 salvage). The two recoverable sums ($45,000 plus $80,000) add up to $125,000, but Walsh has received $60,000 from Jones that must be subtracted from its entitlement.

B. a. If Walsh is relegated to its reliance interest, perhaps because Walsh is unable to prove what its profit would be, Walsh would be entitled to its sunk costs which it cannot salvage—$80,000 ($90,000 minus $10,000 salvage). Because Walsh has received $60,000, it is entitled to judgment for $20,000.

C. c. If Construction Co. were to be awarded the expectation interest under the contract, it would be in bad shape, because the expectation is that if it completed the contract it would be at a loss of $50,000. Reliance interest recovery would yield $75,000. It had incurred costs of $125,000 and received $50,000. Combining these numbers yields $75,000. The Restitution interest yields the reasonable value of Construction Co.'s work, which is one half of $300,000 ($150,000). From this, we subtract the payments received of $50,000. The bottom line is $100,000.

D. d. The calculations done in the prior answer provide the answer here.

Because the job would be done at a loss, Construction Co. has no expectation of a profit. Therefore, its expectancy interest would be limited to what it has spent in reliance on the contract—$125,000. From this, the $50,000 down payment must be subtracted. Recovery would be $75,000. This is precisely the reliance damages. Restitutionary recovery would give Construction Co. the value of the work performed. Since the value of the total job is $300,000, and it is half done, the value of the work done is $150,000. Again, the down payment would be subtracted. Judgment would be for $100,000.

CHAPTER IX. AVOIDANCE OR REFORMATION FOR MISCONDUCT OR MISTAKE

1. ***False.*** The answer might be "True" if *B* were a carpenter, but absent a specific showing that *B,* a lawyer, was knowledgeable about lumber prices, it cannot be said that the mistake was obvious to *B.*

2. ***False.*** Today, relief from mistake is not denied merely because the mistake is unilateral.

3. ***False.*** Negligence is not a bar to relief for mistake.

4. ***True.*** *B* has changed position by building the deck. The case is different from the XYZ stock case used in the illustration. Although *B* is enriched by having a deck at a cheap cost for lumber, there is no practical way for *B* to restore the lumber. In the XYZ case, money can be paid back.

5. The heirs would be unsuccessful if they sought to set aside the contract on grounds of unconscionability. Because of the interest-free financing, there is a great disparity between the value of the property ($40,000) and the present value of a promise to pay that sum over 40 years. Although such disparity can be circumstantial evidence of unconscionable conduct, it is rebutted by the circumstances that indicate a partially donative intent by Mrs. Klaus.

The evidence may well tend to show that Mrs. Klaus intended to benefit "*Lutheran* religious and educational purposes" rather than religious and educational purposes *in general*. Nonetheless, the contract does not so state. This evidence would be admissible in an action for reformation where the parol evidence rule is inapplicable. For the action to succeed, however, it is not sufficient to prove Mrs. Klaus' lack of interest in furthering the work of non-Lutheran groups, nor is it sufficient to prove that Mrs. Klaus affirmatively intended to benefit only Lutheran groups. It must be shown that it was *agreed* between the parties that the use of the land would be limited to Lutheran organizations. It must also be shown that the writing failed to reflect this agreement because of the misconduct of the Association or because of mistake. Did the Association deliberately palm off the writing as reflecting the agreement (if there was one) to limit the land to Lutheran uses? If so, reformation will be granted. Similarly, if it can be shown that both parties were under the mistaken belief that the contract limited the use of the land in accordance with the still hypothetical agreement, reformation would be available. The prospects for success appear minimal based on the summary of the evidence given in the problem. There is no reference to the essential fact—that there be an agreement that, because of fraud or mistake, was not incorporated into the writing. It should be pointed out that if such evidence were to be found, say, by discovery, there would be no economic benefit to the heirs by a decree of reformation. The intent of their ancestor, would, however, be carried out.

A remedy that would produce economic benefits to the heirs would be the avoidance of the contract and recovery of the land. If the contract is recorded with the registry of deeds (or its local equivalent) a decree of cancellation would be required. It is again doubtful whether this remedy is available to the heirs. There is nothing to indicate that the Association misrepresented any fact to Mrs. Klaus or that it misrepresented the content or legal effect of the writing. If so, there would be a basis for avoiding the contract. The mere fact that Mrs. Klaus mistakenly assumed that the land would be used solely by Lutheran organizations is not a sufficient basis for avoidance. Her mistaken belief (if indeed it can be proved she had this belief) that the contract restricted the use to such organizations is not grounds for rescission unless it can be proved that this belief was induced by the Association or shared by the Association.

Assuming there were grounds for rescission or reformation, there is a possible affirmative defense. Neither remedy will be allowed on grounds of mistake (as opposed to misrepresentation) if there is a change of position by the Association. The announced deal with the Alliance may be such a change of position. Indeed, if a contract has been entered into with the Alliance, these remedies would be unavailable to the Klaus heirs even if misrepresentation were proved, providing the Alliance is a good faith purchaser for value and without notice of the equities of the heirs.

CHAPTER X. THIRD PARTY BENEFICIARIES

1. ***False.*** Generally, a promisor may not raise defenses that the promisee has against the beneficiary.

2. ***True.*** *T*'s rights against *A* are dependent upon the intent of *B* and *A* to benefit *T*. Such intent is excluded by the quoted term.

3. When Enterprise promised Starr to pay $100,000 to State Bank to satisfy Starr's obligation to the Bank, the Bank became a third party intended creditor beneficiary of the contract between Enterprise and Starr. Performance of Enterprise's promise to pay directly to the Bank would clearly benefit the Bank and is intended by the contract. Similarly, the warranty holders are intended creditor beneficiaries inasmuch as the contract requires Enterprise to honor justified warranty claims presented by them.

The absence of notification is of no relevance. The absence of knowledge of the contract is equally irrelevant on the facts. Notice of the existence of the promise for the benefit of the third party is not needed. Notice is relevant on the issue of whether Starr and Enterprise could have modified or rescinded the agreement by mutual agreement, but that issue does not arise under the facts.

In the action by State Bank, Enterprise can raise against the State Bank any defense it has against Starr, based on the general rule that the promisor may raise against the beneficiary any defense it has against the promisee. The obvious potential defense is that of avoidance of the contract on the ground of Starr's material misrepresentation of fact. Enterprise, however, can use this against Starr only by way of defense. State Bank is not liable for any damages suffered by Enterprise beyond the amount of Starr's obligation to State Bank.

For the same reasons, Enterprise can raise against the warranty holders the same defenses it has against Starr and State Bank.

4. Ms. *T* is clearly an intended beneficiary of Mrs. *S*'s promise to convey the real property, as performance runs directly to her. She is apparently a donee beneficiary as the facts fail to indicate any obligation owed by Mr. *B* to Ms. *T*. Her rights have vested as she knows of the contract and has assented to it, but this fact is not relevant under the circumstances.

If Ms. *T* would pursue her action against Mrs. *S*, the promisor. Mrs. *S* would have the defense of non-payment. Clearly, as a constructive concurrent condition to her duty to convey, payment must be tendered, and the facts indicate this has not and will not happen.

If Ms. *T* were to pursue an action against B's estate, the estate can point out that Mr. *B*'s intention was to provide Ms. *T* with a gift. Delivery of the gift never was effected and there is no obligation for the estate to complete a gift.

CHAPTER XI. ASSIGNMENT AND DELEGATION

1. ***False.*** Although there is some common law authority to the effect that an anti-assignment clause can nullify a purported assignment, this transaction is now governed by Article 9 of the UCC which invalidates any term that purports to restrain the assignability of a right to the payment of money ("account") whether earned or expected to be earned.

2. ***False.*** *See* explanation to the previous question.

3. ***False.*** The New York view is "first in time, first in right." C has a remedy of restitution against D.

4. ***True.*** Under the UCC a filing system has been inaugurated. If the assignee has received an assignment of a significant part of the outstanding accounts of *S,* the first assignee who has given value and who has filed prevails.

5. ***False.*** An assignment is created by words of present transfer. (Do not confuse this rule with the notion that an anti-assignment clause is construed, unless the circumstances indicate to the contrary, as merely forbidding delegation.)

6. ***True.*** Whenever one party to a sale of goods contract delegates all his or her duties, the other contracting party has reasonable grounds for insecurity and may demand assurances of both the delegant and the delegate.

7. ***False.*** The duty is to deliver footballs of certain specifications. *B* has no substantial interest in having *S* personally perform.

8. ***True.*** If *B* deals with *X,* without protesting *S*'s repudiation, *B* is deemed to have agreed to a novation.

9. (a) The initial question is the effect of the anti-assignment clause. Article 2 of the UCC, which applies because the contract is for the sale of goods, provides that unless the contrary intention is manifested, an anti-assignment clause is to be construed as barring only the delegation of duties. Consequently, the assignment is not barred by the anti-assignment clause.

Under the UCC, as at common law, rights are not assignable if the assignment would materially change the duties of the obligee. Abel's duties are not changed. Non-assignability also exists if the obligee's burden or risk is materially changed or if the obligee's chances of getting return performance are materially impaired. None of these rules affects the case at bar. Abel is still entitled to cash and Baker's note. This last credit risk is one Abel voluntarily undertook.

Under UCC Article 2, an assignment in general terms is deemed to be an assignment coupled with a delegation and assumption of duties. Here the delegation is barred by the anti-assignment clause. Therefore, the delegation is ineffective, but is not a material breach unless persisted in. Abel's remedy for the uncertainty created by the transaction between Baker and Caleb would be to demand assurances of each of them. Consequently, Abel's letter of March 6th was an over-reaction and a repudiation, entitling Caleb to bring an immediate action for anticipatory breach.

In such an action the plaintiff's tender of performance is excused, but plaintiff must show that but for the repudiation plaintiff would have been ready, willing and able to perform on the date performance was due. Caleb thus may recover on a showing of the source from which the cash payment was to come and that Baker's note would have been tendered.

(b) Abel's retraction is timely. There is no indication that either Caleb or Baker changed position in reliance upon the repudiation or stated that the contract was at an end. Consequently, Abel may retract, reinstating the duties of all parties.

Both Caleb and Baker would be liable. Baker is liable on the original contract. It is simply impossible for an obligor to transfer or divest an obligation except with the consent of the obligee.

Caleb's liability is less clear. As stated earlier, general words of assignment also carry with it a delegation and assumption of duties. Such delegation is barred by the anti-assignment clause. Arguably, however, when Abel retracts, Abel is waiving the non-delegability of the duties and more likely the non-assumability of the duties. Since an assumption of liability can only benefit Abel, such a waiver is probably in accord with Abel's real intent.

Of course, Caleb's refusal of delivery was a material breach. In contracts for the sale of goods, refusal to accept delivery within the contract term is a material breach which justifies cancellation of the contract and triggers a right to demand damages for total breach.

Appendix B

Practice Examinations

MULTIPLE CHOICE QUESTIONS

For the purposes of this test, you are to assume that the only statutes in effect are the UCC, all applicable statutes of frauds, and the statute of limitations, but you are not expected to know the content of the statute of limitations.

1. On March 31, *B* loaned *C* $500. On April 1, *A* wrote *B* as follows: "Please lend to *C*, at his request, from time to time during the next six months, whatever *C* requires, but not to exceed a total of $5,000, and I will see to it that you are paid. (Signed) *A*." On April 3, *B* replied: "I undertake to make the loans to *C* in accordance with your offer. (Signed *B*)." *A* received the letter on April 3.

   a. *B*'s reply of April 2 created a contract between *A* and *B* when the letter of reply was mailed.

   b. *B*'s reply of April 2 created a contract between *A* and *B* when it was received by *A*.

   c. *A* is not liable to *B* on the loan of March 31.

   d. Two of the above statements are correct.

   e. The statements made in (a), (b), and (c) are all correct.

   f. None of the above statements is correct.

2. *B*, in Chicago, called *X* in New York City, knowing that *X* was going to make a trip to Chicago and said, "if you will agree to pick up my son at Memorial Sloan Kettering Hospital on Thursday morning and escort him to Chicago, I will meet you at the airport and pay for your trip and I authorize you to fly first class." *X* agreed. The cost of *X*'s airline ticket was $900.

   a. If *X* already intended to fly to Chicago on Thursday, *X*'s promise to escort *B*'s son would nevertheless furnish consideration to support *B*'s promise.

   b. If *X*'s employer had already agreed to pay for *X*'s travel expenses, because *X* was going to Chicago on company business, *B*'s promise was not supported by consideration.

   c. If *X* attempted to recover from *B*, *B* would have the defense of the statute of frauds because the flight cost more than $500.

   d. Two of the above statements are correct.

   e. The statements made in (a), (b), and (c) are all correct.

f. None of the above statements is correct.

3. On May 1, 1979, Model entered into a contract with Brush, a portrait painter, whereby Brush agreed to paint Model's portrait for $3,000 of which $1,000 was to be paid immediately, $1,000 on June 1, and $1,000 on completion of the portrait, provided Model was satisfied with it. Brush promised to commence the work on May 4 and to complete it on or before June 20. The $1,000 was paid and Brush began to work. He continued diligently to work until June 4 when he, Brush, was dissatisfied with the painting and said he would not complete it. Model had not then made the second payment of $1,000.

a. The satisfaction clause in the contract gave rise to an illusory promise.

b. Model had the right to start suit on June 4 against Brush for damages for breach of contract.

c. If the painting had been destroyed by fire when half completed without the fault of Brush or Model, Brush would have the defense of impossibility of performance.

d. Two of the above statements are correct.

e. The statements made in (a), (b), and (c) are all correct.

f. None of the above statements is correct.

4. *A* called *B*, his nephew, and stated: "If you move into my house and take care of me for the rest of my life, you shall have free board and lodging and my estate will pay you $200,000 upon my death." After the phone call, *B* moved into *A*'s house and cared for *A* for five years. At that point, *A* evicted *B* from the house without cause. *A* died the following year.

a. In most jurisdictions, *A* would have the defense of the statute of frauds.

b. Since the express condition attached to *A*'s promise was not performed, *A*'s estate is liable not in contract but in quasi-contract.

c. *B*'s moving into the house and beginning to take care of *A* made *A*'s offer irrevocable.

d. Two of the above statements are correct.

e. The statements made in (a), (b), and (c) are all correct.

f. None of the above statements is correct.

5. X Corp., on June 1, entered into an oral contract to construct a ten-mile length of Z Railroad Company's railroad line running along the flank of a mountain for a fee of $12,000,000. The parties agreed that the work was to be completed within 3 years. Z agreed to pay X Corp. $1,000,000 at the completion of each mile, and an additional payment of $2,000,000 at the end.

a. This was a divisible contract.

b. The contract was within the one-year statute of frauds.

c. In the absence of the railroad's agreement to make periodic payments or a custom to make such payments, X Corp. would not be entitled to any payment until it had completed the work.

d. Two of the above statements are correct.

e. The statements made in (a), (b), and (c) are all correct.

f. None of the above statements is correct.

6. John and Alice had a child who was born out of wedlock in a state that did not require John to support the child. Thereafter, Alice obtained a position with a company that was 200 miles away. Her contract with the company was for a five-year period and required her to move within 20 miles of the job site. When John learned of this, he considered the move to be in the best interests of all concerned, and, in consideration of Alice's moving, promised to make certain child-support payments to her until the child became 21. Alice moved. John died two years after making the agreement without having made any payments.

a. If John's promise was oral it could not be enforced for that reason.

b. Alice could claim that the promise was enforceable under a theory of moral obligation as articulated in the Restatement (Second).

c. Many jurisdictions would hold that John's promise is not enforceable because Alice furnished no consideration.

d. If there was a binding arrangement between John and Alice, John's death would discharge the obligation.

e. All of the above statements are correct.

f. Three of the statements made in (a), (b), (c) and (d) are correct.

g. Two of the statements made in (a), (b), (c) and (d) are correct.

h. None of the above statements is correct.

7. On Dec. 7, Dan lost his dog, Rover. He placed an advertisement in the New York Times on Dec. 8, 9 and 10 in which he stated he would pay $500 for the return of the dog. Dan caused a notice of revocation to be placed in the Times on January 2, 3, and 4. Pam saw the December notice but never saw any of the January notices.

a. If Pam found and returned the dog on January 5, her acceptance would be effective.

b. The death of the dog before it was returned would terminate the offer.

c. If Pam, knowing of the offer, found and returned Rover on Dec. 11, with primary motive of earning a girl scout merit badge, she would not be entitled to the reward.

d. If Pam started to look for the dog prior to January 2, the offer would not be revocable as to her.

e. All of the above statements are correct.

f. Three of the statements made in (a), (b), (c) and (d) are correct.

g. Two of the statements made in (a), (b), (c) and (d) are correct.

h. None of the above statements is correct.

8. On January 2, 2004, *S* and *B* entered into a written contract, subscribed by both of them, by which *B* promised to pay *S* $8,000 for a certain lot, $1,000 upon signing the contract (which *B* paid), $1,000 on Jan. 2, 2005, $1,000 on Jan. 2, 2006, $1,000 on Jan. 2, 2007, when *B* was to receive the deed, and the balance of $4,000 on Jan. 2, 2008. *S* promised to deliver the deed on the making of the 2007 payment.

a. The contract was divisible.

b. *B*'s promise to make the 2005 payment was unconditional.

c. *B*'s promise to make the 2007 payment was a dependent one.

d. Two of the above statements are correct.

e. The statements made in (a), (b), and (c) are all correct.

f. None of the above statements is correct.

9. *A* and *B* entered into a written contract, subscribed by both parties, whereby *A* agreed to sell and *B* agreed to buy 400 tons of coal at $75 per ton to be delivered in four equal monthly installments on the first day of each month starting on Feb. 1. Payment for each installment was to be made 20 days after delivery. *A* delivered the first installment on Feb. 1, as per the contract. *B* did not pay for this installment. On Feb. 16, *A* made a written assignment of rights under its coal contract to *C*, for value, as security for a loan. *B* learned of this assignment on Feb. 20.

a. If *B* had paid *A* the price for the first installment on Feb. 18, *B* would be discharged of liability to *C* as to that installment.

b. If *B* had accepted delivery of, but had not paid *A* the price for, the first installment and *B* had a claim for damages based on breach of warranty because of the defective quality of the coal delivered on Feb. 1, *B* could assert the claim to defeat or diminish *C*'s recovery in an action by *C* to recover the price of the first installment.

c. If *A* failed to deliver the installment due on March 1, *B* could successfully assert this failure to defeat or diminish *C*'s recovery in an action by *C* to recover the price for the first installment.

d. Two of the above statements are correct.

e. The statements made in (a), (b), and (c) are all correct.

f. None of the above statements is correct.

10. *A* offers to sell a specific automobile to *B*. Before *B* can accept, the automobile is destroyed through no fault of either party.

a. The facts present a problem relating to the doctrine of termination of offers.

b. The facts present a problem relating to the doctrine of supervening impossibility.

c. The facts present a problem relating to the doctrine of existing impossibility.

d. The facts present a problem relating to the doctrine of prospective inability to perform.

e. All of the above statements are correct.

f. Three of the statements made in (a), (b), (c) and (d) are correct.

g. Two of the statements made in (a), (b), (c) and (d) are correct.

h. None of the above statements is correct.

11. *A* makes an offer to sell a specified automobile to *B*. *B* tells *C* of the offer. *C* sends a letter stating that she accepts, and *B* agrees to sell the automobile to *C*.

a. There is no contract because an offer is not assignable.

b. There is a contract because *C* may accept a non-personal offer.

c. There is a contract because there was a delegation of duties that resulted in a novation.

d. Two of the above statements are correct.

e. The statements made in (a), (b), and (c) are all correct.

f. None of the above statements is correct.

12. *S* offered to sell *B* certain goods at a 10% discount from the market price for so long as *B* desired to purchase such goods from *S*. *B* said, "I accept your offer."

a. The agreement is void.

b. If the agreement is void, the net effect of the agreement would be that *S* made an offer looking to a series of contracts.

c. The agreement does not violate the one-year statute of frauds.

d. Two of the above statements are correct.

e. The statements made in (a), (b) and (c) are all correct.

f. None of the above statements is correct.

13. *A* owed *B* $5,000 and entered into an agreement with *C*, who orally agreed to assume the obligation of *A*. There was no consideration for *C*'s promise to assume.

a. *C*'s promise is not enforceable by *A*.

b. *B* is a third party intended beneficiary of *C*'s promise made to *A*.

c. Even if *B* is a third party intended beneficiary of *C*'s promise made to *A*, *B* may not enforce the promise.

d. Two of the above statements are correct.

e. The statements in (a), (b), and (c) are all correct.

f. None of the above statements is correct.

14. On January 2, *S* and *B* entered into oral agreement under which *S* was to supply *B* with *B*'s requirements of oil for one year commencing January 3rd, for the oil burner in *B*'s one-family house. *B* promised to pay the market price at the time of delivery.

a. *B*'s promise is illusory because *B* could convert to gas and not have any requirements.

b. The agreement is within the one-year statute of frauds.

c. The agreement could be orally modified without consideration.

d. Two of the statements are correct.

e. The statements made in (a), (b), and (c) are all correct.

f. None of the above statements is correct.

15. *A* was injured in a train wreck. *A* and the general manager of the railroad entered into an agreement whereby in consideration of $1,000 paid to *A* and the promise of a job for life as gate tender at $800 per month. *A* released the railroad from all his claims. After three years in such a job, *A* became hopelessly bedridden by "Lou Gehrig's disease" and was dismissed by the railroad.

a. The railroad was never bound by this promise of employment.

b. Even if the railroad was bound initially, it is now legally discharged.

c. Even if the railroad was bound, in most jurisdictions, the statute of frauds would prevent enforcement by the employee.

d. Two of the above statements are correct.

e. Statements (a), (b) and (c) are all correct.

f. None of the above statements is correct.

16. *S* sold and delivered 1,000 lawnmowers to *B*, payable in three monthly installments of $55.00 each. If *B* fails to make timely payment of the first installment, *S*

a. may sue immediately only for the past due installment.

b. may sue immediately for the entire purchase price, including installments due in the future.

c. must wait until the last installment is overdue before commencing any action.

d. Two of the above statements are correct.

e. Statements (a), (b) and (c) are all correct.

f. None of the above statements is correct.

17. *X* rendered carpentry services to *C* at *B*'s request. The price of the services was not discussed. The reasonable value of these services was $500.

a. *A* subsequent promise by *B* to pay $500 for the services would be unenforceable because *B* received no benefit.

b. *A* subsequent promise, by whichever of the parties is liable to pay for the services, to pay $600 would be unenforceable for lack of consideration.

c. Statements (a) and (b) are both correct.

d. Neither statement (a) nor (b) is correct.

18. *A*'s car is in *B*'s garage pursuant to a written lease of garage space. The lease concludes with a merger clause. Later, *A* offers by mail to sell to *B* the car for $4,500, saying: "I am so sure that you will accept that you need not trouble to write me."

a. If *B* makes no reply, but does not intend to accept, there is no contract.

b. If *B* makes no reply, intending to accept, there is a contract.

c. The parol evidence rule would make it impossible to prove that there is a contract if *B* fails to sign a writing.

d. Two of the above statements are correct.

e. Statements (a) and (b) and (c) are all correct.

f. None of the above statements is correct.

19. *A* agreed to make certain alterations on *B*'s house for $35,000.

a. *A* would be entitled to periodic payments in the absence of a provision therefor in the contract and in the absence of a custom to that effect.

b. *A*'s substantial performance is a constructive condition to *B*'s duty to pay.

c. If *A* hired a plumbing subcontractor to do the plumbing work and the building was destroyed by fire through no fault of *A*, when the plumbing was 45% completed, the plumbing subcontractor could successfully sue *A* for breach of contract.

d. Two of the above statements are correct.

e. The statements made in (a), (b) and (c) are all correct.

f. None of the above statements is correct.

20. On March 1, *A* and *B* entered into a written agreement subscribed by both parties by the terms of which *A* was to act as a valet for *B* for one year starting April 1, and *B* was to pay him $26,000 per year payable $500 weekly.

a. This would amount to hiring at will.

b. If *B* wrongfully repudiated the arrangement on April 15, and *A* died on April 30, *A*'s estate would not be entitled to damages for the period beyond April 30.

c. If *A* wrongfully repudiated the arrangement on April 15, and *A* died on April 30, *B* could recover damages for the entire period of nonperformance.

d. Two of the above statements are correct.

e. The statements made in (a), (b) and (c) are all correct.

f. None of the above statements is correct.

21. *A* and *B* entered into a contract by the terms of which *A* was to build a house for *B* on *A*'s property. When the house was complete, *A* was to convey to *B* for a designated price.

a. If the house was nearly completed when it was destroyed in a riot, *A* would have the defense of impossibility or impracticability.

b. *A* would be entitled to periodic payments as the building progressed.

c. Payment and delivery of the deed are concurrent conditions.

d. Two of the above statements are correct.

e. The statements made in (a), (b), and (c) are all correct.

f. None of the above statements is correct.

22. *A* offered to pay *B* $5,000 for a portrait of *A*'s son, *C*, if *B* promised to paint the portrait to *A*'s personal satisfaction. *B* so promised. *A*'s offer also promised *B* that *C* would pose for the portrait so that *B* could paint a living likeness.

a. *A*'s promise is conditioned by an express condition of personal satisfaction.

b. If *A* is dissatisfied with the portrait, *A* has a cause of action against *B*.

c. If *A*'s son, *C*, died before the portrait was commenced, *A* and *B* would be discharged from their obligations.

d. Two of the above statements are correct.

e. The statements made in (a), (b) and (c) are all correct.

f. None of the above statements is correct.

23. *A* owes *B* $1,000 here and now undisputedly due. *B* agrees to discharge the debt now in exchange for *A*'s promise to pay $950 in two months and *A* so promises.

a. The agreement between *A* and *B*, if valid, would be an executory accord.

b. The agreement between *A* and *B*, if valid, would be a substituted agreement.

c. The agreement between *A* and *B* was void.

d. Statements (a) and (c) are correct.

e. Statements (b) and (c) are correct.

f. The statements made in (a), (b) and (c) are all correct.

g. None of the above statements is correct.

24. *A*, a producer who wished to put on a theatrical performance, hired *B*, an inexperienced actor, to play a minor part. Under the relevant law, *A* needed a license to put on the performance. The license was for the protection of the public. At the time *B* entered into the contract, *B* was unaware that *A* did not have a license or even that a license was required. When *B* became aware of these matters she refused to perform.

a. *A* can enforce the contract because *B* is not a member of the public.

b. *B* could recover on the contract because she was unaware that *A* did not have a license.

c. *B* could recover on the contract because she could justifiably rely on *A*'s superior knowledge of the law.

d. Two of the above statements are correct.

e. The statements in (a), (b), and (c) are correct.

f. None of the above statements is correct.

25. At *B*'s request, *A* promised *B* to smuggle certain goods into the country. *B* promised in exchange to paint *A*'s house.

a. The agreement is void.

b. If *B* performed, *B* could recover under the doctrine of severability.

c. If *B* performed, *B* could recover under the doctrine of *locus poenitentiae*.

d. Two of the above statements are correct.

e. All of the statements in (a), (b) or (c) are all correct.

f. None of the above statements is correct.

26. Choose the most correct of d, e, f, and g.

a. The Parol Evidence Rule does not have any application to subsequent agreements.

b. The UCC has a section that under certain circumstances excludes modification or rescission without a signed writing.

c. The UCC has a section that under certain circumstances validates an oral modification of a contract even though the modification is without consideration.

d. One of the above statements is correct.

e. Two of the statements in (a), (b), and (c) are correct.

f. The statements in (a), (b) and (c) are all correct.

g. None of the above statements is correct.

27. *A* owed *B* $1,000, collection of which was barred by the statute of limitations.

a. *B* may recover the balance of the $1,000 if *A* makes a part payment of $100.

b. *B* may recover the $1,000 if *A* orally promises to pay the sum in exchange for *B*'s promise to deliver a theater ticket worth $50.

c. *B* may recover the $1,000 if *A* unconditionally acknowledges the debt in a signed writing.

d. All of the above are correct.

e. Two of the statements made in (a), (b) and (c) are correct.

f. None of the above statements is correct.

28. *A* owed *B* $1,000, collection of which was barred by the statute of limitations, but *A* was unaware that period of limitations had passed.

a. If *C*, without consideration, orally promised *A* to pay the debt, *B* may recover $1,000 from *C*.

b. If *C*, without consideration, promised *A* in writing to pay the debt, *B* may recover $1,000 from *C*.

c. Both of the above statements are correct.

d. Neither (a) nor (b) is correct.

29. *A* and *B* entered into an oral contract in November of 2008 by which *A* and *B* agreed that *B* was to have the exclusive right to act as sales representative for *A*'s beer in Raintree County for one year commencing on Jan. 1, and *B* was to exercise best efforts to promote the sale of *A*'s beer and was to receive a commission of 5%, payable monthly, on all sales made during the year.

a. The agreement is too vague and indefinite to be enforced.

b. The agreement contravenes the one-year statute of frauds.

c. If *A* and *B* continued to perform beyond December 31, it could be inferred that the parties agreed to be bound for another year.

d. Two of the above statements are correct.

e. The statements made in (a), (b) and (c) are all correct.

f. None of the above statements is correct.

30. Defendant issued a disability policy to plaintiff promising payment of $500 a week for total disability and $150 a week for partial disability as defined in the policy.

a. If plaintiff became permanently totally disabled, but the defendant wrongly concluded that plaintiff was faking the disability and refused to pay anything, plaintiff could sue for total breach.

b. Assume plaintiff and defendant had a good faith dispute as to the degree of plaintiff's disability, and the defendant sent a check to the plaintiff for $3,000 with a legend clearly stating that, if plaintiff cashed it, plaintiff accepted it in full payment of all rights against defendant. If plaintiff deposited it, there would be an accord and satisfaction.

c. The insurance policy was a divisible contract.

d. Two of the above statements are correct.

e. None of the above statements is correct.

31. Under Article 2 of the Uniform Commercial Code:

a. Unless the circumstances indicate the contrary, a prohibition of assignment of "the contract" is to be construed as barring only the delegation to the assignee of the assignor's performance.

b. An assignment of "the contract" is an assignment of rights and unless the language or the circumstances indicate the contrary, it is also a delegation of performance of the duties.

c. The other party may treat any assignment that delegates performance as creating reasonable grounds for insecurity.

d. Two of the above statements are correct.

e. The statements made in (a), (b) and (c) are all correct.

f. None of the above statements is correct.

32. *A*, who is not a merchant, in a subscribed writing, offered to sell a specific antique car to *B*, if *B* gave *A* her promissory note in the amount of $50,000. By its terms, in consideration of $250, the offer was not to be withdrawn for 100 days.

a. The offer is revocable because it exceeds three months.

b. The offer is revocable because *A* is not a merchant.

c. If *B* assigned her rights and delegated her duties to *C*, and *C* tendered *C*'s promissory note in the amount of $50,000 to *A*, *A* would be required to accept it and deliver the car to *C*.

d. Two of the above statements are correct.

e. The statements made in (a), (b), and (c) are all correct.

f. None of the above statements is correct.

33. *S* and *B* entered into an oral contract for the sale of goods for 1,000 widgets at a price of $1.00 per widget. Delivery was to be made six months after the contract was made. Before delivery, the parties orally agreed that the price would be raised to $1.05 per widget and only 400 widgets should be supplied.

a. The second oral agreement is a modification that need not be supported by consideration to be effective.

b. The second oral agreement is supported by consideration.

c. Neither agreement is enforceable because of the UCC statute of frauds.

d. Two of the above statements are correct.

e. The statements made in (a), (b), and (c) are all correct.

f. None of the above statements is correct.

34. *A* and *S* entered into a written agreement, subscribed by both parties, by the terms of which *A* was to receive 5% of the gross receipts (payable annually) received by *S*, if *A* induced *C* corporation to enter into a five-year requirements contract with *S*.

a. If *A* succeeded because *A* bribed *C*'s purchasing agent, *A* could not recover from *S*.

b. If *A* succeeded without bribing anyone, and the agreement between *A* and *S* was oral, *S* would have the defense of the statute of frauds.

c. If, at the end of the first year, *S* repudiated the written contract, A could bring an action for total breach.

d. Two of the above statements are correct.

e. The statements made in (a), (b), and (c) are all correct.

f. None of the above statements is correct.

35. *A* agreed to work for *B* as a valet for six months. After two months of performance, *B* asked *A* if *A* would be willing to terminate their agreement and work for *C* for the remaining four months. *A* agreed as did *C*.

a. *B* continued to remain liable to *A*.

b. *B* could not have transferred his rights under the contract to *C* without *A*'s consent.

c. If *B* had died before the second agreement mentioned, *A* would have been obliged to serve *B*'s executor.

d. Two of the above statements are correct.

e. The statements made in (a), (b) and (c) are all correct.

f. None of the above statements is correct.

36. *A*, an architect, contracted, on February 1, with *Z* to prepare plans for the construction of a building. *A* agreed to start work on the plans by June 1. On May 1, *A* suffered a stroke. *Z* telephoned to determine if *A* would be able to perform. *A* told *Z* that *A*'s doctors had prognosticated that *A* would be disabled from working for at least ten months. *Z* then contracted on May 15 with *B* for preparation of the plans. *A*'s doctors were, however, wrong in their prognosis and, on June 1, *A* was ready, willing and able to perform.

a. In an action by *A* against *Z*, *Z* has the defense of prospective inability to perform.

b. In an action by *B* against *Z* (assuming *Z* refused to honor the contract with *B*), *Z* has the defense of impossibility of performance by virtue of the prior contract with *A*.

c. Both of the statements (a) and (b) are correct.

d. Neither of the statements in (a) and (b) is correct.

37. *A* hired *B* as a clerk on the day shift for a six-month term. The parties subscribed a detailed printed form contract that contained a merger clause. The salary blank was filled into read that *B* would receive $500 per week.

a. In fact, the parties orally agreed that $550 per week would be paid and that the writing would not show this, as other clerks in the office might discover that *B* was receiving a higher salary than they were receiving. *B* may enforce the promise of a salary of $550 per week.

b. In fact, the parties orally agreed that *B* would not be bound on the contract unless *B* could obtain transportation in a carpool on specified terms and conditions. *A* may enforce the contract even though such transportation is not available.

c. One month after entering into the contract, the parties orally agreed that *B* would work the night shift for the balance of the contract term and would receive $600 per week. *B* may enforce this promise.

d. None of the above statements is correct.

e. Each of the statements made in (a), (b) and (c) is correct.

f. Two of the statements made in (a), (b) and (c) are correct.

38. *B* contracted in a subscribed writing, on February 1, to purchase a house and lot from *S*. Title was to be conveyed free of any encumbrance on June 1. A title search, made on

March 1, revealed that a mortgage existed as a lien on the premises and had existed for three years prior to contracting.

a. *B* may cancel the contract on the grounds of prospective inability to perform.

b. *B* may sue for anticipatory breach.

c. *B* writes to *S* on March 1: "I will take title despite the mortgage"; and, on March 3, *B* writes to *S*, "I have reconsidered. I will not take title unless the mortgage lien is removed." *B* is obligated to take title encumbered by the mortgage.

d. All of the statements made in (a), (b) and (c) are correct.

e. Two of the statements made in (a), (b) and (c) are correct.

f. None of the statements made in (a), (b) and (c) is correct.

39. On February 1, *A* distributed printed announcements that on June 1 an auction would be held at his premises of certain paintings "to be sold to the highest bidder."

a. If *B* comes to New York from Chicago to attend the auction, and on the morning of June 1, *A* announces that the auction is canceled, *B* has no cause of action for breach of contract.

b. If the auction is held as announced, the auction is without reserve.

c. If the auction is announced to be with reserve and the seller, secretly acting through an agent, is the highest bidder on an item, the highest bidder who is not the seller's agent may take the goods at the "last good faith bid."

d. The statements in (a), (b) and (c) are all correct.

e. Two of the statements in (a), (b) and (c) are all correct.

f. None of the statements in (a), (b) and (c) is correct.

40. *B* purchased a tractor from *S*, financing the purchase price by signing a note and giving the seller a security interest in the tractor. Subsequently *B* sold the tractor to *Y*.

a. If *Y* assumed the debt, in an action by *S*, absent language or circumstances that showed a contrary intention, *Y* may raise the defense that *B* misrepresented the condition of the tractor.

b. If in the agreement between *B* and *Y*, *Y* had promised *B* to pay off the indebtedness to *S*, but the agreement contained a clause stating "*S* shall have no right to enforce this agreement," *S* would be barred from recovering judgment from *Y*.

c. If *Y* assumed the debt, absent language or circumstances that showed a contrary intention, in an action by *S* against *Y*, *Y* may properly raise as a defense against *S* the fact that the tractor was defective when *S* sold it to *B*.

d. The statements made in (a), (b) and (c) are all correct.

e. Two of the statements made in (a), (b) and (c) are correct.

f. None of the statements made in (a), (b) and (c) is correct.

41. *B* contracted in a subscribed writing on February 1 to purchase a house and lot from *S*. Title was to be conveyed on June 1. Time was stated in the contract to be of the essence and the contract recited valid and sufficient reasons why time should be of the essence.

a. Transfer of title by *S* on June 1, is an express condition to *B*'s duty to pay the price.

b. Transfer of title by *S* on June 1, is a constructive condition to *B*'s duty to pay the price.

c. Failure by *S* to tender a sufficient conveyance on June 1, is a failure of condition but not a breach of contract.

d. Failure by *S* to tender a sufficient conveyance on June 1, is a breach of contract but not a failure of condition.

e. Three of the statements made in (a), (b), (c) and (d) are correct.

f. Two of the statements made in (a), (b), (c) and (d) are correct.

g. None of the statements made in (a), (b), (c) and (d) is correct.

42. *S* mailed an offer to *B* to sell 50 widgets at a specified price. *B* immediately mailed a letter of acceptance. The letter was delayed and arrived 5 days later. *S* died a day before the letter was delivered. *B*, who was unaware of *S*'s death immediately after dispatching the letter of acceptance changed position in reliance on the existence of the contract of purchase and made this known to *S*'s executor before the executor could take any action.

a. *S*'s offer terminated immediately upon his death and therefore no contract was formed.

b. *S*'s executor is not entitled to use impossibility of performance as a defense to an action by *B* on the contract.

c. *A* valid contract arose upon *B*'s mailing of a letter of acceptance.

d. Two of the above statements are correct.

e. The statements made in (a), (b), and (c) are all correct.

f. None of the above statements is correct.

ANSWERS TO MULTIPLE CHOICE QUESTIONS

1. c. Both a and b are incorrect. *A*'s offer to guarantee payment of loans made to *C* is an offer to a unilateral contract even under the modern approach. The offeree may accept by promise only if (1) the offer is unambiguously an offer to a bilateral contract, or (2) is indifferent to the manner acceptance. "Please lend" is unambiguously a request for a performance, not for a promise to perform. Choice c is correct, as the loan had been made prior to the offer. Therefore, it does not come within the terms of the offer, and, even if it came within the terms of the offer, there was no consideration for the guaranty of the past loan.

2. a. The offer need not be the sole inducement for the conduct agreed to. Choice b is incorrect; although *X* may have had a preexisting duty to go to Chicago, he had no duty to escort *B*'s son. Choice c is incorrect; the $500 threshold amount is for the sale of goods. *B*'s promise is not within any of the statutes of frauds.

3. b. Brush's statement that he would not complete the painting is an anticipatory repudiation—an unequivocal refusal to perform. It was unjustified; Model's failure to pay an installment was a breach and a prospective inability, perhaps justifying a suspension of performance, not a cancellation. (Also, there was no clause providing for Brush's satisfaction.) Choice a is incorrect because conditions of personal satisfaction are permitted. Their apparently illusory nature is restricted by obligations of good faith. Choice c is incorrect, because the painting could have been finished before the fire, and, secondly, could have been restarted and completed after the fire.

4. c. The offer unambiguously looks to a unilateral contract. Under the modern and prevailing view an offer to a unilateral contract becomes irrevocable when the offeree commences performance. Choice a is incorrect because most jurisdictions hold that a performance measured by a lifetime is not within the one-year statute of frauds because the person could die within a year from the making of the contract. Moreover, because the proposed contract is unilateral, the contract itself is made only on full performance of the requested act. It would be made at the instant of the promisor's death. Choice b is incorrect because the condition would be excused, and an action could proceed on the contract.

5. c. Statements a and b are incorrect. The contract is clearly not divisible. Note that the final payment is tied to completion of the entire project. Thus, $1,000,000 is not the agreed exchange for each mile. The contract is not within the one-year statute of frauds because it was legally possible to finish the job within one year without breaching the contract. Choice c is correct because, in the absence of contrary agreement, performance of the service must be substantially performed before the promised compensation is earned.

6. c. Under the classical view, Alice furnished no consideration because in moving she was performing her preexisting duty to her employer. Many jurisdictions follow this view. Choice a is incorrect, because if the child were to die within one year of the making of the contract, the essential purpose of the contract would have been fulfilled. Choice b is incorrect; the moral obligation theory of the Restatement (Second) requires that the moral obligation stem from a material benefit received by the promisor. Choice d is incorrect because debts are not discharged by the death of the debtor.

7. b. This answer is correct because the death or destruction of a person or thing necessary for performance terminates the offer. Return of a dog's corpse would not be the return of the dog. Choice a is incorrect; the revocation by equal publication of an advertised offer is effective. Choice c is incorrect; mixed motives for accepting offers do not detract from the validity of the acceptance. Choice d is incorrect; starting to look for the dog is not part performance; it is mere preparation for performance and would not make the offer irrevocable.

8. d. Choice b is correct because there were no conditions tied to the duty to pay. Choice c is correct because it was conditioned on the tender of the deed; where performances by both parties are due at the same time, they are constructively conditioned on each other. Choice a is incorrect; divisibility would exist if the payment were the agreed exchange for some distinct performance by the other.

9. e. Choices a, b and c are each correct. Choice a is correct because the obligor is free to continue to pay the obligee until the obligor receives notice of the assignment. Choice b is correct because, under Article 9 of the UCC, the obligor may raise any defense or counter-claim it has against the assignor that arises under the same contract that the assignee claims under. Although we speak of counter-claim, the more accurate terminology is "recoupment." A recoupment is defensive only and can only be used to defeat or diminish the assignee's recovery. Choice c is correct for the same reason as choice b. Because the counter-claim arises out of the same contract it is immaterial whether it accrued before or after the notice of assignment.

10. g. Choices a and c are each correct. Choice a is correct because an offer terminates if a person or thing essential to performance is destroyed prior to its acceptance. Choice c is correct because if *B* is unaware of the destruction of the automobile, no contract is formed, if at the time the offer is accepted, the contract is impossible or impracticable to perform. Choices b and d could be engaged if there were an existing contract.

11. f. None of the statements is correct. There is a contract because *C*'s purported acceptance is a manifestation of willingness to enter into a contract and, thus, is an offer which *B* accepted. While it is true that offers are not assignable, on the total facts that rule is inapplicable. Choice b is wrong, *C* cannot accept any kind of an offer not made to *C*. Choice c is wrong, a novation is a variety of substituted contract; here there was no prior contract to substitute.

12. d. Choices a and c are both correct. Choice a is correct because *B* has not made a binding promise. *B* has made no commitment to buy, and, indeed, was not asked to make any commitment. *S*'s promise is also illusory making choice b incorrect. *S* has not committed itself to anything; essentially the offered deal is that if *B* orders goods from *S*, and *S* sells the goods to *B*, the price will be at a 10% discount. The reason why *S*'s promise is not an offer is that no quantity term exists. Choice c is correct. Assume that *B* orders goods and *S* fills the order, a contract is made on the basis of *S*'s promise of a discount. Would the one-year provision prevent proof of the promise? No, because each purchase and sale would be a separate contract.

13. e. Choices a, b, and c are all correct. The promise cannot be enforced by *A*, because there was no consideration for the promise. For the same reason, choice c is correct. The general rule is that the promisor may assert any defense against the beneficiary that he or she has against the promisee. No exceptions apply to these facts. Choice b is correct. The promise, although it was not legally binding, was performable by the direct payment by *C* to *B*. This makes *B* an intended beneficiary.

14. c. Choice a is incorrect. *B* has provided consideration by committing himself not to buy oil from any other supplier. Choice b is incorrect. The contract is performable within precisely a year. The law disregards the day on which the contract is made; consequently, Jan 2 is not counted. Choice c is correct. Oil is a good governed by UCC Article 2 which permits modifications without consideration.

15. b. Choice a is incorrect. Promises of permanent or lifetime employment are binding if the employee provides a consideration above and beyond the performance of services. This fact pattern typifies the kind of consideration that supports such a promise—the release of a tort claim.

Choice b is correct. Although lifetime employment is promised, performance of the promise is constructively conditioned on the employee's doing the work. Choice c is incorrect. The measuring period of the contract is *A*'s lifetime. This period could be less than one year.

16. a. If the only remaining duty under a contract is the payment of a liquidated debt in the future, a repudiation or failure to pay an installment does not operate to accelerate the debt. This is unfortunate but true. Consequently, b is incorrect. Because the failure to make the payment is a breach, an immediate action for partial breach is permitted. Thus, c is incorrect.

17. d. Choice a is incorrect. When *B* asks a carpenter to do work for himself or another, *B* is impliedly promising to pay the carpenter, unless, of course, *B* is merely acting as *C*'s agent. But the facts do not indicate any such agency. Choice b is incorrect. *A* promise to pay a sum certain for an unliquidated debt is binding without further consideration. There is some authority to the effect that the promise will not be enforced to the extent it is disproportionate to the amount reasonably due. The disparity between $500 value and the $600 promise does not rise to the kind of disproportion those authorities have in mind.

18. d. Choices a and b are correct. *A*'s offer makes *B*'s silence ambiguous. Because *A* has authorized silence as acceptance, if *B* intends to accept, a contract is formed. Because

A cannot impose a duty on *B* to reply, if *B* does not intend to accept, no contract is made. Choice c is incorrect. The parol evidence rule has no application to any terms agreed to subsequent to a written agreement.

19. b. Choice b is correct. The common law rule is clear that, unless otherwise agreed, work must precede payment. Thus, choice a is incorrect. Choice b is correct, because the rule that work must precede payment is the basis of creating a constructive condition of substantial performance. Choice c is incorrect because destruction of the building makes the subcontractor's performance impossible. There is no breach of contract. The plumbing subcontractor can recover but not in a contract action. Because the contract is not divisible, recovery is in the restitutionary action of quasi contract.

20. b. Choice a is incorrect. Because most hirings are at will, a few students get the wrong impression to the effect that *all* hirings are at will. Hirings are presumptively at will; the presumption here is rebutted by the express written contract providing for a one-year duration. Choice b is correct. In order to recover, *A*'s estate would have to show that *A* would have been ready, willing, and able to perform but for the repudiation. This it cannot do. Choice c is incorrect. Under the prevailing view, impossibility of performance that supervenes after a repudiation is taken into consideration in the measurement of damages. Consequently, *A*'s death excuses the estate from any liability, but also curtails the estate's right to damages.

21. c. Choice a is incorrect. The risk of loss of a building under construction is on the contractor. Choice b is incorrect. Periodic payments need not be made unless the parties agree upon periodic payments. Choice c is correct. Because payment and conveyance are to be made upon completion, the promises are constructively conditioned on each other, i.e., "dependent."

22. d. Choices b and c are correct. Choice a is incorrect because while *B* promised to paint to *A*'s satisfaction, no express condition is stated in the facts. The facts mention only a promise. Any condition of *A*'s satisfaction would be a constructive condition, not an express condition. Precisely because *B* promised to satisfy, *A* would have a cause of action against *B* if *B* failed to perform the promise. Choice c is correct. The contract required *C*'s posing for the portrait, therefore his death makes performance impossible.

23. e. Choices b and c are correct. Choice a is incorrect because the agreement is to discharge the debt *now*. An executory accord is an agreement to discharge a debt when a later performance is rendered. Consequently, the agreement, if binding, is a substituted contract—choice b. Choice c is also correct, because the agreement lacks consideration. Under the rule of Foakes v. Beer, payment (or promise of payment) of part of a liquidated debt is not consideration for discharge of the balance.

24. d. Choice a is incorrect. The contract is unenforceable by *A* because the licensing provision is for the benefit of the public and enforcement would legitimize the illegal activity. Nonetheless, statements b, and c are correct. *B* has a cause of action for breach because she was unaware of facts making the contract void—choice b. An additional reason why *B* has a cause of action is that *B* can rely on a theatrical producer to know the fundamental laws that affect the legality of theatrical productions—choice c.

25. a. Choice a is correct, because the only consideration supplied by *A* was the promise of performing a criminal act. Choice b is incorrect; *B*'s promise is not severable from the consideration for it. Choice c is incorrect. The doctrine of *locus poenitentiae* has to do with a situation where one party withdraws from an illegal agreement.

26. f. Choice a is correct because the parol evidence rule only bars certain prior and contemporaneous statements and writings. Choices b and c are also correct. *See* UCC § 2–209.

27. d. Choices a, b, and c are all correct. Choice c is correct because most state statutes provide that a written promise or acknowledgment is required to revive a debt barred by the statute of limitations without fresh consideration. Choice a is correct because part payment is regarded as the evidentiary equivalent of a writing. Choice b is correct because there is fresh consideration and a new contract that has no writing requirement.

28. d. The new promise that revives a debt discharged by the statute of limitations must be made by the debtor or the debtor's agent to the creditor or the creditor's agent. The promise made by *C* to *A* makes *B* a third party intended beneficiary of the promise, but the promise by *C* is not binding. There is no consideration for it and *C* can raise the defense of lack of consideration against the beneficiary.

29. d. Choices b and c are correct. Choice a is incorrect, exclusive dealing arrangements of this kind are common and are enforced. Choice b is correct. The agreement is to last over 13 months from its formation. The one-year period is calculated from the formation of the contract. Choice c is correct. When parties continue to perform after the expiration of their contract, the contract renews for the same duration as its original term. The fact that the original contract is within the statute of frauds is no problem, because the parties have fully performed it. The renewal contract is not within the one-year section because performance will be exactly one year from the renewal.

30. b. Choice b is correct because the language on the check is an offer, and the cashing of it constitutes the satisfaction of plaintiff's claim. The consideration consists of the settlement of a good faith and reasonable dispute. Choice a is incorrect. If the only remaining performances under a contract consist of payment of a fixed amount of money at a fixed time or fixed times in the future, the repudiation of the obligation to pay is not a total breach. Choice c is incorrect. The policy is definitely not divisible; divisibility requires that within the contract there be a performance exchanged for payment (or some other performance) that is its agreed equivalent. The installment payments owed by the insurer have no agreed equivalents.

31. e. Statements a, b, and c are all correct. Each of them is based on UCC § 2–210.

32. f. Choice a is incorrect. UCC Article 2 limits options *without consideration* to three months. Here there was consideration. Choice b is incorrect. Under Article 2, there are special rules for making irrevocable offers *without consideration* relating to merchants and to a special signature requirement (§ 2–205). Choice c is incorrect. Although option contracts are assignable, the execution of a credit instrument is a non-delegable performance. The offer was based on *B*'s credit, not *C*'s. Consequently, *C*'s tender is deficient.

33. d. Choice a is correct because UCC Article 2 provides that a modification of a contract for the sale of goods needs no consideration. Choice b is also correct. There is a change of duties on both sides. *S* will receive a higher unit price and *B* need accept fewer widgets. Choice c is incorrect. The contract as modified is for a price that is less than $500.

34. d. Choice a is correct because a contract performed by illegal activity is tainted with illegality. Choice b is incorrect. Under the prevailing view, full performance by *A* would take the contract out of the statute of frauds. Choice c is correct. A repudiation is a total breach unless the only remaining obligation of the promisor is to pay money at fixed times in the future. Here, *S* owes a duty to *A* to pay money, but also owes *A* the duty to

fulfill *C*'s requirements in good faith. *S*'s duty to *C* is also a duty to *A* because *S* owes *A* the duty of cooperation.

35. b. Choice b is correct because the relationship between valet and employer is one in which there is great physical proximity and personal interaction. Therefore, *B*'s rights to *A*'s services are non-assignable. For exactly the same reason, choice c is incorrect. An employment contract that involves a personal relationship is discharged by the death of the employer or the employee. Choice a is incorrect. The statement of facts spells out a novation. The deal was subject to the condition that *A* agree to "terminate" the agreement with *B*. And *A* agreed. This ended *B*'s liability.

36. a. Choice a is correct. *Z*'s telephone call was in legal contemplation a demand for assurance. *Z* justifiably relied on the information supplied by *A*. Choice b is incorrect. *Z*'s obligation is to pay money. Performance of the obligation is not impossible.

37. c. Choice c is correct. The parties are free orally to modify a contract that, as modified, is not within the statute of frauds. There is consideration on both sides. *A* agrees to pay more money; *B* agrees to work under different conditions than previously agreed. Choice b is incorrect. *B* is free to show that a condition precedent to the existence of the contract existed and has failed. Choice a is incorrect. The writing cannot be reformed because the deviation from the oral agreement is intentional. The rule allowing contracts to be shown to be sham is not applicable. That rule applies to sham contracts, not sham contractual terms.

38. f. Choice a is incorrect. Cancellation would be too precipitous under any view of the matter. There is plenty of opportunity for *S* to perfect title; e.g., by paying off the mortgage. Under the view of the Restatement (Second), *B* should inform *S* of the problem and ask for assurances. Choice b is incorrect. *S* has not done anything after the contract was made to repudiate by words or to disable herself from performance. Choice c is incorrect. Although *B* has communicated a waiver, the waiver is retractable until such time as there has been a material change of position by *S*. No such change of position is stated.

39. a. The announcement that an auction will be held is deemed a statement of intention. Consequently, choice a is correct. Choice b is incorrect. The rules for the sale of goods by auction appear in UCC § 2–328. The default rule is that an auction is with reserve. Choice c is incorrect. Because the seller had reserved the right not to sell, the seller may do this either directly or by a subterfuge. The quoted language applies only if the auction is without reserve.

40. e. Choice a and b are both correct. As to choice a, *S* is a third party creditor beneficiary of *Y*'s promise. *S*'s rights against *Y* are derivative of the contract between *B* and *Y*. Consequently, any defense that *Y* has against *B*, Y may assert against *S*. Choice b is also correct. Again, *S*'s rights against *Y* derive from the contract between *B* and *Y* and they had the power which they exercised to provide that third parties do not have enforceable rights in their agreement. Choice c is incorrect. Absent indicia of another intention, the promisor in a third party beneficiary contract who assumed a specific obligation cannot raise defenses that the promisee might have against the beneficiary.

41. a. Choice a is correct because the phrase "time is of the essence" is standard language to express the idea that performance on time is an express condition. Choice b is incorrect, because the contract makes performance on time an express condition, there is no need for the court to construct a condition to the same effect. Choices c and d are both wrong for the reason that failure to perform on time is both a breach of contract and a failure of condition.

42. c. Choice a is incorrect because a contract arose upon dispatch of the acceptance while *S* was still alive. Choice b is correct. Impossibility is no defense to this contract of sale unless *S* was to have personally hand-crafted the widgets. Choice c is correct under the mailbox rule.

COMPREHENSIVE ESSAY EXAMINATION QUESTIONS

QUESTION 1

Owner retained Broker to find a buyer who would purchase a designated house and lot. The written and subscribed contract between Owner and Broker provided that a commission of $1,400 would be payable in 14 monthly installments to commence "when the broker produced a purchaser who is ready willing and able to purchase." Broker succeeded in finding a purchaser who entered into a written contract of sale with Owner and who had sufficient funds to make the purchase. Broker brought an action for $1,400 and moved for summary judgment.

Owner submitted an answering affidavit that stated in substance (1) that the parties orally agreed that the commission would be paid on the closing of title in a lump sum; (2) that title failed to close because the purchaser refused to proceed upon learning of a cloud on title; (3) that the contract authorized Broker to search title but Broker did not search title and neither party was aware of the cloud on title; and (4) that the house was destroyed by fire between the time the contract was signed and the closing of title.

Rule on the motion for summary judgment, discussing the issues involved.

QUESTION 2

Special Interests, Inc., (SI), a duly registered lawful lobbying organization, conducted a fund-raising drive, soliciting pledges from those who shared its views. It received this signed pledge from Pledgor: "In consideration of SI's valuable services to the nation, heretofore and in the future, I pledge $5,000 to SI, payable in six months."

Pledgor owned a grinching machine. Lessee orally offered to lease the machine. Pledgor was receptive, saying: "I'll let you have the machine for five years if you agree to pay me $500 a month and pay SI the $5,000 that I pledged last week." Lessee said, "Okay, but I want the right to cancel if I'm not satisfied with the machine. I'll take it on a trial basis for 3 months." Pledgor said nothing further, and helped Lessee load the machine onto Lessee's truck.

After a week, Pledgor told Lessee not to pay the $5,000 to SI, but to pay it directly to Pledgor. Lessee agreed.

Several weeks later, after Lessee put the machine into operation, Lessee angrily told Pledgor that the machine "doesn't grinch worth a darn." Pledgor replied that the only problem was that Lessee did not know the first thing about the art of using finely calibrated machinery. At the end of this stormy telephone conversation Lessee said that only as much rent as the machine proved to be worth would be paid. Pledgor then went to the site of the machine, repossessed it, and sued immediately for damages. SI subsequently brought suit against Pledgor and Lessee. The actions have been consolidated and will be tried together.

What are the rights of the parties? Discuss.

QUESTION 3

This question is based on a question that appeared on the New Jersey Bar Examination.

H owns Hotel and Tee owns an adjacent 18 hole Golf Course.

H desired to arrange golfing privileges at Tee's golf course for Hotel's guests. In December 1980 *H* told Tee that if Hotel's guests were permitted to use Golf Course free of charge, *H* would pay Tee $2,500 per month during the season. Tee replied that this would be acceptable "if it is for a five year term and if you purchase all of Hotel's meat requirements from my brother-in-law, Butcher." *H* agreed. The two men wrote out and subscribed the following

> "Agreed: Guests at Hotel may use Golf Course free of charge.
>
> *H* shall pay Tee $2,500 per month. Duration as per verbal agreement.
>
> *H* shall purchase Hotel's meat requirements from Butcher."

The parties operated under the agreement for a year. Tee then told *H* that the monthly payments would have to be increased to $3,000, "because your guests are overcrowding the course and my lawyer says our deal isn't binding. You have 10 days to decide or I will cancel." Five days later Sport, the proprietor of a sporting goods store located in Hotel, wrote Tee: "I hear you are considering canceling your deal with *H*. If you do, it will hurt my sales of golf equipment. If you agree not to cancel during the life of the agreement, I'll pay you $300 per month." Tee wrote back: "I accept," and in January 1982 Sport commenced paying Tee $300 per month. *H* continued to pay $2,500 per month to Tee.

Late in the second year of the agreement, Tee announced plans to erect a large resort hotel on land presently occupied by 9 of the 18 holes on Golf Course. *H* was upset at the announcement and *H* and Sport refused to make any further payments and *H* told Butcher that *H* no longer would buy meat from Butcher. Butcher had recently spent $10,000 expanding refrigeration capacity to provide Hotel with better services.

What are the rights of the parties at each stage of the events set out above? Discuss.

QUESTION 4—CALIFORNIA BAR EXAM COMPREHENSIVE QUESTION

Katy and Mike operated a motorcycle dealership under the name K & M. I Cycles orally agreed to supply motorcycles to K & M for resale at a price 5% less than Cycles' factory list prices. The term of the agreement was for the succeeding five-year period but could be terminated at any time by either party. Cycles immediately sent a written signed confirmation of the agreement which, however, omitted the 5% discount provision. K & M never received the written confirmation.

Soon after these events, Katy and Mike terminated their business relationship. They executed a document by which Mike assigned all his rights in K & M contracts to Katy, and by which Katy agreed to be solely liable for all of K & M's business obligations. A copy of the signed document was delivered to Cycles. Cycles continued to ship motorcycles to K & M.

A year after receiving the copy of the document, Cycles sent Katy a statement for $40,000, the factory list price for the latest shipment of motorcycles accepted by Katy. Katy sent Cycles a check for $30,000 with a letter stating that the check was sent in full payment of the statement because Cycles had billed her at prices which were too high. Cycles deposited the check and immediately sent protest letters to Katy and Mike demanding payment of $10,000 and canceling the agreement to supply motorcycles on the ground that the agreement was not binding and, alternatively, that it was invalidated because Mike had left the dealership.

1. To what relief, if any, is Katy entitled against Cycles? Discuss.
2. To what relief, if any, is Cycles entitled against:
   (a) Katy? Discuss.

(b) Mike? Discuss.

QUESTION 5

In January 1998, Owens (*O*) contacted constructor (*C*), a licensed building contractor, for a price at which *C* would remodel and redecorate *O*'s historical mansion pursuant to the plans and specifications prepared by an architect. *C* presented *O* with a simple written document stating that *C* would do the work pursuant to the plans and specifications of the architect for $572,000. The document also contained a detailed schedule for accomplishing the work and for progress payments keyed to certain milestones on the schedule. *O* told *C* that she would not haggle over the price provided *C* would warrant the work for three years. *C* replied that "three years is well beyond industry standards, but my work is better than standard and I will warrant this work for three years." *O* then said, "I know your work is better than standard, that's why I sought you out. We have a deal." They shook hands and parted.

The work proceeded in accordance with the schedule, but *C* ran into problems having nothing to do with *O*'s mansion restoration project. The stock market crash wiped out the small fortune *C* had amassed. An owner of a project *C* was working on was behind in payments and then went bankrupt. Although *C* filed a lien, *C* was desperately short of cash. *C* contacted Xerxes (*X*), a licensed contractor who was known to be flush with cash, but was short on current work-in-progress. After a discussion, *X* agreed with *C* to take over the Owens job and to pay *C* immediately any sums that *O* owed plus one-third of *C*'s projected profit.

Pursuant to the agreement, *X* took over the project and made the payments to *C*. Because the subcontractors who were on site were the same as before, *O* was unaware of *X*'s deal with *C* until the next scheduled payment was due when *X* informed *O* of the deal, which *C* confirmed. *O*, who is a perfectionist in all things, went to the job site, pointed out certain decorating details that were not to her satisfaction and demanded they be done over or else the next payment would not be made. *X* checked out the complaints with some contractors who were knowledgeable about this sort of thing, and they confirmed *X*'s contention that the work was done in a good skilled manner. *O* refused to make the scheduled payment. *X* left the job which was ultimately completed by another contractor at a considerably higher overall cost. *X* sues *O* and *C* for damages. *O* counterclaims against *X* and also crossclaims against *C*. Raise and resolve the issues involved in these lawsuits.

QUESTION 6. SHORT ESSAY

Garbage, Inc., operated a waste transfer station. It had an oral agreement with Blair, its attorney, to pay Blair $2,500 a month for 5 years for services Blair had rendered. Garbage sold this station to Trash, Inc. for $500,000 pursuant to a written contract subscribed by both parties. In addition, Trash orally agreed to assume Garbage's liability to Blair until the waste station ceased to operate or for five years, whichever occurred first. One year later, Blair sent Garbage a letter releasing Garbage from further liability for fees. Because of financial pressures, Trash stopped paying Blair. Raise and resolve the contracts issues in this fact pattern.

QUESTION 7. SHORT ESSAY

Century 21 operates an automobile race track. It distributed a letter to various race drivers including Sigrist to the effect that at the end of the season a bonus of would be paid to the driver who had accumulated the most points in his or her division at the end of the racing season. Sigrist entered the "Figure 8" division races. On August 13, after 6 races in the Figure 8 division, Century 21 decided that no further races would be held in that division because there were too few entries to put on a good show for the spectators.

At that point, Sigrist was the point leader in that division. Races in other divisions continued for a month, after which an end-of-season dinner was held for all the racing contestants and a trophy was given and a bonus of $20,000 paid to the point leaders of every division, except Sigrist, who was given only a trophy. He sues claiming an entitlement to a bonus. Raise and resolve the issues presented.

QUESTION 8. SHORT ESSAY

Plaintiff, while an employee of Chase Manhattan Bank and with the bank's written approval, enrolled in the Fordham University M.B.A. evening program for the trimester that began in September. The bank's personnel manual, titled "Human Resources Guide," provided for reimbursement "to active staff members" of tuition expenses for approved university courses at the end of the courses taken, provided that the employee had obtained a grade of C or better. Plaintiff paid Fordham's tuition in September. On October 9th, plaintiff was discharged as part of a large personnel reduction. When she received her transcript of grades in January, all of which were C or better, she provided the bank with a copy and requested reimbursement of tuition. The bank refused to reimburse. She sues. Decide the case.

QUESTION 9. SHORT ESSAY

Tenant was a permanent resident of a residential hotel. The owner (Landlord #1) wished to gut the building and create a modern transient hotel in the premises and obtained a building permit for that purpose. The owner brought an eviction action against Tenant which was settled by agreement. Tenant agreed to vacate the premises for a maximum of two years during which Landlord #1 would gut and reconstruct the building and certain designated rooms would be made available to her in the reconstructed building. She was to be paid at the rate of $18,000 per year during the time she was out of possession. She vacated. The building was sold to Landlord #2 who gutted the building. Whereupon the Building Department issued a stop-work order, canceled the building permit and told Landlord #2 that no new permit would issue unless the building were redesigned from a hotel to premises containing 51% apartment space and 49% hotel space. No lending institution is willing to finance such construction. The building stands as a shell. Five years after she vacated the building Tenant, who has been paid $36,000, sues both Landlord #1 and Landlord #2 for damages. Decide the case.

QUESTION 10. SHORT ESSAY

At an auction conducted pursuant to an order of the Bankruptcy Court, *B* was the high bidder on certain machinery owned by Wonderbold, a bankrupt. The auctioneer accepted *B*'s high bid, and the sale was approved by the Bankruptcy Court. Delivery and payment were to take place on January 31. *T* brought a proceeding to enjoin the sale, claiming certain rights in the machinery. Pending disposition of *T*'s claim, the Court ordered a stay of delivery. On February 14, following the scheduled delivery date, *B* wants to cancel because the proceeding determining *T*'s claim might take up to a year to determine and *B* would rather buy similar goods elsewhere than deal with the uncertainty. (a) What are the prospects of such a cancellation without liability on *B*'s part? (b) What are the possibilities of *B* recovering a judgment for damages against Wonderbold's bankruptcy estate?

QUESTION 11

Buyer contacted Seller about purchasing coin-operated video arcade-game machines. After reviewing Seller's products, Buyer selected Model K22 and asked what the unit price would be if Buyer ordered about 200 of them for its chain of motels. Seller was happy to know that the prospective sale was for a motel chain. Consumers would be introduced to them when staying at one of buyer's motels and some of them would enjoy them enough to order the model for home use. On February 1, Seller sent buyer a form titled "Proposal." In the quantity box on the form, Seller entered "200" and in the price box it entered "$2,300 per unit; buyer pays shipping costs." This price was the lowest it could offer without taking a loss on each sale. No further communications were made until April 1, when Buyer replied by letter, saying "We are pleased to accept your proposal. Please enter our order for 125 of your Model K22's. It is the custom of the motel industry to arbitrate all disputes. Consequently, we deem your proposal to incorporate this custom."

A few days after the dispatch of this letter, Buyer became aware of a new entry into the market of a new video arcade-game machine that was a smashing success with video-game fans. It sent a fax to Seller, stating "Disregard our letter of April 1. We apologize for creating some confusion, but our lawyers tell us that the letter is pointless and for more than one reason created no obligations for either of us."

(a) After unsuccessfully trying to make telephone contact with the individuals at Buyer's offices with whom they had dealt, Seller commenced suit, seeking damages, in state court. Buyer moved to stay the action and for a court order ordering arbitration. Decide the motion.

(b) Assume that the merits have been tried either before an arbitrator or by the court. What should the decision be?

Assume the facts stated above, except that Buyer did not send the fax and no litigation occurred. Instead, Seller wrote stating, "We have 125 model K22's ready to go. Give us shipping instructions. Upon receipt of this letter, Buyer replied, We have assigned the contract to the XYZ Medical Associates. They run a string of nursing homes around the country. We have forwarded your request for shipping instructions to them."

(c) The information Buyer gave Seller in this letter is factually correct. How does this information affect the rights of the parties?

MORE COMPREHENSIVE QUESTIONS

Note that the answers to the next questions are very thorough, much more thorough than an examinee would be expected to provide. These answers were prepared by a law professor to guide the grading of the essays. Despite their origin, they should be useful to the student who is facing a comprehensive essay question.

QUESTION 12

A, Inc., contracted to build a hi-rise building for *B* in an urban center, at a cost of $72,000,000. Zelda, an architect retained by *B*, prepared the plans. *B* agreed to pay *A* "upon Zelda's certification that the contract has been performed in accordance with its terms."

Upon excavation, the water table was found just below the surface. The area was shown as a swamp on maps printed when the location was still rural. These maps are frequently consulted by architects and builders, but these maps were not consulted in this case.

A told *B* it would quit unless *B* promised payment for the increased costs caused by the water level. *B* agreed to pay such costs.

A then agreed with, *C*, a Dutch building firm experienced in coping with water, whereby *C* agreed to complete the job. *C* performed, using supervisory engineers licensed only in the Netherlands, although State law required that engineers be licensed by the State.

Zelda, after discovering that the exterior glass was not the brand specified in the contract, refused to certify completion although the glass was regarded in the trade as just as good as the specified brand.

A sues *B* in a contract action for the unpaid price plus the additional costs of coping with the water. What contentions would *B* raise and what is the likelihood of success for each of these? *C* sues *A*. What contentions would *A* and *B* raise and what is the likelihood of success for each of these? Do not discuss anything other than contractual relief.

QUESTION 13

Hatfield, a Californian, inherited woodland in Kentucky. He had little idea of its extent or quality. The land contained rare old-growth black walnut trees worth up to $20,000 each for furniture veneer. He approached McCoy, a Kentuckian, who knew local land and timber values and knew the Hatfield tract. McCoy told Hatfield—accurately—that local acreage generally brought $1,300 to $1,500 an acre. He did not reveal that the Hatfield tract was worth much more than the average. He offered $1,500 an acre if Hatfield had good title. Hatfield accepted. Attempting to evidence what they had agreed upon, they signed the following:

> "1. McCoy agrees to pay Hatfield $1,500 per acre for land conveyed to McCoy and Hatfield agrees to convey any or all his Kentucky acreage on demand."
>
> "2. Upon the signing of this agreement, $1,500 is to be paid to Title Abstract Co. to hold until title to the first acre of land is delivered to McCoy. If no conveyance is executed within 90 days, this agreement becomes void and the $1,500 shall be returned to McCoy. This agreement is non-retractable for 90 days."

McCoy immediately ordered a survey and title search at a cost to him of $750. These showed that Hatfield had 10 marketable acres. Soon thereafter, and 20 days after signing the agreement, McCoy received an e-mail from Hatfield stating, "I terminate our deal." McCoy's tender of $15,000 was refused. He seeks legal and equitable relief. What result? Discuss all relevant possible claims and defenses.

QUESTION 14

Jim orally agreed to work for Jane for $70,000 a year as Jane's accountant for 5 years, "provided that if Jim's services do not satisfy Jane, Jane may terminate the employment at any time." The terms of the agreement were typed on Jane's letterhead and placed in Jane's files.

Two years later, Jim, a normally temperate person, had too much to drink at a company picnic and became boisterous. Jane told Jim that he was fired. Subsequently, Jim indicated to Jane that if he was not reinstated in his job he would retain an attorney to sue for breach of contract.

During ensuing negotiations Jane handed Jim a signed paper headed, "Final Offer," stating that Jim accepted a position with Jane's office in New Zealand for the balance of the five-year term. With obvious reluctance, Jim wrote, "I accept" and signed the paper.

Several weeks later, the New Zealand consulate denied Jim a visa on the ground that, under a regulation promulgated a day earlier, visas would be denied whenever there were sufficient unemployed residents to fill the applicant's job opening.

What are the rights of Jim against Jane at each stage of their relationship? Discuss.

QUESTION 15

Assume that franchises are governed by the UCC and no other statute regulating franchises is in effect.

RS, Inc. manufactures converters that permit AM-FM radios to broadcast shortwave signals. RS advertised in a national publication, stating: "We offer permanent dealerships. Our dealers will gross a minimum of $100,000 yearly from sales of our converter."

Williston replied to the ad, and, after an interview, signed a writing (also signed by RS's sales manager) which stated:

I. In consideration of $1.00 in hand paid to RS, receipt of which is acknowledged, RS appoints Williston as a franchisee for the sale of the RS converter.

II. Williston will not sell any other brand of converter.

III. RS warrants that its products delivered under this agreement will comply with all government regulations. No other warranties are given.

IV. RS will supply Williston with converters to an extent consistent with its production plans and actual capacity. All orders from Williston, therefore, are subject to determination by us.

The parties acted under this agreement for twelve months, after which Williston received a letter from RS giving him three days notice of termination of the franchise. Williston had grossed only $12,000 from the sale of the RS converter. This small gross is attributable, in part, to the fact that many of the converters did not work and Williston refunded the purchase price to its customers in such cases.

What are the rights of Williston? Discuss all contracts issues raised by these facts in coming to your conclusion.

SAMPLE ANSWERS TO COMPREHENSIVE QUESTIONS

ANSWER 1

Summary judgment denied. Resolution of the dispute hinges upon questions of fact.

Item 1 of the affidavit does not indicate whether the oral agreement was made before or after the written contract was signed.

(a) If the oral agreement was prior to, or contemporaneous with, the written contract, it would be ineffective and barred by the parol evidence rule. The oral agreement directly contradicts the written contract.

(b) If the oral agreement was made subsequent to the written contract, it would have effectively modified the contract. The parol evidence rule does not bar evidence of agreements made subsequent to the writing. The modification is supported by consideration, as there is new detriment on each side. Broker's payments rights are postponed. Owner's payment duty is changed inasmuch as payment must be in one lump sum rather than in installments. The statute of frauds presents no obstacle to enforcement, except in those few states that require a brokerage contract to be in writing. The contract, originally not performable within one year, as modified, is performable within a year. Although it relates to real property, it is not a contract for the conveyance of any interest in real property. Therefore, it is not within the real property statute of frauds.

Consequently, the motion cannot be granted without knowing when the oral agreement was allegedly made.

Item 2 indicates that seller's title may be unmarketable. As between seller and buyer whether buyer was justified in refusing to proceed depends on whether title is curable or not. This question of fact also has an impact upon the Broker's rights. If the written contract stands as written, Broker has complied with all conditions precedent to Broker's right to a commission. When a purchaser, with sufficient financial ability to purchase, signs a contract of sale the purchaser's ability and willingness to perform are established. If the brokerage contract was modified to postpone payment until closing of title, a different condition is imposed. It has been held that time-of-payment clauses in brokerage contracts ("when clauses") create conditions to the broker's right to payment. Unless the condition is excused, the broker's right to payment has not become absolute under the allegedly modified agreement. The condition would be excused, however, if the cloud on title were curable and seller failed to cure. Even if the title were incurable, the condition may be excused on the theory that the seller when listing the property for sale impliedly warranted marketable title. However, this implied warranty may have been negated by facts alleged in item 3 of the affidavit.

Item 3 alleges that Broker was authorized to search title. On the face of it this is not a condition to Broker's rights nor a promise on Broker's part. Its legal effect is ambiguous. Only by a process of interpretation involving parol evidence can it be determined whether the authorization was intended to expressly or impliedly condition Broker's rights on making a search to determine the marketability of Owner's title.

Item 4 describes the destruction of the building by fire. If the written contract stands unmodified, this allegation does not affect Broker's rights. Broker's rights became absolute. The rights of Broker are not discharged by impossibility as it is not impossible for Owner to pay. Frustration of purpose is no defense as Broker has fully performed. If the contract had been modified as alleged in Item 1, and assuming Owner was not at fault in causing the fire, the purpose of the parties may have been frustrated by an event the non-occurrence of which was a basic assumption of the parties. Whether this is the fact can only be determined after a full evidentiary hearing. Also to be explored is the question of whether the buyer, at the time of the fire, had already indicated that he or she was cancelling the contract.

Assuming it is determined that the broker is entitled to judgment on the original written contract, Broker would only be entitled to the sums due at the time of trial. When a party has fully performed and is entitled to payments at fixed times in the future the law only permits recovery of payments due up to time of trial. A material breach does not accelerate the due dates of debts.

ANSWER 2

The first question presented is whether the pledge is binding. If it is, SI may recover from Pledgor regardless of any assumption by Lessee. The promise to pay must be supported by consideration or its equivalent. Past valuable services are not consideration, because they were not bargained for in exchange for the promise. The services "in the future" could serve as consideration if SI has promised to continue to render its services. The facts do not so indicate. Nonetheless, SI's acceptance of the pledge may well be taken as an implied promise to continue its services. The implication of such a promise may depend upon further information concerning SI's handling of the pledge.

If no promise is implied, the pledge may possibly be upheld under the doctrine of promissory estoppel. Under the rule of the Restatement, Second, of Contracts, a charitable pledge is enforceable without consideration and without proof of reliance by the promisee on the promise. This rule is, in part, founded on a recognition of the important societal role of private charities in this country. However, SI is not a charity. It is doubtful whether SI could successfully invoke the Restatement rule here discussed.

Another approach to the pledge is to look at it as an offer that requests a performance (future service to the nation). If SI has performed any service subsequent to, and with knowledge of, the pledge, the offer becomes irrevocable. This approach has been taken by courts that do not accept the doctrine of promissory estoppel. Again, however, the context has been the charitable pledge and SI is not a charity, but the principle could be applicable to non-charitable pledges.

The lease is valid. Lessee's counter-offer was accepted on the spot. Although Pledgor did not reply in words to Lessee's counter-offer, Pledgor's conduct in assisting Lessee to move the machine is implicitly an expression of assent.

There is, however, a division of authority as to whether this valid lease is enforceable. A five-year lease of personalty is within the one-year statute of frauds. However, this lease gives Lessee an option to terminate upon dissatisfaction within three months. Many courts would rule that exercise of this option would result in a discharge of the contract rather than its full performance. Under this view, the contract would be unenforceable for want of a writing. Many courts would instead rule that the exercise of the option to terminate would be one of the alternative ways full performance could take place. In these jurisdictions, no writing would be required.

By the end of the telephone conversation Lessee had repudiated the contract, justifying Pledgor's cancellation of the contract. If Lessee was dissatisfied with the machine, Lessee had the option to terminate, but this does not carry with it the right to state dissatisfaction and to reduce the price. The statement was an unequivocal repudiation of duties under the contract. Consequently, subject to the possible defense of the statute of frauds, Lessee is liable to Pledgor for total breach.

SI's rights against Pledgor have been discussed. SI's relationship with Lessee is analytically more complex. When Lessee promised Pledgor to pay the $5,000 to SI, SI became a third-party beneficiary of Lessee's contract. When Pledgor and Lessee agreed to modify the contract so that SI's rights would be destroyed, this was permissible unless SI's rights had vested. There is no indication that SI even knew of the assumption of the obligation. Knowledge of the promise by the third party beneficiary is minimum standard of vesting, according to most authorities, for anyone other than an infant.

Even if the rights of SI have vested, they are subject to any defenses that Lessee has against Pledgor. This includes Lessee's possible statute of frauds defense and any defenses that Lessee may have based on the alleged unsatisfactory quality of the leased machinery.

A last and, difficult, question is whether Lessee can raise against SI the contention that Pledgor was not bound by its pledge to SI because SI supplied no consideration. Leading cases, such as Rouse v. United States, indicate that the promisor may not usually raise defenses against the beneficiary that the promisee could raise against the beneficiary. Such defenses are available only when the contract can be interpreted as containing a provision that the promisor's obligation is conditioned on the promisee being liable to the beneficiary. There is no basis for such an interpretation in the case at bar.

ANSWER 3

1. *H* made an offer. Tee made a counter-offer which *H* accepted on the spot, forming an oral contract. It is not a problem that Tee's single promise to allow the use of the golf-

course by *H*'s guests is exchanged for two promises by *H*. One consideration can support multiple promises.

2. The oral contract is within the statute of frauds and thus unenforceable unless it is sufficiently memorialized. The written memorandum must contain all of the essential terms agreed upon. Although there is a reference to duration and parol evidence is admissible to clarify vague or indefinite terms, it seems doubtful that a term that merely refers to "as per oral agreement" has sufficient content to satisfy the statute. Parol evidence would supply the term, not clarify it.

3. Tee's later demand was unjustified, but was perhaps not a repudiation because it was conditional. There is authority, however, to the effect that a demand conditioned on an act that goes beyond the contract constitutes a repudiation. In any event, Tee retracted in timely fashion; Tee failed to carry out its threat to cancel.

4. There is a consideration problem with respect to the agreement between Sport and Tee. Assuming Tee was bound by the contract with *H*, the traditional rule is that a promise to perform a preexisting duty owed to the other party or to a third person is not consideration. (The Restatements disagree.) Nonetheless, Tee may have provided consideration by retracting the threat to cancel. Assuming Tee's lawyer advised Tee that the contract was unenforceable, Tee's good faith is established and, in view of the statute of frauds problem, the contention of the right to cancel is not unreasonable. That the course is overcrowded is a foreseeable risk assumed by Tee and not even plausibly a ground for cancellation.

5. The contract between Sport and Tee suffers from the same statute of frauds difficulty as does the original writing between *H* and Tee. Since Sport's letter refers to the original contract, the original memorandum can be treated as part of the memorandum between Sport and Tee. Arguably, however, the duration term is not sufficiently reduced to writing.

6. Assuming Tee does not have a statute of frauds defense, Tee's announcement of its plans to build a resort hotel is not yet a repudiation, nor is it a sufficient expression of prospective unwillingness to perform to justify cancellation by *H*. Tee has not announced when the hotel is to be built. Depending on the tenor of the announcement, *H* may be justified in suspending performance and demanding assurances from Tee.

7. Because the original contract between *H* and Tee called for performances that would be rendered directly to Butcher (paying for meat or, at a minimum, not buying meat from others). Butcher is an intended third-party beneficiary of the contract between *H* and Tee. (Since the contract gives Butcher rights but no duties, it is an option contract.) As a third party intended beneficiary, Butcher's rights have vested. Butcher knows of the contract and has relied upon it. Nonetheless, despite vesting, Butcher's rights against *H* are subject to any defense that *H* has against Tee other than those arising from subsequent voluntary agreements between *H* and Tee. Potential defenses are the statute of frauds and Tee's prospective unwillingness to carry out the contract.

8. Butcher has no contractual rights against Tee. From all appearances, Butcher is a donee beneficiary, inasmuch as we are not informed of any obligor-obligee relationship between these brothers-in-law. Under the contract, Butcher was the beneficiary of orders and payments from *H*, not Tee. Butcher was only an incidental beneficiary of Tee's promised performance. It is also clear that a donee beneficiary has no cause of action against Tee in Tee's capacity of promisee.

ANSWER 4—MODEL ANSWER TO CALIFORNIA BAR EXAMINATION QUESTION

What follows is a "model answer," slightly edited for this edition. This model is beyond what an examiner expects from a student for a grade of A+. It does, however, illustrate the goal against which an examinee's paper is graded. Matter within square brackets has been added for this edition.

Point One: The agreement is not binding for a five-year term on Cycles. It is, however, not terminable except on a reasonable period of notice.

As a common law proposition, the agreement would likely be held void for lack of consideration. A promise terminable at the will of a promisor has been regarded as illusory. *Miami Coca-Cola Bottling Co. v. Orange Crush Co.,* 296 F. 693 (5th Cir.1924). Since reasonable notice was not given by Cycles, *absent other defenses,* it is liable for damages suffered by Katy for a reasonable period of time after notice of termination. Reasonableness depends primarily on factors unknown to us, such as the period of time needed to make alternative business arrangements and to recoup one's investment in the dealership. *See generally,* Gellhorn, *Limitations on Contract Termination Rights,* 57 Duke L.J. 465 (1967).

Section 2–207 of the UCC, dealing with additional or different terms contained in a written confirmation, is not relevant to this set of facts as that section presupposes receipt of the confirmation. UCC § 2–207(2)(c).

Point Two: As to the claim of Katy and Mike, Cycles' written confirmation satisfies the writing requirement of the Sales, and can satisfy, under certain circumstances, the One Year statute of frauds.

The agreement is for the sale of goods and must satisfy the UCC statute of frauds. It is within the one-year statute of frauds as well. Thus, the transaction would have to meet the terms of both provisions. *Restatement of Contracts* § 178, Comment b; *Restatement (Second) of Contracts* § 110, Comment b. [Recent cases are to the contrary, taking the position that only the UCC needs to be satisfied.]

The Sales Provision is clearly met. The confirmation meets the test of UCC—Sales § 2–201(1) that there be "some writing sufficient to indicate that a contract for sale has been made between the parties and signed by the party against whom enforcement is sought. . . ."

The statute is satisfied even though an important term (5% discount) is omitted. "A writing is not insufficient because it omits or incorrectly states a term agreed upon." UCC § 2–201(1).

The contract cannot be performed within a one year term and is, therefore, within the one-year statute of frauds. Although either party can terminate within the year, under the majority view, termination *discharges* the contract, so that it cannot be said that the contract is "fully performed" if the hypothetical termination takes place. *Restatement (Second) of Contracts* § 130, Comment b. *J. Perillo, Contracts* § 19.21 (7th ed. 2014). Unlike the UCC statute of frauds, the one-year provision requires that all material terms agreed upon be included in the memorandum. The omission of the 5% discount provision would appear to be a fatal omission. However, the omission can be rectified in two ways. First, if the omission was accidental, under the majority view, the writing can be reformed to reflect the true agreement of the parties. *J. Perillo, Contracts* § 19.28 (7th ed. 2014). Second, since the clause unilaterally benefits the buyers, they may cure any statute of frauds problem by renouncing the benefit of the clause. *Restatement of Contracts* § 221;

Restatement (Second) of Contracts § 147. The one-year statute of frauds requires a signature "by the party to be charged." The signed confirmation meets this test. It is enforceable against Cycles despite the fact it was not signed by any other party. *Restatement, Contracts* § 211; *Restatement (Second) of Contracts* § 135. The statutes are satisfied although the only writing that can be found is the copy in Cycles' own files and although the other parties were unaware of the writing. *Transit Advertisers Inc. v. New York, N.H. & H.R.R.*, 194 F.2d 907, 31 A.L.R.2d 1102 (2d Cir.), cert. denied, 344 U.S. 817 (1952).

Point Three: As to the claim of Cycles against Katy and Mike, the confirmation does not satisfy the statute of frauds, but Cycles' claim for payment of goods received and accepted takes the case out of the writing requirements of the statute of frauds.

Under UCC § 2–201(2), a non-signing merchant party loses the defense of the statute of frauds if he or she fails to contest a written confirmation within 10 days of receipt. Since K & M never received the confirmation, they have not lost the defense in this way. However, UCC § 2–201(3) provides that, despite the absence of sufficient written evidence of a contract, the contract is enforceable "with respect to goods . . . which have been received and accepted."

As for the one-year statute of frauds, full performance takes the contract out of the statute of frauds. *Restatement (Second) of Contracts* § 130 and Comment d. Full performance by one party of a divisible portion of a contract permits contractual recovery of the corresponding price for the performance. *Blue Valley Creamery Co. v. Consolidated Products Co.*, 81 F.2d 182 (8th Cir.1936); *see* Note, 71 A.L.R. 479, 492. Since Cycles seeks payment for a divisible portion of the contract—a discrete delivery of goods for an apportioned price (*Gill v. Johnstown Lumber Co.*, 151 Pa. 534, 25 A. 120 (1892)), the statute of frauds is not a defense.

Point Four: Mike's "assignment" to Katy carried with it an improper delegation of duties. Cycles, however, has lost the power to object to the delegation by waiver.

According to the UCC § 2–210(4), general language of assignment carries with it a delegation of duties unless other language or the circumstances dictates a contrary interpretation. Mike's general language of assignment coupled with his leaving the business clearly indicates an intent to delegate.

The delegation is, however, improper. Under UCC § 2–210(1) a delegation is improper if the obligee has a substantial interest in having the original contracting parties perform. It is clear that in a franchising (albeit non-exclusive) arrangement such as is present here, Cycles has a substantial interest in determining the individuals who will operate a Cycles dealership. *Paige v. Faure*, 229 N.Y. 114, 127 N.E. 898 (1920) (pre-code but good law);J. Perillo, Contracts § 18.28 (7th ed. 2014).

Despite the impropriety of the delegation, Cycles, with notice of the delegation, dealt with Katy. Consequently, it waived the non-delegability of Mike's duties. *Seale v. Bates*, 145 Colo. 430, 359 P.2d 356 (1961).

Point Five: Despite Katy's agreement to be solely liable for contract obligations, Mike remains liable on the Cycles contract.

Although Katy agreed to be solely liable on K & M contracts, it is fundamental that such an agreement could have no effect on the rights of Cycles against Mike. Consequently, assuming a valid cause of action, Cycles may obtain judgment against both Katy and Mike. *Copeland v. Beard*, 217 Ala. 216, 115 So. 389 (1928); *Erickson v. Grande Ronde Lumber Co.*, 162 Or. 556, 94 P.2d 139 (1939). The fact that Katy is primarily, and Mike secondarily, liable is of interest but of no relevance to the resolution of any problem in this lawsuit.

Point Six: Cycles did not enter into an accord and satisfaction when it cashed Katy's check under protest.

At common law it was the general rule that when a debtor tendered a check for less than the amount claimed by his creditor, clearly indicating that it was tendered in full satisfaction of the creditor's claim, the depositing of the check acted as an acceptance of the debtor's offer to an accord and satisfaction. "Protest will then be unavailing if the money is retained." *Hudson v. Yonkers Fruit Co.,* 258 N.Y. 168, 179 N.E. 373 (1932) (Cardozo, C.J.). The creditor is estopped from claiming that the check was tortiously cashed. Despite the absence of assent, estoppel creates the fiction of mutual assent. However, for a valid accord and satisfaction, another element—consideration—is also needed. In cases such as this, the consideration is often the compromise of a good faith dispute. Nothing in the facts clearly indicates such a dispute. Dissatisfaction with the prices charged under the contract is not a bona fide dispute unless, perhaps, if the prices are fixed in bad faith. UCC § 2–305(2).

All of the above, however, is preamble to the UCC which drastically changes the common law. UCC § 1–207 permits the creditor to accept the debtor's conditional check under protest, reserving rights, and permitting the cashing of the check without accepting the offer to an accord and satisfaction. [This answer is no longer correct, because most later cases have held that UCC 1–207 does not apply to a full-payment check. Moreover, the Commissioner on Uniform State Laws have revised the UCC to state that 1–207 does not apply to an accord and satisfaction and almost every state has enacted the revision.]

ANSWER 5

The offer was in writing. A contemporaneous oral term was agreed upon and the contract formed by oral assent. Certainly, under a liberal approach to the parol evidence rule the very existence of the oral warranty proves that there is no total integration. Even under the most conservative views of the parol evidence rule it is doubtful that there is a total integration. We are told that the writing is simple and there is no indication whatsoever that *O* ever signed it. Unless it contained a merger clause, it is unlikely that the parol evidence rule presents any obstacle to the admission of evidence of the oral warranty.—a consistent additional term.

The oral warranty is not performable within a year. Presumably, it requires *C* to cure defects that surface within the three-year term. Because it is clearly a material term, the entire contract is unenforceable.

Assuming the contract is enforceable or the defense is waived, is the assignment to *X* valid? The assignment is coupled with a delegation. If the delegation is invalid, then the assignment falls with it. The oral testimony points to *O*'s belief that she will get a superior result if *C* supervises the job. Yet the contract requires only compliance with the architect's specifications and drawings. *C* could have turned over supervision to a hired hand. The facts make it clear that the same subcontractors were employed by *X*. Thus, the duties are delegable, there was no improper delegation, and the assignment is valid.

Even if the duties were non-delegable, *O* waived her rights to object. When she discovered the delegation, she asked *X* to redo certain work. She did not object to the delegation. She objected to the quality of the work.

Were her objections sound? There is no indication that the contract contains a provision providing that *O* must be satisfied. That being so, her claim of personal dissatisfaction is not relevant and her statement that she would not pay is, under the modern view, a repudiation, justifying *X*'s cancellation. Although her refusal to pay was conditional, and under one view therefore not a repudiation, it was conditioned on a task—redoing the work—to which she was not entitled, coupled with a present breach. *X* has an action for total breach.

In the event *O* was justified in her reaction, and the contractors consulted by *X* were incorrect, X has materially breached and *X* is liable to *O* for total breach. How does *X* become liable to *O*? Under the modern view, when there is a total assignment of all rights under a contract coupled with the delegation of all of its duties, the assignee-delegate implicitly assumes the duties of the contract.

If *X* has breached the contract, *O* has an action against both *X* and *C* as *C* cannot transfer his duties and no novation has occurred. *X*, as well as *C*, can raise the defense of the statute of frauds. "The assignee stands in the shoes of the assignor." [This maxim misled a number of students. It signifies that the assignee has the rights of and is subject to the defenses against the assignor. It does *not* mean that the assignee takes on the duties of the assignor. Generally, assignees do not assume the duties of the assignor. The previous paragraph presents an exception.]

X v. C. There seems to be no basis for any liability by *C* to *X*. An assignor does not impliedly warrant that the other contracting party, (*O*), will perform.

[A number of students discussed *C*'s financial difficulties as a ground for impossibility. The stock market periodically crashes and thus the crash was foreseeable. Clients go bankrupt with some frequency. More important than foreseeability is that the parties do not share *C*'s assumption of risks of his investments and business dealings. There is no credible impossibility issue. A case has held that a buyer whose wealth had mostly been entrusted to Bernard Madoff had no defense.]

ANSWER 6

In some jurisdictions, the oral agreement between Garbage and Blair was unenforceable under the one-year statute of frauds. In others, because Blair had fully performed, the promise would no longer be within the statute, but Blair would have a quasi-contractual action for the balance of the reasonable value of services rendered.

When Trash promised to assume Garbage's liability to Blair, Blair became a third-party beneficiary. The same consideration (conveyance of the transfer station) that supports the rest of the contract supports the promise to pay Blair who is a third-party beneficiary of this promise.

Although Trash has assumed Garbage's liability to Blair, Garbage remains secondarily liable to Blair. The assumption of liability does not release the original obligor's (Garbage's) liability to the beneficiary.

May Trash raise the defense of the statute of frauds if it is available to Garbage? This is a close call. The issue is whether Trash agreed to pay a specific sum; if so, the defense is unavailable. If Trash agreed to pay only to the extent the promisee was liable, the defense is available. If in doubt, the first interpretation is much preferred.

Trash's oral promise to assume liability to Blair may run afoul of the parol evidence rule. We do not know the content of the written contract, but if it is a total integration, Trash may have a complete defense based on the parol evidence rule.

Trash's promise does not run afoul of the one-year statute of frauds, as the station could be shut down within a year, thereby full performance would have been rendered within a year.

The letter sent by Blair to Garbage is not effective under common law because it is not supported by consideration. In some jurisdictions, a written signed release is effective, and in such jurisdictions the letter can operate as a release. In any event, the release of Garbage would have no effect on the liability, if any, of Trash. Garbage and Trash's liability to Blair stems from separate contracts. They are severally liable.

ANSWER 7

The letters to Sigrist and other race car drivers constituted offers to unilateral contracts. The amassing of the most points constitutes both the act of acceptance and the consideration for Century 21's promise. Under the modern approach such an offer cannot be revoked after there has been a commencement of performance of the requested act.

If Century had not purported to revoke the offer by canceling the figure 8 division races, it is not certain that Sigrist would have won the most points. Because Century impeded the determination of the season winner, the uncertainty must be construed against it.

Alternatively, we could conclude that Sigrist had fully performed. What is a season? If the race impresario chooses to cut the racing season short, doesn't that decision define the season?

There is an indefiniteness problem. The offer did not specify the amount of the bonus, but the awarding of $20,000 to each of the other division winners seems to clarify the indefiniteness.

Sigrist should recover $20,000 unless Century 21 can show that its breach freed up time for Sigrist to earn money doing substantially the same kind of racing in other arenas. In which case, the amount that Sigrist earned or could have earned in such races would be subtracted from Sigrist's recovery.

ANSWER 8

Is the bank's personnel manual an offer? Although there are cases to the contrary, personnel manuals that promise some of the terms of employment are treated as offers to unilateral contracts. When Plaintiff enrolled in the MBA program, this was performance of the act of acceptance, or perhaps, only part performance. More likely it was full performance by enrolling and paying, obtaining a satisfactory grade being merely a condition to the bank's promise. If it was only part performance, under the modern view the promise was binding on the bank as an option contract. Even under the ancient view she would be entitled to reimbursement in quasi-contract.

While the bank will argue that her being an "active staff" member at the time of the requested reimbursement was a further condition, this argument can be met in at least two ways. (1) By dismissing her from employment, the bank prevented the condition from happening. (2) By the process of interpretation: she was an active staff member at the time she performed. The requirement that she attain grades of C or better is a condition that she has fulfilled. If the phrase is ambiguous, it should be construed against the bank as the drafter of the manual.

ANSWER 9

There is no indication that Landlord #2 assumed the obligations of the contract, or even knew of the contract. Absent such an express or implied assumption, Landlord #2 has no liability.

Landlord #1 has made a promise that has not been performed. Has the supervening order of the Building Department discharged the contract by the impossibility doctrine? The performance of the promise to this tenant is not impossible, it is only financially difficult and perhaps extremely unwise to carry out. The tenant is entitled to damages.

ANSWER 10

B may cancel under the perfect tender rule. Wonderbold's bankruptcy estate has not delivered as scheduled and the UCC's general principle is that of perfect tender. Failure to tender performance when due generally justifies *B*, as buyer, to cancel the contract. A limited exception exists under the impracticability sections of the UCC. However, the buyer need not accept the goods if a delay in performance that is excused under these provisions is for a material or indefinite period. Clearly, *B* is faced with an indefinite delay and may terminate the contract.

B has a prima facie case to recover damages for breach of contract. The bankruptcy estate may have the defense that performance was impossible because of the court's injunction against delivery. This defense may be available, if it meets the impracticability criteria of the UCC, i.e., that there was no express assumption of the risk, the risk was not reasonably foreseeable, and the injunction was not the fault of the estate. If the estate fails to establish that it should be excused, it is liable for damages for non-delivery.

ANSWER 11

Buyer's initial communication was an inquiry asking for a price on a specific number of a specific product.

Seller's "Proposal" was an offer. This aspect of the case is much like the *Fairmount* case. In response to an inquiry, the seller states a price for the specific quantity of goods sought by the buyer.

Buyer's response was a counter-offer. It was sent after an unreasonable amount of time. Thus, it was not "seasonable" as required by UCC 2–207. And it contained a different quantity term. A departure from a core term such as quantity is not a "definite expression of acceptance." Consequently, it is not an acceptance. It operates as an offer because it manifests an intent to contract, is sufficiently definite in its terms. The arbitration clause is part of this counter-offer.

Buyer's fax operates as a revocation upon its receipt.

(a) Because there was no agreement there is no contract. Motion granted.

(b) Seller's response is a definite and seasonable expression of acceptance of Buyer's counter-offer. Consequently, any dispute between the parties must be brought before an arbitrator.

(c) Is the assignment effective? It certainly does not materially change the duty of the seller. It has to ship to other addresses, but since Buyer is responsible for shipping costs it does not matter whether shipments are to be made in the same county or made to the Aleutian Islands. It does not increase the burden or risk imposed by the contract—Buyer remains liable for the price and shipping costs if the assignee fails to pay. Does it materially impair Seller's chance of obtaining return performance? Here Seller is in for a disappointment. In pricing the product at cost, it was expecting to receive its product's exposure to the mobile sort of individuals who frequent motels and the frequent turnover of such individuals. Instead, the product will be used by the relative immobile, disabled individuals who are the clients of nursing homes. Yet, nothing in the correspondence indicates that Buyer was aware of this thinking. Such subjective motive will not be taken into account by the arbitrator. The assignment is valid.

ANSWER 12

ANALYSIS

Legal Problems: (1) Was *B*'s promise to pay for the increased costs supported by consideration or the equivalent?

(2) Did *A* properly delegate its duties to *C*, and did it assign its rights to *C*?

(3) Will the unlicensed status of *C*'s engineers prevent recovery?

(4) Will the use of an improper brand of glass and consequent refusal by the architect to certify completion prevent recovery.

DISCUSSION

POINT ONE: B*'s defense of lack of consideration for the promise to pay for the increased costs is likely to succeed.*

As a general rule, a promise by one contracting party to pay an additional sum to the other for the performance of his contractual duty is void for lack of consideration. *J. Perillo, Contracts* § 4.9 (7th ed. 2014). Such consideration would exist if *A* had the legal right to refuse to proceed further upon discovery of the underground lake. Despite two plausible theories, *B* had no right to recover unless a minority view is adopted.

The first plausible argument is *B*'s theory that cancellation of the contract would be justified because there was a breach of implied warranty that the plans were adequate for the site. Such a warranty is normally implied, but the builder may not rely upon the warranty if the builder has reason to know of the inadequacy of the plans. *Perillo, supra at* § 13.3. Because information regarding site conditions was available to *B*, *B* did not have the right to cancel for breach of warranty.

Second, *B* may argue that the parties were mutually mistaken about the soil conditions thereby giving *B* the right to avoid the contract. This too fails. Because soil conditions were not checked despite the feasibility of such checking, the facts show conscious ignorance rather than mutual mistake. *Perillo, supra at* § 9.26(b).

In certain jurisdictions, a modification requires no new consideration. These jurisdictions are in a distinct minority. Nevertheless, the minority view is supported by the Restatement (Second) of Contracts § 89. *See Perillo, supra at* § 5.14. The Restatement requires that the modification be fair and reasonable in the light of unanticipated difficulties. These criteria appear to be met.

POINT TWO: The duties were properly delegated but C may not recover against B unless C is an assignee of A.

Generally speaking, duties under a construction contract are delegable. Although *A* has delegated its overall duty of completion of the job, rather than follow the usual pattern of sub-contracting parts of the job, the delegation is proper because the duties are regarded as mechanical. *Perillo, supra at* § 18.28. Of course, *A* continues to remain liable for the due performance of these duties.

Even if the duties were fully performed, however, it is doubtful if *C* may recover from *B*. The facts do not indicate any assignment of rights by *A* to *C*. If there is no assignment, *C* must look solely to *A* for payment and has no rights against *B*. No assignment can be implied merely from the delegation of duties and unrevised UCC § 1–206 requires a writing for enforcement of an assignment in excess of $5,000. Consequently, even if there were an oral assignment it would not be enforceable without such a writing.

POINT THREE: *The defense of an illegality based on the use of unlicensed Personnel is likely to fail in whole or in part.*

Engineers are licensed for the protection of the public against fraud and incompetence. Legislatures do not usually provide for civil consequences of the violation of licensing statutes. Normally, but not uniformly, where professional services are rendered in violation of a licensing statute, recovery for these services will be denied on the rationale that denial of relief will further the intent of the legislature. Where the violation of the statute is relatively technical, as where the person has an out-of-state license, the courts are more reluctant to deny recovery.

However, this is not an action by unlicensed engineers to recover. Rather, it is an action by a construction firm to recover for the erection of a building. The services of unlicensed personnel are only a component of the amount claimed. Consequently, the illegality may be over-looked as "too remote" (*Perillo, supra at* § 22.3–22.5) or, the illegality may be deemed "divisible" (*Perillo, supra at* § 22.6) and recovery denied only for the value of the illegal services.

POINT FOUR: *Although the use of a different brand of glass is not likely to be a material breach, in the majority of jurisdictions the refusal of the architect to certify approval will prevent recovery.*

All examiners are likely to be aware of Judge Cardozo's opinion in Jacob & Youngs, Inc v. Kent, 230 N.Y. 239, 129 N.E. 889 (1921). In that case, the builder utilized Cohoes instead of Reading brand pipe. The court ruled that the breach was not material. Consequently, the builder had rendered substantial performance, and recovery was allowed because substantial performance satisfies the constructive condition that services be performed before payment is due.

In this case, however, payment is not to be made until Zelda, an independent professional, certifies completion of the work. Such a clause is normally construed as an express condition. The majority rule is that strict compliance with express conditions must be shown prior to a contractual recovery. *Perillo, supra at* § 11.37(c). Although conditions can be excused on a variety of grounds (hindrance, waiver, etc.), no such ground appears here.

ANSWER 13

ANALYSIS

(1) In an action at law would the parol evidence rule bar evidence that the writing did not accurately evidence the parties' agreement? If so, does the writing create a contract or only an offer? If the evidence is not barred, will the agreement be unenforceable under the statute of frauds?

(2) Is the language in the writing with respect to non-retractability effective? What is the effect of action in reliance upon the writing?

(3) Is McCoy's non-disclosure of the timber value of the land fraudulent?

(4) Will the statute of frauds or the parol evidence rule bar reformation of the writing in equity?

(5) Will equity grant specific performance where there is a lack of full disclosure by the plaintiff?

POINT ONE: The written agreement, taken alone, is not enforceable at law. Evidence of the oral agreement is barred by the parol evidence rule. Consequently, the writing states an offer, not a contract. Alternatively, if the evidence is not barred by the parol evidence rule, the agreement is unenforceable under the statute of frauds.

A contract for the sale of woodland is clearly within the real property statute of frauds. To comply with the statute, the writing must contain the material terms actually agreed upon. These terms were the mutual promises of purchase and sale. These terms are not accurately contained in the writing. The writing contains no promise by McCoy to purchase the realty. It gives him a right to purchase on demand. Such a right is essentially a power of acceptance of Hatfield's promise to convey. Hatfield's written promise is then, in law, an offer. *Restatement, Contracts (Second)* § 24.

Although the writing does not accurately reflect the parties' agreement, the parol evidence rule does not come into play unless there is a contract. The evidence of their oral agreement is admissible to establish that the writing fails to satisfy the statute of frauds requirement that all the material terms be contained in the writing. Consequently, McCoy's action will be dismissed as the statute is not satisfied. This conclusion is reached without consideration of the possible availability of the remedy of reformation.

POINT TWO: The offer is revocable. The promise of irrevocability is supported neither by consideration nor by promissory estoppel. The promise, however, is a basis for a quasi-contractual action for recovery of $750 or a promissory estoppel action for the same amount.

The writing claims to be "non-retractable." The law is well settled that an offer that states that it is irrevocable can nevertheless be revoked, unless a consideration (or a substitute therefore) be given in exchange for the engagement to keep the offer open. *Dickinson v. Dodds*, 2 Ch. D. 463 (1876). In which case, the offer is an option contract. McCoy may well argue that the $1,500 down payment is sufficient consideration to support an engagement to keep the offer open for 90 days. The fallacy with this argument is that there is nothing to indicate (and it is unlikely) that this refundable sum was bargained for in exchange for the promise of irrevocability. *Bard v. Kent*, 19 Cal. 2d 449, 122 P.2d 8 (1942).

It is possible for a promise of irrevocability to be supported by promissory estoppel. If an action or forbearance is foreseeably induced by a promise, the promise is binding if injustice can be avoided only by enforcement of the promise. *Restatement (Second) of Contracts* § 90; *Id.* § 87. The only action shown by the facts in reliance on the promise is the incurrence of $750 worth of obligations to search title and to survey the premises. Since this amount is small in relation to McCoy's expectation interest, no compelling case for "injustice" has been made out, especially since the $750 is recoverable in a quasi-contractual action. When there is a contract that is unenforceable under a statute of frauds, a party who has partly performed the contract or who had incurred reliance expenditures because of the contract is entitled to restitution measured by his or her detriment. *Randolph v. Castle*, 190 Ky. 776, 228 S.W. 418 (1921); *Perillo, supra at* § 19.44. Even under the doctrine of promissory estoppel, relief can be limited as justice requires. Consequently, even assuming applicability of promissory estoppel, recovery can be limited to $750. *Hoffman v. Red Owl Stores*, 26 Wis. 2d 683, 133 N.W.2d 267 (1965); *Restatement, Contracts (Second)* § 90(1); *Id.* § 87.

POINT THREE: McCoy's action at law will be dismissed because Hatfield has the affirmative defense of fraudulent non-disclosure.

McCoy knew the Hatfield tract and knew land and timber values. Consequently, McCoy knew of the extremely valuable timber resources on the tract. Generally speaking, a purchaser has no duty at law to disclose to the seller any special knowledge he or she has of the subject matter. *Laidlaw v. Organ*, 15 U.S. 178 (1817). An exception to this rule is where the purchaser discloses partial information, lack of full disclosure may constitute misrepresentation. *Kannavos v. Annino*, 356 Mass. 42, 247 N.E.2d 708 (1969). When McCoy told Hatfield that land generally sold in the area from $1,300 to $1,500 an acre, McCoy undertook to disclose all relevant information including the special circumstances that obviously related to the value of Hatfield's land.

POINT FOUR: Reformation is available in Equity despite the Statute of Frauds and Parol Evidence Rule.

Setting aside any peculiarly equitable defenses, McCoy can successfully ask a court of equity to reform the writing. Reformation is available to rectify a writing that unintentionally fails to reflect the parties' true agreement. Since the facts indicate the parties attempted to evidence their true agreement, it is clear that the variance was unintentional. Here the parties were mistaken as to the legal effect of their writing. This is one of the standard instances where reformation is available. *Pasotex Petroleum Co. v. Cameron* 283, F.2d 63 (10th Cir. 1960). According to the majority of jurisdictions, the statute of frauds does not bar reformation of a writing evidencing a contract within the statute. *Restatement, Contracts (Second)* § 156. All jurisdictions agree that the parol evidence rule is not applicable in a reformation action. *General Discount Corp. v. Sadowski*, 183 F.2d 542, 547 (6th Cir. 1950).

POINT FIVE: Even assuming the contract is not voidable for fraudulent non-disclosure, Equity will not order specific performance where there is a lack of full and fair disclosure.

Specific performance is a discretionary remedy. It will be withheld whenever the plaintiff has been guilty of inequitable conduct with respect to the transaction. Failure to disclose pertinent facts unknown to the other party is a ground for refusal of such relief. *Kleinberg v. Ratett*, 252 N.Y. 236, 169 N.E.289 (1929). This includes facts with respect to the value of the subject matter, *Margraf v. Muir*, 57 N.Y. 155 (1874), such as a purchaser's knowledge of mineral deposits or other similar facts unknown to the seller.

ANSWER 14

ANALYSIS

Issues: (1) Is an employment agreement valid where the employee commits himself to a five-year term but the employer reserves the power to terminate if she is not satisfied with the employee's services?

(2) Is excessive drinking by an employee at one company picnic either a material breach of contract or grounds for invoking a condition of satisfaction with the employee's services?

(3) Is the statute of frauds satisfied by a memorandum typed on employer's letterhead.

(4) Does a new and inconsistent employment agreement between the parties discharge the contractual and remedial rights under the original contract? What is the effect of reluctant assent to the new agreement?

(5) What is the effect of changed regulations of a foreign government that makes performance illegal?

DISCUSSION

POINT ONE: The initial agreement is valid despite the apparent lack of commitment on the part of Jane. A return promise will be implied, and the condition of satisfaction does not make the implied promise illusory.

Although the agreement does not appear to contain any express promise of employment by Jane, the agreement is "instinct with obligation." *Wood v. Lucy, Lady Duff-Gordon*, 222 N.Y. 88, 118 N.E. 214 (1917). It is unlikely that Jim would have committed himself to Jane unless he had reason to understand that a commitment had been made to him. Moreover, the existence of a termination clause is decisive. Its existence establishes an understanding that there was a commitment that could be terminated. In the light of all the known circumstances, it is apparent that it was understood that Jane was bound for a five-year term.

The condition of satisfaction does not make Jane's obligation illusory. Jane cannot arbitrarily invoke the clause. The condition is interpreted to mean that the expression of dissatisfaction must be made in good faith, and, where personal taste, fancy or judgment is not involved, reasonably. *Western Hills, Oregon, Ltd. v. Pfau*, 265 Or. 137, 508 P.2d 201 (1973). Irrespective of which category is involved on these facts, the commitment is not illusory and provides consideration for Jim's promise.

POINT TWO: Excessive drinking and boisterousness at a company picnic is neither a material breach of contract nor grounds for invoking the termination clause.

In an employment contract there is an implied promise of sobriety during the performance of one's duties and also while on company premises. The breach of this obligation by Jim must, however, be viewed in relation to the five-year term of the employment and also in relation to two years of service about which no complaint is made. *Hadden v. Consolidated Edison Co.*, 34 N.Y.2d 88, 312 N.E.2d 445 (1974). Viewed in these contexts, the breach clearly is not material.

When Jane fired Jim she could not claim that she was invoking the condition of satisfaction. There is no indication that Jim's services were in any way unsatisfactory either measured on an objective standard or from the viewpoint of Jane's subjective standard. The misconduct did not relate to Jim's services.

POINT THREE: The statute of frauds is satisfied despite the fact that it is not "signed" in the ordinary meaning of the term. The typing of a memorandum of the contract on Jane's letterhead for Jane's internal files sufficiently authenticates the writing so that the letterhead is deemed the signature.

A "signature" is any mark placed upon a writing by a party with intent to authenticate the writing; that is, indicates that the party assents to and adopts the writing. *Restatement (Second) of Contracts* § 134. Courts have been generous in finding that pre-printed stationery bearing the name of the party to be charged constitutes a signature if it can be shown that the stationery was used with the consent of that party. *See* Annots., 112 *A.L.R.* 937, 171 *A.L.R.* 334. Of course, since Jim has not signed a written memorandum, it is not binding on him. Basically, this is irrelevant as Jane is not seeking to hold Jim to the agreement.

POINT FOUR: Jane's offer of employment in New Zealand was an offer to an accord and satisfaction. When accepted by Jim, the prior contract and any remedial rights flowing from any breach were discharged.

At the time of Jane's offer to Jim of employment in New Zealand, there was a dispute between the parties. Nothing indicates that either party was in bad faith. Each claimed that the other was in breach. Implicitly each surrendered a right to pursue an action for breach against the other. The surrender of a claim asserted in good faith and not palpably unreasonable constitutes consideration. *Restatement, (Second) of Contracts* § 74. Consequently, the contractual relations of the parties are governed solely by the new contract. The fact that Jim signed with reluctance does not curtail its legal effect.

Grumbling assent is assent. *Johnson v. Federal Union Surety Co.*, 187 Mich. 454, 153 N.W. 788 (1915).

POINT FIVE: The rights of Jim and Jane under the substituted contract are discharged by virtue of supervening illegality which rendered performance impossible.

There is nothing to indicate that the substituted contract was illegal when made or that either of the parties assumed any special risks of changes in New Zealand law. Consequently, under the modern view, the contract is discharged by virtue of supervening impossibility caused by a change in foreign law. *Perillo, supra at* § 13.5. The older view (*Jacobs Marcus & Co. v. Credit Lyonnais*, 12 Q.B.D. 589 (1884)) to the effect that supervening illegality under foreign law is not a defense has largely been discarded.

ANSWER 15

ANALYSIS

Legal Problems:

(1) Was there consideration for RS's promise in the agreement?

(2) Was there consideration for Williston's promises or did the agreement fail for lack of mutuality?

(3) Did the absence of price and duration terms make the agreement too indefinite to be binding?

(4) Was Williston protected by the "permanent dealership" language of the ad?

(5) Was Williston protected by the "$100,000 yearly" language of the ad?

(6) Did the negation of warranties clause of the writing exclude the warranty of merchantability?

DISCUSSION

POINT ONE: RS's defense of lack of consideration will fail. Despite the possible insufficiency of the recited $1.00 as consideration because of its token and possibly sham nature, Williston's undertaking not to buy converters elsewhere supplies sufficient consideration for RS's obligations.

Consideration is detriment suffered by the promisee, or some third person on her behalf, that has been bargained for in exchange for the promise. *Perillo, supra at* § 4.2. The recited consideration is $1.00. It staggers the imagination that RS entered into the agreement in exchange for $1.00. Moreover, it is very likely that the $1.00 was not in fact paid. Nonetheless, the orthodox view has been that the appearance of a bargain is sufficient, but more recent authority favors the view that a bargain-in-fact must exist. *Perillo, supra at* § 4.6. If the $1.00 was not paid, there are further divergent views within the orthodox view that the appearance of a bargain in sufficient as consideration. There is, however, no need to select among these views on the facts presented, because there is consideration elsewhere in the agreement.

It is well established that if there is bargained-for detriment elsewhere in the agreement, the agreement will stand despite the insufficiency of the recited consideration. *Thomas v. Thomas*, [1842] 2 Q.B. 851, 114 Eng. Rep. 330.

Here, Williston's undertaking to refrain from selling any other brand of converter is such detriment. *Lima Locomotive & Mach. Co. v. National Steel Castings Co.*, 155 F. 77 (6th Cir.1907).

POINT TWO: RS's defense that it has provided no consideration and that consequently there is no mutuality of obligation, will also fail. Although RS's promises appear illusory, RS's apparently unfettered discretion to withhold deliveries is restricted by intelligent interpretation and by application of provisions of the UCC.

RS's basic commitment to supply converters ordered by Williston is severely hedged. Acceptance of orders is contingent upon is "production plans and actual capacity." Moreover, the next sentence of the agreement appears to further undercut its commitment by leaving acceptance of orders to its entire discretion. If this were the correct interpretation, RS's promise would be illusory. An illusory promise is not detrimental. Under the rule that both parties to bilateral contract must provide consideration otherwise the "contract" is void, RS would have a total defense to a breach of contract action. *Perillo, supra at* § 4.12(4).

This, however, is not the appropriate interpretation or conclusion. It is clear that the parties intended legal consequences. Legal terminology such as "franchisee," "consideration," and "warrant" demonstrate a clear intent to contract. That intent should be effectuated if it does not do violence to the language of the agreement. RS's ability to refuse to accept orders must be read in context. An order can be refused only if RS *cannot* fill an order because it lacks production capacity or because of a conflict with its production plans.

These plans cannot be whimsical. Under UCC § 2–306(2) an exclusive dealing arrangement imposes an obligation upon RS to use best efforts to supply the goods and upon Williston an obligation to use best efforts to promote their sale. This is in addition to the obligation of the parties of the parties to perform in good faith imposed by the UCC.

For the reasons given, RS's commitment is not illusory. It does not have arbitrary power to determine whether it will perform of not.

POINT THREE: Despite the absence of price and duration terms, the agreement is not too indefinite to be a legally binding contract. Gap-fillers supplied by the UCC will supply a requisite that a reasonable price be charged and that a reasonable period of notice of termination be given. There appears to be a breach of the latter term.

The UCC greatly downgrades the certainty of terms requirement of the common law. UCC § 2–204(3). Even under common law, the absence of a price term is not fatal. The implication is that a reasonable price is intended. *Perillo, supra at* § 2.9, and UCC § 2–305. In a franchising situation. this would normally be deemed that price which the franchisor charged franchisees generally. Although no duration is agreed upon in the signed writing, (the "permanent dealership" term in the ad is discussed in the next point), the UCC provides that where there is a continuing relationship of seller-buyer, the agreement may be terminated only upon a reasonable period of notice. UCC § 2–309(3). "Reasonableness" in this context takes into account that the terminated party requires a period of time to recoup its investment or to make substitute arrangements, or both. *See Perillo, supra at* § 4.12(b). Although reasonableness is a question of fact, three days would appear to be an unreasonably short period of notice.

POINT FOUR: The term contained in the ad with respect to "permanent dealership," does not give Williston any protection beyond the notice of termination provision of the UCC discussed in point three.

Aside from problems with respect to the parol evidence rule (discussed in point five), the term "permanent" utilized in the ad gives Williston no rights. The term, frequently seen in "help wanted" and other ads has been judicially construed to convey merely a statement of present intention, a representation rather than a promise. It indicates that RS presently envisions a long-term relationship. It does not prevent a change of policy. *Perillo, supra at* § 2.9(a)(3).

POINT FIVE: The $100,000 yearly gross stated in the ad may well be a contractually binding promise. The parol evidence rule will not bar evidence of the ad.

The signed agreement is clearly not a total integration. It contains no merger clause. Although there are various standards for determining whether there is a total integration in the absence of a merger clause, under all tests it would be fairly obvious that such a succinct document was not designed to govern all aspects of their relationship. Consequently, the advertisement is admissible into evidence. *See Perillo, supra at* §§ 3.3–3.5 (discussing integration). The language is promissory: "will gross a minimum." See, *e.g., Willis v. Allied Insulation Co.*, 174 So. 2d 858 (La. App. 1965). The only question is whether it is negated by other parol evidence of what the parties agreed upon at the time of the interview.

POINT SIX: Although these has been a negation of express warranties, the writing does not exclude implied warranties, especially the implied warranty of merchantability which has been breached.

According to UCC § 2–316(2) an implied warranty of merchantability cannot be excluded unless the term "merchantability" is mentioned in the writing. Since this has not been done, such a warranty attaches to the sale. A converter that does not work is non-merchantable as it is not fit for the ordinary purpose for which a converter is used. UCC § 2–314(2). Consequently, Williston is entitled to all damages attributable to the purchase and resale of non-functioning converters.

Appendix C

Glossary

A

Accord and Satisfaction There are two kinds of accords and satisfactions. Type I involves an agreement (the accord—also called an executory accord) to settle a claim followed by its performance discharging the claim (the satisfaction). Type II involves the immediate discharge of a claim by a new contract. This kind of accord and satisfaction is called a substituted contract. *See also* **Executory Accord**.

Account An account is a right to payment which is not evidenced by an instrument or chattel paper and certain other exceptions, whether or not it has been earned by performance. UCC § 9–102. The person who owes the duty of payment is an **Account Debtor**.

Account Stated An "account stated" arises where there have been transactions between debtor and creditor resulting in the creation of matured debts and where the parties by agreement compute a balance that the debtor promises to pay and the creditor promises to accept in full payment for the items of account. Frequently, the agreement arises by implication, as where a statement of account is sent to the debtor who fails to contest it within a reasonable time.

Aleatory Contract An "aleatory contract" is where the performance on one or both sides of a contract is conditioned on a fortuitous event. Examples include insurance contracts and wagers.

Anticipatory Repudiation Four actions that constitute "repudiation":

a. positive statement (to promisee or other person having a right under the contract) indicating the promisor will not or cannot substantially perform;

b. transfer (or contracting to transfer) to a third person of anything essential for substantial performance by promisor;

c. any other voluntary act that renders substantial performance impossible or apparently impossible.

d. under the UCC and some common law cases, the failure to respond satisfactorily to a justified demand for assurances.

A repudiation is "anticipatory" if the repudiation takes place before the time for performance.

Assignment (compared with "Delegation" and "Assumption")

a. ***Assignment** (of Rights).* An "assignment" is a manifestation of intent by the owner of a contractual right to effectuate a present transfer of an interest in the right to the assignee. An assignment extinguishes the right in the assignor, unless the assignment is intended to create merely a security interest. While an outright assignment extinguishes the assignor's rights, it cannot extinguish the assignor's duties.

b. ***Delegation*** *(of Duties).* A "delegation" involves the appointment by the obligor of another to render performance on obligor's behalf. Unlike an assignment, a delegation is not a transfer. A delegation does not eliminate the original contractual obligations of the delegant unless the promisee by a "novation" discharges the delegant from the duty to see to it that the promised performance is rendered. *See* **Novation**.

c. ***Assumption*** *(of Duties).* Not every delegation involves an "assumption" of duties by the delegate. Such an assumption occurs if the delegate makes a promise that is intended to benefit the person to whom the duty is owed. An assumption does not affect the delegant's continuing duty of seeing that the performance is rendered.

Assumpsit This is the name of the common law writ for the enforcement of contracts that were not expressed in sealed instruments (where the writ of Covenant was employed) and that did not result in a debt (for which the writ of Debt was employed). Eventually, assumpsit swallowed up the other contractual writs.

Avoidance The act of disaffirming a valid contract that is voidable for lack of capacity, duress, misrepresentation, etc.

B

Bilateral Contract (compared with Unilateral Contract)

a. ***"Bilateral" Contract.*** Exists if both parties have made promises to each other.

b. ***"Unilateral" Contract.*** Exists if one party has promised to perform (offer) and the other party creates the contract (acceptance) by rendering the requested performance rather than by making a return promise.

Boilerplate Originally, this was a printer's term referring to printed matter that was permanently imbedded in a plate for constant reuse; e.g., the masthead of a newspaper. Later, it came to be used for standard terms that are constantly repeated in form contracts and are not negotiated. Now, it also includes standard terms spat out by a word processor.

C

Cancellation *See* **Rescission**.

Chancery and Chancellor A court of chancery is a court of Equity. The judge in such a court is a chancellor or vice-chancellor. *See* **Equity**.

Capacity When a party to an agreement is deemed to lack the "capacity" to enter into a binding contract, the agreement is void or voidable. Classes that have historically been deemed to lack capacity include: (1) infants and (2) persons mentally infirm.

Common Law This term has a number of meanings depending on context. (a) It is used to distinguish the legal system of England and those countries whose law is historically rooted in English law from the law of other countries; e.g., Islamic Law and the law of Civil Law countries whose law descends from the Roman Law. (b) "Common Law" is used to distinguish case developed by the courts of common law from case law that derives from courts of Equity. (c) "Common law" is used to distinguish judge-made law from statutory law.

Condition (compared with Promise)

a. ***Condition*** An act or event, other than the lapse of time, that qualifies a duty to render a promised performance. A condition may be "precedent," "concurrent" or "subsequent." It may be express, implied-in-fact, or constructive. When a promise is conditional, it is sometimes called a "dependent promise."

b. ***Promise*** Defined in Restatement (Second) Contracts § 2 as a manifestation of intention to act or refrain from acting in a specified way. A promise is said to be "absolute" (independent or unconditional) if nothing but a lapse of time is necessary to make its performance due immediately.

c. ***Constructive Conditions*** (Imposed by Law) "Constructive" conditions are constructed by law to meet the ends of justice, as opposed to "express" conditions that are either spelled out or implied-in-fact (by being gathered from the contract terms and the surrounding circumstances as a matter of interpretation).

Consequential Damages There is an old poem concerning a king who stopped off at a blacksmith's shop to shoe his horse. The smith affixed a shoe carelessly so that the shoe was missing a nail. This caused the horse to stumble. The king did not arrive at a crucial battle on time; his forces lost the battle and he lost his throne. "For want of a nail a kingdom was lost." This illustrates consequential damages caused by the blacksmith. Such damages are also known as "special" or "indirect" damages. These are damages that go beyond the value of the promised performance. *See* **General Damages**.

Consideration The essence of "consideration" is legal detriment that has been bargained for by the promisor and exchanged by the promisee for the promise.

Contract "A contract is a promise, or set of promises, for the breach of which the law gives a remedy, or the performance of which the law in some way recognizes as a duty."

Contra Proferentem This is the name of a rule that states that if a writing is unclear it should be construed against the drafter. This rule should only be employed after genuine attempts to ascertain the meaning of the writing have been exhausted.

Counter-Offer An offeree may decide not to accept the original offer and to instead make an offer on different terms, as to which the original offeree then becomes the offeror, and the original offeror becomes the offeree. The effect of a counter-offer is to terminate the counter offeror's power to subsequently accept the original offer.

Course of Dealing "A course of dealing is a sequence of previous conduct between the parties to a particular transaction [that] is fairly to be regarded as establishing a common basis of understanding for interpreting their expressions and other conduct." UCC § 1–205(1), revised § 1–303(b).

Course of Performance When a contract involves repeated occasions for performance by either party with knowledge of the nature of the performance and opportunity for objection to it by the other, any course of performance accepted or acquiesced in without objection shall be relevant to determine the meaning of the agreement. UCC § 2–208, revised § 1–303 (a). The same thought is sometimes labeled as "practical construction."

Covenant In modern usage, "covenant" is a synonym for "promise." Under the system of common law writs, "covenant" was the appropriate writ for an action on a sealed instrument.

Creditor Beneficiary ***See*** **Donee Beneficiary.**

D

Debt A debt is an obligation to pay money. Under the writ system "debt" was the appropriate writ for an action for nonpayment of a debt.

Delegation (of Duties) *See* **Assignment**.

Dependent Promise See **Condition**.

Detriment As used in consideration doctrine, detriment is doing or promising to do what one has no legal duty to do, or forbearing or promising to forbear from doing what one has a legal right to do. In promissory estoppel doctrine, detriment is sometimes used to connote the actual suffering of some harm. In this context, this book uses the term "injurious reliance" rather than "detrimental reliance."

Disaffirmance This word is a synonym for "avoidance." It is mostly used in the context of avoiding a contract for lack of capacity.

Divisible Contract A contract is divisible if: (1) performance by each party is divided into two or more parts; and (2) the performance of each party by one party is the agreed exchange for a corresponding part by the other party.

Donee Beneficiary If the promisee (in a third party beneficiary situation) enters into a contract with the purpose of having a gift conferred upon a third party, the third party is a "donee beneficiary." The third party is a "creditor beneficiary" if the purpose of the promisee in extracting the promise from the promisor is to discharge an obligation that the promisee owes or believes is owed to the third party.

E

Efficient Breach Some economic theorists hold that if a party breaches, and is still better off after paying damages to compensate the victim of the breach, the result is economically efficient because, considered as a unit, the parties are better off because of the breach and the breach makes no party worse off. Consequently, the party who will benefit from the breach should breach. The theory is highly flawed.

Ejusdem generis A rule of interpretation that states that where a clause enumerates specific things, general words following the enumeration are interpreted to be restricted to things **of the same kind** as those specifically listed.

Enforceable Contract When a promisee is entitled to either a money judgment or specific performance because of a breach, the contract is said to be "enforceable." See **Unenforceable Contract**.

Equitable Estoppel Where a person by words or conduct represents a fact to be true, and the other party reasonably changes position in reliance on the representation, the representer will be precluded from proving the untruth of the representation. E.g., if a party whose signature has been forged affirms that the signature is genuine, the party will be precluded from proving the forgery if the other party has changed position in reliance on it.

Equity A system of law administered in the past by chancellors. The system originated as a way of administering justice in situations where the more rigid system of common law failed to mete out justice. Although in most states the equity and common law are now procedurally integrated in unified court systems, different rules prevail depending on the historical origin of the remedy sought. The principal equitable remedy in contract litigation is specific performance. Another remedy, important to contract law is reformation.

Executed A promise that has not fully been performed is an executory promise. When it is fully performed it is **executed.** The word "executed" is ambiguous, however. A frequent usage is to say, "I executed the contract," meaning "I signed the contract."

Executory Accord An "executory accord" is an agreement embodying a promise, express or implied, to accept at some future time a stipulated performance in satisfaction or discharge, in whole or in part, of any present claim, cause of action or obligation, and a return promise, express or implied, to render such performance. *See also* **Accord and Satisfaction**.

Express Contract When the parties manifest their agreement by words, the contract is said to be "express."

***Expressio unius est exclusio alterius* (expression of one thing is exclusion of another)** A rule of interpretation to the effect if specifics are mentioned, unmentioned specifics are not included. Thus, if a contract for the sale of a house states "living room couch and end tables included," the coffee table is excluded.

F

Foakes v. Beer, Rule of Under the rule of *Foakes v. Beer,* a debtor's part payment of a total amount undisputedly due is not consideration to support a contract based on the creditor's promise to discharge the remaining amount due. One qualification to this rule, stated in *Pinnell's Case* (1602), is that a slightly different performance (e.g., payment one day earlier, or tossing in a "hawk, horse, or robe") is sufficient detriment to support a finding of consideration for the creditor's promise to discharge the debt.

Force Majeure A French term frequently used to describe a clause that deals with excuses stemming from supervening events such as war, strikes, riots, etc., that impede the performance of a contract.

Forfeiture Narrowly used, this term applies to the divestiture of a property interest without compensation. More broadly, it is used to encompass the inability, under the classical view, of a breaching party to recover the value of work done.

Frustration of Purpose (Venture) Where the object of one of the parties is the basis upon which both parties contract, the duties of performance are constructively conditioned upon the attainment of this object. This doctrine arose in the "coronation cases" involving contracts to license the use of various premises to view a coronation procession that was canceled.

G

General Damages Damages that flow ordinarily or naturally from a breach are known as general damages; e.g., if a seller breaches the obligation to deliver, general damages are the buyer's additional costs to cover, or the difference between the market price and the contract price.

Good Faith Honesty constitutes good faith. Under the UCC's definition, in sale of goods cases, good faith in the case of a merchant means honesty *and* the observance of reasonable commercial standards of fair dealing.

H

Hadley v. Baxendale, Rule of Under the rule of *Hadley v. Baxendale,* "special" or "consequential" damages (as opposed to "general" damages that so obviously result from a breach that all contracting parties are deemed to have contemplated them) will only be awarded if they were in the parties' contemplation, at the time of contracting, as a probable consequence of a breach of contract.

I

Implied-in-fact Contract When the parties manifest their agreement by conduct, the contract is said to be "implied-in-fact."

Implied-in-law A contract implied-in-law is not a contract at all, but an obligation imposed by law to do justice even though it is clear that no promise was ever made or intended. *See* **Quasi Contract**.

Impossibility of Performance The doctrine of "impossibility of performance" is an exception to the general rule that the promisor must either perform, or pay damages for failure to perform, no matter how burdensome performance has become because of unforeseen circumstances. While the doctrine has evolved around various specific categories, one basic part of the doctrine is that the impossibility of performance must be objective rather than merely subjective.

Impracticability Where circumstances so change since the time of contracting that the contract can only be performed in a manner that is radically different from originally contemplated and at tremendous extra cost, performance may be impracticable and the rules governing impossibility of performance apply.

Incidental Beneficiary A person who is a donee or creditor (third party) beneficiary of a contract is entitled, under certain circumstances, to enforce the contract. Since there will often be many people indirectly or even directly benefitted by any given contractual performance, the term "incidental beneficiary" is used to describe those persons who would benefit by the performance but who were not intended by the parties to be benefitted and who thus cannot enforce the contract.

In Pari Delicto Under this doctrine, a party who has performed under an illegal bargain is entitled to a quasi-contractual recovery if this party is not guilty of serious moral turpitude and, although blameworthy, is not equally as guilty as the other party to the illegal bargain. Such a party is said to be "not in pari delicto."

Integration A writing that embodies one or more terms of a contract with finality is an integration. If it is final *and* complete, it is a **total integration**. If the writing is final and incomplete, it is a **partial integration**.

L

Liquidated Damages Clause If the court upholds a clause that determines in advance what the damages for breach will be, it is called a "liquidated damages clause." If such a clause is struck down, it is usually then called a "penalty clause." The traditional criteria of a liquidated damages clause are: (1) injury caused by the breach must be difficult or impossible to estimate accurately; (2) parties must have intended that the agreed payment be for the loss, rather than as a deterrent to breach; (3) the stipulated amount of damages must be a reasonable estimate of the probable loss.

Liquidated Debt A debt is liquidated if it is undisputed, presently due, and certain in amount or can be made certain by the rules of arithmetic.

Locus Poenitentiae (room for repentance) While a court will usually leave the parties to an illegal contract where it finds them, the doctrine of "locus poenitentiae" permits a party, even one "in pari delicto" (*see supra*), to disavow an illegal contract and obtain restitution if the party acts in time to prevent the illegal purpose for which the bargain was made, and if the mere making of the illegal bargain does not itself involve serious moral turpitude.

M

Mailbox Rule This is a nickname for the rule of *Adams v. Lindsell* to the effect that, where mailing an acceptance is a reasonable means of accepting an offer, the acceptance is effective on dispatch.

Merger Clause This is a clause in a written contract to the effect that the writing fully expresses all the parties promises and that there are no promises in addition to those contained in the writing. Generally, courts will honor the clause and treat the writing as a total integration. *See* **Integration**. Often, merger clauses will also say that neither party is relying on any representation of fact made by the other. This is an effort to prevent either a fraud action or an attempt to avoid the contract. Such efforts are less successful.

Mirror Image Rule This is also known as the **Ribbon Matching Rule**. This rule states that if an acceptance varies from the terms of the offer in any detail it constitutes a counter-offer.

Mitigation of Damages A party who is entitled to recover for a breach of contract may not recover for those damages that the party could have been avoided by a reasonable effort without undue risk, expense or humiliation. This is the doctrine of "mitigation of damages" or "avoidable consequences."

N

Noscitur a sociis (known by one's associates) A rule of interpretation to the effect that a term takes on a coloration from the verbal context.

Novation A contract is a "novation" if it: (1) discharges immediately a previous contractual duty or a duty to make compensation; and (2) creates a new contractual duty; and (3) includes as a party one who neither owed the previous duty nor was entitled to its performance.

O

Objective Test An objective test of intention looks to the outward manifestation of intent, rather than what the party who spoke or wrote the words had in mind.

Obligor A party under an obligation is an obligor. The person to whom the obligation is owed is an **Obligee**.

Offer An offer is a promise to do or refrain from doing some specified thing in the future conditioned upon the promisee's acceptance. The offer creates a "power of acceptance" that permits the offeree to accept the offer thereby transforming the offeror's promise into a contractual obligation.

Option A binding promise to keep an offer open; an irrevocable offer.

Output Contract This is a contract whereby a seller promises to deliver its entire production of a product to the buyer. These are commonly mining contracts and contracts for the sale of by-products of industrial production.

P

Pari Delicto *See* **In Pari Delicto**.

Parol Evidence Rule Under the "parol evidence rule," prior and contemporaneous oral expressions and prior written expressions are not admissible to vary or contradict the terms of a writing that both parties intended to be the final and complete integration of their agreement. This rule is subject to many exceptions and qualifications.

Penalty Clause *See* **Liquidated Damages Clause**.

Practical Construction *See* **Course of Performance**.

Pre-Existing Duty Under the "pre-existing duty" rule, a party who merely does or promises to do something he or she is already legally obligated to do or who refrains from doing or promises to refrain from doing something he or she is already legally obligated to refrain from doing has incurred no detriment for purposes of determining whether his or her act or forbearance constitutes consideration.

Promise *See* **Conditions**.

Promissory Estoppel Section 90 of the Restatement (Second) of Contracts states "A promise that the promisor should reasonably expect to induce action or forbearance on the part of the promisee or a third person and that does induce such action or forbearance is binding if injustice can be avoided only by enforcement of the promise." This is the doctrine of "promissory estoppel."

Punitive Damages These are damages that are intended to punish a wrongdoer as a deterrent to repetition of the wrong and as a deterrent to others. In classic contract law, such damages are not available for a breach unless the breach involves an independent tort; today, in some jurisdictions, they are available in rare cases of malicious or oppressive breaches.

Q

Quasi Contract A quasi contract is a fictitious contract constructed by the law to provide a remedial device to give redress to deserving parties who are not protected by a contract. For example, where an enforceable contract is not created because of indefiniteness or a statute of frauds, a party who partly performs can get redress in quasi contract. It is also employed where a contract is avoided because of fraud or the like and where a contract is discharged for impracticability. A quasi contract is sometimes called a contract implied-in-law.

R

Reliance Damages These are costs incurred because of the contract that cannot be salvaged.

Requirements Contract A contract to supply all the buyer's needs of a certain product or service is a requirements contract. Examples are a contract to supply all the coal needed to operate a steel mill, all the bricks required for a construction project, or to process all of the bauxite mined by the seller.

Rescission A "rescission" is an agreement between the parties to end the contract before full performance; a "termination" is the discharge of duties by the exercise of a power granted by the contract; a "cancellation" is one party's putting an end to the contract by reason of a breach by the other party. These are the definitions of the UCC. Unfortunately, the three terms are often interchanged indiscriminately.

Release A "release" is a writing manifesting an intention to discharge another from an existing or asserted duty. Historically, releases were under seal and required no consideration. Today, in many jurisdictions that have abolished the effectiveness of the seal, no consideration is needed, but others require consideration.

Restitution As explained by the Restatement of Restitution, restitution is an amalgam of rights and remedies available at law and in equity. Principally, restitution describes relief in quasi contract (an action at law), and the imposition of constructive trusts (a form of equitable relief). In a contract context it also describes a remedy that is an alternative to damages—giving the aggrieved party a judgment against a breaching party for sufficient sum of money to restore the status quo ante, or specifically restoring property that was transferred to the breaching party.

S

Satisfaction (Accord and,) A "satisfaction" in the context of an "accord and satisfaction" is the performance of an executory accord (*see* **Executory Accord**) or the making of a substituted contract.

Seasonable An act is seasonable if it is timely. The term covers both the situation when a specified time is stated in a document such as an offer or a contract, but also where the document is silent. In that case, the law usually sets a standard of a "reasonable" time for the act to be seasonable.

Security Interest A creditor's interest in the borrower's property (such as a lender's interest in an automobile it has financed) is a security interest.

Signature A signature is any mark or sign that is written, printed, stamped, photographed, engraved, or otherwise placed on any writing with the intent to authenticate the writing.

Special Damages *See* **Consequential Damages**.

Specific Performance This is a remedy forged by courts of equity and is available if the remedy at law is inadequate. It consists of an order by the court addressed to a party to perform or be held in contempt.

Substantial Performance Where a party is guilty of an immaterial breach, but has otherwise fully performed, the party has substantially performed. This means that this party may recover on the contract with a set-off for the other party's damages. It also means that this party has not materially breached and therefore the other party cannot cancel.

T

Temporary Frustration or Impossibility A "temporary frustration" (of purpose) or "temporary impossibility" merely suspends the duty of performance until the impossibility or frustrating event ceases. However, the duty of performance is discharged if, after cessation of the temporary frustration or impossibility, the burden of the promised performance would be substantially different than if there had been no such temporary frustration or impossibility.

Tender A valid tender requires an offer to perform, readiness and ability to perform and actual production of the thing to be delivered.

Termination *See* **Rescission**.

Third Party Beneficiary *See* **Donee Beneficiary**.

"Time is of the Essence" This is a standard phrase showing that the parties agree that performance on time is an express condition. Failure to receive performance on time therefore allows the aggrieved party to cancel the contract.

Trade Usage *See* **Usage**.

U

Unconscionable While courts will usually not look into the adequacy of consideration (thus permitting great differences between the value of the promise made and the detriment incurred), the UCC has borrowed an equity concept in stating that enforcement of a contract or part of it may be refused "if the court as a matter of law finds the contract or any clause of the contract to have been unconscionable." Unfair bargaining has been called **Procedural Unconscionability** and oppressive terms have been called **Substantive Unconscionability**.

Unenforceable Contract When a contract has some legal consequences but may not be enforced in an action for damages or specific performance in the face of certain defenses such as a statute of frauds or a statute of limitations, the contract is "unenforceable."

Unilateral Contract Bilateral Contract.

Usage A usage is any practice or method of dealing or terminology having such regularity of observance in a place, vocation or trade as to justify an expectation that it will be observed with respect to the transaction in question.

Ut res magis valeat quam pereat "That the thing may have effect rather than be destroyed." A maxim of interpretation that expresses a preference that an agreement be deemed valid and operative rather than void.

V

Void Contract When an agreement produces no legal obligation upon the part of a promisor, it is sometimes said to be a "void" contract; it is more exact to say that no contract has been created.

Voidable Contract When one or more of the parties has the power to elect to avoid the legal relations created by the contract or the power by ratification to extinguish the power of avoidance, the contract is said to be "voidable." Voidable contracts include:

a. contracts involving minors or others that lack capacity to contract, and

b. contracts involving duress, undue influence, misrepresentation, or mistake.

Table of Cases

Index